IN THE
SHADOW OF
MT. DIABLO

IN THE
SHADOW OF
MT. DIABLO

THE SHOCKING TRUE
IDENTITY OF
THE ZODIAC KILLER

MIKE RODELLI

Indigo River Publishing
3 West Garden Street, Ste. 718
Pensacola, FL 32502
www.indigoriverpublishing.com

First edition published 2017 as *The Hunt for Zodiac: The Inconceivable Double Life of a Notorious Serial Killer.* Revised edition 2021.
Printed in the United States of America

In the Shadow of Mt. Diablo: The Shocking True Identity of the Zodiac Killer
Mike Rodelli, author
ISBN: 978-1-950906-87-1 | LCCN 2020921261

Cover & Interior design by Robin Vuchnich

Cover image of Mt. Diablo by **Robert Clay/Alamy Stock Photo**

Special discounts are available on quantity purchases by corporations, associations, and others. For details, contact the publisher at the address above. Orders by US trade bookstores and wholesalers: Please contact the publisher at the address above.

With Indigo River Publishing, you can always expect great books, strong voices, and meaningful messages. Most importantly, you'll always find . . . words worth reading.

Dedicated to the memories of my mom and dad,
Ann and Joseph Rodelli

Find something more important than you are and dedicate your life to it.
—Philosopher Dan Dennett

CONTENTS

PREFACE

FROM DECEMBER 1968 UNTIL JULY 1974, a man who called himself the Zodiac terrorized the people of the San Francisco Bay Area with cold-blooded murders and chilling hand-printed letters to the editors of the local newspapers. In these letters, he boasted of his crimes and threatened unspeakable mayhem. He taunted and ridiculed his police pursuers. He even hinted that he was leaving clues to his true identity.

After killing five people and then writing about his exploits under his now infamous pen name, the Zodiac has been called a "sexual sadist," a "sexual killer without the sex," and a "loser who was compensating for his feelings of inadequacy." None of these characterizations is the truth, and when you learn the truth about his identity, it will surely shock you as much as it did me.

In June 1999, I had what I thought to be a simple-minded idea to use the killer's own behavior as a weapon to identify him. That idea led to just one name. Through various discoveries made from June 1999 until January 2000, I felt that I had solved the Zodiac case: there simply seemed to be too many stunning and disturbing circumstances pointing at my suspect for him *not* to be the Zodiac. I was certain that, with the assistance of the local police, I'd have the case completely wrapped up within a few months. Instead, that one name set me on a quest that would slowly but inexorably consume the next twenty years of my life.

I was forced at various times to be my own behavioral profiler, my own "internet detective," and use the World Wide Web to piece together the evidence to prove my case. I had to be my own forensic scientist and challenge the DNA evidence that had allegedly been developed from one of Zodiac's many letters. The question was, Would I be able to successfully overcome this DNA and prove that I had solved the case? Eventually I also had to become my own police interrogator when I interviewed my wealthy suspect at his request in a memorable face-to-face meeting in 2006.

The most important step in identifying the Zodiac is to redefine him through behavioral profiling techniques that were not available to the police in the 1960s. That profile is based on the killer's crime scenes and how he interacted with his victims. We'll undertake that task in chapter 17. It is based on my interviews with a forensic psychologist and crime scene analyst, Mr. Richard Walter, who is one of the founders of the prestigious cold-case-solving group, the Vidocq Society of Philadelphia. Mr. Walter is one of a small handful of elite profilers in the world and is known by Scotland Yard as "the living Sherlock Holmes." As a result of an inaccurate profile of the Zodiac, people both inside and outside of law enforcement have been looking for the killer in all the wrong places since 1969. As Mr. Walter said to me several years ago, "You can't find something if you don't know what you are looking for."

We will also redefine Zodiac through a clear obsession he had. This obsession pervades every one of his crime scenes. It is also in many of his letters to the press, and even the crimes for which Zodiac took credit but may not have committed. When combined with the updated profile, this obsession clearly and decisively points the finger of suspicion squarely at the man named in this book and dismisses all of the other three thousand or so suspects who have been named since the search for Zodiac began in 1969.

In addition to the challenges I naturally faced on my journey, I've also had incredible experiences. In developing the name of my suspect, I happened upon an entire secret world that lay hidden just beneath the surface of this mind-bending case for a generation. I have learned amazing things and made many lasting friends since 1999. These include a retired and now deceased Superior Court judge from Solano County, California, who helped guide me through the political maze that is Northern California law enforcement. In 2001 he called mine the "only true prime suspect" ever developed in the history of the investigation.

Other individuals assisted me as well. One is a former investigator for the San Francisco City Attorney's Office, whose counsel and insights over the years were of inestimable assistance. Another was a man who was widely considered the "dean" of private investigators in San Francisco. There were also three amateur investigators from Europe whom I've never met in person, but who became my staunchest allies and supporters at a time when I most needed them. Last but by no means least was retired Vallejo, California, Police Department detective Jim Dean, who investigated the Zodiac crimes in the 1970s. His badge opened the door to the pair of us interviewing several key eyewitnesses who were completely inaccessible to the average "amateur researcher." One of these cornerstone eyewitnesses had never told his story to anyone outside of law enforcement for *over thirty years.* Jim and I spoke to him beginning on a memorable day in September 2003, and what a story it turned out to be! Hearing that story directly from this eyewitness was a once-in-a-lifetime experience for both Jim and me.

In the chapters where I present the circumstantial case I have assembled over the years, I provide extensive footnoting and include a number of exhibits in support of my theory. The evidence I present comes from books, newspaper and magazine articles, birth and death records, European genealogical records, maps, other publicly available information, and even as unlikely a place as horse racing results charts from the *Daily Racing Form*. The reason I so carefully document my evidence is twofold: First, my suspect was an upstanding citizen of San Francisco who I believed had committed a series of heinous crimes. Therefore, it was incumbent upon me, in making such accusations, to be prepared to completely substantiate my claims with the facts that had led me, as well as many others, to conclude that this man was the Zodiac. Second, I also wanted to make my case not about me and what

I personally thought but about *the objective facts that comprise my case*. In this way, anybody could put himself in my shoes, assess the evidence for himself, and draw his own conclusions.

In short, I've tried to make this the most heavily researched and thoroughly documented book ever written on the Zodiac mystery, one that, I believe, will bring the case to a definitive conclusion. This is in direct contrast to many other books and newspaper articles I have read on the case, in which someone might simply present handwriting from canceled checks and ask us to conclude that the writer was Zodiac. Or they might alter the 1969 wanted poster sketch of Zodiac to look like "their" suspect and then marvel at the resemblance or propose a dizzying case based on mathematics against a man who lived some three thousand miles from the crime scenes and was never placed at any of them. Or they may confidently name a suspect who was "proven" in a 2014 book to be the Zodiac with handwriting from a marriage document that I easily proved not to be the suspect's handwriting at all!

I will do my utmost to take you along with me on this journey, painting in fine brush strokes wherever possible and in much broader ones when need be. I hope that you find the trip through my research on the Zodiac case as endlessly fascinating today as I found it while I was living it. It is research that brought me to unbelievable heights of discovery, led me to disaster on national television in 2002, and ultimately led me to what I believe to be the absolute truth about the identity of the heartless, power-hungry, and egotistical man who called himself Zodiac. My goal in this book is what it's been since 1999: to put the truth as I see it about the identity of the Zodiac before the public. That truth may not be what people expected in their wildest dreams, nor what anyone who knew my suspect could have imagined in their worst nightmares, but it is the unvarnished truth as I see it.

The proof that I will present on the identity of the Zodiac within these pages represents the only circumstantial case ever put forth by any individual in over fifty years that has been endorsed in print by a man like Richard Walter, who is called upon by police departments from across the country and around the world to help solve their most difficult and perplexing cold cases.

Mike Rodelli
October 2017
Revised April 2020

PROLOGUE

THE SUN SHONE BRIGHTLY as I stood on the east side of Van Ness Avenue in San Francisco a few blocks north of Market Street. The date was September 27, 2006. This area, which in its glory days was known as Auto Row for the number of new car dealerships that called it home, now hosted a smattering of different types of businesses, from diners to electronics stores, that had popped up in the years since many of the dealers had left for greener pastures and lower rents.

Specifically, I found myself standing opposite 901 North Van Ness. The building, a huge glass-and-marble edifice, was designed in 1926 by Bernard Maybeck, a famous Bay Area architect, as a Packard showroom for auto dealer Earle C. Anthony. Designated as a San Francisco landmark, 901 Van Ness now houses British Motor Car Distributors, which imports and sells British marques of all types, like Land Rover, Jaguar, and Bentley.

Before crossing the street, I drew a deep breath. And for a good reason. This was arguably the most important day of my entire life. I was about to interview the owner of British Motor Car Distributors, who had driven his first British car in a chance encounter with an MG-TC in New Orleans in 1946 and had been a wildly successful importer ever since. But I wasn't there to ask him about his long and storied career as a car dealer, horse breeder, sportsman, and entrepreneur. Rather, I was there at his request to ask him some questions in order to determine if he also, as I had suspected for seven years, was San Francisco's most notorious serial killer.

Before I begin to describe the man who was the Zodiac in chapter 13, we must first learn as much as we can about the killer by what he revealed about himself at his crime scenes and through his taunting letters to the press. We therefore begin our quest for his identity on a lonely stretch of back road in Solano County, California, on a cold early-winter's night.

PART ONE
LAKE HERMAN ROAD

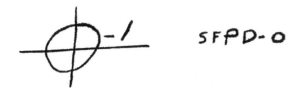

IN THE BEGINNING: DAVID FARADAY
AND BETTY LOU JENSEN

WHEN DECEMBER 20, 1968, rolled around it brought with it the promise of the end of one of the most tumultuous years in American history. It was a year in which both Martin Luther King, Jr., and Robert F. Kennedy had been gunned down in cold blood, and in which there were violent confrontations between youthful protesters like Abbie Hoffman's Yippies and Mayor Richard Daley's police at the Democratic National Convention in Chicago. The war in Vietnam was raging on amid loud and sometimes bloody protests at home. The failed wartime policy of escalation had led in March to the essential abdication of President Lyndon Johnson, who chose not to run for re-election after the January Tet Offensive by the North Vietnamese stunned the nation and revealed our vulnerabilities.

In Vallejo, California, a small, family-oriented city of roughly sixty-five thousand people situated twenty-five miles northeast of San Francisco, December 20 meant there were a mere five shopping days until Christmas. As the three astronauts of *Apollo 8* prepared to soar toward man's first rendezvous with the moon, spirits were high both in Vallejo and across the nation. But the violence that marred 1968 was not yet done with Vallejo, or with the people of the San Francisco Bay Area. Before this cold, clear, essentially moonless night was over, an unspeakably cowardly, brutal, and senseless crime would occur. It was a seemingly motiveless attack that shocked and confused Vallejoans by its sheer cold-bloodedness. By August of 1969, however, it took on even greater proportions as it became clear that this had been the opening act of an enigmatic, ruthless, and bizarre serial killer who would inflict a reign of terror over the entire region for the next six years.

The deaths of seventeen-year-old David Faraday and sixteen-year-old Betty Lou Jensen were not unlike those of two star-crossed lovers from a Shakespearean tragedy, and of all the murders in this brutal series of crimes, theirs may be the ones steeped in the bitterest of irony. David was one of the finest and most community-oriented young men at Vallejo High School and seemed to be a born leader. Betty Lou was an outgoing and friendly young lady who had a strict Christian Science upbringing. She went to rival Hogan High School across town.

Having met only the week before, David and Betty Lou made plans to go on their first "official" date on December 20. The brown-and-tan Faraday family 1961 Rambler arrived right on time, at 8:00 PM, at Betty Lou's house on Ridgewood Drive. The couple proceeded to tell her parents a little white lie to disguise their actual plans for that night. They said they were heading to a Christmas carol concert at her school, a concert that had actually been held the previous week. They then left, promising Mr. and Mrs. Jensen that they would be home by 11:00 PM, not knowing that if they had kept that promise, they would have lived to see December 21.

Nobody knows their exact movements that evening, but at some point David drove the Rambler east and headed out of Vallejo. Their ultimate destination was a lovers' lane in the unincorporated area of Solano County between Vallejo and the city of Benicia, an isolated area traversed by a dark, unlit thoroughfare. Its name is now legendary in Zodiac lore: Lake Herman Road.

Traveling along Lake Herman Road today is like taking a trip back in time. Although there have been recent rumors of possible development, this area remains essentially unchanged since that long-ago December night. Lake Herman Road was well known for its remarkable, impenetrable darkness. The spot that David had picked out for the couple's first date was about three miles east of Columbus Parkway, a road that skirts the eastern border of Vallejo. It was a nondescript roadside parking area in front of a high, somewhat rickety-looking chain-link rollback fence known as Gate #10 that was set well off the main road. The dirt access road beyond the gate led to a police firing range and a water pumping station that fed lake water to the city of Benicia. Since it was both secluded and dark, it was a popular location for young lovers. In those days and at that hour, there was very little traffic on Lake Herman Road.

Meanwhile, another man with plans to go to Lake Herman Road was just completing his own preparations for the evening. He was now dressed in dark clothing and ready to make his years of planning into a cold, stunning reality. He checked the magazine of his gun one last time to make sure it was fully loaded. He knew that the firing mechanism was ready to perform flawlessly, having cleaned it obsessively for the past several weeks, a skill he had been taught as a US Navy pilot in World War II. The man had also installed a special sighting mechanism that he knew he would need that night after having driven down Lake Herman Road many times in the past. He went out to the car he had procured for the evening, one of the legion of nondescript vehicles to which he had unfettered access. He felt confident that, even if someone happened to spot this car that night, it could never be traced back to him.

Before Betty Lou and David arrived at Gate #10, raccoon hunters Frank Gasser and Robert Connley were looking for small game down near the pumping station. It was an especially cold night, the temperature hovering just over twenty degrees. The hunters got there at 9:00 PM coming west on Lake Herman Road from the direction of Benicia. As they passed the turnout for the pumping station, where David and Betty Lou would later park, they noticed a four-door white 1960 Chevy Impala sitting unoccupied there. About the same time that the hunters passed, sheepherder Bingo Wesher was driving out of Gate #10 after tending his flock and saw the same car, describing it as a white Chevy coupe.

This white 1960 Chevy would become part of the legend that would grow around the Zodiac case, since this may have been the car driven that night by the Zodiac. However, since neither Wesher nor the hunters had any reason to jot down the car's plate number, the police were frustratingly unable to follow up on this potentially important lead.

David and Betty Lou arrived at the entrance to the Benicia pumping station sometime between 9:30 and 10:15 PM. They parked in the western part of the turnout facing south toward Gate #10. Because the moon was just a minute crescent barely out of its new phase with only 1 percent of its surface visible[1] and there were no street lights, the area was steeped in almost complete darkness. Just as it remains to this day, the parking area was nothing more than a roughly semicircular patch of dirt on the south side of the road.

Had it been light out, David and Betty Lou would have been able to clearly see the twin peaks of a local landmark, Mt. Diablo, looming in the distance in front of them. Mt. Diablo is visible from all over the Bay Area. Because of the way the terrain south of the turnout at Gate #10 is sculpted, creating a "visual funnel" of sorts, from this particular spot, Mt. Diablo looms large over the landscape. Mt. Diablo would play a sinister role in the events that were to be set in motion on December 20, and the "visual funnel" at Gate #10 may well have influenced the decision of the killer to choose this particular location for his first crimes.

Had David and Betty Lou known what happened here at 9:30 PM that evening, they might have thought twice about staying. Another

1   https://www.calendar-12.com/moon_calendar/1968/december

young couple had pulled off the road at the exact same spot in order for the driver to familiarize himself with the car's controls. The white Impala that had been there at 9:00 PM had apparently already left. The twenty-two-year-old driver was at the wheel of a new foreign sports car for the first time and had never before seen a dashboard with toggle switches on it.

In the police report on the incident, the young man said that a blue Plymouth Valiant drove toward them from the direction of Benicia. After it passed them, the car suddenly stopped and reversed, slowly backing down Lake Herman Road toward them. Sensing danger, the young man put the sports car in gear and took off down the road headed toward Benicia. He told police that there were two Caucasian passengers in the car, but he couldn't describe either of them. The other car followed them, but not at a dangerously close distance. When the two cars arrived at the east end of Lake Herman Road, the young man used his car's superior cornering ability to make a quick right onto a road that led to Benicia. The other car went straight along Lake Herman Road heading toward the on-ramp for Route 680. Considering there might be a confrontation with the occupants of the other car, the young man decided it was best to just drive home.

Finally alone in the turnout, David and Betty Lou made small talk about school and the upcoming Christmas season. David edged closer to Betty Lou, who suddenly asked if it was all right if she smoked. She rolled down her window a few inches and nervously slid ever so slightly away from David's advances. She eased closer to her door to direct the smoke out of the car. The cold night air now found a place to work its way into the vehicle. David turned on the engine and engaged the heater to ward off the chill, and the car became warm enough that both of them were able to remove their coats. It was now about 10:15 PM. As they peered out into the night sky, the teenaged couple may have seen their entire lives stretching out before them with worlds of possibilities.

In reality, they had about an hour left to live.

Were it not for the momentous events of December 20, 1968, the mundane details of people driving back and forth on a small byway on an otherwise ordinary night would've been lost to history long ago and of little consequence to anyone. However, because of what was about to happen, every tiny nuance about the precise movements of these individuals and what they did or did not see that night has become fodder for untold thousands of message-board posts. Every conceivable aspect of each individual's contribution to either the timing or the knowledge base of the events of that night has been recorded. Some of these innocent witnesses even became suspects themselves as amateur investigators picked apart their stories on the internet looking for the slightest of inconsistencies.

Only a few cars passed by the couple's Rambler on the lonely stretch of rural byway that night. The first was a young couple that was also looking for solitude on Lake Herman Road. They first spotted Faraday's car at about 10:15 PM. The girl in the car, whom I'll call Joan, later said she realized it was David Faraday who was parked in the turnout because she recognized his brown-and-tan Rambler. Seeing that this "make-out spot" was already occupied, Joan and her boyfriend continued on to the east end of Lake Herman Road.

Upon reaching the eastern end of the desolate road, they turned around and drove back toward Vallejo, passing David and Betty Lou's car once again. This was about 10:30 PM. The station wagon was still in the turnout. Had David and Betty Lou not been parked there first, Joan and her boyfriend may well have been the ones to fall victim to the tragedy that lay ahead. Had she and her friend chosen to park elsewhere in the spacious turnout, their very presence may well have prevented that tragedy from happening at all.

Another set of eyewitnesses also came forward. One of them was Peggy Your. She and her husband passed by the area just before 11:00 PM. The two hunters also viewed Faraday's Rambler as they left the area a few minutes later, shortly after eleven. With minor discrepancies as to the exact position of the car, both Peggy Your and the hunters stated they saw the Rambler still parked in the turnout.

At 11:00 PM David and Betty Lou were already due back at the Jensen home. However, it was such a beautiful night and they were having such fun talking with each other that they decided it would be all right to stay out just a little longer. As they talked and held hands, a car pulled up next to them around ten minutes later and parked about ten feet to their right, thus positioning itself between the Rambler and the rollaway gate, cutting off its lights and engine. With no interior lights on, it was impossible to tell who it might be in the inky blackness of Lake Herman Road. David and Betty Lou weren't concerned enough to leave. They likely assumed it was just some other high school kids coming out to join them for some late Friday-night fun.

The man in the other car sat silently in the dark, looking at the luminescent dial of his watch. It wasn't quite time for him to act. As he did this, a car approached from Vallejo. Was it the police coming out to check on things? What if they thought he was making a drug deal with the other car and asked him if they could search his vehicle? They'd certainly find out who he was, and he was not someone who easily fit the usual description of someone innocently parking on Lake Herman Road this late at night. He cursed himself for his miscalculation and unconsciously held his breath until the car passed by about 11:14 PM. But the vehicle was not a police car. James Owen, an oil refinery worker on his way to Benicia for the night shift, was behind the wheel. While Owen would later recall seeing David's Rambler and another car at the scene, he would not remember the make or model of the second car. When he failed to do so, the man who would later call himself the Zodiac caught the first of what would be several lucky breaks in his lethal career.

After the car passed, the man looked once again at his watch and waited patiently until it was time to act. He double-checked to make sure his dome light switch was off and carefully opened the car door. He emerged into the darkness and faced the other vehicle. David and

Betty Lou may have heard the other car's door open, but could not see the occupant.

The unknown, silent man had obviously planned for this evening, especially for the forbidding darkness of the area. He'd driven to this desolate spot numerous times before, just as he'd driven high-performance sports cars down many other lonely and dark roads in the Bay Area beginning in the late 1940s, to rehearse in the pitch-black conditions. He would later boast about having improvised a flashlight sighting mechanism that would be effective in the type of darkness in which he knew a standard gun sight would be useless. His repeated boasting on this topic would prove both his pride in this device and his familiarity with the area.

Betty Lou's window may have been rolled down already from when she was smoking, or she may have rolled it down to call out to see if the person in the other car was someone she or David knew. But she was greeted with only the sight of a small, thin beam of light pointed directly at them. David also saw it and immediately wondered if it was the police. Did they use such small flashlights? Wouldn't it be great if the Jensens found out they hadn't gone to the Christmas concert by their getting busted by the cops? He and Betty Lou weren't doing anything illegal. Why was that flashlight so small? It was after eleven. David was going to be in big trouble with Mr. Jensen.

Meanwhile, about three miles down Lake Herman Road toward Vallejo, Stella Medeiros had arrived at her home around 10:50 PM. She immediately received a call from her young son, who had just seen a movie in Benicia and needed a ride home. A little while later, she piled her young daughter and mother-in-law into her car, leaving just after 11:15 PM. She drove the two and seven tenths miles to the pumping station at a leisurely pace. The police would later calculate that it took her about three minutes at thirty to thirty-five miles per hour to reach Gate #10. What she was about to see would both change her life and haunt her dreams forever.

When her car reached the top of the hill east of the Marshall Ranch, Medeiros noticed the body of a young man lying next to the passenger's side of the station wagon. She then spotted what looked like a child lying about thirty feet behind the car. There was a lot of blood. Reflexively, her foot slammed down on the accelerator, and she careened down Lake Herman Road looking for someone, anyone, who could help these poor young people.

When she got to the intersection with Old Lake Herman Road, which runs south from Lake Herman Road about thirteen hundred feet east of the pumping station, she made a right turn and sped toward downtown Benicia. She made a left at the bottom of the hill and headed east desperately scanning the area for a sign of life. At a gas station, she noticed a Benicia police car. She told Captain Dan Pitta and Officer William Warner what she had seen and where, and the police car exploded to life and headed toward the eastern end of Lake Herman Road, its siren blaring, the officers wondering what exactly awaited them. If some madman had hurt these people, might he still be lurking there in the darkness?

When the officers arrived the full scope of the tragedy was apparent. There was a teenaged girl sprawled on her right side twenty-eight feet from the rear bumper of the car and toward the passenger's side. She lay motionless with multiple bullet wounds in her back and a sickeningly large pool of blood flowing from her onto the dirt and gravel. Her head was facing east, toward the car; her feet west, toward Vallejo. Though these nitty-gritty details were just something to enter into the police reports at the time, they would become very important seven months later. She would shortly be pronounced DOS—dead on scene—by a local doctor who came to the site to examine her.

David was lying faceup at a right angle to the station wagon with his feet against the rear passenger's-side wheel. He had been shot one time through the left ear, the bullet penetrating his skull diagonally from left to right and forward through his brain. A large pool of blood had formed under and around his head. He was still breathing, as the officers could see condensation flowing into the cold night air with every labored gasp he took. Pitta and Warner immediately summoned an ambulance to take David Faraday to Vallejo General Hospital on Tennessee Street in downtown Vallejo.

They then made a chalk outline of David's body. Pitta also called for an investigator from the Solano County Sheriff's Office (SO), since the crime had taken place in an unincorporated area of the county, outside the jurisdiction of Benicia PD. The officers then set about looking for evidence. They eventually found ten .22-caliber Super-X long-rifle shell casings scattered around the scene, one of which was recovered from the front passenger-side floorboard of the car. However, they found little else.

In 1968 murder had to have a motive—anger, jealousy, greed, revenge, robbery. In those days victims usually knew their killers as well. Sergeant Les Lundblad and Deputy Russ Butterbach, two investigators from the Solano County SO who were called to the scene by Capt. Pitta, quickly ruled out the most obvious motives in the Jensen-Faraday attack—robbery or sexual assault of the female victim. And through painstaking interviews with the various witnesses, they established that the time frame during which the murders were committed was extremely narrow, approximately 11:14 to 11:20 PM, though one could quibble over the exact time range. Lundblad also heard from two sets of eyewitnesses, Bingo Wesher and the two hunters, that there had been a white 1960s' Chevy in the area of the murder scene around 9:00 PM.

Betty Lou Jensen was already dead by the time police arrived. David Faraday died en route to the hospital. They had fallen victim to a heartless gunman simply because they were in the wrong place and stayed there until the wrong time. They had lost their promising young lives on their first date to satisfy the sick needs of an evil but brilliant man who would subsequently prove that his purpose was not only to simply murder but also to instill fear and dread in the people of the Bay Area for years to come.

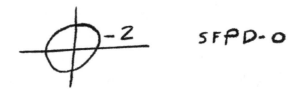

Lake Herman Road
Research

AS I BEGAN MY OWN RESEARCH into the Zodiac crime scenes, questions arose about certain aspects of the Jensen-Faraday murders. The first was with the statement of the young man driving the sports car who had parked at the eventual Lake Herman Road crime scene at 9:30 PM. He, along with his unnamed date that night, were frightened by the car that had followed them to the Benicia end of Lake Herman Road after initially driving past them.

In 2005 the man described the car he and his girlfriend were in as being "either an MG or a Triumph," both *British* makes.[2] As it turned out, the new sports car in which the pair was riding that night may well have been what attracted the attention of their tormenter in the first place. The toggle switches with which the young man was familiarizing himself when he pulled into the Gate #10 turnout were characteristic of

---

2   Male witness in statement to retired CHiP officer Lyndon Lafferty, retired naval intelligence officer Jerry Johnson, and retired VPD detective Jim Dean, January 2005.

imported sports cars and consistent with British makes, like the MG or Triumph the young man said he was driving, but not of American cars. The female passenger who owned the sports car was reportedly from Napa but was apparently living in San Francisco at the time.

The biggest question that this witness could answer today is, From which dealership was his date's British sports car purchased? Where was that dealership located? In San Francisco, where the young lady lived at the time, Vallejo, Napa, or elsewhere? If we presume for a moment that their pursuer was, in fact, the man who would later attack Faraday and Jensen and identify himself as the Zodiac, these are questions that could prove to be crucial to the case *and to the reason their car was targeted that night.*

(Note to reader: you can read my reconstruction of the Lake Herman Road crime scene, as well as other content, on my website, www.mikerodelli.com.)

...

In 2002 I befriended Russ Butterbach, one of the Solano County Sheriff's Office deputies who responded to Captain Pitta when he called for assistance. He and his rookie partner, Wayne Waterman, were sent to Vallejo General Hospital on the night of the Jensen-Faraday murders. Waterman had been on the job just forty days. Having been sent to interview Faraday about the incident, they learned that he had been DOA at the hospital. They inventoried his personal effects and took custody of them. Deputy Roger Wilson was called to photograph the body. Butterbach had noticed one odd thing: The boy was holding his red-stoned Vallejo High School 1969 class ring in an unnatural way. The tips of his thumb and ring finger of his left hand were forced together in an O, or loop. The ring had also been moved up onto the second knuckle of his ring finger. Normally, a ring is worn at the base of the first knuckle and flush against the palm. This caught Butterbach's eye. It seemed to him as if Faraday may have been trying to prevent someone from taking the ring from him.[3]

In the 1960s it was common for a high school boy to give his class ring to his girlfriend. She would then usually wrap wool around the band of the ring to make it small enough to fit her own finger. Wearing it was a sign that they were going steady. Had David Faraday planned to give his ring to Betty Lou that night? A friend of the couple, whom Zodiac researcher Tom Voigt interviewed in 2003, said that David had intended to do just that on December 20, 1968.[4] If so, his final act after being shot had been to fight heroically with his killer for the possession of the ring. Was this a last sign of his affection for Betty Lou before slowly drifting into unconsciousness?

As soon as Butterbach told me about his observation, I felt that the position of David's hand must have been much more than the product of coincidence or posturing after the injury to his brain. I knew from having studied neuroanatomy in college that a shot through the left side of the brain should potentially affect only the limbs of the *right* side of the body. The ring had been in David's left hand. A thought then flashed through my mind that evidently had not occurred to Butterbach in 1968: I immediately got angry and wondered what would have happened if Russ had bagged the ring that night and sent it to the lab. After all, even if logic seemed to dictate that Faraday should've been immediately unconscious after receiving his head wound, there was at least a suggestion that there had been a struggle for possession of that ring at some point.

I now asked myself, Did the killer wear gloves that night or not? Might he have grabbed the ring by placing his thumb on the top and his fingers on the bottom of it and then attempted to pull it off Faraday's finger? *And if so, might the killer's thumbprint at one point have been on*

---

3   There is a phenomenon called *cadaveric spasm* that occurs after death and can cause the hand to clench. However, this usually results in a closed fist, not the unusual configuration that Butterbach noted.

4   "The Lake Herman Road Tragedy," http://zodiackiller.com/LHR2.html.

the smooth red stone of that Vallejo High School class ring? Unfortunately, by the early 2000s, through handling, cleaning, and the evaporation of potential oils from the hand, it was probably long past the time that the ring could have been dusted for prints.

...

In April 2001, I received a thick folder representing the surviving police reports from the Solano County Sheriff's Office. Within those documents were many reports on the "usual suspects" of the day, at whom police looked as the possible perpetrator of the Jensen-Faraday murders. Accompanying a good number of these reports were samples of the writings of these men, in the form of confessions, parole letters, et cetera. Nearly all such letters I read were so poorly written by people who were barely literate that none of them could conceivably have aspired to writing the taunting letters from the killer that would soon begin to arrive.

...

The day after the murders the *Vallejo Times-Herald* carried a front-page article about the Jensen-Faraday tragedy. "Vallejo Teenagers Are Shot to Death near Lake Herman," the piece announced. Tucked innocuously to the left of this article was another piece, this one announcing news that wasn't nearly as significant to the average reader as a double homicide.[5] Called to my attention by researcher Chris MacRae of Canada, it discussed Vallejo's "sister city" program, which saw Vallejo forming a partnership with cities in foreign lands that, like Vallejo, had a strong association with shipping, ocean trade, et cetera. The article announced that the next week, Vallejo would be adding a second sister

---

5   Anonymous, "New Sister City Officials to Visit," *Vallejo Times-Herald*, December 21, 1968, p. 1.

city, Akashi, Japan, to the budding program. The very first sister city in that program, which had partnered with Vallejo some eight years earlier and was the *only* "sister" to Vallejo on December 20, 1968, was a small, unassuming seafaring town sitting on a fjord on the west coast of Scandinavia.

Its name, as mentioned in the article, was Trondheim, Norway.

PART TWO
BLUE ROCK SPRINGS

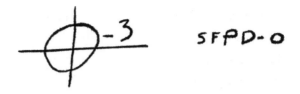

No Escape: Darlene Ferrin and Mike Mageau

DARLENE FERRIN, a twenty-two-year-old Vallejo, California, resident, was a young woman of the Age of Aquarius. Of that there can be no doubt. She had by such a young age already been married, divorced, and remarried. She was also the mother of a young daughter, who was born in 1968. Darlene had once hitchhiked across the United States and back and had allegedly witnessed a murder somewhere. She worked as a waitress at a local restaurant called Terry's Waffle House, a popular hangout in Vallejo. She was attractive, outgoing, full of life, and very popular with her customers. Some of them she allegedly dated, even after becoming a wife for the second time and a mother. Her husband, Dean, seemed not to be too perturbed by her behavior. Maybe he felt she needed to get it out of her system. After all, it *was* the Age of Aquarius.

One of the people Darlene knew from around town was nineteen-year-old Mike Mageau. He, along with his identical twin brother, Stephen, reportedly vied for Darlene's attention. The Mageaus went to the same school that Darlene had attended, Hogan High School. Mike was tall and exceedingly thin. He had a habit of trying to hide his scrawny physique by wearing several layers of clothing even on hot early-summer days in Vallejo. This habit would later lead to speculation on other, possibly darker motives for his unusual way of dressing.

On the night of July 4, 1969, Darlene was seemingly being pulled in many different directions at once while leaving her young daughter in the company of two teenaged babysitters. The police reports from that night detail a dizzying series of plans, broken engagements, and erratic movements that seem to argue against any rhyme or reason to her comings and goings, as some would later allege. The night was a microcosm of her helter-skelter lifestyle.

According to police reports, even though she had been charged by Dean and some friends with procuring fireworks for an impromptu Fourth of July celebration, Darlene made the five-minute drive to Mike Mageau's home. This happened between 11:30 PM and midnight. Some of the odd details that would dog this aspect of the case are that Mageau, in his apparent haste to get into Darlene's car, reportedly left the TV on, the lights blazing, and the door to his house open. Why he did this is unclear. However, these facts, combined with Mageau's unusual manner of dressing, have led to speculation that there was a nefarious reason for his leaving his home in such a rush. Was it a possible drug deal for which the pair was running late? Was Mike a burglar wearing layers of clothes that he could shed to change his appearance after committing a crime? It hardly seems that way given how randomly the events unfolded that night. In Mike's version of the events, which *could* have been self-serving, he and Darlene had planned at one point to go to San Francisco for a movie.

According to the police reports, Mageau stated that both he and Darlene were hungry, so they decided to get a quick bite to eat at Mr. Ed's, a local fast-food hangout on Springs Road west of Mageau's home. But Darlene said there was something urgent she wanted to speak to him about, something apparently more important than eating. So, at

Mike's suggestion, she made a quick U-turn just east of Mr. Ed's and doubled back toward the eastern side of Vallejo. Mike suggested they go to Blue Rock Springs Park. The park, which was across the street from the nine-hole Blue Rock Springs executive golf course, was a popular place for family picnics, Frisbee tossing, and other pleasurable outings during daylight hours. While a family venue during the day, this remote and desolate area on the outskirts of Vallejo became a lovers' lane and a drug-dealing haven by night.

Sometime just before midnight, Darlene drove northeast past the Lake Herman Road turnoff on Columbus Parkway, the same road that David Faraday had so tragically used six months earlier. She continued north on Columbus and entered the southernmost portion of the oval parking lot of Blue Rock Springs Park. The lot was separated from the grassy park area by large stones and logs that formed its eastern perimeter. The couple was just four miles from Gate #10 on Lake Herman Road, where the Jensen-Faraday tragedy had occurred the previous December—a seemingly random crime that was beginning to fade into the past. She parked, turned off the engine, and turned on the radio. Darlene's sister, Pam, would later allege that Darlene was chased to this spot. But other details of the events of that night, along with common sense and Mageau's police report, seem to indicate otherwise.

For whatever reason, Darlene drove to this area and parked her brown 1960 Corvair shortly before midnight. She and Mike were sitting in the car talking when three groups of kids celebrating the waning minutes of the Fourth came by in quick succession. Shortly after they left another car pulled into the lot after coming north on Columbus, from the direction of Vallejo. The small car parked alongside them about six to eight feet away on their left and slightly behind. It was just before midnight on July 4. The driver sat there for a short while with the headlights off. He then drove out of the lot, heading back in the direction from which he had come. Mike asked Darlene if she knew who had just pulled behind them. According to Mageau, she replied in a dismissive manner, leaving Mike to wonder later if she had known who it was and hadn't been particularly concerned, or if she had just been blowing the incident off as being insignificant.

A few minutes later, at what was subsequently determined to have been just after midnight on July 5, 1969, the same car returned and pulled about ten feet behind Darlene and Mike and offset slightly to the passenger's side. The driver left the headlights on this time. Someone got out of the car and, in contrast to the weak pencil flashlight that the man at the Lake Herman crime scene had used, turned on a large, blinding flashlight and walked around to Mike's side of the vehicle. The man was also carrying more firepower this time.

Mike assumed from the positioning of the car and the use of the flashlight that it was a Vallejo police officer patrolling the park, which was officially closed after dark. He and Darlene were going to be busted for being there, and Dean would probably find out that they had been together. Mike dutifully began reaching for his ID and advised Darlene to do the same. But when the man made it to the driver's side he didn't ask for Mike's driver's license through the rolled-down window. In fact, he didn't say a word. Instead, total mayhem was about to break loose within the confines of the compact car. According to Mike, the man just started firing a gun at them, and then he "kept on firing."

The first shot was a "free" shot at Mike, who was an unsuspecting, stationary target. The shooter missed hitting him in the skull, the presumed target, and the bullet smashed through his right cheek, lacerating his tongue and shattering his jaw. The bullet then passed through him and hit Darlene in her right side. Mike found himself cornered inside the vehicle with the madman silently pumping bullets into both him and Darlene. Trapped inside the Corvair, the couple could do nothing but scream, throw up their hands, thrash violently about, and contort their bodies in a vain effort to ward off the barrage of bullets. The shooter was blocking his exit, and there was only one place for Mike to go to try to escape the point-blank fire. With his fear surging, he somehow managed to propel himself backward over the front seat. However, since the Corvair was only a two-door vehicle, Mike had unwittingly made himself a sitting duck for the shooter. He had placed himself in the rear of the car from which there was no exit. With Mike's body out of his way, the killer began shooting into Darlene as she sat helplessly behind the wheel of the car. Blood sprayed all over the interior of the Corvair.

Apparently sated, the man slowly walked back to his car. As he did, from either anguish, pain, or both, Mike let out an agonizing scream into the night. This had the unintended effect of letting the killer know that his job was not yet complete. The killer slowly walked back to the car and fired twice more at Mike, who was lying on the back seat trying desperately to use his legs to ward off the deadly shots. Mageau took another bullet in the knee and one in his back. Although the man was shooting the equivalent of fish in a barrel, miraculously, he did not fatally wound Mike. The stranger fired two more rounds at Darlene; then he walked away as silently as he had approached.

His missing the initial head shot at Mageau at point-blank range may indicate that the shooter was not that handy with a gun. Although he had hit Betty Lou Jensen five times in the back, he had barely hit the long storage-compartment window of Faraday's station wagon and apparently missed the passenger's-side rear window of Faraday's car. (See my reconstruction of the Jensen-Faraday murders on www.mikerodelli. com.) This lack of skill is something about which the killer would later subconsciously hint by stating that at Lake Herman he had "sprayed" the bullets like a "water hose" at the fleeing girl, something an expert marksman would never have to do—or admit to doing, in any case.

When the carnage finally ceased, Mike had been hit by four bullets and Darlene by five rounds, one or more of which had initially passed through Mike. With your life flashing before your eyes, even a few moments can seem like an eternity and fewer than a dozen rounds seem like a fusillade of ten times that number.

Shortly after the shooter left, a carful of kids out cruising the area arrived at the park in search of some friends. Their headlights illuminated Mike, who was covered in blood. He told the frightened group about the attack, and they quickly left to phone the Vallejo Police Department.

Help arrived in the form of Officer Dick Hoffman of the VPD. He had been patrolling the area in an unmarked car and found Mike Mageau lying outside the car and Darlene Ferrin pushed up against the driver's-side door. When Mageau tried to tell Hoffman what had happened in those harrowing moments, blood took the place of words. Soon, a car containing VPD sergeants John Lynch and Ed Rust arrived on the scene. The pair would become the lead investigators in the case.

An ambulance was immediately summoned to the scene.

When the pair arrived at Kaiser Hospital, Darlene was quickly wheeled into the ER. She was pronounced DOA at 12:38 AM. Mike, although gravely wounded, was taken immediately into surgery and survived. In preparing Mike for surgery, the doctors noted his unconventional manner of dressing, especially for this hot July 4–5 night. He had on no fewer than three pairs of pants, three sweaters, and a long-sleeved button-down shirt. As discussed earlier, this would become fodder for speculation as to exactly why he had dressed in this manner and what the couple was really doing in the park that night.

After shooting the kids at Blue Rock Springs, the killer had one more piece of business to attend to before heading home for the night.

...

At 12:40 AM a man picked up the receiver of a pay phone, dialed O for the operator and asked for the Vallejo Police Department. When he was put through, he had a chilling message for dispatcher Nancy Slover and the rest of the VPD. Spoken in a monotone as if he were reading from a script, the man said, "I want to report a double murder. If you will go one mile east on Columbus Parkway to the public park, you'll find kids in a brown car. They were shot with a nine-millimeter Luger. I also killed those kids last year." As he spoke, Slover tried to jump in and get more details to keep him on the line so the call might be traced. When she did so, the man would speak more forcefully and drown her out. He was clearly not to be interrupted. At the end of this unprecedented and frightening call, the man's voice suddenly became more taunting and he said, "Good-bye," starting on a high note and ending in a chilling bass. Then the voice was replaced by dead silence.

After the call Slover sat in a state of shock before pulling herself together and quickly writing down from memory the caller's exact words. She then immediately initiated a trace on the call and ran for a supervisor.

The interesting thing about the directions the caller provided is that Columbus Parkway doesn't run east to west. However, as Zodiac researcher Ed Neil pointed out to me in 1999, it does run *northwest to southeast*. So, in order to go one mile *east* to arrive at Blue Rock Springs Park, you have to start out one mile *northwest* of that location. The place that takes you to is the intersection of Columbus Parkway and an obscure dead-end byway named St. John's Mine Road.

Why did Zodiac pick that remote location as his starting point? That's one of the many mysteries surrounding the case. Later, I'll propose a possible reason for this seemingly inexplicable and arbitrary starting point.

Several minutes later the call was traced back to a phone booth located at Joe's Union 76 Station in Vallejo. The police were both shocked and angered because this particular station was one they knew very well. It was located at the intersection of Tuolumne Street and Springs Road in Vallejo, just a few hundred feet from VPD headquarters where Slover had taken the call! In addition to the call itself, the close location from which it was made showed that this was a brazen killer who was making it personal by rubbing VPD's nose in both the Blue Rock Springs and Lake Herman crimes. He was essentially going onto their home turf to taunt them about both attacks.

...

Mageau would later describe his attacker as being on the short side, possibly five foot eight or so. He was also young, heavyset, and alone.

In a conversation I had with Ed Rust in 2013, he emphasized that the man Mageau saw could not have been anywhere near six feet tall, since his head had barely been higher than the low-profile Corvair in which Mageau had been sitting.[6] Mageau said at that time that although the man was short, he was solidly built—"beefy"—and around two hundred pounds. He described him as having a large face with no glasses. His hair was light brown, nearly blond, and curly. It has never been made clear that Mageau knew the difference between *curly* hair and *wavy* hair. He was driving a car that closely resembled Darlene's Corvair, either the exact same model or possibly a Renault make.

Mageau, who was severely traumatized, emphasized that he only got to see his attacker in profile. His description was so seemingly unreliable and flexible that years later he would pick out a man named Arthur Leigh (pronounced lē) Allen, the main suspect of author Robert Graysmith's *Zodiac* who was named Robert Hall Starr in that work. Allen was six feet tall and nearly bald in 1969 (Exhibit 1). Allen would have towered over the Corvair.

However, one man immediately came to the fore as a possible suspect: a bartender who had made amorous advances toward Darlene. That lead quickly fizzled out after a thorough investigation, leaving investigators with yet another puzzling and seemingly senseless crime to solve, with one man now claiming responsibility for both this attack and the Jensen-Faraday murders.

---

6   Vallejo Police Sgt. Ed Rust (Ret.), personal communication, 2011. Rust stated that, in his hospital interview with Mike Mageau the day after he was shot, Mageau was adamant that the perpetrator, as measured against the Corvair that Mike had been sitting in, was no more than 5'8".

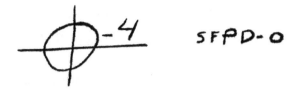

BLUE ROCK SPRINGS RESEARCH

WHEN A SERIAL MURDER CASE, like that of the Zodiac, remains unsolved for fifty years, it's bound to grow in complexity, as conjecture and myth slowly attach themselves like remoras to a shark. Every year, amateur researchers, newsmen, and even family members of the victims come along with new testimony, theories, or stories, some of which are based on fact and others on fantasy, attention-seeking, overactive imaginations, or failing memories. Nowhere is this more evident than in the case of the murder of Darlene Ferrin. What appears to be a straight-forward ambush by an unknown assailant, similar to what happened at Lake Herman just over six months prior, has grown into a story that defies efforts to unravel it to get to the truth about what happened that night.

Speculation that started with Robert Graysmith's 1986 book, *Zodiac,* persists to this day—that Darlene and Mike were chased, or "herded," to the spot where they ended up. However, had Darlene been forced to this area by this driver, why didn't she simply pull away before the car returned after it initially left? The fact that she didn't leave the parking lot and go to a safe place seems to prove that she wasn't chased out of Vallejo to Blue Rock Springs. This idea of her being herded to the park is part of the burgeoning mythology that has built up since the attack.

Over the years, so many rumors and theories on the death of Darlene Ferrin have arisen that it would take an entire book to chase them all down. There was the rumor that Darlene was the "key" to the entire Zodiac case and that she had given the killer the nickname "the Zodiac." Then there are people who called police and said that Darlene was a witch and/or was involved with a witch from San Francisco. There's also been speculation that after Darlene and Dean purchased a home in Vallejo, they had a "painting party" in order to freshen it up. One of the attendees is rumored to have been an odd and taciturn man named Lee, who many have speculated was none other than Arthur *Leigh* Allen, the main suspect in Graysmith's 1986 book. Other lines of thought have a police officer or someone from a satanic cult being her killer. None of these assertions has ever been proven.

The Vallejo PD investigation was spinning its wheels three weeks after the Blue Rock Springs attack when suddenly there was a major development. This breakthrough, however, wasn't brought about by the efforts of the investigators. Rather, it came from the killer himself communicating once again. But this time he chose the US mail as his medium, not the phone company. And his audience was not the police themselves but the local newspapers. The case was about to evolve to a new level that would eventually make it one of the most enigmatic and talked about mysteries in the history of crime.

PART THREE
THE FIRST LETTERS ARRIVE

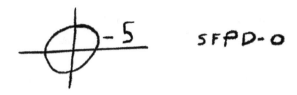

Credit Where It Is Due:
Zodiac Emerges

ON FRIDAY, AUGUST 1, 1969, a little less than one month after the attack at Blue Rock Springs, Carol Fisher sat at her desk at the Bay Area's largest circulation newspaper, the *San Francisco Chronicle*. Letter opener poised at the ready, she stared at the virtual tidal wave of letters to the editor that inundated the paper every day. Freshly back from her summer vacation, Carol's unenviable job was to winnow these letters to the half dozen or so the paper would include in the next day's edition.[7]

The correspondence the paper received day in and day out was usually replete with people's gripes about the habits of the hippies still occupying the Haight, pet peeves about privileged politicians, and an assortment of mostly harebrained ideas of how to improve the quality of life in the post–Summer of Love era. In other words, nothing even remotely newsworthy. Certainly nothing to rival a story like the one

---

7 The following account is based on events described in Robert Graysmith's *Zodiac* and in the David Fincher movie *Zodiac* (2007), which was based on Graysmith's book.

that had just gripped the world—Neil Armstrong and Buzz Aldrin landing safely on the moon—ever came out of her little corner of the newspaper.

But that was about to change.

Today was to be no ordinary day. In fact, one letter sitting in the pile in front of her would be the only one of the untold thousands of letters she would read during her career that would immediately change her life. The words "Please Rush to Editor" were dashed off on both sides of the envelope, and it had twice the postage needed to mail it. This single letter would plunge the *San Francisco Chronicle*'s readership and the entire Bay Area into a profoundly dark period that would hang like a malevolent fog from the Golden Gate over the populace for more than a generation.

Carol Fisher didn't know it at the time, but two other area newspapers, the *San Francisco Examiner* and the *Vallejo Times-Herald*, had also received similar letters that morning. When specific parts of each of these three letters were combined, as the writer would instruct, they would cause a huge explosion that would rock the Bay Area like chemicals in some mad scientist's laboratory.

In a nearby room, the editorial staff of the paper had begun to assemble to discuss its August 2, 1969, edition. It was a relatively slow news day in the Bay Area. Since colleges and universities were deep into their summer breaks, clashes between students and police, like the recent People's Park incident that had created a war-zone-like feel in Berkeley in May, as well as anti-Vietnam protests, were in a period of remission. Meanwhile, the hippie population in the city had thinned considerably from its 1967 levels, as more hardcore drugs, like heroin and speed, had inevitably replaced the harmless hallucinogens that had fueled their movement in its more utopian moments.

Grizzled veterans of the business, like editors Al Hyman and Templeton Peck, took up their accustomed positions at the conference table alongside the metro and national editors. The men discussed the day's news—from the SEC announcing that a record $7.1 billion in corporate securities were offered in the second quarter of 1969 to Elvis Presley holding a press conference that day in Las Vegas. Suddenly there was an urgent rap on the door that jolted everyone out of their discussions. That knock preceded a wild-eyed Carol Fisher bursting into the room brandishing a letter.

The usually unflappable Peck, taken by surprise, stared at her for a moment, not quite understanding the intrusion. What was so pressing about a damn letter to the editor? Then he accepted the document and read it quietly to himself.

"Jesus Christ!" he muttered upon digesting part of its contents. He then read the letter out loud. The two-page missive was written in blue felt-tip pen on narrow, odd-sized stationery later determined to be monarch-sized paper, ten and a half by seven and a quarter inches. (Note: since all the letters sent by the killer are readily available on the net, I do not reproduce them here.) The overall appearance of the letter suggested that it had been written in haste, not carefully composed. It was full of strange misspellings of common words, like "frunt" and "Christmass."[8] Many of the lines ran steeply downhill to the right, as if they had fallen off some invisible cliff. And there were a few other characteristics of the writing: the lowercase d was so slanted that it looked as if it were going to tip over to the right. But the most noticeable thing was his letter k, which was made with three strokes instead of the usual two. In subsequent letters, the man's letter f was written so that it looked like a candy cane in its exaggerated execution. Surely, the letter writer's handwriting would be easily recognized by using the letter K alone.

The missive provided a laundry list of facts that constituted an admission of cold-blooded murder and was clearly intended to pose a taunting challenge both to the reader and the police. Like so many shots from a gun, the author spat out one specific detail after another about two deadly lovers'-lane attacks that had taken place in the Vallejo

---

8   Interestingly, although Zodiac appeared to be semiliterate due to his many outrageous misspellings, conversely, he knew how to use a semi-colon, as evidenced by their presence, especially in some of his early letters.

area. The first was of the murder the previous month near a "golf course"; that is, Blue Rock Springs Park adjacent to Blue Rock Springs golf course. The other was of the attack during the previous Christmas season. The roster of facts the author provided included the types of ammunition used, the number of shots fired, the positions of the bodies, a specific wound one victim received, and even the type of clothing one of the victims had been wearing. The writer clearly knew what he was talking about and claimed that, other than himself, only the police could confirm these statements. The tone of the letter could best be described as assertive—like that of a person with power who was accustomed to barking orders to underlings. The author stated that he had also sent letters to the rival *San Francisco Examiner* across town and the *Vallejo Times-Herald*. The letter writer provided no name for himself, and the letter was unsigned except for a stark, frightening crossed-circle symbol that seemed to resemble the gun sight on a rifle.

This symbol would later be interpreted many different ways as more and more people from different backgrounds saw it over the next several decades. One interpretation that seemed to get lost in the mix was that the symbol closely resembled what is known in Viking/Norse culture as "Odin's cross."[9] (Exhibit 2). Odin is the highest god in the Norse pantheon and would also be associated with another symbol the killer would place on a letter some fifteen months later. The nascent trail that began with Vallejo's sister-city relationship with an obscure Norwegian town had just picked up another small Norse-related stepping stone.

Because of the distance, not so much geographically but socially, between Vallejo in the North Bay and San Francisco, nobody in the editorial room was even aware of the attacks the writer alleged, and wondered if they were real or fabricated.

There was one more page in the envelope: a sheet containing seventeen perfectly aligned columns and eight maniacally neat rows of symbols. In stark contrast to the sloppiness of the letter, the presentation

---

9   Eduard Versluijs, personal communication, 2000.

of this block of code was immaculate. The exceptionally neat nature of the artwork, or draftsmanship, whispered of meticulousness and obsession. The author stated that this array of characters was part of a cryptogram message and that the *Chronicle* had received one-third of the complete encoded message. Simple math dictated that the other two newspapers had received the missing parts of the code with their letters, which the letter writer confirmed. The author chillingly stated that the cipher contained his "idenity [*sic*]." For years to come, this would be interpreted by many to mean that the killer's *name* must be contained in the coded message. People seemed oblivious to the fact that a clue to one's identity can take many forms.

The letter concluded with a threat: if the paper did not print its portion of the cipher by that afternoon, August 1, the killer would spend the weekend cruising the area and killing a dozen innocent people. Given that the letter had been postmarked July 31 and didn't arrive until August 1, printing it that day was a physical impossibility. However, the date August 1 would become one of many interesting ones in the case that related to the suspect I was to develop just short of thirty years to the day after this letter arrived.

When Peck finished reading, there was stone silence in the room. What were they supposed to do? Nothing like this had ever happened at the *San Francisco Chronicle*—or at any other newspaper, for that matter. Was this man serious? Was it a prank? The writer certainly sounded matter of fact and deadly serious. Was he a lunatic or a mental patient? Should they run the letter? If they did, would other cranks be encouraged to crawl out of the woodwork and send all manner of craziness for the paper to print? But what if he was serious? If they didn't run it, would people's lives actually be at risk? This was potentially serious stuff.

They had a big decision to make. Peck asked that the owner of the *Chronicle*, Charles DeYoung Thieriot, join them to discuss the letter and how to handle it.

After Thieriot joined the group, all the previous debate about whether or not to run the letter seemed to fade into the walnut-paneled walls of the room. The question now was not if but on what page to run the letter. Peck suggested they make copies of everything and then call the police and allow them to take custody of the original evidence.

Nothing much was said about the underlying reason they decided to print the letter. The notion of saving lives by doing so sounded noble. However, there was another unspoken, and even unspeakable, reason for their decision. They were all newspapermen. They all recognized that a newspaper is first and foremost a business and running this story would be good for the paper's bottom line. A shocking piece about a man who first confesses to murder and then dares the public to discover his true identity by decoding a cipher was sure to mean a huge spike in circulation. The notion that someone might identify the alleged killer either through his handwriting or by decoding the madman's message was reason enough for the paper to move forward. The threat of more violence by the letter writer served as justification to do so.

The *San Francisco Chronicle* acceded to the professed killer's demands. But so as not to give in to all of his whims, Thieriot denied him the front-page coverage he so brazenly tried to wrest from them. The story, "Coded Clue in Murder," ran on page four the next day, August 2, a day later than the letter writer had demanded. In the meantime, the three newspapers forwarded the letters to the police, who in turn provided copies of the three blocks of symbols to the FBI and the Office of Naval Intelligence for decoding.

The Sunday combined edition of the *San Francisco Examiner* and *San Francisco Chronicle* printed all three blocks of code, which has become known as the "Three-Part Cipher," thus giving the public the opportunity to become partners in solving the case. This attracted the attention of a couple, Donald and Bettye Harden of Salinas. Mr. Harden was a history teacher looking for something to give him some mental stimulation on his summer break, so he and his wife decided to try their hand at the code. The first problem they encountered was that it didn't appear the killer had provided a clue to how the three blocks should be arranged to attempt to decode them. Which one came first?[10]

Harden and his wife became immersed in the code. Hours later they noticed it was getting dark; the entire day had flown by without a solution. So they went to bed and slept on the problem, attacking it again with renewed determination the next day. They stuck to the task, with Bettye in particular refusing to give up. Through sheer perseverance, they eventually had the idea to look for double symbols representing the letter *l* in the word *kill*. Even though the author had used multiple symbols to disguise various letters, amazingly, he had used symbols for the letter *l that closely resembled navy semaphore flags.* They were similar enough to each other to allow the Hardens to recognize the *i-l-l* pattern in such words as *kill* and solve the bizarre message, which read as follows (the killer's spelling errors are left intact):

> I like killing people because it is so much fun. It is more fun than killing wild game in the forrest because man is the most dangeroue anamal of all. To kill something gives me the most thrilling experience. It is even better than getting your rocks off with a girl. The best part of it is that when I die I will be reborn in Paradice and all the I have killed will become my slaves. I will not give you my name because you will try to sloi down or stop my collecting of slaves for my afterlife.

---

10 In fact, Zodiac had provided a clue to how to arrange the three blocks. It lay in the manner in which he named the three newspapers in the same order in each of his three letters. When the code blocks were arranged in the order in which the newspapers were always named—*Vallejo Times–Herald, San Francisco, Examiner* and then *San Francisco Chronicle*—they were arranged properly. This clue was not revealed until I happened to discover it in 2013. In 1969, however, the Hardens had no idea which block came first, second, or third, compounding the difficulty of their task.

At the end of message were eighteen symbols that appeared to be gibberish:

EBORIETEMETHHPITI

The Vallejo Police Department sent the decoded message to the FBI for authentication. After it was verified to the satisfaction of Chief Jack Stiltz, the solution was printed in the newspapers, and resourceful puzzle solvers throughout the Bay Area began treating the eighteen letters at the end of the code as an anagram. They anagrammed the letters and proposed various possible names, none of which checked out. Some, like "Robert Emmet the Hippie," were missing letters. Others made little sense.

As the public began to digest this letter, some possible leads developed. One reader said that the concept of man as "the most dangerous animal of all" may have come from the 1924 short story "The Most Dangerous Game," by Richard O'Connell. Because this story had been widely read by untold numbers of high school students and had even been made into an RKO movie in 1932, this possible lead couldn't help the police narrow down the list of suspects. However, it did possibly give some insight into the killer's mindset.

Another bizarre and frightening concept was the notion of this man killing people in order to make them his "slaves in the afterlife." Robert Graysmith indicated that this idea may have been rooted in "southeastern Asian civilization or devil-worshiping cults."[11] Another possible origin that people may have missed at the time was one that had already reared its head with the crossed circle and its relationship to Odin's cross: *"Slaves in the afterlife" also has roots in Viking/Norse culture.* Other possible references to Norse culture would appear in Zodiac's many subsequent letters. Some of these references were obscure and cryptic ones that would remain hidden until as late as 2014, when I discovered them. Others, though, as we will see, were obvious. The mention of "slaves in

---

11   Graysmith, p. 60.

the afterlife" along with Odin's cross and Vallejo's sister-city relationship with Trondheim began a slowly emerging pattern of Norse references in the locations of Zodiac's crimes and also in his letters.

At Viking funerals it was not uncommon for the deceased to be sent off into his afterlife in Valhalla on a ship that was set afire and cast out to sea. The master was often dispatched with a female slave who was killed and placed on the boat with him. She was to serve him in his afterlife just as she had during his life on Earth. In Gunnel Friberg's 2000 book, *Myth, Might, and Man*, he states, "It also happened that slaves were killed at burial ceremonies to accompany their masters into the realm of the dead."[12]

One thing police keyed in on at the time was the writer's use of the phrase "getting your rocks off." They felt that this phrase, which was apparently not in common use in 1969, may have been a clue that Zodiac was an older individual. In fact, other potential clues later on would point in the same direction.

One of the cleverest moves the police made early in this game was to try to draw the killer out by publicly challenging his knowledge of the Solano County crime scenes. Chief Stiltz of the Vallejo Police Department stated that he needed to see "more facts" to be convinced of the letter writer's credentials. The killer eagerly obliged by penning a second letter to the *San Francisco Examiner*, received August 4, 1969. This was technically his fourth letter, given that the first letter was mailed in three parts. In this letter, the killer provided a name for himself that would prove to be every bit as chilling and puzzling as his seemingly motiveless crimes. The letter foreshadowed all of the killer's confirmed mailings of the next year and a half by starting with a chilling line that in the future would herald the arrival of a new communication from the killer: **"This is the Zodiac speaking."**

Where did this odd name come from? What led this man to call himself the Zodiac? This phrase, "This is the Zodiac speaking," was

12   Gunnel Friberg, *Myth, Might, and Man*, (Stockholm: Riksantikvarieämbetets Förl., 2000), p. 11.

similar to the way a "polite and polished [British] gentleman" might have answered the phone, as stated in a 2009 article by Mark Hewitt, who himself had British roots.[13] And where did the name Zodiac originate? Of course, many people assumed it had to do with astrology. Some pointed out that there was a Dr. Zodiac in the 1939 movie *Charlie Chan at Treasure Island,* which took place in San Francisco. This was yet another possible reference to old movies that bears further scrutiny later in this book.

San Francisco Police Department (SFPD) chief of detectives Martin Lee would later speculate that the name Zodiac suggested that they might find some pattern to the Zodiac murder dates in the field of astrology. In the end, he was right about there being a pattern, but Lee would have been shocked beyond words to learn what the actual basis for that pattern was.

In his August 4, 1969, letter, the writer provided more details about the December and July murders he had committed, in order to prove he was the killer. One such statement stands out. The killer wrote of his attack on Mike Mageau at Blue Rock Springs, "When I fired the first shot at his head, he leaped backwards at the same time thus spoiling my aim." As stated earlier, Mageau made it clear that he'd thought the man was a police officer coming to see what they were up to and that Mike had even fished around for his ID and asked Darlene to do the same. So he was totally unprepared for the first shot. The statement by Zodiac therefore appears to be his attempt at making an excuse for being the poor shot that I believe he demonstrated himself to be, first by barely hitting the long window of Faraday's station wagon and then by completely missing the rear passenger's-side window of the Rambler at Lake Herman and shooting into the roof of the car. He didn't want to admit that he had tried to blow the boy's head off but had missed and ended up making a nonfatal shot to his mouth and jaw.

---

13   Mark Hewitt, "The Zodiac's Connection to Britain," *Radians and Inches,* vol. 1, no. 1: 28 September 2009, p. 6.

He also did a very interesting thing: to further prove he had committed the murders, he revealed that, in order to hit his victims in the impenetrable darkness of Lake Herman Road, he'd taped a small pencil flashlight onto the end of his gun as a sighting mechanism. He would boast about his gun sight once more in a future letter. But why mention something that nobody on the scene of the crime could possibly verify existed, since light beams leave no trace? The answer is that he was clearly very proud of his ingenuity in solving the problem of how to carry out his deadly attack in the complete darkness of the Lake Herman area.

After the flurry of interest and fear this story generated in early August 1969, it slowly began to slip beneath the consciousness of the public when there were no new developments. It was replaced by such stories as the seven horrific murders committed in Los Angeles by the Manson Family on August 9 and 10 and the Woodstock Festival, which started on August 15. But despite his silence, the Zodiac wasn't finished doing murder and mayhem in Northern California. Seven weeks later, on an early autumn afternoon in the wine country of Napa County, California, a couple would come face-to-face with a man who had intruded into their lives with two intentions: to first frighten them with his appearance and then to kill them. There was just one problem with his plan: since neither of them had spent the summer of 1969 in Northern California, they had no idea who the Zodiac Killer was.

PART FOUR
LAKE BERRYESSA

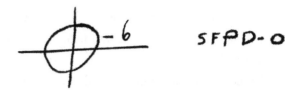

HORROR ON THE SHORELINE: CECELIA SHEPARD AND BRYAN HARTNELL

"That sign on the hood was real distinctive to me because I didn't know what it meant."
—victim Bryan Hartnell in article by L. Pierce Carson, "Hartnell: 'I Refused to Die,'" *The Napa Register*, October 7, 1969, p. 9a

AFTER THE TWO AMBUSH ATTACKS in Vallejo in December 1968 and July 1969 and the series of taunting letters in July and August, Zodiac fell silent for over a month. But that silence wasn't an indication that he was anywhere near finished terrorizing the region. In fact, he'd only been warming up. His next attack was carefully planned to include a frightening element intended to cause the maximum amount of fear and intimidation in his victims through their attacker's appearance.

On college campuses across the country, September means the start of a fresh school year and all the excitement and promise that it holds. In the early fall of 1969, Bryan Hartnell was a very tall and lean twenty-year-old pre-law student at Pacific Union College, a Seventh Day Adventist school in Angwin, California. He was so tall, in fact, that he had difficulty judging the height of others. Since almost everyone was shorter than he was, he had little frame of reference. Or as he put it, it was "always down, never up." Bespectacled and with brown hair, he hailed from a small city outside Portland, Oregon, called Troutdale, where he'd spent the summer that year. He drove a white 1956 Volkswagen Karmann-Ghia. Bryan was in his third year at PUC, and while studying pre-law he was also taking a class in sociology. These were rather sad days for Bryan because a pretty, petite, twenty-two-year-old blonde-haired music major he'd met at Pacific Union two years before had decided to relocate to be closer to her family and to attend the University of California at Riverside.

Her name was Cecelia Shepard, and she was from Loma Linda in Southern California.

During the time Bryan and Cecelia attended school together, they had become close friends. She was in Angwin to pack some belongings, so she and Bryan decided to spend one last day together. They eventually decided to go to Lake Berryessa, a manmade recreation area that had been created by flooding a nearby valley. At 5:15 PM Bryan honked and waved as they drove into the area and passed by a couple they knew who were heading south to the Rancho Monticello Resort on the lake. Bryan and Cecelia found a quiet spot on the western shore of the lake and made a U-turn to park on the east side of Knoxville Road.

It was a long trek from the side of the road to a point of land with three oak trees set in a wide configuration. The taller tree to the south was about seventy-five feet from the other two, which were about twenty feet from each other on the northernmost tip of the peninsula (Exhibit 3). The south side formed a little levee of sorts that was elevated above the high water mark during most of the rainy season and served as a footpath to get to the peninsula during periods of high water. They had laid out their picnic blanket on a piece of land that became an island in the height of the rainy season when a tongue of water crept in from the north and created a small channel that separated the peninsula from the mainland. The island, which ran north–south at right angles to the levee, was unusual in that it was humpbacked, so that the couple was actually perched on top of a mound. They were about fifteen hundred feet from their car.

Bryan and Cecelia couldn't have been there for much more than an hour when Cecelia noticed they had company. They were lying in the shade of the two trees on the northern point as the sun began to cast elongated shadows around them. Bryan was lying on ground that sloped down toward the lake, which allowed him to look out east over the water, while Cecelia was on her stomach at an angle to him. She lay on his left, or north, side facing southwest with her head resting on his chest. She could clearly see the area of the park to their south, toward the levee where they'd walked onto the peninsula.

On that still afternoon, the couple was lazily reminiscing about the good times they'd had at PUC while enjoying the lake and each other's company. Suddenly, Cecelia became distracted and didn't answer a question Bryan had put to her. "There's a man over there," she said. Bryan assumed from the direction in which Cecelia was looking that "over there" meant the next piece of land south on the shoreline, which was characterized by jutting pieces of land separated by coves that bit deeply into the spaces between them. This would've placed the individual she saw about eight hundred to nine hundred feet away from them. Bryan made a dismissive comment about her sighting, and they drifted back into their conversation. Cecelia remarked that the man had gone behind a tree. Bryan assumed the man was relieving himself on the distant shoreline. The first inkling Bryan got that there was any danger at hand was when Cecelia said, "Oh my God! He's coming towards us and he has a gun."

When Bryan looked up, it was with the grim realization that the man Cecelia had been describing was not on the opposite side of the cove but had emerged from behind the larger tree on the southern part of their peninsula. He was essentially right on top of them. Instantly standing to face the intruder, Bryan found himself looking upon an odd and frightening presence.

The man was dressed as some kind of bizarre commando, and he was walking quickly toward them. He extended a black gun in his right hand toward the couple. The color of the gun made it blend in with the rest of the man's outfit: a dark shirt, black "old-fashioned" pleated pants that were tucked into black military-style boots, and black gloves. Over his head he had a rectangular black hood with a hole for his mouth and eyeholes that were covered with clip-on sunglasses. Despite the gravity of the situation, the hood was somewhat comical in that its shape mimicked an inverted grocery bag. Underneath the hood he had on a second pair of glasses. Why did he go so far to cover his eyes? Were they distinctive in some way? A bib came down over the front of the costume. The only flash of white in the entire outfit was a three- or four-inch symmetrical crossed circle emblazoned on the bib. The symbol meant nothing to Bryan or Cecelia. Around his waist the man wore a belt containing a holster on the right side for the gun and a wooden sheath on his left side holding a long, approximately twelve-inch, thin-bladed knife sharpened on both sides. It resembled a bayonet or bread knife and looked somewhat crude and homemade.

To Bryan the man looked as if he'd just walked out of a store that sold Halloween costumes. Where else would someone have found such a getup? The costume gave the man the look of an executioner who had emerged from some medieval nightmare. Bryan spotted a shock of dark brown hair through the eyeholes of the hood. The hair was either greasy or wet with perspiration, which wouldn't be surprising for someone dressed entirely in black on an extremely hot day.

But it was that symbol on the man's bib that caught Bryan's attention. The crossed circle appeared to have been carefully and maybe even professionally embroidered onto the garment in white thread. Bryan was impressed by the care with which it had been sewn into the black fabric, not just carelessly thrown on with white paint. Had Cecelia and Bryan lived in Northern California during the summer months instead of Southern California and Oregon respectively, they may have recognized the crossed circle as being identical to the ones used to sign the Zodiac's taunting messages from July and August. But as it stood, they were completely clueless. Zodiac's attempt to parlay his measure of fame from the summer of 1969 into terror in September had fallen flat with these two new victims.

Cecelia and Bryan kept staring in disbelief at the apparition looming before them. What did he want? The late afternoon sun still shimmered on the water, but all of a sudden the couple no longer heard birds chirping in the two trees above them; in fact, there was nothing but dead silence. Then from under the hood came a voice: "I just want your money and your car keys."

So it was just a robbery after all. Thank goodness! While the man's disguise seemed elaborate and bizarrely threatening, his motive was nonetheless pretty mundane. Bryan exhaled a sigh of relief.

The voice assured them, "Just do what I say and nobody gets hurt." This allowed the couple to relax a little. He was just going to rob them despite his appearance and having not one but two weapons. If they cooperated, everything would be OK. Was the man telling them the truth, or was the robbery angle simply a ploy to ensure their cooperation? This likely didn't occur to a couple that was hoping against hope for the best. But there was a problem.

"I've only got a few cents on me," Bryan sheepishly replied. This statement was met with steely silence. Bryan, searching for a way to placate the man, added, "I could write you a check."

"There's no time," the man insisted. "I'm an escaped convict from Montana, and I killed a guard getting out of prison. My car is hot, and I need to get to Mexico." The costumed man may have mentioned the name of an obscure penal facility in Montana, Deer Lodge State Prison. However, there's enough controversy over this point to call this possibility into question.

Now Bryan and Cecelia became a bit more concerned. The man had admittedly already killed someone. This changed the game considerably. He was also apparently desperate, another bad sign. Cecelia was too frightened to talk, so Bryan picked up the conversation for both of them. And talk he did. Since he was taking that sociology course that semester, he felt that maybe he could defuse the situation by conversing with the man. The man had put him at such ease with the robbery angle that Bryan, sensing no other motive, had hoped to write a class paper about his experience with the robber after it was over, as he admitted later.[14]

Knowing the man had killed before, Bryan made small talk with him—anything to keep the man distracted. As long as he was talking, Bryan reasoned, he would not be shooting anyone or unsheathing that terrifyingly long-bladed knife. After all, the man had told them that all he wanted was money and Bryan's car.

The man ordered Bryan onto his knees, reached into his jacket, and pulled out precut lengths of the hollow plastic rope that was commonly used for clotheslines in the 1960s. He then ordered Cecelia to tie Bryan up, and she promptly did so, intentionally tying him very loosely. She was hoping that if the opportunity arose, he could break free and take on the man to disarm him. But that opportunity never presented itself.

The man then said, "I need to get you *both* tied up." He then proceeded to bind Cecelia's hands and retie the bindings on Bryan's hands so that they were painfully tight. Bryan could sense the feeling slowly fading from his hands. With that, the man ordered the couple onto their stomachs.

Bryan would later tell Napa SO sergeant John Robertson about the man's unusual manner of speaking. He didn't have any recognizable accent that Bryan had ever heard before. Rather his voice was "distinctive" and when he spoke the words "just came out." He struggled to describe the man's unique manner of speaking, but in a 1989 interview for the TV show *Crimes of the Century*, Hartnell stated that it was "lifeless and without expression."[15] One thing we do know is that the

---

14   David Fincher, *This Is the Zodiac Speaking*, "Lake Berryessa," Paramount Home Entertainment, 2008.

15   Handwritten notes, producer of *Crimes of the Century: The Zodiac Killer*, 1989.

man spoke very slowly and deliberately. Bryan indicated it was something he "couldn't repeat" and likened it to a song. He said, "Sometimes
you know what you're going to say, but you just can't sing the melody
worth a darn."[16] Bryan described the manner of speaking as a "drawl."[17]
However, he apparently didn't recognize it as being a Southern drawl or
a Boston accent, since he didn't report it as such in the police interview.
There is a discussion of a potential suspect in the Napa police reports
who was later questioned and released specifically because he had a
"definite very fast manner of speaking which was *completely opposed to
the victim's statement concerning the suspect's voice*"[18] (italics mine). This
implies that the man Bryan described clearly had a noticeably *slow,
deliberate manner of speaking.*

Even though he was looking down the barrel of a gun, Bryan
bristled at the notion of being tied up hand and foot and incapacitated.
He didn't see the reason for such a move if the man were simply going
to take their money and their car and then leave. How would they get
off the peninsula? It was going to be dark soon. Apparently, the possibility of being murdered was not on Bryan's mind. He was thinking of
nothing more than getting back to civilization after the man drove off
with his "cherry" Karmann-Ghia and headed for the border.

Hartnell voiced an objection. But the costumed man wasn't open to
debating the issue. He pointed his gun at Bryan and ordered him onto
his stomach. He proceeded to hogtie the pair with the precut lengths
of hollow plastic clothesline that he produced from under his jacket.
When he was finished, the man holstered his gun. Relieved, Hartnell
assumed the man was about to leave; then he suddenly caught a flash
of metal reflecting the setting sun: the man had unsheathed that long
knife. Almost immediately Hartnell felt it entering his back six times in

---

16 "Interview of John Robertson, Det/Sgt., Napa County Sheriff's Department with Bryan Calvin Hartnell, 27 September 1969," p. 15.

17 ibid.

18 "Napa County Sheriff's Office Supplementary Crime Report," October 5,
1969, p. 13.

quick succession, with one stab wound coming dangerously close to his heart. The killer then turned his attack on Cecelia, who had seen what had happened to Bryan and was frantic with fear. She sobbed, pleaded, rolled, and struggled against her bindings to try to avoid the rapidly rising and falling blade of her frenzied attacker. The man managed to stab her ten times through her blood-curdling screams. Bryan, still conscious, lay still and played dead, hoping the man wouldn't stab him yet again. Apparently satisfied, the man simply walked away.

He never even took Bryan's wallet, car keys, or pocket change.

Given their loss of blood, it took the couple several minutes to extricate themselves from their bindings. The slipperiness of their blood on the plastic rope actually helped loosen the cords. However, in addition to overhandling of the evidence over the years, it made potential touch-DNA analyses in the distant future a virtual exercise in futility due to contamination of their blood with any DNA left by the killer.[19] Bryan sat up and yelled as best he could across the water. A few boats passed by without stopping. He was finally able to get the attention of a man and his young son in a small rowboat equipped with an outboard motor. The fisherman seemed to be ignoring them when he stopped and listened for a minute, but then sped off to the north. Unbeknownst to Bryan, the man's destination was the Rancho Monticello Resort on the lake. He was going to get help.

That help came in the form of park ranger Bill White, who had been out on patrol when he heard a radio call about the stabbings. He immediately headed to the resort, and then he and resort employees Archie White and his wife and Mr. Fong sprang into action. They took off in a speedboat and arrived on the scene to find Cecelia rocking back and forth on her knees. She was in tremendous pain. Through their agony, the couple gave a description of the strange man who had done this to them.

---

19 There is a photo in the *Napa Register* from October 1, 1969, of the two SO detectives handling the clothesline, thus adding their DNA to that of Hartnell and Shepard, as well as possibly to that of their attacker.

Meanwhile, at 7:40 PM, a call came in to the Napa Police Department. A young officer, Dave Slaight, answered the phone. The caller seemed to be a civilian reporting the tragedy that had taken place at Lake Berryessa. He said in a calm voice, "I want to report a murder . . . no, a double murder. They are two miles north of park headquarters. They were driving a white Volkswagen Karmann-Ghia." Slaight asked his location so he could dispatch someone to meet him. The man then calmly said, "I'm the one that did it," and he let the receiver drop.

Officer Slaight was attempting to have the taunting phone call traced when a local news reporter located the booth the killer had used. It was adjacent to the Napa Car Wash and, similar to the phone booth in Vallejo, just blocks from the Napa Police Department. The phone booth was protected by sheriff's office personnel until criminologist Hal Snook was able to get there and process the scene. For some reason, the prints on the phone were quite wet and seemed to remain so for a long time. Could someone who was so cool in the way in which he both carried out the crime and made the phone call have had hands that were sweating that much? Of course, in a public phone booth you're going to find many finger and palm prints. Several were lifted from the phone and the receiver, but they never matched any suspect. No standard print card has palm prints. The only way to make a comparison to the palms from the phone booth is to identify a suspect *first* and then obtain his palm prints for comparison. However, occasionally law enforcement has what are called *major case prints* on file for that individual, which include palm prints.

Cecelia described a Caucasian man with brown hair who was six feet tall and two hundred or more pounds.[20] This differs greatly from the five-foot-seven-to-five-foot-eight assailant that Mike Mageau had described fewer than three months earlier. Cecelia said she never saw his eyes, which, as Bryan also pointed out, were concealed behind two pairs of glasses.

---

20   Fincher, 2008.

Bryan Hartnell described a large man with a stomach that hung over his belt. However, in later years, he stated that the man was wearing a jacket that may have had a lining that would've made him look bigger than he was. It was also possible that the precut lengths of rope tucked inside the jacket created that illusion. So the attacker may not have been as heavy as Hartnell originally believed. The term *bulky*, which Cecelia used to describe the man's build, may therefore have come from the man wearing sweaters or other clothing under his windbreaker to disguise his actual weight. (In a 1969 interview from his hospital bed aired on the 2019 HLN show *Very Scary People*, Bryan Hartnell said that the man was of "short to medium height" and "pouchy.")

Napa County Sheriff's Office detective Ken Narlow and his wife, Marie, had just finished eating dinner when the phone suddenly rang. It was 8:20 PM. Narlow and his partner, Det. Richard Lonergan, were ordered to Queen of the Valley Hospital after the Shepard-Hartnell attack. Sadly, although they had been attacked about 6:30 PM, the ambulance carrying the victims didn't arrive at the hospital until 8:50 PM. By then, Cecelia was unconscious and would die two days later from blood loss. Hartnell, not as gravely injured, was able to answer a few questions before he went into surgery. Eventually he made a full recovery, returned to school, and became a successful lawyer in Southern California.

At the lake, detectives made two major discoveries: First, they located a set of footprints leading to and from the crime scene. These were later identified as coming from size 10.5 "wing walker" shoes. Wing walkers were military issue and used by service members who needed antistatic shoes to, as the name implies, walk on the wings of military aircraft for servicing, refueling, et cetera. They were only available to air force and navy personnel. This started the police thinking that Zodiac may have had a military background. Although the ground at Lake Berryessa hardly lends itself to being compacted in most areas, the prints were left in a sandy spot near the levee. Using different individuals from among the police officials gathered there, Narlow and Lonergan were able to estimate that, based on the depth of the compaction of the soil by the killer and one of the deputies, the unknown assailant weighed approximately 230 pounds.[21]

The second discovery was more bizarre. When the investigators examined Bryan's Karmann-Ghia, they discovered that the killer had written a message on the passenger's-side door in black felt-tip pen. The message was a calling card of sorts, similar to the way a gang might tag or mark its turf. It began with an autograph in the form of the killer's crossed-circle symbol, followed by the dates and location of his previous two attacks. He again ignored the fact that the Lake Herman murders had taken place in unincorporated Solano County, not Vallejo. He then wrote down the current date, "Sept 27-69," and at the very bottom, the words "by knife."

Where did the killer get this unique idea? How could the notion of doing such an unusual thing occur to someone? Had the man possibly seen it before in some other context? As soon as the police saw that symbol, they knew that the man known as the Zodiac, who had been terrifying couples in Solano County, had now moved north to their quiet city.

---

21   If Zodiac intentionally bulked himself up that day to look heavier, when he made the transition from the hardpan ground that characterizes 99 percent of the terrain at the lake to that patch of soft ground, he may have essentially jumped up and down on one foot to leave deep shoe impressions and perpetuate the illusion of being heavy in what was likely the only patch of such ground on the levee that day.

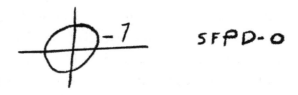

Lake Berryessa Research

THE FIRST TIME I WENT to examine the location of the Lake Berryessa attack, I didn't initially find the correct spot. It was October of 2000, and about two months before I began to build what would eventually become my unofficial team of retired investigators and other law enforcement officials by calling and emailing them. One was Detective Ken Narlow (Ret.), who had headed the investigation of the Lake Berryessa attack for the Napa Sheriff's Office in 1969. While maintaining a healthy skepticism about my work, Ken would become a close friend, advisor, and ally of mine until his death in 2010. When I went out to visit the Bay Area the first time, Ken kindly offered to take me to the Berryessa crime scene. I proceeded to Ken's house in the city of Napa, and Ken drove us up to the lake. We arrived in the late morning and parked. Since the parking area had been reconfigured over the last ten years, Ken was unsure of his bearings.

Based on my then colleague Ed Neil's recommendation, we went to an area provided on a map in Robert Graysmith's *Zodiac*, which detailed the attack site. There was a small island very close to the shore but separated by a narrow channel of cold October water. I traversed the channel and wandered around the island for a bit while Ken wandered north. The piece of land looked nothing like what I recalled from the description in Graysmith's book. By then Ed had arrived, and while we were talking Ken came back to us and said that this didn't look like the correct spot. Ken said it was farther north, so we hopped into the cars and, sure enough, the correct site was at the next cove up.

A park ranger was locking the gate when we got there. It was closing time. As a result, Ed and I didn't get to go out to the tip of the peninsula where Hartnell and Shepard had been attacked in 1969 with Ken and learn the details of the attack from him firsthand. This was unfortunate, because, despite having been to the attack site many times, Graysmith not only got the map wrong, he also had the details of the crime wrong. This would lead to my having misconceptions for many years about what had truly happened on September 27, 1969.

During the course of our visit, Ed and I learned an interesting fact that no other Zodiac researchers knew: the place where the attack took place had been given a name by the local park rangers. They called it Zodiac Island.

What neither Bryan Hartnell, Cecelia Shepard, nor the police knew on September 27, 1969, was that there was a man who lived not far from Lake Berryessa. While his main residence was in the city of San Francisco, he also owned a horse ranch in Oakville, about halfway between the lake and the city of Napa, where the killer made his phone call. This ranch would have been a convenient place for Zodiac to stop and change his blood-splattered costume before heading into Napa to make his call to the police. This man loved fast cars and undoubtedly enjoyed navigating high-performance sports cars on the hilly, winding back roads of Napa County. He was a man who admittedly lived for speed. At various times he had owned speedboats on both Lake Tahoe and San Francisco Bay. However, in 2006, he would deny ever having visited Lake Berryessa, even though it was known as "the Speedboat

Capital of Northern California." And there was something else that was very interesting about this man, as we'll see in a later chapter: he had a strong relationship with the Karmann-Ghia Bryan Hartnell had driven that day. In addition, the date September 27 held a special significance to him. Finally, the man also sold British cars like MGs and Triumphs, just like the car Zodiac may have pursued at Lake Herman Road on the night of December 20, 1968. But none of these facts would see the light of day for some thirty years.

...

The important thing to remember about the attack at Lake Berryessa is that Bryan Hartnell only survived because of sheer luck; one of his stab wounds missed piercing his heart by only a few millimeters. Had Hartnell and Shepard immediately succumbed to their multiple stab wounds, as Zodiac clearly intended, there would've been no record nor any evidence that a hooded attacker wearing a bizarre outfit had stabbed the two young students. And when Zodiac stated in his phone call to the Napa police after the crime that he wanted to report a *double* murder, he reveals that he hadn't intended to leave behind any survivors to describe the events at Lake Berryessa that day.

So the question becomes, Why did Zodiac wear this bizarre outfit? It may be that his intention that day was to frighten his victims before killing them, believing they would recognize his crossed-circle symbol from all the news reports the previous month. He would then finish them off. It was only by sheer chance that neither Hartnell nor Shepard recognized the strange symbol on the killer's chest. By being out of Northern California that summer, they may have deprived Zodiac of part of the excitement he'd hoped to derive from wearing his costume that day.

About three weeks after the attack on Bryan Hartnell and Cecelia Shepard, a letter arrived at the offices of the Napa Sheriff's Office. But this letter was not from the Zodiac. Instead, it was from Thomas

Kinkead, the chief of police of Riverside, California, which lies some 430 miles southeast of San Francisco. The letter concerned similarities that Kinkead had noticed between the Zodiac crimes and subsequent letters and the letters that followed the murder of an eighteen-year-old coed named Cheri Jo Bates in the city of Riverside in October 1966.

Was Cheri Jo Bates actually the first victim of the Zodiac Killer, having been murdered over two years before Zodiac's Lake Herman Road murders? Kinkead apparently thought it was a possibility.

...

When I asked world-renowned behavioral profiler Richard Walter about the Lake Berryessa crime, he indicated that what he felt had happened was that Zodiac, bored with the two previous execution-style attacks, indulged in some fantasy at Lake Berryessa. Thus the outlandish disguise, the story about being an escaped convict, and the somewhat lengthy conversation with the victims. Although he stabbed Cecelia Shepard, this was still a power-assertive crime. According to Mr. Walter, there was no evidence of sadism in the form of picquerism; that is, the paraphilia of recreationally stabbing someone for sexual pleasure. In contrast, Zodiac's stab wounds to Cecelia seemed purposeful, not recreational. But after trying this new approach, the killer apparently found that it didn't sufficiently satisfy his psychological needs. Therefore, for his next crime just two weeks later, he would return to yet another execution. But this time, he would up the stakes considerably. However, before we examine that crime, we must first follow the diversion suggested by Chief Kinkead's letter and head those 430 miles south of the Bay Area to Riverside, California, and the October 30, 1966, murder of Cheri Jo Bates.

PART FIVE
Riverside

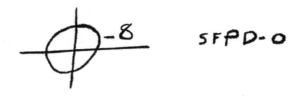

Before the Beginning: Cheri Jo Bates

SOMETIMES FATE CAN TURN on the seemingly inconsequential and mundane details of everyday life. Such was the case of a young college student from Riverside, California, named Cheri Jo Bates. The only difference between Cheri Jo possibly lying on the beach basking in the sun on the unusually warm day of October 30, 1966, and lying dead in a driveway between two buildings on her college campus was a lost set of notes for a school project.

Cheri Jo was an eighteen-year-old college freshman attending Riverside City College. However, in terms of the Zodiac case, like Vallejo and Trondheim in Norway, they might as well be sister cities. Cheri Jo, unlike some people her age, had definite plans for her future. She had recently broken up with one boyfriend and was now seeing a football player, Dennis Highland, who had left his Inland Empire city of 150,000 to attend San Francisco State University. Unlike Dennis, Cheri Jo had decided to stay close to home for school. This Sunday had started out like any other but would end in a way that nobody could possibly have predicted. It left Cheri Jo at the epicenter of one of the most enduring mysteries in Southern California—one that in late 1970 would become inextricably linked to the most famous unsolved serial killer case in the Golden State.

Cheri Jo's Sunday began the usual way, with church services followed by breakfast at a local diner with her father, Joseph. After that, Joseph said he wanted to head toward San Diego and its cool beaches. They were beckoning him that hot fall day, when temperatures neared one hundred degrees and would make for uncomfortable trick-or-treating and melted Hershey's Kisses in children's goodie bags the next day. Cheri Jo declined his offer to accompany him, saying she had to finish a report on the Electoral College for one of her classes. Annoyingly, she couldn't find the note cards she had written based on books she'd read from the RCC library. That meant a trip to check out these books all over again in order to recreate the research for her report from scratch.

Meanwhile, big preparations were being made for a huge event that was taking place on the other side of town. Sunday, October 30 was the day of the 1966 *Los Angeles Times* Grand Prix auto race, previously known as the Riverside Grand Prix. Cars and people from all over the world were massing to see a showdown featuring New Zealander Bruce McLaren as the pole sitter and such luminaries as Americans Phil Hill and A. J. Foyt at the now defunct Riverside International Raceway. From the perspective of the Zodiac case, however, the two most notable people who may have attended this event were from Northern California.

While children in Riverside were trying on their costumes for the next day's festivities, Cheri Jo had to get her paper done, and that meant a trip to the RCC campus. The library was open until 9:00 PM that Sunday with an hour dinner break between 5:00 and 6:00 PM. Cheri Jo left a fateful note for her father on the refrigerator that read, "Dad— Went to RCC Library," and headed out the door to her lime-green Volkswagen Beetle. And that was the last anyone ever heard from Cheri Jo Bates.

While she was in the library, a man with at least some automotive knowledge stealthily approached her car and did something sinister. He opened the engine compartment located in the rear of the vehicle, removed the middle wire that connected the distributor to the ignition coil, and then removed both the coil and the condenser. Afterward, he simply waited for these carefully calculated moves to have the desired effect.

When she returned from the library, Cheri Jo placed three newly checked-out books in the car. She then settled into the driver's seat and turned the key. The area around her was pitch dark, so when she heard the reassuring whir of her starter, she felt confident that she would soon be in the light and comfort of her home. But there was a problem. The little engine kept turning over, but it wouldn't start. And after a few minutes of unsuccessful attempts, the battery was starting to run down.

Just then, a man appeared as if from nowhere and approached her from the passenger's side. He had noticed her plight and was coming to her assistance. The man opened the rear compartment of the car and fidgeted with the engine for a few moments, while Cheri Jo stayed in the driver's seat waiting for his signal to try the engine again. He gave her the cue, and she turned the key, but the engine still wouldn't catch. By now the battery was nearly dead. The man seemed to be so nice, reassuring, and helpful. He asked if she'd like to accompany him back to his own car so he could give her a lift to a gas station for help.

Cheri Jo Bates was almost phobically afraid of the dark. In order to reach the man's car, they would have to traverse a few hundred feet of unlit real estate. So the first question that comes to mind is, Was the man someone Cheri Jo knew, either well or casually, from the campus or elsewhere, or was he a complete stranger? Some people have said that, due to her profound fear of the dark, it must have been someone with whom she was acquainted. It's also possible that the man was so glib and knowledgeable about cars that he was immediately reassuring. Perhaps she felt instantly comfortable with his friendly manner and didn't sense any ulterior motive. After all, he *had* tried to help her get her VW started.

Here's where the timeline gets muddled. The library closed at 9:00 PM. Cheri Jo's encounter with her eventual assailant probably took place no later than 9:15 PM or so. However, it wasn't until about 10:30 PM that a local resident said she heard a "terrible scream" followed by silence. Then there was yet another scream. This was followed by the sound of an old car starting up. The lady who heard the screams presumably didn't wish to get involved in whatever had happened and didn't call the police. It's now believed that those screams mark the precise moment of the murder.

So what happened during the time period between Cheri Jo first encountering the man and the screams at 10:30 PM or so, which were presumed to have come from the death scene? Apparently, a lengthy interaction took place between the two. Some of it probably took place at the location where her car was, but more likely it took place as they walked and then continued at or near the site of the murder. Is this further evidence that Cheri Jo knew her killer and felt comfortable conversing with him?

Whatever the case, at some point things went terribly wrong for Cheri Jo. A fierce struggle ensued in a driveway between two dark, unoccupied buildings on the campus and violently churned up the ground. As one detective later put it, the ground was like a "freshly plowed field." Cheri Jo put up a valiant fight, but ultimately, she lost her struggle for life. The next day at about 6:30 AM, an RCC employee operating a street cleaner found her body and called police.

Cheri Jo Bates, clad in red Capri pants, sandals, and a faded yellow blouse, was lying facedown in the dirt driveway with her oversized straw bag partially under her body. She had many defensive wounds on her hands, and fingernail scrapings taken later would reveal that her attacker was a Caucasian. Several strands of brown hair were found clutched in her hand, embedded in a clot of blood near the base of her thumb. This would become crucial physical evidence of the highest order when DNA science was created many years later, since it was 99 percent certain that the hair had come from her attacker. The cause of death was two deep slash wounds across her throat, which severed her jugular vein. Even though the available crime scene photos are in black and white, one can still tell that there was a lot of blood on the ground around the body. Although she was facedown, the fact that there were leaves in her hair and that her ankles were crossed seem to indicate that she had originally been lying on her back and that the killer had rolled her over on her face, probably by using his foot to push her body over after she was dead. He then stabbed her one time in the back.

About ten feet from her body police found a Timex watch. It was assumed by detectives that it had been stripped off the killer's wrist during the struggle, since the pin holding the band to the case of the watch was missing. However, the more intriguing and sobering speculation about it having been intentionally planted there by her attacker as a clue would come much later.

Given that Cheri Jo was approached by someone who had at least some degree of automotive knowledge, there has always been discourse that the perpetrator was someone who had come to town to attend the *Los Angeles Times* Grand Prix. But while the killer clearly knew how to disable a car, this is not proof in and of itself that he was in any way associated with the race. This possibility is quite tantalizing, though, and would also suggest that the man was likely a stranger to Cheri Jo.

When investigators examined her car, they found it unlocked with the windows rolled down and the keys in the ignition. This was reportedly highly unusual for Cheri Jo, who always locked her precious Beetle. There were also the three library books date stamped with that day's date on the back seat. When the car was examined for evidence, police found several sets of prints and some greasy palm prints. Most were later identified as having come from Mr. Bates, her brother, or other people Cheri Jo knew, like her mechanic. Since the police couldn't tell *when* the fingerprints were deposited on the car, one has to wonder if they ever investigated any of those people. Simply knowing there was a logical reason for those prints to be where they were didn't necessarily mean they were placed on the car innocently by those individuals.

Exactly one month after the Bates murder a letter, called The Confession, was sent to the *Riverside Press-Enterprise*. The author demonstrated some savvy about not getting apprehended by using a multilayered "sandwich" of paper and carbon paper to type the letter. He then sent one of the middle copies so as to obscure the specific characteristics of the typewriter he'd used. In the letter, the one fact that only the author could've known is the brief reference to a phone call presumably made to the police after the murder. Over the course of the past fifty years, why would the Riverside Police Department not confirm this call even though the best chance at this point of solving the case may lie in the public investigation into her murder? Why doesn't RPD engage the public by releasing some information that may be useful to amateur investigators?

The letter was a first-person account of what supposedly happened that night. The killer showed himself to be someone who fantasized about different types of women—brunettes, blondes, et cetera. He was also eager for us to know how clever his evil plot truly was. He said that he first disconnected the middle wire of the distributor; that is, the one leading to the coil. This specific detail had not been released in the local newspaper. However, an early account did say that the condenser and coil had been "torn out," and the only way to get the coil out is to disconnect that middle wire. So the detail about the middle wire, which *was* published in a small and obscure article in the *New York Times* on November 1, 1966,[22] didn't prove in and of itself that the killer had inside information about the crime. The author then said he'd led Bates to her death like a "lamb going to slaughter." He boasted that the churned ground of the driveway was the result of his having had a "good time," as opposed to his losing control of his struggling victim, which led to a chaotic and disorganized crime scene.

---

22 Anonymous, "Girl Student, 18, on Coast Is Found Slain on Campus," *New York Times*, November 1, 1966, p. 10.

In about January of 1968, the Riverside Police Department developed a suspect in the only unsolved homicide case in their city's history. He was an ex-boyfriend of Cheri Jo's. She had jilted him for Dennis Highland. Over the years, RPD seemed to become fixated on their suspect, making one wonder if they had lost their objectivity in considering the possibility of other suspects. In the amateur community, people often staunchly defend their pet suspects, but should such a thing exist in a police investigation? This appeared to be especially true after the Zodiac's name surfaced when *San Francisco Chronicle* reporter Paul Avery received Zodiac's October 1970 Halloween card and threat. Why was the RPD seemingly unwilling to consider other suspects in the Bates murder?

Exactly six months after the Bates murder, on April 30, 1967, an unknown author sent three letters: one to the RPD, one to the *Riverside Press-Enterprise* newspaper, and, chillingly, the last to Joseph Bates at his home address. That letter was published in the *Press* and other newspapers after Cheri Jo's death in those more innocent days. These letters each contained twice the postage necessary to send them. Two of the letters said, "BATES HAD TO DIE THERE WILL BE MORE." The one sent to Mr. Bates started, "She Had To Die." The writer was ghoulishly confident that Joseph would know what the letter was about. The signature on the letter was a squiggle that looked like a stylized *Z* but that has naturally been interpreted in numerous ways over the years.

A few months after the Bates murder, a janitor in RCC made an unusual find. In a storage room he located a student desk that had been kept there for several months. On the underside of the desk someone had scratched out a gory poem that's clearly about suicide, although many interpret it as being related to the Bates murder. In November 1970, when the Bates case was linked to the Zodiac crimes, the California State Questioned Documents expert Sherwood Morrill determined that the handwriting on the three "Bates Had to Die" letters and that on the desk bottom matched the hand printing of the Zodiac.

Thus came about the connection between the murder of Cheri Jo Bates and the later crimes of the Zodiac in the Bay Area. They are still linked to this day.

...

So how can the murder of Cheri Jo Bates be solved today? One possibility is that the RPD at least consider theories that have been investigated and carefully researched, including those by amateur researchers. Did RPD make a strategic mistake early on by essentially decreeing that their suspect was responsible for the murder of Cheri Jo Bates and then entrenching itself in that position despite exonerating evidence? Why didn't they consider other suspects in Cheri Jo's death? The odd thing is that in October 1969, a year before the Bates case was linked by handwriting to the Zodiac case, the RPD sent the aforementioned letter from Chief Thomas Kincaid to Chief Don Townsend of the Napa Sheriff's Office. The letter pointed out the similarities between the Bates case and the Lake Berryessa attack by Zodiac. For unknown reasons, after the Bates case was linked to the Zodiac case in 1970, RPD became enamored with the idea of their "local boy" as Bates's killer and seemed to close their minds to any other possible solution, *especially* one involving the Zodiac.

The problem with their suspect is, ironically, high-quality DNA evidence from those strands of hair that were found embedded in a blood clot in Cheri Jo's hand after her death. In March 2000, the FBI's criminalistics lab developed mitochondrial DNA (mt-DNA) from that hair. The location of the hair in her hand associated with blood from the attack leaves virtually no doubt as to its source: it almost inevitably came from the person who killed Ms. Bates and was torn out during the struggle. Later in 2000, RPD picked up their suspect as he arrived in Riverside at a local airport and served a warrant for his DNA. When the results came back, the mt-DNA did not match. All the eggs RPD had put in that basket for thirty years now shattered, and the investigation was left at square one.

That same year, in a peculiar move, a detective for RPD fed what turned out to be inaccurate information about their suspect to an amateur investigator that was immediately posted on the Net. The official told the amateur that Bates had been stabbed forty-two times. This had the effect of making the crime sound like a crime of passion and reinforced their notion that whoever killed Ms. Bates knew her personally and likely had strong feelings toward her. This matched RPD's suspect. Oddly enough, this statement wasn't supported by the information later found in the actual Bates autopsy report. The RPD official also told the amateur investigator additional unlikely stories. Was the circulation of inaccurate information a strategy of RPD's to hopefully draw the killer out?

Over fifty years after the crime was committed, the most likely way in which the Bates case will ever be solved is if RPD reverses its course and accepts that their suspect was cleared via the comparison to mt-DNA. The evidence possesses a pedigree that virtually assures it came from the murderer. More importantly, it should release useful information to the public in order to allow other investigators to help solve this case. Circulating accurate information would enable others to help RPD, which may have limited time and resources, to continue to work on this cold case.

Another thing that can be done is to release information on any DNA analyses that were presumably done on the three "Bates Had to Die" letters and other evidence. The first question is, Do the stamps show evidence of having been licked? If so, they may contain saliva and DNA-bearing cells. The reason for knowing if the stamp and envelopes were licked will become obvious when I discuss DNA in the Zodiac case in chapter 21. If the Bates letters were licked, DNA can be obtained from them for comparison to any new suspects that come along. If they were *not* licked, this might be an important clue that would provide a potentially crucial link between these letters and the Zodiac letters from the Bay Area, for reasons that will also become clear later.

The final thing that may help RPD to solve this case is to utilize the most sensitive new techniques for impressed writing to analyze the "Bates Had to Die" letters. These techniques may provide useful information that may have been pressed into the paper by someone writing on an overlying sheet, something like a name or a phone number, for example. This approach was suggested years ago by my colleague Eduard Versluijs, who also had an interesting theory: he wondered if the three-ring loose-leaf paper the sender used for the "Bates Had to Die" letters may have come from a notebook that Bates may have had in her car and which the killer took as a souvenir. In such a case, might there be impressed writing on one of the "Bates Had to Die" letters that came from the victim herself, thus proving that the paper came from her own possessions? There is always concern that analysis could damage the unique and irreplaceable evidence. However, the method used for this technique is completely nondestructive. Therefore, there's no reason not to utilize impressed writing to the fullest extent possible.

It is my hope that at least some of these suggestions will be used to help solve the murder of Cheri Jo Bates and honor her memory after all these years.

...

Profiling information I'll share in chapter 17 will cast doubt on whether the Zodiac actually murdered Cheri Jo Bates. But that doesn't mean that the Riverside murder didn't influence Zodiac and his later career. By solving it, we may not discover an indirect link between the Bates killer and Zodiac himself, an idea suggested by Dr. Mike Kelleher in the late 1990s. It also doesn't mean that Zodiac didn't write some of the Riverside letters. The one thing I've always cautioned when comparing the 1966 Bates case and the later Zodiac case is "chickens and eggs." Just because both killers wrote letters about their crimes, used double postage on their letters, and may have used automotive ruses to approach victims doesn't mean that Bates's killer and the Zodiac are necessarily one and the same. That's because by the time Zodiac began his career *all of these facts about the Riverside murder were known to the public.* Zodiac may have so admired the Riverside killer, either by knowing him or simply admiring him from afar, that he modeled his own lethal career after him and copied some of his techniques.

One man who said he was in Riverside on the weekend of October 29–30, 1966, was Robert Graysmith's suspect, Arthur Leigh Allen. Allen was known to be a racing fan and even owned a British Austin-Healey sports car. But like so many of the things Allen said, nobody was ever able to prove conclusively that he was telling the truth.

There is another man, one who *definitely was* present in Riverside on the weekend of October 29–30, 1966, and who was also visiting from the Bay Area. He came from Presidio Heights. In fact, he lived a block or so from the intersection of Washington Street and Maple Street, Zodiac's original destination given to cab driver Paul Stine. The reason he was in Riverside is that he had a car entered in the *Los Angeles Times* Grand Prix, although it scratched out of the event the day before when the driver, Bob Bondurant, refused to race it for safety reasons.[23] The man also bore one more distinction: he was one of the largest Volkswagen dealers on the West Coast. So when a crime was committed that involved the disabling of a Volkswagen Beetle, of which he sold untold numbers in the 1960s, this crime may have immediately piqued his interest, and he may have stored the Bates murder away in his mind as one that had a special place in his worldview. As indicated earlier, regardless of who killed her, it's tempting to link the Bates murder to someone attending the road race that day, because an automotive ruse was used to lure her to her death. This is especially true knowing that the three "Bates Had to Die" letters were mailed in Riverside on April 30, 1967, the weekend of yet another big auto race at the Riverside

23   Bob Bondurant, personal communication, 2000.

International Raceway. However, no definite link between the letters and the auto race has ever been proven.

In August 2015, I corresponded with a government official from Riverside who said he grew up with Cheri Jo. He said that at the time of her murder even the kids in her peer group thought that her ex-boyfriend was the guilty party. The police clearly thought so too. But according to the mt-DNA results from 2000, they were all wrong. After that elimination I recall hearing that the hairs from Cheri Jo's palm that the FBI tested for mt-DNA might have belonged to one of the detectives who worked the crime scene. Given that they were found clutched in her hand in a clot of blood and were presumably ripped out of someone's head, as suggested by the absence of any root structure, does anyone seriously believe that the strands of hair from a detective's head conveniently fell out and right into the blood clot in her hand?

In 2015 RPD reportedly sent some of the Bates evidence out for further testing.[24] This is a good start. But sharing the information they have obtained with the public might help to develop new leads. Amateur investigators need to know:

- Was there a phone call made to the police shortly after her murder, as alleged in The Confession?
- Do the three "Bates Had to Die" envelopes test positive for amylase/saliva?
- If so, was DNA extracted from them?
- If so, does the DNA match across all those letters, thus proving that what was analyzed came from the letter writer?
- Was there impressed writing on the "Bates Had to Die" letters?
- Were any copies of the Confession letter tested for impressed writing, in case the sender was careless and used paper that had information impressed into it?

---

24 "Unlocking a Very Cold Case," March 2015, www.inlandempiremagazine.com.

PART SIX
PRESIDIO HEIGHTS

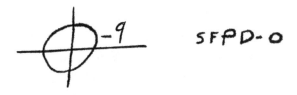

"A Place Where Nothing Ever Happens": Paul Stine

TO THOSE INTERESTED IN THE CASE of the Zodiac, there is a famous intersection in San Francisco. It's dominated on its northwest corner by a massive edifice called Le Petit Trianon. If you ask the average San Franciscan where this intersection is, however, an overwhelming majority of them, 97 percent in fact, would most likely shrug their shoulders. At least that was the opinion of Inspector Vince Repetto (Ret.), who was in charge of the Zodiac investigation for SFPD in the mid-1990s.[25][26] And that would surely go double for anyone who resided in other parts of the Bay Area, such as Solano, Napa, or Marin Counties. That's because the intersection of Washington and Maple Streets is in Presidio Heights, the home of some of the city's wealthiest citizens. Houses are not called just houses in this exclusive neighborhood, they

---

25   SFPD Insp. Vince Repetto (Ret.), personal communication, 2010.

26   My colleague Jim Dean told me that, despite having grown up in San Francisco, he had no idea where the intersection of Washington Street and Maple Street was until he started working with me on the Zodiac case and we went to the site together in 2003.

are referred to as mansions. Presidio Heights is far off the beaten path of cable cars, electric buses, Alcatraz tours, Coit Tower, the seafood restaurants on Fisherman's Wharf, and other attractions that adorn the postcards tourists send home while on vacation in the city. For that reason, unless you've been to that intersection, you'd have virtually no way, nor any reason, to know of its existence.

One man in particular had been there before. And he felt pretty comfortable at the intersection of Washington and Maple Streets. So comfortable, in fact, that he decided to kill someone there with the supreme confidence that he could do so and literally get away with murder. This strongly suggests that he had more than just a passing familiarity with this intersection and the surrounding neighborhood. The big question has always been, How?

...

Driving a hack is not a glamorous job by any means today, and it wasn't so in the fall of 1969. But then neither is grinding out the classroom hours and the dissertation required to earn a PhD in English. But that was what twenty-nine year-old Paul Lee Stine was doing two years removed from the famous Summer of Love. Prematurely balding and with bad eyesight, he needed heavy, horn-rimmed glasses with thick lenses to navigate the streets of the city. Stine was attending San Francisco State University and driving a cab on the side. He was married and lived at 1842 Fell Street with the panhandle of Golden Gate Park essentially serving as his front yard. He wasn't scheduled to work on the night of October 11, 1969. However, fate intervened when he got a call from the dispatcher for Yellow Cab and learned that an opportunity had presented itself to pick up a few extra bucks toward the rent by filling a vacancy on the night shift. He figured that since it was a Saturday night, maybe he'd do well working the theater district, where such plays as *Hair* were drawing huge throngs.

Stine had only managed a couple of fares and had just a few dollars in his pocket when the time came for him to position himself on Geary Street. Soon such places as the Curran Theater would regurgitate the masses of people they had swallowed up at 8:00 PM. And many of the well-heeled theater goers would need rides home to places that weren't serviced by a cable car or municipal bus line. Places like Presidio Heights.

Stine was parked near Union Square while waiting for the shows to end. As ten o'clock approached and the streets began to fill, he received a radio call. He was to head out west of Presidio Heights to Ninth Avenue, in the outer Richmond District of the city, to pick up a fare. This was just his luck. Now that he was buried in traffic, he had to make a trek across town. He wondered where that call was fifteen minutes ago.

As Stine pulled away from the curb, he was suddenly hailed by a man with short reddish-brown hair and horn-rimmed glasses and dressed in a dark-colored parka and rust-colored pants. When the man said he wished to go to a location in Presidio Heights, Stine felt that his luck that night was changing for the better. Presidio Heights just happened to be on the way to the fare to which he was headed in outer Richmond. He could therefore make a little extra money on the drive out west of the city.

The fare asked if he could sit in the front seat. It was later alleged that Stine would generally only allow people he knew to sit in the front of the cab with him. However, the confident demeanor of the man and the fact that he was headed to a tony neighborhood may have put the cabbie at ease, and he invited the man to sit next to him. Stine grabbed his fare book and dutifully wrote down the destination: Washington and Maple Streets, the obscure corner of Le Petit Trianon. The cab slowly pulled into traffic. Stine must have been an honest driver, since he could have dropped the new fare off on his way to his radio call and simply pocketed the money for himself. Who would have known? But Stine apparently was not that type of person, so he started the cab's meter. Little did he know that his seemingly innocent fare-book entry would fuel massive debate for many years to come.

Stine skillfully navigated his way first north, then west—Geary, Van Ness, and then eventually west on California, the southernmost east–west street of the five that comprise Presidio Heights. Next he went right on Divisidero and then swung a left on Washington for the trip out nine blocks to Maple Street.[27] When the cab arrived at Maple Street, Stine was instructed to pull over to the curb on the northeast corner. As he did, a dog walker or jogger unexpectedly rounded the corner coming up Maple Street to Washington Street. He was to the right and immediately ahead of the cab. Spotting that individual, the fare suddenly indicated that he was visiting a friend and had only been to his home a few times, and that was during daylight hours. He may have indicated that this corner suddenly didn't look familiar to him, and he asked the cabbie to go another block. When the cab arrived at the next corner, Cherry Street (Exhibit 4), the man may have feigned unfamiliarity with this intersection as well. He asked Stine to put the cab in PARK so he could take a look around and make sure he was in the right place. Meanwhile, the fare discreetly scanned the streets for any sign of potential witnesses to what he was about to do. Stine may have turned his head to the left to try to see the number on the house on the corner. He wanted to help his passenger so he could move on to pick up his other waiting fare. When he did so, the passenger took that opportunity to jam a 9 mm semiautomatic against the right side of Stine's face just in front of his ear. Stine apparently reached in front of his face with his left hand in a vain effort to ward off the inevitable before the man pulled the trigger. With the muzzle of the gun flush to the skin, the sound of the powerful 9 mm shot was almost entirely

---

27   In 2018 Ted Gross, who grew up in Presidio Heights and played in the Julius Kahn Playground as a child, said that a veteran cabbie would have more likely taken this route: Geary to Franklin, Franklin to Pine, Pine to Presidio, and then either Presidio to Washington or Presidio to California to Maple Street. This is because the lights on both Franklin and Pine are synchronized, making the drive west faster.

absorbed into Stine's head. There was no need for a silencer. Blood started to flow freely from the wound.

Across the street, at 3898 Washington Street, some kids were holding a small party. Three members of the Robbins family, the children of a local doctor, and some friends were on an upper floor. To show that they lived in no ordinary neighborhood, their parents were at a dinner soiree being held at no less than the Belgian embassy a block away to the north, at Cherry and Jackson Streets. Even though it was October and the outside temperature was in the fifties, the room started to get hot. The oldest teen, sixteen-year-old Lindsey Robbins,[28] decided to open a window to let in some cool night air. This simple act would profoundly change his young life forever.

As Lindsey peered out the window to the street below, he saw two figures and commotion in the front seat of Yellow Cab 912, which was parked directly across the street from his vantage point. At first amused, he called everyone in the room to the window because he felt that the cabbie was drunk and couldn't sit up straight. He thought the passenger was actually trying to help the driver get back behind the wheel so he could continue his shift. Then the bright dome light of the cab, which Lindsey would describe in 2003 as being like a floodlight, revealed the massive amount of blood on the cabbie's face and head.

Contrary to what Robert Graysmith reported in *Zodiac*, Lindsey in 2003 stated that there was no fog that night,[29] and the light burning brightly inside the cab made it easy to observe what was going on. According to Lindsey, both he and his fourteen-year-old sister, Rebecca, had 20/20 vision and an unobstructed line of sight. The two would become the key observers of the events in and around the cab that evening. The younger kids also gathered around the window and stared in stunned silence.

---

28 Many of the details in this chapter and the next come from an exclusive series of interviews my colleague Jim Dean did with Mr. Robbins and his sister Rebecca beginning in September 2003.

29 Graysmith, p. 84.

Inside the cab, Stine had been killed instantly. It was then time for the killer to go to work. He first laid Stine across his lap and then sat the dead driver up and maneuvered him around several times for some unknown reason. Rebecca would later say that she also thought the man was trying to sit Stine upright, but he kept slumping over. This happened several times. Lindsey voiced a similar thing, stating he thought the passenger was trying to get the cabbie back behind the wheel. The man with the short reddish-brown hair then reached into Stine's pants pocket and took his wallet containing his driver's license. He also may have snatched the fare and tip money that was in his other pocket. But as we'll see later, that was not necessarily so. After grabbing Stine's keys out of the ignition he slid out the front passenger's-side door.

Lindsey decided to dash downstairs to the darkened living room to get a look at the man at street level so as to better judge his height. Lindsey knew that the man couldn't have seen him in the dark first-floor room—even if he looked right at him. This was in contrast to Rebecca, who was in a room with lights on. As Lindsey did this, he yelled out to his sister that he was going to grab his father's World War II bayonet and go out to help the cab driver. He believed the killer had used a knife, not a gun, since nobody had heard a gunshot. He was talked out of this potentially tragic decision by Rebecca, who stayed by herself at the upper-floor window and never took her eyes off the man across the street.

Detractors of their description of the man they observed have said that, from that elevated position, Rebecca would not have been able to correctly judge the man's height. But since Graysmith never interviewed these witnesses and they'd never spoken to anyone other than my colleague retired VPD detective Jim Dean, until 2003 no amateur investigator ever knew that Lindsey had gone downstairs and could see the man *at street level*. In addition, Rebecca actually had the catbird's seat from her elevated position, and with the light blazing brightly in the cab, she had a perfect view of the man's face. Both she and Lindsey remained calm throughout the ordeal and methodically watched the man, making mental notes of his appearance.

As the kids watched in horror, the man walked slowly and deliberately around to the driver's side of the car, seemingly unaware that anyone was watching him. As he did so, he came even closer to their position, and they carefully noted the features of his face. He had what looked to them like an off-white rag in his hand that he was using to wipe down portions of the outside of the cab. Rebecca watched him as he opened the door, grabbed the cabbie, and tried to sit him up behind the wheel one last time. He also reached into the cab with the rag and wiped it some more. As he did, he may have braced himself with his right hand on the post separating the front and rear doors on the driver's side. The man seemed not to have a care in the world as he methodically went about his gory business.

Finally succeeding in getting the cabbie in the position he wanted, the killer walked around to the front of the car. He then casually escaped north on Cherry Street in the direction of the dark, heavily tree-lined Presidio. Alarmingly to the kids, he was now heading straight in the direction of the Belgian embassy, where Dr. and Mrs. Robbins were still at the dinner party.

However, *escaped* may be the wrong word to describe Zodiac's actions. In an article on Sunday, October 12, the *Chronicle* ran a story with the headline "Cabbie Slain in Presidio Heights." In it, obviously not yet knowing the facts, they stated that after the murder the killer "dashed" up Cherry Street to the safety of the Presidio. This was a logical assumption under normal circumstances. But, as with many other assumptions people have made about the Zodiac, this one is dead wrong, because despite having brazenly shot and killed Stine in a residential neighborhood in the shadow of several houses, the killer was definitely in no hurry. Far from exhibiting the behavior of a frightened animal expecting danger around every corner and proceeding quickly and stealthily toward safety, it was as if the man were out for a casual Sunday stroll in the park.

At Lindsey's direction, one of the kids picked up a phone and frantically called the police to report the crime. To this day, nobody is really sure how the ensuing misunderstanding took place or why. However, a huge error in the description of the perpetrator was about to be made that would forever affect the life of one San Francisco police officer in particular and help fuel a major controversy that swirls around the case to this day.

"SFPD Dispatch. What is your emergency?" the voice at the other end of the line said.

"There is a man fighting with a cab driver at the corner of Washington Street and Cherry," said the petrified caller.

The caller provided a description of the man: thirty-five to forty-five years old, short brown hair, possibly with reddish tint, and wearing glasses. The caller informed the police that the crime was still in progress. The police dispatcher immediately put out a call for the nearest units to proceed to the area. The dispatcher indicated that the perpetrator was an NMA—a Negro male adult—instead of the WMA, or white male adult, the kids had apparently described. This all-points bulletin (APB) went out over all three police radio channels and was heard by all units. Lindsey Robbins would later tell Jim Dean that he had no idea how this horrible mistake happened, but that he didn't believe the error was on their end. And it's difficult to imagine how even a child seeing a white man would have described him as being black regardless of what emotional state he or she was in.

After the killer left the car and started walking north on Cherry Street toward Jackson Street and the safety of the dark Presidio beyond, Lindsey ran out of the house. He carefully watched to make sure the man didn't turn around and head back toward him. Lindsey then bravely crossed Washington Street and stood on the northeast corner of Cherry, not far from the cab, to watch the man as he casually walked away to the north.

The closest SFPD patrol car to the scene was manned by Officers Frank Peda and Armond Pelissetti, who later in his career became a homicide inspector. Luckily, they were able to respond quickly to the APB. Siren screeching and lights flashing, they skidded to a halt at the corner of Cherry and Washington Streets and parked in the crosswalk of the intersection facing east, toward the cab. Their arrival distracted Lindsey, who was still tracking the man as he arrived at Jackson Street. Lindsey turned around and pointed the police officers toward the man walking casually up Cherry Street.

"He's getting away! He's getting away! He's right there," Lindsey said, gesturing frantically toward the receding figure to the north.

When Lindsey turned and looked back up clear, fogless Cherry Street, the man was gone. He didn't see the direction in which the man had walked when he'd gotten to the corner of Jackson Street—east, west, or north.

Officer Pelissetti leapt from the cruiser. By this time, the other kids, including Rebecca and the younger Robbins brother, had spilled out onto the street. Their natural curiosity was drawing them inexorably toward whatever was in that cab, however gruesome and traumatizing it might be. At the same time, Lindsey was still yelling to the cops and pointing animatedly toward Jackson Street. He didn't know why they didn't immediately take off in pursuit of the man who had done whatever had befallen the cab driver.

In the confusion, Officer Pelissetti wasn't sure what had happened. He understandably needed to take a step back and assess the situation and get his bearings before he went chasing after anyone. He was able to get a description of the man from the kids. That's when he learned that SFPD Dispatch had made a potentially disastrous error and that the cab robber was actually a white male. The officer quickly went back to his car radio and announced to all the units listening to his channel that they were actually looking for a WMA—a white male adult. Pelissetti's report didn't go out over all three of the radio channels like the initial APB did, since individual patrol cars are tuned to the radio channel that serves only their portion of the city. The one he and Peda had been monitoring was for the west side of the city only. Central

Dispatch would have to relay the call and alert the cars on the other two channels with another APB. This delay would compound the problem that began with the original mistaken APB of a black male.

Meanwhile, SFPD officer Don Fouke was patrolling an area a few miles east of the crime scene. Like Pelissetti and Peda, Fouke was working out of the Richmond District Station House, just west of downtown San Francisco, and since his regular partner was off that evening, Fouke was assigned to ride with Officer Eric Zelms, a young but very courageous and dedicated rookie police officer. (Zelms would give his life in the line of duty on New Year's Day 1970, just over two months from this night.) Retired SFPD inspector Vince Repetto called Zelms a "go-getter." Officers Fouke and Zelms were about to be thrust into the glaring, hot spotlight of the Zodiac case.

Fouke and Zelms were east of the crime scene on Presidio Boulevard headed northbound and had just passed Washington Street when they heard the original APB call from Dispatch of a Negro male adult suspect on their channel. Fouke, who was at the wheel, immediately swung the car west to join the search for the killer.

The two cops sped along Jackson Street, one block north of Washington, further and further into the uncertainty that lay ahead. At every intersection he came to, Fouke told me in 2004, he would slow down in case another car was coming through so he didn't T-bone anyone. When the patrol car reached the intersection of Jackson Street and Maple Street, Fouke was slowing down. When he passed through the intersection and the car began to go up a grade toward Cherry Street, its headlights shined onto a white male walking east down the north side of Jackson Street. It was the last block before the expansive, leafy, and very dark southern boundary of the Presidio of San Francisco, which lay just behind the houses on the north side of the street. The man was about one hundred feet west of the corner of Maple Street. Fouke took a look at the man. He emphasized that he was still looking for a Negro male adult when he spotted him.

The Caucasian male was neatly dressed and clearly didn't fit the description from the APB of a black suspect. According to Officer Fouke, he also appeared to fit seamlessly into the neighborhood and didn't seem at all out of place in this wealthy enclave. In conversations I had with Fouke, it became clear that he was quite class conscious and felt that you did not trouble the wealthy residents of Presidio Heights unless you had a very good reason for doing so. The man was in no hurry and kept his head down as he walked. When he got to a residence just west of Maple Street, at 3712 Jackson Street, he casually turned left and began to ascend a flight of stairs to that residence in such a natural, easy fashion that Fouke presumed he lived there.

Fouke's description strongly reinforces what the kids from Washington and Cherry Streets said about the man they saw. They felt that he was never in a hurry and didn't seem to be aware that anyone was watching him. The very fact that Fouke and Zelms were able to surprise the man and did so by approaching him from the *front* clearly suggests that he didn't think anyone had seen him at the crime scene or that anyone would be looking for him. Had the man been afraid of the police flooding the neighborhood, as soon as he saw a pair of headlights approaching him from afar, he presumably would've taken some evasive action, like ducking down behind a parked car, before Fouke could have a chance to spot him.

Officer Fouke described the man he saw as follows: a white male adult, thirty-five to forty-five years of age, five feet ten inches tall, 180–210 pounds and barrel chested, with a medium complexion, a crew cut, and light-colored hair possibly graying in the back, and wearing glasses. He had on a dark blue waist-length coat with elastic on the cuffs and a flap-down collar and brown-and-rust-colored pleated pants that were baggy in the rear. Fouke felt the pants were "unusual" for that time period, being old-fashioned and out of style. The man was wearing low-cut shoes, which Fouke referred to as engineering-type boots. He walked in a "shuffling lope," which would later evolve within the Zodiac community into a "lumbering gait." Fouke later described the way the man walked as a semi-limp.[30] The man was slightly bent forward as he made his way down Jackson Street, and Fouke guessed that he was of Welsh ancestry. Fouke later amended his description of the man's ancestry to "Northern European" in an audiotaped interview he did with Jim Dean and me in December 2005.[31]

After determining that this wasn't the man he was looking for, Officer Fouke stepped on the accelerator and headed west toward Cherry Street and the crime scene. Zodiac had caught yet another lucky break with the bungled description of an "NMA" that went over the air that evening.

Meanwhile, Officer Pelissetti had been examining the cab. He indicated that he saw Stine slumped across the seat with his head toward the floor on the passenger's side. Clearly, Stine had fallen over again after being propped up by the killer. There was blood everywhere in the front of the cab and also covering Stine. His eyes were open and unblinking. Given that fact and the amount of blood in the vehicle, Pelissetti instinctively knew he was dead.

After examining the cab, speaking to the kids, and changing the description of the perpetrator from black to white, Officer Pelissetti made a fateful decision. It was a decision that would become extremely critical to my research decades later and put this officer at odds with my ideas on the identity of the Zodiac. It would also be a decision rife with controversy and confusion, as his story seemed to evolve in significant ways over time. And beginning in January of 2004, it would pit Pelissetti against me in a battle to determine the truth about the killer's identity.

In a 2007 interview for the movie *Zodiac*, on which he advised,[32] he indicated that he decided to take off in pursuit of the man who had robbed and shot the cab driver. Officer Pelissetti slowly walked up

30   Fincher, *This Is the Zodiac Speaking*, "San Francisco," 2008.

31   SFPD officer Don Fouke, personal communication to Det. Jim Dean (Ret.), December 2005. Northern Europe encompasses the countries of Norway, Denmark, and Sweden, in addition to such places as Wales.

32   Fincher, 2007.

Cherry Street, presumably using the techniques the department had shown him in training to make sure that he "did not get [his] head blown off." Erring on the side of caution, he ignored what Lindsey had told him about seeing the man get all the way to the southeast corner of Jackson and Cherry Streets before losing sight of him. As a result, he was carefully searching an area that the killer had already passed.

As Pelissetti cautiously made his way up the block, the patrol car carrying Officers Fouke and Zelms rounded the corner from Jackson Street, and they stopped. Having spotted the man near Maple Street seconds earlier, Fouke had a brief conversation with Pelissetti and found they were looking for a white male. At about that same time, the corrected APB description from SFPD Dispatch finally came over the air on the channel Fouke was monitoring that evening, a different channel than the one over which it had been initially broadcast by Pelissetti. Fouke muttered something to himself about the white male they'd just passed near Maple, made a three-point turn, and took off north on Cherry and then turned left on Jackson Street, toward the Arguello Boulevard gate into the Presidio. Fouke may have been embarrassed by the fact that he may have driven right by the killer near Maple Street. Therefore, he apparently didn't say anything loudly enough for Pelissetti to hear. This probably left Pelissetti wondering why Fouke had taken off so abruptly and where he was headed. Pelissetti continued up the block, and when he got to the corner he decided to turn right and go east toward Maple, staying on the south side of Jackson Street.

Officer Pelissetti stated in the documentary accompanying the director's cut of the movie *Zodiac* that when he arrived at the corner of Jackson and Maple Streets, he decided to turn right to go south, back to Washington Street. As he did so, he ran into a man who was out walking his dog. I'll have much more to say about this seemingly innocuous "dog walker" in chapter 18.

Meanwhile, an ambulance had been dispatched to the corner of Washington and Cherry Streets and the attendant declared Stine DOS at 10:05 PM. With Stine now officially pronounced dead, this cleared the way for a homicide team to be called out to this tranquil, wealthy neighborhood where, as Rebecca Robbins said, "nothing ever happened." This night would therefore surely remain seared in the memories of anyone who lived in Presidio Heights when Zodiac struck in their insulated community. But as we'll see, at least one man, the "dog walker" mentioned earlier, would later claim not to remember much of anything about this particular night even though he had a very good reason to have done so.

I learned years later that the SFPD homicide team of Insps. Gus Coreris and John Fotinos, "the Greeks," as they were collectively known around the department, were supposed to be the on-call homicide team on October 11, 1969, and would have caught the Stine murder case. However, Coreris told me that he was going on vacation the next week, so the case was assigned to the next team in line, SFPD homicide inspectors Dave Toschi and Bill Armstrong. A call went out to Toschi at about 10:15 PM.[33] He called Armstrong to tell him about the murder and that he was on his way to pick him up. Toschi dressed, grabbed some coffee to get him through what he knew was going to be a long night, and went to meet his partner at his home on Park Presidio, south of the area where Toschi lived. Meanwhile, the Greeks were given the crucial task of wrangling the youthful eyewitnesses and getting them together with SFPD sketch artist Juan Morales.

When Insps. Toschi and Armstrong arrived on scene, probably no earlier than 10:45 PM, they learned the full name of the victim, Paul Lee Stine. A Yellow Cab dispatcher had to identify him because the man's wallet and ID were missing. These missing items and money were presumably taken by the killer. However, in 2010, an SFPD source told me that in those days ambulance drivers were notorious for "appropriating" the possessions of deceased victims, apparently thinking that the victims no longer needed their money. So if the ambulance attendants assumed this was just another routine cab robbery gone awry, it's possible that it

33 http://blog.sfgate.com/djennings/2009/10/07/40-years-of-zodiac-the-cold-case-that-haunts-dave-toschi/

was not Zodiac who took the missing money from Stine's pockets but an ambulance or morgue worker.

Stine had been killed with a single 9 mm bullet to the head, the casing for which Insp. Toschi found on the floor of the cab. A forensics team was carefully going over the vehicle for prints. They knew before they even started what they were in for: every crime scene technician in the world knows that cabs, like the phone booths in Vallejo and Napa, are a forensics nightmare because so many people ride in them, drive them, touch them, and clean them. You could theoretically use up all the powder in your fingerprint kit developing prints from a taxi. However, two sets of prints on cab 912 stood out from the rest.

One set of prints on the cab was on the passenger's-side front door handle. These were from the very distal tips of the middle and ring fingers of a right hand. To envision what distal tips are, simply stick your arm straight out in front of you as if you were sleepwalking and head straight for a wall. The parts of your fingers that will hit first are the distal tips. It's hard to envision how these prints got on the door handle, except to say that the *least* likely way seems to be by someone casually opening this door.

The other prints of interest were located on the post separating the front and rear doors on the driver's side of the cab. On this post were prints from the lower finger joints and upper palm of a right hand. As luck would have it, these were yet more prints that aren't easily comparable, since they, too, aren't taken on a standard fingerprint card. In my conversations over the years with SFPD officials, they've all said that most of the cab prints were fragmentary and that the cab prints were only inclusionary, not exclusionary. This means that, while you can rule a suspect in with these prints if they match, *you cannot rule that suspect out if they don't.* Given Rebecca Robbins's observation about Zodiac bracing himself on the cab to lean in, it's possible that the prints on the post between the front and rear doors may have been left by the killer, but SFPD still stipulates, for reasons only they know, that the cab prints are used only for the inclusion of suspects.

SFPD has indicated that it took elimination prints from all the on-scene personnel, thus allowing them to say that the prints from the cab did not belong to anyone who was in or around the cab for the department. However, as part of my research, I've learned that it may not be that simple. In 2006, I spoke to a retired SFPD officer. He said that policemen were very curious in those days about seeing dead bodies and that they would often stray far from their assigned beats to catch a glimpse of a deceased victim. He said they would sneak away for a quick peek at the scene, and if they were ever asked by their superior officers what they were doing on the scene of the murder, they would say rather disingenuously that they went to look at the dead person for "training purposes," so that if such a thing ever happened on their beat, they'd be prepared and know just how to handle the event. In other words, they were just satisfying their morbid curiosity. He felt that before Insps. Toschi and Armstrong arrived on scene, which may have been as much as an hour or so after the crime had taken place, it would've been possible for all sorts of SFPD patrol cars to have pulled up to that scene and for numerous people to have touched the cab. It would've been impossible to keep track of them all. In fact, Insp. Vince Repetto told me in 2011 that there were "lots of people" around the cab that night.

SFPD inspector Bill Armstrong in the 1991 affidavit for a search warrant for Arthur Leigh Allen's home: "There were so many fingerprints in this public cab, that *it is unknown that, if in fact* [sic], *they have Zodiac's fingerprints at the crime scene or not*" (italics mine). In other words, they don't know if the cab prints are from the killer or not. That is presumably why the prints are considered to be of value only to rule someone in, not to rule someone out, as being Zodiac.

...

Inspectors Coreris and Fotinos would get the kids together with SFPD sketch artist Juan Morales over the next few days. When the initial wanted poster came out on October 13, the police did not yet know that the man who had killed Stine was anyone other than your run-of-the-mill petty criminal with no ulterior motive. It described the perpetrator as a "cab robber" who was youthful, at twenty-five to thirty years old, and five feet eight to five feet nine inches tall with reddish-brown hair in a crew cut, heavy rimmed glasses, and a navy-blue or black jacket. Insp. Toschi would later say that the sketch was prepared hastily and only released at the insistence of the chief. He said that the kids were screaming and in a panic. That may have been true of the younger kids but clearly not of Lindsey and Rebecca based on their conversations with Jim Dean in 2003. Did Toschi ever even talk to them? Insp. Coreris said in 2002 of Toschi and his comments about the quality of the sketches, "He wasn't there." Insp. Coreris knew the Robbins kids and felt that the sketches were accurate. Jim Dean's 2003 conversation with them supports this point of view.

A few days later, after Zodiac took credit for the crime, Dr. Robbins called SFPD and requested that Morales come back to their house because his daughter Rebecca felt that she could come up with a better likeness of the man. After all, she'd had the longest uninterrupted view of the killer. She sat down one-on-one with Morales and together they created a new sketch. Lindsey Robbins said that when the two sketches, which were both done by the youthful eyewitnesses without any input from Officer Fouke, essentially matched, they knew they had nailed the likeness of the killer.

On October 18, 1969, an amended sketch based on Rebecca's recollections was put out on a new wanted poster. This time, the crime listed on the poster was murder and the man was described as being a bit older, thirty-five to forty-five years of age, and five feet, eight inches tall (which was more in line with Mike Mageau's estimate at Blue Rock Springs than with the hulking man at Lake Berryessa). He had a heavy build, short brown hair (note the change from a "crew cut") possibly with a reddish tint, and glasses. It also identified the perpetrator: "Zodiac."

...

It was after the murder of Paul Stine in the big city, where a phantom killer struck and then simply disappeared into thin air, that people suddenly became aware of the Zodiac Killer. The story started to get major play in the San Francisco newspapers, and the murder opened the floodgates of suspects pouring into the police on a daily basis. And, of course, in killing someone in the big city, this deluge of publicity had been the killer's goal. The conventional wisdom was that Zodiac was a known criminal. Whoever he was, Zodiac was certainly a "psychopath" and had undoubtedly come from San Francisco's seedier areas, which are not far from where Stine picked up his fare. Although he had killed Stine at the corner of Washington Street and Cherry Street, and in doing so seemed very familiar with the neighborhood of Presidio Heights, the killer certainly could not have been one of the privileged few who dined on filet mignon in that exclusive neighborhood on a nightly basis. Or at least that's what everyone assumed in 1969.

Zodiac had committed a series of brutal murders. First, there was the assault on Jensen and Faraday at a remote and dark lovers' lane. Then there was the attack on Ferrin and Mageau at a lovers' lane nearer to the populated area of Vallejo. Next was the accosting of Shepard and Hartnell in a bizarre costume on an exposed peninsula during daylight hours. Finally there was the murder of Stine right under the noses of homeowners in Presidio Heights. With each murder, the Zodiac showed a clear progression of risk. With each of his crimes, the killer had become more and more brazen. However, the extent of that brazenness wouldn't be fully appreciated until I learned the killer's true identity and the clues he had left behind for someone to find.

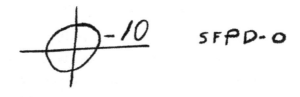

PRESIDIO HEIGHTS RESEARCH

WHEN I STARTED doing my own research on the murder of Paul Stine by the Zodiac, I found it to be a fertile crime in which to mine for new information. In 2001, I befriended retired Solano County Superior Court judge Eric Uldall. He had studied the Zodiac case all of his life, starting when he was a young prosecutor. He told me that he was in the Richmond District on the evening that cabbie Paul Stine was murdered. Judge Uldall was visiting a friend about eight blocks west of Presidio Heights. He said that, even at that distance from the crime scene, he saw police officers going through the bushes near the home he was visiting.

Captain Martin Lee, the head of detectives for SFPD in 1969, said of the search, "A mouse could not have escaped our attention." That may be true. But what about a "mouse" that blended into the surroundings and *belonged* in Presidio Heights—like possibly a resident of that wealthy neighborhood? This would, after all, qualify as someone who fit "seamlessly" into the neighborhood, as Officer Fouke had stated about the man he saw at Jackson and Maple Streets.

The suspect I will name in this book fits the description of someone who blended into the neighborhood. In fact, he lived there. This man was also out walking on the streets of that neighborhood shortly after Stine was murdered when he encountered an SFPD officer who was looking for the person who had murdered Paul Stine.

In 2003, I was introduced to investigator Tim Armistead of the City Attorney's Office in San Francisco. He told me that, whoever Stine's fare was that night, he seemed to know that the quickest way out of downtown and to the west side of the city, specifically to Presidio Heights, was to hail a cab in the theater district. Along with the Zodiac's apparent knowledge of Presidio Heights, which I'll explore in much greater detail later in this book, and more precisely his apparent knowledge of the intersection to which Zodiac directed Paul Stine, Washington Street and Maple Street, this hints that the man had strong ties to the city of San Francisco, as opposed to him being a commuter from another part of the Bay Area or a traveler from a distant part of California.

In June 2004, Jim Dean and I went to the intersection of Washington Street and Cherry Street at night. I stood across the street near the house where the kids had watched the events of October 11, 1969. With a light on in the car, I could see Jim clearly in the front seat. And when Zodiac got out of the car and walked to the driver's side that night in 1969, he brought himself seven or eight feet *closer* to the vantage point Lindsey and Rebecca had. My own opinion after conducting this exercise is that the kids would have had every opportunity to observe and later accurately describe the Zodiac that night.

This brings into question the concept of Zodiac being a "big man," someone like suspects Arthur Leigh Allen or Ross Sullivan. In an interview I did with Officer Donald Fouke in 2005, he allowed for a plus or minus of fifty pounds on the man's weight due to the loose-fitting jacket he was wearing, which may have disguised his true physique. Also, in a

1989 interview for the TV show *Crimes of the Century*, Bryan Hartnell stated that, due to the loose-fitting windbreaker Zodiac wore at Lake Berryessa, Hartnell had "grossly misjudged his height and weight." He stated that the killer could have been "big or small."[34] The term *barrel chested*, which Fouke used to describe the man he saw, is interesting. It may suggest that the man had noticeably *bulked up his upper body under his jacket* possibly to disguise his true weight. In a subsequent letter, Zodiac stated that he was wearing a "descise" on the night of the Stine murder. Had he been accosted by the police, which *nearly* happened with Officers Fouke and Zelms, it would've been foolhardy for him to have worn any sort of facial disguise, such as makeup, a clay nose, or a fake moustache. That would certainly have been noticeable were he taken in for questioning and would've made the authorities understandably suspicious. So the concept of the man altering his height with lifts in his shoes and possibly his weight by wearing three sweaters under the loose jacket is plausible in terms of a disguise. And those sweaters might have made him appear barrel chested. If he were stopped by the police, they couldn't prove he was lying if he said he was warding off the cold and "did not take the cool temperatures of early fall very well."

I was at a classic car gathering in 2009 and found a car with a similar old-fashioned push-button door mechanism (Exhibit 5) as Stine's Ford Galaxie. I wrapped my hand around the handle and did so in such a way as to have the distal tips of my fingers pressed against the inner side of the handle; that is, the side of the handle that was facing *away* from me. I then attempted to push the button that opens the door with my thumb and learned this was a painful and completely unnatural way to accomplish a simple task. As you put pressure on your thumb to press down on the button at the end of the handle, you tighten the muscles of your hand, making a fist, and in doing so drive the sensitive tips of your fingers hard into the metal of the handle. Why anyone would have opened a door like this is beyond comprehension. So if those are

---

34   Handwritten notes of interview with Bryan Hartnell by producer, *Crimes of the Century: The Zodiac Killer.*

Zodiac's prints on the inside part of the handle of Stine's cab, they seem to have gotten there in some way other than by his casually opening the front door of the car. Distal tips, like the palm prints found at the Napa phone booth after the Lake Berryessa attack, are also not taken on a standard print card.

...

It has been alleged for years that Officer Fouke stopped and spoke to the man he and rookie officer Eric Zelms drove past on Jackson Street, but Fouke is adamant that this is simply not true. He also categorically denies being responsible for or even contributing to the "Amended" wanted poster sketch. Amateurs have constantly questioned his denial about not having done his own sketch, but Lindsey Robbins's emphatic assertion that *both* sketches are the work of the Stine eyewitnesses supports Fouke's claims on this point.

...

Why did Robert Graysmith say in his 1986 book, *Zodiac*, that the streets were "wet with fog" and the air "misty" on October 11, 1969? He's certainly not describing the virtually ideal viewing conditions that Lindsey Robbins described. And hadn't Lindsey watched the killer as he walked all the way up to Jackson Street, about two hundred feet away? How could he have done so if the area were enshrouded in fog? Officer Fouke would later also tell me that there was no fog that night. The crime scene photos don't portray any obscuring mist in the air. And why didn't Graysmith ever even attempt to interview the Robbins kids *or* Officer Fouke, whom retired VPD detective Jim Dean called the "cornerstone" eyewitnesses in the Zodiac case? When Officer Fouke called Graysmith to protest how his story was portrayed in *Zodiac*, why did Graysmith not follow through on his promise to interview Fouke for his *second* book? The Stine eyewitnesses and Officer Fouke were, after all, the key eyewitnesses in the Zodiac case for a good reason: both had seen Zodiac without a hood.

The answer to this question seems obvious. Just look at the two wanted poster sketches the kids produced. Because he never interviewed him, Graysmith undoubtedly thought that Officer Don Fouke may have had a hand in creating the two sketches. *Neither one of those sketches looks even remotely like Graysmith's main suspect, Arthur Leigh Allen* (Exhibit 1). In fact, when Lindsey and Officer Fouke were shown photos of Allen in the 1980s, they both completely laughed off the possibility that Allen was the man they saw that night. I believe that Graysmith avoided these witnesses so as not to undermine the narrative he was creating about Allen being the Zodiac. Whatever his reason for doing so, by not trying to interview the Robbins kids and Fouke, Graysmith deprived the public of some of the most crucial evidence in the entire Zodiac investigation, until Jim Dean spoke to Lindsey and Rebecca after a chance encounter Jim and I would have in 2003.

PART SEVEN
Communicating in Earnest

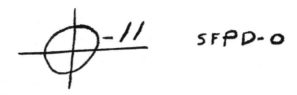

"I've Been Too Clever for You": Fall 1969–Spring 1971 Letters

ON TUESDAY, OCTOBER 14, 1969, just three days after the murder of cabbie Paul Stine, the *San Francisco Chronicle*'s Carol Fisher was once again at work sifting through the day's letters to the editor. She opened one envelope that had been postmarked in San Francisco the day before and was disgusted to find that someone had mailed her a piece of striped cloth that appeared to have been torn from a larger piece of material. What's worse was that the cloth was dirty—stained with some rust-colored substance. She shook her head and said, "What are people thinking these days?" It must be some sort of sick joke, she mused. Then she read the letter inside and let out a loud gasp.

He had written to them again.

The letter from the Zodiac was yet another confession. This time, however, he was taking credit for a crime that had occurred not in Solano or Napa Counties in the North Bay but for the murder of cab driver Paul Stine right in her city.[35] She immediately recalled the small

---

35 Zodiac did not send any letters to the press after the attack at Lake Ber-

article she had read on the front page of the Sunday paper mentioning his death. A crime that everyone had assumed was just a botched robbery was actually much, much more than that. As she read the letter, she realized that the cloth she had just handled was allegedly a blood-stained piece of Stine's shirt. A sudden wave of nausea overcame her. Like the writing on the car door at Lake Berryessa, Zodiac had once again demonstrated his dark inventiveness by finding a way to create yet another unique clue for the crime history books. It was similar to Jack the Ripper tearing off a piece of an apron from one of his victims to call attention to the so-called Goulston Street graffito. When she got to the last lines of the letter, her eyes widened and she realized that somebody had to do something, and quickly. She rushed the letter directly to editor Templeton Peck, who called SFPD.

When SFPD received the letter, they immediately called the morgue and asked if there was a piece of Stine's shirt missing. The technician called back and said that a huge portion of the tail of Stine's shirt was simply gone. He apologized that the lab hadn't noticed this when it processed the clothing on Saturday night. But then, like writing the message on the door of Hartnell's car, something like this was completely unprecedented, so why *would* anyone be on the lookout for a missing shirttail? SFPD inspector Dave Toschi immediately understood that the missing piece of Stine's shirt was the "rag" the kids had seen the killer use to wipe down Stine's cab. However, the letter they received, which became known as the "Stine letter," not only contained a bloody swatch of cloth. The killer also made the horrifying threat that he was going to shoot up a school bus full of innocent kids.

One of the most important things this letter confirms is that, despite the large police and military presence in Presidio Heights as well as the work of the search dogs, the Zodiac did not leave the area of the park that night. For years, there has been widespread speculation

---

ryessa. The note on the door of Hartnell's car, in fact, stands as the only written reference the killer ever made to that crime.

that Zodiac had parked his car on Maple Street and was walking back to it when he was spotted by SFPD officer Don Fouke. Afterward, he simply drove away and was miles from the scene long before the police search even began. But this letter tells us something different if we read it carefully, as my brother John did in 2005. At the time, John was a lieutenant for the New York Police Department.

John noted that Zodiac referenced the *sounds*, not the sights, of the police search. He referred to the "motor cicles [*sic*]" making a racket while racing each other in the park. This proves he was in the area that night. In stating this, Zodiac sounded like some cranky resident who was upset by the noisy intrusion the motorcycles made into his otherwise peaceful, upscale neighborhood. Providing the sounds of the police search is a theme he would carry over into a subsequent letter as well. According to Jim Dean, who is among other things a firearms expert, Zodiac may well have been extremely sensitive to even the slightest of sounds after subjecting his ears to the explosive report of a 9 mm handgun being discharged in an enclosed space like a cab. It has been widely believed that Zodiac simply read newspaper accounts of the search and then culled details from them to write the letter. That explanation makes perfect sense in theory. However, there had been no articles about the shooting on Sunday or Monday that mentioned the presence of motorcycles or referenced the *sounds* of the police search that night.

By providing the police and public with this information, Zodiac proved he had been there the whole time. He had been watching. He had been listening. But where was he? Chief Martin Lee of SFPD was adamant that the killer could not have eluded the manhunt after the Stine murder. And yet Zodiac did evade them while being able to provide details of their search. In providing the specifics that he did about his presence in the search area, the killer also clearly wanted to make the police look as bumbling and incompetent as possible.

Zodiac described the actions of the motorcycle drivers using the unusual term *road races*. This isn't something the average person would be expected to say. The implication of this terminology is that the letter writer was familiar with auto/motorcycle racing and may even have been involved in staging such events, such as *holding* road races.

So how did Zodiac stay in the area long enough to describe the police search and yet not be subject to being caught? I will explore the possible answer to this question later.

...

The threat to shoot up a school bus of course created a difficult dilemma for the police. Do you keep the threat quiet and hope the killer is bluffing, or do you risk the wrath of the populace if such an attack takes place and nobody is prepared for it? Or finally, do you tell everyone about it and take the chance of causing widespread panic? They decided to keep a lid on the news for the moment but knew they probably couldn't keep that lid on forever. Behind the scenes, especially in Napa County[36] where school buses covered hundreds of miles of lonely and desolate back roads every day, plans were made for drivers to keep the bus moving if a tire were to be shot out. Police cars and helicopters began following buses in the mornings and afternoons, and some police personnel and volunteers even began riding shotgun on the buses themselves. By the end of the week, the threat had leaked out in the newspapers and the widespread panic that would envelop the area began. In all, it was both a frightening and memorable experience for grade school and high school students in the area during the fall of 1969, and one which I'm sure they all still vividly recall with a cold shudder to this day.

Once again in the Stine letter, Zodiac continued to show his tendency toward British usage. The word *kiddies,* the phrase *I shall,* and the notion of searching the park "properly" are all cited as examples of this in the Hewitt article.[37] Mark Hewitt calls the British connection

36 Ted Gross, personal communication, 2018.

37 Hewitt, p. 2.

"pervasive" in the Zodiac letters. Once again, with all the references to the sounds of the motorcycles and a school bus as a target for his shooting threat, cars and vehicles were prominently featured in this letter.

The next two letters from the killer came in rapid succession in early November. The first, dated November 8, 1969, was a sick, tongue-in-cheek greeting card in which the killer ironically apologized for not having written sooner, as if everyone in the Bay Area were hanging on his every word. The letter contained a second piece of Stine's bloody shirt for authentication purposes as well as a new block of cipher that has come to be known as the 340-Character Code. The letter itself was nicknamed the Dripping Pen Card.

The newspaper immediately printed the new missive, as well as the new coded message that accompanied it. The code was once again an obsessively neatly aligned block of seventeen columns with twenty rows, thus giving the coded message its name—the 340-Character Code. It was a nearly perfect work of art in its construction with one glaring exception: in row six Zodiac had crossed out a character, a *K*, and replaced it with a backward version of that letter. Code breakers from around the Bay Area, the FBI, the CIA, Naval Intelligence, and the general public set themselves to the task of solving the cryptogram in earnest. But this time, it proved to be much more resistant to their efforts. In fact, as of the fall of 2020, this code has never been definitively broken, like the Three-Part Cipher was by the Hardens.

An entire book could be written about this code and the efforts to coax its message from it. But suffice it to say, every idea and methodology imaginable has been used to try to get it to yield its message, assuming it has one. Many cryptographers believe it does contain a message based on patterns they see in the characters. However, as yet the efforts have been to no avail. But then again, maybe this code had a *very* different purpose than to simply convey a message that is 340 characters in length, as we'll see later.

Of particular interest is the word **"Thing"** written on the inside of the greeting card. One intriguing aspect is that this is the *only* word in all of his letters that Zodiac gave such dramatic emphasis by writing it in extremely bold letters. In 2001, I was reading a book on the Vikings[38] and was surprised to learn that the word *Thing* is actually a Viking/ Norse term. The term is also spelled with a capital *T*. If you look closely, you can see that the author of the Dripping Pen Card initially wrote the word with a lowercase *t* before correcting himself and making it a capital letter. (It is possible that using a capital *T* may have given away Zodiac's familiarity with Norse/Viking culture.) A Thing relates to a gathering of free men to enact laws and mete out punishment to violators. Such punishments might include the chopping off of a hand or the lopping off of an ear for a heinous offense. Like the men gathered at a Thing, Zodiac was, in effect, acting as judge, jury, and executioner in his crimes. So, in essence, when he killed people he was literally doing his *"Thing"* in the true Viking sense of the word. And there was one more feature of this letter that I noticed.

In 2000, I made an observation about the "eleven o'clock" and "one o'clock" circles that Zodiac used in his letters and in his signature. When Zodiac wrote a letter *o* or wrote his crossed-circle symbol within the *body* of a letter, he made it as an "eleven o'clock" circle, one that opened and closed at (or close to) that position on a clock face (Exhibit 6a). However, when he *signed* his letters with his crossed-circle symbol, he made it as a one o'clock circle, which opened and closed on the opposite side of the twelve o'clock position of the clock face (Exhibit 6b). This was a fairly consistent pattern, which even applies to crossed circles that are not signatures but rather are embedded within the body of a letter (Exhibit 6a.) The version of the November 8 letter that I used was from Graysmith's book, and the signature circle, which I later learned was a publishing/printing anomaly, *appeared* to be upside down. Unaware of that piece of information at the time, I assumed that you had to turn the card 180 degrees in order to get a one o'clock, "signature"-type, circle. So I turned the card upside down and made a startling observation.

---

38   Johannes Bronsted, *The Vikings* (Middlesex, England: Penguin Books, 1960), pp. 242–3.

I looked carefully at the six exclamation points that followed the word "**Thing**." If you closely examine the dots beneath the points, they seem to form a pattern: there are two heavily shaded dots followed by three stippled dots and finally a slash/line that doubles for a dot. The manner in which they were made clearly suggests intent by the writer for them to appear different from one another and form this pattern. If you read that series with the card inverted, it is "1-3-2" (Exhibit 7). Several months later, a strange incident involving the abduction of Kathleen Johns and her baby daughter took place near Modesto, California— on a lonely stretch of **Highway 132**. Zodiac later took credit for this abduction. The 1 in "1-3-2" even resembles the actual number, in that it's the only one of the "dots" that is not a dot but a small line.

An eerie feeling came over me: Was Zodiac planting a clue to a crime he would commit four months into the future?

...

Zodiac's next letter followed hot on the heels of this one, being post-marked November 9. Called the Bus Bomb Letter, it was seven pages in length. The killer started out this letter by announcing he had killed seven people. However, the police could only account for five victims at the time.

In the Bus Bomb Letter Zodiac indicated that he was angry at the police for the perceived lies they were telling about him in the press. An article by *San Francisco Chronicle* reporter Paul Avery had labeled Zodiac a "latent homosexual" and, for good measure, a "liar." Zodiac didn't seem to take kindly to these barbs.

Zodiac then proceeded to throw a huge monkey wrench into the investigation. He stated that in the future he wouldn't take credit for his murders. Rather, he would stage them to look like robberies, "fake accidents," or anger killings. Now the police wouldn't know who was a Zodiac victim and who was not. Some might not even be identified as murder victims at all!

The killer then went on to assert his superiority over his pursuers once again, indicating that he hadn't left any fingerprints behind him at the Stine crime scene. He claimed to have coated his fingertips with airplane glue to obscure his prints. However, no "blank" prints were reported to have been found on the cab, so there was no proof that he had actually taken this step. He also revealed his method for purchasing weapons so that they couldn't be traced to him, stating that one of his guns had been purchased "out of state" and the other through the US mail prior to a 1968 ban on such purchases following the assassination of Sen. Robert Kennedy that June. Zodiac taunted the police by saying that the reason he was wiping down the cab was to leave fake "clews" for them to chase down. Some researchers took this to mean that Zodiac had cut off someone's fingers and was using them to leave behind prints from a dead man, though there is no evidence that he carried out such a ghoulish exercise.

The killer next indicated that he was wearing a "descise" when he killed and that, while he did look like the SFPD wanted poster sketches, he only looked that way when he was out to kill. So of what could this disguise have consisted? As discussed earlier, it wouldn't be much trouble for a man with an average build to alter his appearance to make himself look heavier. And a couple of lifts in his shoes could also make him appear to be taller. Conversely, it's very difficult if not impossible for a tall and heavy man, like Arthur Allen, to make himself appear both shorter and thinner than he actually is. Arthur Allen, who was the primary suspect in the case for over thirty years, weighed 230 pounds and was over six feet tall.

Zodiac then made more allusions to the police search on the night of the Stine murder that are revealing. He once again described the sounds, not the sights, of the search. This was the theme he had started in his October 13 letter, when he spoke about motorcycles making noise by holding "road races." In the current letter, instead of confirming the search lights that Martin Lee had discussed, the killer made reference to the fact that the police were using fire trucks to mask the sound of their patrol cars going through the neighborhood. He also described two groups of "barking" search dogs that went by over a ten-minute interval. Then he indicated that he'd heard motorcycles going by about 150 feet away from his position heading from "south to north west [*sic*]."

The latter is an interesting reference. All of the cross streets in Presidio Heights run in a slight but distinct southeast–northwest direction (Exhibit 4). In other words, when Zodiac gave that description, he could easily have been saying that the motorcycles were going up one of the north–south streets into the area of the Kahn Playground. There is no entry into the park at the end of either Cherry or Maple Streets due to a three-foot drop-off at the end of both streets. However, as in 1969, there is an opening in a stone gate at the north end of Spruce Street that would have given the motorcycles access to the park. Spruce Street was in the area of the police search that night. Therefore, when Zodiac says that he heard the motorcycles going by from "south to north west," he could easily have been saying that they were headed up Spruce Street into the park.

At three different points in this letter, Zodiac stated that he had disappeared "into the park." He went out of his way to paint a word picture in the minds of the police and public that the Presidio, and specifically the area of the Kahn Playground, was his destination after killing Stine. But was it a case of the famous line from Shakespeare's *Hamlet*, "He doth protest too much"? Was Zodiac headed somewhere *else* in the Presidio Heights neighborhood that night, but was seemingly overanxious for everyone to *believe* that he had disappeared into the park? After all, the park was searched thoroughly and nothing was found, yet Zodiac was able to describe the sounds of the search. So where exactly was he?

In the next part of the letter, Zodiac chides the police for thinking he was serious when he said he would kill school kids by picking them off with a gun. What he really intended to do was to blow them up with a "bus bomb" consisting of five bags of ammonia nitrate fertilizer, stove oil, and gravel for shrapnel. He provided a recipe for the bomb, detailing its component parts. One particularly interesting aspect of the bomb was its power source—a six-volt car battery. At the time, six-volt batteries were what you might find in an imported sports car, such as British-made marques like the MG or Triumph the young man was driving at Lake Herman, not a 1960s' US-made vehicle. US-made cars from that era used *twelve-volt batteries*.

This threat of course set off new alarm bells in the Bay Area after the shock of the initial school bus threat from the Stine letter had slowly begun to subside. The bomb was set up with a timer in order to have the mechanism active at the right time to hit a school bus—seven in the morning, as opposed to seven at night. It also had an electric eye system, like the one you might see at the foul line in a bowling alley. There had to be an elevation change between the light source and the reflector, with the reflector being set up higher than the receptor, so that the bomb could target only high-profile vehicles like buses. A bus would interrupt the beam of light, thus detonating the device, but lower-carriage cars would be allowed to pass safely by. This meant that the most likely place for the bomb to be set up was somewhere along the lonely tangle of byways in Napa County where there were many roadside cliffs. Search teams were sent out to scour the area, looking for anything suspicious. As mentioned in Graysmith's *Zodiac*, despite the fact that the bomb resembled something out of a Rube Goldberg cartoon (Goldberg was famous for creating obscenely and comically complex methods for accomplishing life's simple chores), experts felt that it could be made to work.[39]

The two bus threats—to either shoot up or blow up school-children—combined to cause a panic in the Bay Area that cut right across class lines. Whether you lived on Nob Hill in San Francisco or in Richmond in Contra Costa County, you probably had a child who rode a bus to school, or knew someone who did. These threats affected everyone throughout Northern California and caused many kids to have nightmares that the Zodiac was coming to get them. And since

---

39   Graysmith (1986), p. 126.

no bomb was ever found, the threat appeared to be yet another way of creating headaches and tremendous overtime expenditures for the local governments as the police feverishly scanned the hillsides of Napa County and elsewhere for the infernal device.

On the last page of the November 9 letter, Zodiac's signature circle is not only quadruple its normal size but the author also put small *x*s along its periphery at positions equivalent to the six-, eight-, nine-, ten-, and eleven o'clock positions. These marks have variously been interpreted as months of the year, signs of the Zodiac based on numbering the months, or any number of other things. Until someone can come up with an ironclad system for interpreting the *x*s that's consistent with some other aspect of the case, this figure will remain open to rampant interpretation.

In the November 9 letter, the killer said that the police didn't know if the bomb was already on-site or if it was being stored in his *basement*. This reference finally provided the police with a promising lead: due to the igneous, rocky nature of the land in the Bay Area, not many homes had basements. Research was done along these lines but never led to an arrest of a man with a bus bomb hidden in his home.

The references to a basement or cellar may have had a much different connotation altogether. In fact, it may have been a very subtle clue to the identity of the killer. However, not only was it an obscure reference but it was, as we'll see later, also in a foreign language: *Norwegian*. References to Norse/Viking culture had already found their way into the Zodiac letters, such as the word *Thing*, Odin's cross, and "slaves in the afterlife." They would continue to accumulate in future letters, with one of the 1974 letters containing the most obvious Norse reference of all.

Once again, the letter contained several iterations of the phrase *I shall*. It also said that if the police tried to bluff him, things could get "*rather* messy," thus reinforcing the British connection. And with the mention of motorcycles, prowl cars, and fire trucks, here again were yet more of the recurring references to cars/vehicles. In addition to these, he had just used a taxi cab as a mobile crime scene and threatened to blow up a school bus with a bomb that was powered by a six-volt car battery, which one might find in a foreign car. More automotive references.

...

Zodiac would soon find himself face-to-face with a new nemesis: reporter Paul Avery of the *San Francisco Chronicle*. Either of his own volition or more likely in consultation with SFPD officials, Avery's job seemed to be to nettle and demean the killer, probably in an effort to anger him and get him to make a false move. In the front-page article that was titled "Zodiac—Portrait of a Killer," but retitled "Zodiac Called a 'Clumsy Criminal'"[40] on the back page of section one, Avery mocks the killer for leaving two victims alive at his four crimes scenes, possibly leaving bloody fingerprints on Stine's cab, and allowing the witnesses in Presidio Heights to see him. He quotes SFPD chief of detectives Lee as calling Zodiac a "liar" when he stated he was in the area when the dog search was going on but then failed to talk about the presence of all the search lights the fire trucks were using. Finally, Avery questioned the killer's manhood in the way he wielded his knife at Lake Berryessa, saying he might be a "latent homosexual."

Zodiac didn't have any direct response for Avery . . . yet. But he did apparently make a mental note of these slights for future reckoning.

On October 22, 1969, a call came in to the Oakland Police Department. The caller, who identified himself as Zodiac, asked that one of two high-profile attorneys be on a local San Francisco morning talk show hosted by Jim Dunbar. The attorneys he requested were F. Lee Bailey of The Boston Strangler fame, or local San Francisco attorney Melvin Belli, known as "the King of Torts," The flamboyant Belli was famous for getting big divorce settlements for the wives of well-heeled husbands possessed of roving eyes. In a photo from the

---

40 Paul Avery, "Zodiac—Portrait of a Killer," *San Francisco Chronicle*, October 18, 1969, p. 1.

1940s, Belli is seen with one of his private investigators, William "Peek-a-Boo" Pennington, trying to revive a female client who had passed out in court—either for effect or possibly from the excitement of the size of the settlement she had just won (Exhibit 8).

The next day, Belli was on the Jim Dunbar morning TV show. A man, who identified himself as Sam, called in a number of times claiming to be Zodiac and stating he suffered from headaches that were only relieved in the most unusual way imaginable: by murdering people. The calls were eventually traced to a mental hospital: Sam was apparently an impostor. Yet a small and obscure article I found in the *Alameda Times-Star* said that the original caller who phoned the Oakland PD provided "undisclosed information" about the case that proved he was the Zodiac. That information, however, wasn't revealed in the article.[41]

It was school kids more so than adults who bore the brunt of Zodiac's threats in the fall of 1969. In addition to worrying that their school buses might be attacked by a crazed gunman, their Halloween fun was cut short when police limited trick-or-treating in Vallejo to daylight hours for fear of an attack. The kids may have begun to hope that the Zodiac would not also somehow cancel Christmas.

...

Paul Avery of the *San Francisco Chronicle* was up to his old tricks once again on November 13. He wrote an article that fired a shot over the killer's bow. He quoted SFPD chief Lee stating that after reviewing the Zodiac letters he felt the killer was "legally sane." This was a veiled way of informing Zodiac that when he was captured he would face the gas chamber and wouldn't be able to escape his fate with an insanity defense. Lee himself also took a jab at the killer by asserting that he

---

41   "Dick Tracy May Point Way to Zodiac Killer," *Alameda Times-Star*, 24 October 1969, p. 1. In 2015, I called the Oakland PD to see if I could learn what that information was. They said that any records they had would have been turned over to SFPD at the time. To me, that was like hearing it had been tossed into a black hole.

probably held some low-level office job in which basically nobody knew he existed. This reference was clearly made to anger the killer into doing something that might reveal him to the police. But had Lee only known the truth about Zodiac's day job, he would have understood just how outrageously off base his statement was.

The articles by Avery in which he taunted the killer were undoubtedly part of a continuing campaign of psychological warfare against Zodiac in his newspaper of choice. Just as Zodiac was using the media to taunt the police, so too were the authorities trying to use Avery and the *San Francisco Chronicle* to get to Zodiac. Their efforts to rile Zodiac up and get the killer to inadvertently reveal himself , however, did not meet with success.

Zodiac's next letter was sent directly to Melvin Belli, who once again found himself a pawn in the killer's literary game with the public and police. The letter was postmarked December 20, the first anniversary of Zodiac's Lake Herman murders. To prove the letter came from the killer, not from some impostor from a mental hospital, he enclosed another bloody swatch of Paul Stine's shirt. The letter was either a legitimate cry for help to his would-be protector or it was yet another tongue-in-cheek joke being played by the killer on the famous attorney. In the letter Zodiac asks Belli for assistance and says that the "thing" inside him won't allow him to reach out himself. The killer reports to Belli that thus far he has been able to keep the entity in check; however, he's not sure how long he can keep the beast confined in its cage. He says that the kids he had threatened to blow up were safe for the moment, which he explains is not because of his benevolence but because of the logistics of rolling out a bomb that requires a lot of digging to set up. He then goes back to threatening to claim victims "nine" and "ten" if he loses his battle for "controol" over the "thing." As if to visually reinforce this point, the letter starts out with hand printing that is very neat and orderly but gets progressively less tidy as the letter continues down the page. With this letter, Zodiac had his fill of Melvin

Belli. He never wrote to him again and would, in fact, make him the butt of his jokes in future letters.

In the first line of this letter, the killer once again used British terminology when he wished Belli a "happy Christmass [*sic*]."

...

The killer then put a cap on his blue felt-tip pen and did not remove it again for exactly four months. What was Zodiac doing during this period? Where was he? What occupied his time and attention so that he did not write any letters? Was he in jail or did he join "Sam" in some mental hospital? Nobody can say for sure, but later on I will propose a theory to explain this gap in the letters.

The next letter, called the "My Name Is" Letter, was postmarked April 20, 1970. In it, Zodiac gave his most tantalizing clue to date: a string of thirteen characters that he said revealed his name. Three of the characters looked like circled 8s, but appear actually to be circled astrological symbols for the birth sign Taurus. So code breakers tried using those purported 8s to find a name in the cipher. Two Zodiac researchers, Lyndon Lafferty and Harvey Hines, succeeded. The problem is that they both used the same technique to arrive at two different names—those of their own suspects.

Lafferty used the alleged circled 8s as a hint to look at letters eight characters to the left, that is, earlier in the alphabet, than the letters they preceded. This led him to the name Grant. Lafferty pursued a man named William Grant for many years. Hines did the opposite in going eight characters to the *right*. This led him to the name Kane. Hines believed that Zodiac was a man named Larry Kane. What both of the solutions tell us is that neither one can be considered valid, since they essentially cancel each other out and prove that if you go looking for a name in the Thirteen-Character Cipher, you can generally find it.

Zodiac then admitted that he was "mildly cerous" (read widely as *curious*) as to how much of a reward was being offered for his capture.

As pointed out by Dr. Mike Kelleher, this was yet another example of Zodiac minimizing his true feelings, like someone from the UK might do. He was actually dying to know that his crimes warranted a huge reward for his capture.[42] He also distanced himself from the murder of an SFPD officer who had been killed at a police station with a bomb. The killer next provided yet another tangible clue into which SFPD inspectors Toschi and Armstrong looked very closely. The killer said that his bus bomb had been a "dud" because he was "swamped out" by the rain that had recently fallen in the area. Since Zodiac had previously said that his bomb was being stored in his basement, did the killer live in an area where there were basements and where there had been recent flooding? This lead ultimately proved to be another in a series of dead ends.

A second page accompanied the code. On it, Zodiac revealed a new configuration for his dastardly bus bomb. This new bomb was again powered by a battery, which this time was explicitly labeled "car bat."

By now, the panic that the first bomb threat had engendered had pretty much worn off. The *San Francisco Chronicle* did not so much as mention the bus bomb. This did not sit well with the killer.

As you will see in chapters 15 and 20, I believe there was an ulterior motive for Zodiac's two bomb diagrams that bordered on genius. This motive had *absolutely* nothing to do with harming schoolchildren or anyone else. What these two diagrams may actually represent are things I believe nobody living in the Bay Area at the time could have possibly imagined in their wildest dreams.

Beginning in 1999 and continuing to 2005, I would make discoveries that led me to believe that Zodiac's two "bus bombs" were not bombs at all but *bombshells*. I believe that, combined, these two diagrams represent the most incredible, wickedly creative, and almost unimaginably daring clues a criminal has ever sent to his pursuers. These clues clearly showed how Zodiac looked down on the intellectual capabilities

---

42 Dr. Michael Kelleher and Dr. David Van Nuys, *This Is the Zodiac Speaking: Into the Mind of a Serial Killer* (New York: Praeger, 2002), p. 133.

and resourcefulness of the police and the public. Zodiac told them they were bus bombs, so that's what everyone accepted them as being. They would go unrecognized for what I believe they truly were for another thirty years.

At the end of the letter, Zodiac provided his first "scorecard": Zodiac—10 SFPD—0. In other words, the killer's body count had now allegedly reached ten victims and SFPD had yet to lay a glove on him. The authorities had no idea who the other victims might have been. Given his threat not to take credit for his murders from his November 9, 1969, letter, there was now no way to know if he had truly killed ten people or not.

After going silent for exactly four months after the Belli letter, the people of the Bay Area did not have to wait long before they heard from the killer after the April 20 letter. He wrote again about a week later, on April 28. This letter has been called the Dragon Card. And for good reason. The killer sent another droll greeting card with two miners on it. One miner was sitting on a donkey and the other was astride a dragon.

In the message on the card, Zodiac once again threatens to use his bus bomb. But he gives the populace a way out: if the newspapers would release the details of the new bus bomb, and if the people of the Bay Area would sport some Zodiac-themed lapel buttons, such as the ones that were popular at the time with the peace symbol or "Black Power," it would improve Zodiac's mood enough that he would relent on the bus-bomb threat. He cautioned the public not to create any "nasty" buttons, such as the one that dug at his favorite target, Melvin Belli, which shows that Zodiac had some special animus reserved for the famed attorney: "Melvin eats bluber [sic]." (This was a takeoff on a button about the author of *Moby Dick*, "*Melville* eats blubber," that was popular at the time.)

On June 19, 1970, SFPD officer Richard Radetich was shot and killed with a .38-caliber slug while writing out a parking ticket in the Height in his squad car. This story was obviously big news in San

Francisco and was covered in the *San Francisco Chronicle* and all the local media outlets.

. . .

After the Dragon Card, the next time the killer would be heard from would be with a letter postmarked June 26, 1970, which is known as the Mt. Diablo Letter. There was no droll greeting card this time, because Zodiac was definitely not in as jovial a mood as he was in his previous letter. The reason was that the citizenry of the Bay Area had not acceded to his demand to wear Zodiac lapel buttons. So to punish them, he stated that he had followed through on his threat and finally deployed his bus bomb. But since school was now out, he couldn't use it until classes resumed in the fall. He then made a thinly veiled confession: "I shot a man sitting in a parked car with a .38." Reading between the lines, he clearly seemed to be taking credit for the Radetich murder. This met with a swift rebuttal from SFPD. They said that they already had a suspect in the case and once again labeled Zodiac a liar. The suspect, however, was never convicted. This wouldn't be the last time the killer may have taken credit for a crime he did not commit.

With the mention of the Radetich murder, since the officer was shot while sitting in his patrol car, here was yet another example of the presence of cars in association with the Zodiac crimes, letters, and in his purported crimes.

Along with the letter, Zodiac sent a portion of a Phillips 66 road map of the Bay Area. The killer singled out the aforementioned Mt. Diablo on this map. With its implied reference to the devil, the name of this mountain in Walnut Creek, California, sounds very foreboding and is in keeping with the Zodiac mystique. In the 1950s, there was a "hill climb" car race for British sports cars that was organized by the suspect named later in this book that went up to the peak of this landmark, thus sealing his association with the location.

The killer drew his crossed circle on the peak of the mountain along with the numbers associated with the face of a clock—0, 3, 6, and 9—with the zero at the twelve o'clock position. At the bottom of the letter, Zodiac provided yet another short cryptogram, known as the 32-Character Cipher. Here he was issuing a challenge and giving the public one last chance to thwart his evil plan. The writer said that the code when coupled with the Phillips 66 map was a clue to where the bomb was buried. And that clue seemed to have something to do with Mt. Diablo. This notion would be reinforced in a later letter. Code breakers and others who loved a challenge put down the 340-Character Code and set out to solve the cryptogram. This was an ingenious move by Zodiac because, in setting people off in search of the bomb, he was able to engage the entire populace of the Bay Area in a giant scavenger hunt. The more people he could entice to try to solve his codes, as he had done before, in July and November of '69 and in April of '70, the more attention he was going to attract to himself. And the one thing Zodiac loved was attention—preferably on the front page of the newspaper. Despite all the attention it received from the public, the 32-Character Cipher has never been definitively solved.

Zodiac mentions that on the map the 0 point is to be set at "Mag. N," or magnetic north. In 1970, magnetic north in the Bay Area was about *seventeen degrees* from true north. This was the same as the number of columns in every one of his coded messages. The number seventeen will also have strong implications for the suspect named in chapter 13.

After the June 26 letter, Zodiac fell silent until July 24, when he was back and talking about the aforementioned Kathleen Johns incident, which had spurred articles in the *Modesto Bee* and *San Francisco Examiner* in March. In the July 24 letter, Zodiac expressed his anger with the fact that nobody was wearing his lapel buttons. So to punish them he stated that he had given a "woeman [*sic*] and her baby a rather intresting [*sic*] ride a few months back." The only incident that seemed to match that description was the Johns incident.

Kathleen Johns was driving her older-model car from her home in San Bernardino to her mother's house in Petaluma on March 22, 1970. As part of her journey, she found herself on a lonely stretch of Highway 132 coming out of Modesto and heading toward Interstate 5, which would take her north. As she drove, another motorist pulled up behind her, flashed his brights on and off, and got her to pull off to the shoulder. He told her that her rear wheel was wobbling and in danger of falling off. Being the Good Samaritan he was, he offered to tighten the lug nuts for her. As she sat in the car, her sleeping baby on the front seat not visible to the man as he spoke through the window, he went to the rear of the car and used his crowbar on the lug nuts. The only problem is that he apparently turned them counterclockwise, loosening not tightening them. He then told her she was all set, got in his car, and pulled away.

Kathleen drove back onto the road but had only gone a short distance when she heard a frightening noise and could feel the rear of the car drop. The wheel had nearly spun off the axle. Out of the darkness once again came the Good Samaritan, who surveyed the situation and kindly offered her a ride to the nearest gas station, which was just up the road. She bundled up her baby and hopped in for the short ride. The man was none too happy to learn that she was toting an infant. When they drove right past the open station, the realization may have immediately hit her that she had been duped.

According to Johns, the man drove her around aimlessly on the back roads of Patterson and the surrounding farmland. He allegedly threatened to kill her and to throw her child out the window before doing so. Kathleen eventually jumped out of the car when the man went the wrong way up a freeway off-ramp. She then fled into a nearby field, cupping her hand over the mouth of her child to keep her from crying. The man played a flashlight over the field for a minute or so before jumping back into his car and fleeing the area as a semi came barreling toward the scene.

Johns, shaken, was taken to the Patterson, California, police department. As the story goes, she was sitting at a desk speaking to an officer about her ordeal when she spotted a wanted poster on the wall. Suddenly her eyes grew wide, and she pointed at the poster. Sobbing uncontrollably, she only managed to get out that the man on the poster was the one who had abducted her. She asked who the man was and what he was wanted for. A look of fear crossing his face, the officer replied that the poster was of the Zodiac.

Later, Johns's car was found on Highway 132. It had been set afire. Zodiac correctly stated in his letter that he had burned the car where he had found it. In the police reports about the incident, Johns never says that the man had threatened her life or that of her baby. Her story has therefore been called into question over the years. Zodiac's claim in the July 24, 1970, letter doesn't contain any information that isn't in the articles that came out after the incident. However, his minimalist manner of taking credit for the crime may reveal his supreme confidence in knowing that he had in fact committed it. By doing so, he had suddenly abandoned his previous pattern from his earlier crimes of either stating facts or sending back pieces of evidence, such as a bloody shirt from the crime scene, that "only he and the police knew" to prove that he had in fact committed the crime.

Was Johns abducted by Zodiac? Here is yet another crime that is related to cars, just like the actual Zodiac attacks and the Radetich case. But did he actually commit the abduction himself, or did he just claim credit for it? The one thing that always sticks in the back of my mind when I ponder this issue is the 1-3-2 pattern of the dots on the November 8 Dripping Pen Card.

The next letter provided the first glimpse of Zodiac's bizarre obsession with a character in a play first performed in the nineteenth century. The letter was postmarked just two days after the Johns letter, July 26, 1970, and is called the Little List Letter.

In this latest letter, Zodiac now says that he will accept any type of Zodiac button, not just a nice one, as long as the people of the Bay Area will wear it in public. If not, he bizarrely threatens to torture the "slaves" he has collected thus far for his afterlife. He then goes on at great length describing the types of woes that await these victims, such as being fed "salt beef" and then not being given any water.

The final form of torture, making billiard players play games in "darkened dungeons" with "crooked cues and twisted cues" is lifted from the libretto of *The Mikado*,[43] a popular light opera written by W. S. Gilbert and Arthur Sullivan in the late 1800s. The lines in the play were sung by the Mikado himself, who was the ruler of all the kingdom. The references to *The Mikado* also serve as a preface for what was to follow on the next pages of the letter: an aria sung by Ko-Ko the Lord High Executioner, who was Zodiac's favorite character to quote from that piece. The song is about finding a victim to sacrifice from the town of Titipu in order to please the Mikado. It seems that Titipu has not been keeping up with its quota for executing people, and someone has to be sacrificed before the emperor arrives for a visit in a few days.

Zodiac purloins essentially the entire song from the play. But interestingly, he gets certain parts wrong. It has been widely theorized that the killer had *heard* the libretto but had not actually been in the play, much to the chagrin of SFPD inspectors, who investigated many actors who had played Ko-Ko in local Gilbert and Sullivan productions. He would therefore never actually have *read* or learned by rote the actual words to these songs. Zodiac replaces some lines with the words he *believes* he has heard, such as saying that he gets annoyed with people who "eat peppermint and phomphit [sic] in your face," instead of "puff it in your face."

Research years later would lead some amateurs to conclude that the recorded libretto that Zodiac used to write the letter potentially came from, of all places, a Groucho Marx version of the song![44] At least the killer had a sense of humor.

---

43 William Gilbert and Arthur Sullivan, 1885.

44 Post by Tahoe 27 on zodiackiller.com message board.

The reference to this Gilbert and Sullivan play may further hint at Zodiac's ties to British culture. Along with his references to automobiles in both his crimes and letters, both British and Norse influences on the Zodiac will become crucial later as I discuss the suspect I name in this book.

In July 1999, I made a mental note that it would be dangerous to discount a suspect as the murderer in the Zodiac case if he were part of a team, as the Gilbert and Sullivan references in *The Mikado* may imply. Just as William S. Gilbert wrote the lyrics to *The Mikado* and Arthur Sullivan wrote the music, what if there were *two* people at work as Zodiac, one who wrote the letters, that is, the "libretto" of the crimes, and one who wrote the "music," or carried out the murders? You could catch the murdering partner but falsely exonerate him if you used handwriting or other evidence from the letters, such as DNA, as the ultimate criterion in assessing his guilt or innocence. This is one reason handwriting and evidence from letters isn't used to solve murder cases. I will delve more deeply into this concept in the last chapter.

Several years later, forensic psychologist Richard Walter would agree with me that you do not eliminate suspects in a homicide case using handwriting. A glaring example of what can happen when you try to solve the Zodiac case using handwriting is the 2014 fiasco caused by the release of a book by Gary Stewart, *The Most Dangerous Animal of All*, in which he produces a marriage certificate with handwriting that he alleges came from his father, Earl Van Best. The handwriting on the certificate was matched to Best essentially beyond all doubt in a sixty-page report by forensic documents examiner Michael Wakshull to the Zodiac. Case closed, right? After learning about this book I contacted the church in Reno, Nevada, where Earl Van Best had been married in 1962 and asked for a sample of the hand printing of the priest who had conducted the service and signed the marriage certificate. Although this priest's signature betrayed nothing, one glance at his hand printing told me that it almost certainly matched the certificate. I was quickly able to prove to even Wakshull's satisfaction that the handwriting on the certificate was that of *the priest who had performed the service, not of Earl Van Best!* The priest is a very unlikely candidate to have been involved in the Zodiac crimes.

Case not closed.

A sentence at the end of the Little List Letter has led to years of speculation about the background and intent of the author. The Zodiac stated, "The Mt. Diablo code concerns Radians & # inches along the radians." The word *radians* raised some eyebrows because it is virtually never used by average people in everyday conversation. Radians are the stuff of engineers, scientists, and automobile engine designers. They are used in place of degrees to measure the rotation of such things as the cam shaft in a racing engine. So how did someone like Zodiac know this obscure word?

The next time the public heard from Zodiac was October 27, 1970, when he sent a Halloween card addressed to his nemesis, Paul Avery. This letter was widely viewed as a threat directed at Avery, who, as discussed earlier, had been used as the mouthpiece of the police to needle the killer and try to get him to make a false move. Developments many years later would lead to questions as to what this letter meant and who the *real* target of the cryptic threat was.

The front of the card had a smiling skeleton. Covering the pubic area was an orange pumpkin the killer had pasted on the card. The skeleton's right hand showed three fingers with the number 14 written on the palm. Some have speculated that this represents the Greek number pi, 3.14, which is the topic of one of the many discussion threads one can find on Zodiac message boards. Suffice it to say, a knowledge of pi would not be uncommon for someone who knows what a radian is, since both are mathematical functions related to circles and circular motion.

The inside of the card had yet another skeleton pasted on it, this one in a position that somewhat resembled a crucifixion. The killer also wrote things on the inside, including "Boo!" But it is the other elements inside the card that are of the most potential significance. The killer had drawn a series of a dozen little eyes, complete with eyelashes, that peer to the reader's right. One of them was in the knothole in what appears to be a tree trunk inside the left margin of the card. Around this knothole the killer had written in white artist's ink what was perceived to be a dire warning to Avery: "PEEK-A-BOO YOU ARE DOOMED!" At the right bottom the killer put his crossed-circle signature, a capital Z, and a bizarre symbol that has sparked debate for nearly fifty years. The "batwing" symbol, which also appears as the return address on the front of the envelope, appeared to Dutch Zodiac researcher Eduard Versluijs in the 1990s to be comprised of two Norse runes—a reversed image of the rune Laguz and the rune Ansuz (Exhibit 9).

Each of these runes has meanings attached to it. For instance, each has a link to a specific Norse god, as well as to secondary meanings that appear to have something to say about the man who sent this letter. I will explore these meanings and what they have to say about the author of the Zodiac letters in chapter 18.

On the back of the card Zodiac created a Scrabble-like composition of the words PARADICE SLAVES written in the form of a cross, along with the words BY FIRE, BY GUN, BY KNIFE, and BY ROPE. These were apparently supposed to describe the various means by which he had claimed his victims. However, there was no Zodiac victim who had been killed by fire as far as the authorities knew.

In February 2014, I wrote to a Norwegian expert on runes to ask him a question. He referred me to Karoline Kjesrud, who told me something unexpected that I found completely amazing. I learned that the batwing symbol, beyond being comprised of two Norse runes, closely resembles an arcane symbol that was used to identify people in Scandinavian countries hundreds of years ago called a *bumerke*, or "house mark." This represents a new and original explanation for the symbol that appears as both the signature *and* the return address on the 1970 Halloween card. To my knowledge, *bumerker* (the plural form of *bumerke*) had never before been proposed as the origin of the batwing symbol over the entire forty-plus-year history of the case.

Bumerker were used to denote the maker of a given product or item and, when inscribed in, say, a tree, to set boundary lines for people's property. A craftsman making a tool might mark it with his bumerke so that people would know who had forged it. If placed on a document, it would represent the signature of the author. This piece of information immediately got my attention. After all, the symbol is used on the Avery card as both a signature *and* a return address. Like a bumerke, it answers the question, Who sent this letter?

Explanations of this symbol over the years have included that it is (1) a construction symbol for a wide flange beam;[45] (2) a cattle brand from Fred Harman's Pagosa Springs, Colorado, Red Ryder Ranch; (3) a cattle brand from the Vincent Fontana/Big Dipper Ranch; (4) and the name of a Zodiac suspect named Grant in a Freemason cipher.[46] Many researchers believe that one of the two cattle brands may be the best explanation for this symbol. A bumerke is often comprised of both lines *and* dots. And often those lines can form Norse runes (Exhibits 10a–d). *It is important to note that neither of the cattle brands proposed to date as the "best" explanations of the winged symbol incorporates any dots in its structure.*

Given its construction and the way a bumerke was used, it appears to be the most logical and appropriate explanation for the winged symbol on the card. This is crucial because once again it reinforces the strong Norse connection that pervades the writings of the Zodiac. And in a future letter that would be sent in February 1974, there would come the ultimate in-your-face Norse reference of all, one so overt that it confirms that Zodiac had strong ties to Norse culture.

Later we'll meet a man who comes from Norway, a place where bumerker were used. He fits all the traits laid out by the hidden meanings behind the two Norse runes in the Avery card bumerke. All the letters in his last name can also be derived from a Zodiac symbol, Odin's

---

45   Graysmith (1986), p. 160.

46   Lyndon Lafferty, *The Zodiac Killer Cover-Up AKA The Silenced Badge* (Vallejo: Mandamus Publishing, 2012), p. 400.

cross. Therefore, the three symbols at the bottom of the Avery card—the Z, the "batwing"/bumerke symbol, and the crossed circle—represent, respectively, (1) "Z for Zodiac," (2) an encapsulated runic description of who the killer was, and, as we'll see later, (3) the killer's last name encoded as a Zodiac symbol.

Written inside this card in white artist's ink is what is presumed to be Zodiac's latest scorecard: "4-TEEN."

As I stated earlier, in 1970, this card was viewed as a threat to the life of Paul Avery, who carried a gun for a period of time after the card arrived. As a result of this implied threat to Avery, Zodiac's wish was finally granted in an unexpected way when the writer's colleagues at the *San Francisco Chronicle* started wearing some Zodiac-inspired lapel buttons, just in case the killer decided to visit them at work. The tongue-in-cheek buttons read, "I Am Not Avery." Apparently willing to go along with the joke and maybe to protect himself from potential harm at the same time, Paul Avery wore one too.

In January of 2015, a message-board poster named Blind Bat revealed one of the most important and exciting new pieces of evidence in the case that I had seen in several years. Although there was no explanation as to how this had happened or what Blind Bat was looking for when she located this piece of information, she had found an ad from the 1946 Oakland, California, yellow pages for a private investigator. The ad was for none other than the private investigator friend of Melvin Belli seen in the 1940s' photo discussed earlier in this chapter, William "Peek- a-Boo" Pennington (Exhibit 11).

Amazingly, this ad seems almost inevitably to have been the inspiration for the Zodiac Halloween card and adds an entirely new dimension to the case. First, there is the Melvin Belli connection. For some reason, Zodiac seemed obsessed with Belli, demanding that he or F. Lee Bailey be on the Dunbar show in October 1969, then writing him a letter on December 20, and finally making him the butt of his "nasty" lapel button, "Melvin eats bluber [*sic*]," in April 1970.

What was the basis for Zodiac's obsession with Melvin Belli? Had he met Belli at some point? Did he know him? Did they move in the same circles? An article from 1952 seems to suggest they did, since they both were invitees to the same dinner party.[47] If so, Zodiac was almost certainly not a "clumsy, small-time office clerk," as SFPD's Martin Lee had portrayed him.

Next, there are the little eyes with eyelashes that are nearly identical to the ones Zodiac drew on the Halloween card. Finally, there is the reference to "Peek-a-Boo" in both Pennington's name and on the Halloween card.

When Zodiac said, "PEEK-A-BOO YOU ARE DOOMED!" on the Halloween card, was he actually cryptically threatening Peek-a-Boo Pennington, *not* Paul Avery? Paul Avery was known to use private investigators, such as San Francisco's David Fechheimer, who would later assist me in locating Officer Don Fouke. When did Pennington retire? Could Avery have also known and used Pennington? There is no mention whatsoever of Avery on the card, but Pennington's nickname does appear on it. I will discuss this ad in more detail in chapter 18.

As a result of the publicity generated by the Halloween card, Paul Avery received a letter from a man in Riverside alerting him of similarities between the Zodiac crimes and the 1966 murder of a college freshman, Cheri Jo Bates. Zodiac was then linked by handwriting on letters sent after the Bates murder to that crime.

...

Beginning in July 1969, the Zodiac showed a facile ability to manipulate the press through his many letters, cryptogram messages, and bomb threats. In fact, the killer's ability to play to the press and use it to get his message out is the main reason we remember his crimes today. But he did so with no learning curve whatsoever. How was he able to do this, and where did these abilities come from? Were the

---

47 Anonymous, "Charles Jones Plan Cocktail Party," *Daily Independent Journal*, October 6, 1952 (located by user Coffee Time, zodiackillersite.com message board).

Zodiac letters his first experience with the media, or might he have had previous episodes, possibly in his personal life, in which he had gotten the local papers to dance to his music of widespread attention seeking?

Later, I will introduce the reader to a man who had his very first taste of getting the media to do his bidding as far back as 1947. In a 2012 book about his life as an entrepreneur he stated that coddling and cozying up to the media was one of the central tenets of a wildly successful business plan. Suffice it to say, by the summer of 1969, this man had many years of experience dealing with and manipulating the media.

...

With the exception of his greeting cards and postcards, all of Zodiac's 1969–71 letters were written on monarch-sized paper. This type of paper is usually favored by businessmen and is often personalized as their private stationery. The suspect I will name wrote to me twice in 1999 on this unusual paper. Whenever I made mention of this, posters on message boards were quick to say that many people write on monarch-sized paper. And while this is certainly true, the point they are forgetting is this: we are not talking about how many members of the general public might use monarch-sized paper. We are talking about *how many Zodiac suspects used it*. That reduces the pool of potential users considerably. To my knowledge, the suspect named in this book is *the only one of the three thousand or more named since 1969 who can be proven to have written even **one** letter on monarch-sized paper.* Assuming he has even heard of it, the plumber, electrician, house painter, or other blue-collar worker living down the street in a middle-class neighborhood most likely does not use this stationery. Monarch-sized stationery, especially when personalized, is generally the realm of the wealthy and the successful, like entrepreneurs who lived in places like Presidio Heights. And, of course, the Zodiac.

...

After the Avery card, Zodiac stopped writing again for over four months. When next he resurfaced, he wrote a letter to the *Los Angeles Times* dated March 13, 1971. This time his "scorecard" showed that he had lost count of his victims, indicating that he had killed "17+" at that point. The killer asserted that he was "crack proof" and admonished the police had "best get off their fat asses and do something." He then used an unusual turn of phrase by warning that the longer the police "fiddle and fart around," the more people will fall victim to him. He said that the reason he wrote to the *Times* was that they "didn't bury him on the back pages" like other newspapers did. In the letter, he gave begrudging credit to Avery for linking him to his "Riverside activity" but taunted that there were "a hell of a lot more down there." Given the cryptic nature of his statement, was he saying that he had actually killed Cheri Jo Bates, who was murdered in Riverside in 1966, and there were more victims in Southern California? Or was he simply saying that his letter writing in the form of the three "Bates Had to Die" letters (see chapter 8) was the "activity" to which he was referring and that there were more letters to the editors of Southern California newspapers to be discovered? The phrase "best get off their fat asses" harkens back once again to the British-isms in the Zodiac letters.

In Mark Hewitt's 2009 article, he explores this topic of British usage in much greater detail. Some British references/influences in the Zodiac letters are as follows: (1) The essential absence of profanity in the letters.[48] When Zodiac could have used strong profanity in the August 7, 1969, letter in describing the incident at the phone booth, he used the comic-book-like expression "dam x@" instead. (2) Zodiac's use of understatement, such as "a rather intresting [*sic*] ride" or "I'm mildly

---

48   This would also be remarked upon with respect to Zodiac's speech pattern at Lake Berryessa by Bryan Hartnell in his interview with Sgt. John Robertson of the Napa Sheriff's Office.

cerous [sic] (curious)." (3) The concept of searching the park "properly," which has a British ring to it (from the October 13, 1969, Stine letter). (4) The use of the phrase "one might say." (5) The consistent use of "I shall," instead of the more common usage in the United States "I will." (6) Zodiac's aforementioned use of "they had best get off their fat asses." (7) The use of "happy Christmass [sic]" in the December 1969 Belli letter. And (8) the use of the word *kiddies*. As per Mr. Hewitt's analysis and experiences growing up in Canada, all of the above references comprise signs of a British influence in Zodiac's writings. *However,* it is the possible origin of Zodiac's signature phrase, "This is the Zodiac speaking," that might be the most revealing. According to Hewitt, he was taught by parents of British descent to answer the phone in a similar manner. Hewitt concludes that Zodiac's ties to England run very deep. For that reason, they are probably not of recent origin; they were therefore likely instilled in the killer many years prior to 1969.

On March 22, 1971, the first anniversary of the abduction of Kathleen Johns and her baby, Zodiac sent a postcard to "Paul Averly" of the *San Francisco Chronicle,* likely intentionally misspelling Avery's name to further antagonize him. Called the Peek through the Pines Card, this unsigned message had a scene taken from an ad for a Nevada condominium complex pasted on its back. The killer stated, "Sought victim 12," even though he had seemed to claim seventeen-plus victims in the *L.A. Times* letter just nine days earlier. Also written on the card is "9-70." This led people to speculate that Zodiac was taking credit for the disappearance of Donna Lass, a nurse in Stateline, Nevada, in September of the previous year. She was then presumably victim number twelve. However, no certain link was ever established between Zodiac and the disappearance of Ms. Lass, despite efforts by some researchers to tie her professionally to a hospital in the Presidio at the time of the Zodiac crimes.

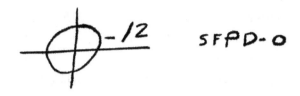

PARTING SHOTS:
THE 1974 LETTERS

THE DAY AFTER CHRISTMAS 1973 Warner Brothers released a movie that introduced the viewing public to the subject of demonic possession and the ritual used by the Catholic Church to expel the devil from the body of one of his victims. *The Exorcist*, starring Ellen Burstyn and Linda Blair, shocked audiences with scenes of a young girl transformed into a monster with a bad complexion who gyrated, levitated, threw up on people, uttered obscene language, and even turned her head in a complete circle. Audiences viewing the movie from coast to coast were naturally horrified. Everyone, that is, except for one man.

On January 29, 1974, someone posted a letter to the editor of the *San Francisco Chronicle* from a San Francisco area mailbox. The letter, which was unsigned, was written in blue felt-tip pen in the seemingly familiar scrawl of the Zodiac.

The author stated that, far from scaring the wits out of him, *The Exorcist* was the "best saterical comidy [*sic*]" he had ever seen. He signed the letter with lyrics lifted once again from an aria by Ko-Ko from *The*

Mikado and warned that if the *San Francisco Chronicle* did not publish his letter, he would "do something nasty," which he reminded everyone he was fully capable of doing. At the bottom of the letter were some arcane characters that looked vaguely Chinese in origin, though they were not from the Chinese alphabet. Of course, these characters were like a Rorschach test. Over the years people, such as Arthur Leigh Allen and an East Coast Ivy League academician, were able to find clues to their favorite suspects in them. Below these characters was the latest running scorecard. The tally, presumably representing the number of victims Zodiac had killed to date, showed that he had been keeping very busy since he was last heard from, in March 1971. It read, "Me-37 SFPD-0."

Unlike all of the other Zodiac letters to date, when this one was treated with ninhydrin to develop fingerprints, something interesting happened. The chemical brought out a swarm of jumbled and super-imposed palm prints on the right side of the letter. Finally, the police had located a solid bit of physical evidence that must have been left by the person who had written the letter as his palm slowly moved down and across the page as he wrote each line. And the palm print evidence indicated that whoever had written this letter had done so with his ungloved right hand.

Over the years, SFPD made a major issue of these prints. But did the Zodiac actually write this letter? The State of California Questioned Documents Examiner, Sherwood Morrill, *the* expert on all things related to handwriting in the Zodiac case, had authenticated this letter as being from the Zodiac. However, in 1978, other handwriting experts would begin to break ranks with Morrill. The *Exorcist* letter was posted the day after the so-called Zebra Killers had made big headlines in San Francisco by shooting five victims. Certainly, Zodiac may not have taken kindly to all the publicity these killers were garnering, and he may have felt the need to reassert himself as the "baddest" man in town. But others, both inside *and* outside of law enforcement, had their own interests in keeping the Zodiac story alive. They also could have conceivably had a motive for writing the letter, since their fortunes were linked in one way or another to the Zodiac story, and they may not have wanted to see the Zebra Killers horn in on the grip Zodiac held over the city.

I will have more to say about the authenticity of the *Exorcist* letter when I discuss DNA in the Zodiac case in chapter 21.

As stated above, the letter was signed with lyrics from Ko-Ko, the Lord High Executioner from *The Mikado*. However, you do not sign letters with lyrics. *The Mikado*, you'll recall, was written by *two* men—Gilbert and Sullivan. If Zodiac wrote this letter, was this yet another cryptic clue that there was both a killer and a letter writer at work behind the scenes of the case?

...

On February 4, 1974, newspaper heiress Patty Hearst was kidnapped by the Symbionese Liberation Army (SLA). Eventually, she would suffer from apparent Stockholm syndrome and transform herself into machine-gun toting "Tania," who realized that she was enamored of the group's philosophy. She even robbed a bank and later shot up the facade of a sporting goods store with the outlaws.

On February 14, the *San Francisco Chronicle* received a short note, signed "a friend," stating that the author knew something nobody else did—that *sla* meant "kill" in the obscure Old Norse language. It seemed that, while everyone in the Bay Area was being exposed to the initialism SLA on a daily basis by mid-February, *only* the author knew its true meaning and he wanted us all to know how smart and insightful he truly was. The letter was authenticated via the handwriting on its envelope as being from the Zodiac. The envelope, in fact, looked extremely similar to the one containing Zodiac's November 8, 1969, Dripping Pen Card. The Sla Letter remained controversial for many years, but the consensus now is that it was sent by the Zodiac.

The simple, straightforward content of the letter became controversial in the 1980s. It seems that the word *sla* in Old Norse, as defined in academic dictionaries, technically does not mean "to kill." It means "to hit" or "to strike." So people said that Zodiac was wrong when he said it meant "kill" and had no idea what he was talking about. But what they failed to appreciate is that this bit of information gives us an important bit of insight into the author: Had he been book educated and learned the meaning of *sla* from a dictionary, then why would he say it meant "kill" when there was no intimation that it did? To me, asserting that the word meant "kill" suggested that whoever Zodiac was, he must have had knowledge that went beyond book learning and dictionary definitions and that he may have learned that *sla* meant "kill" as a slang term—probably by living in Norway or by learning Old Norse from people who had lived there and had a more nuanced knowledge of the language. It may also be a shortened version of *sla ihjel*, which does mean "to kill" in Old Norse. Think of it this way: If someone wanted to learn American English in Norway, he or she would probably have no idea that the words *hit*, *whack*, or *take out* could mean "to kill someone." If they went to an academic English dictionary in Norway, they would learn that to *hit* or *whack* someone means to strike them and to *take out* someone might be to ask the person on a date. But in the US, we have colloquial or slang uses of those words that people who are book taught may not appreciate.

The meaning of a word is in the eye of the person using (or misusing) it. As we will see later, in a 2006 meeting that retired VPD detective Jim Dean and I had with a man whom I will later name as a suspect, he told me that he felt the word *sla* meant "kill." The larger issue that gets lost in the *hit*-versus-*kill* argument is the fact that Zodiac had an inkling that the word *sla* meant *anything* in Old Norse is significant and remains one of the most obvious references to Norwegian culture among many in the Zodiac letters. The author was not an English speaker who had simply looked up *sla* in a dictionary, given that what he provided in the letter was *not* the dictionary definition of the word!

This reference to Old Norse adds yet another layer to the tapestry of Norwegian references in the case, like Odin's cross, "slaves in the afterlife," the word *Thing* and the bumerke/runic return address on the Avery Halloween card.

Eventually, the police were able to corner and kill many members of the SLA in a standoff at a house in Los Angeles. Patty Hearst was arrested and sentenced to prison and eventually released and pardoned. The last I recall hearing of her, she had won a cooking contest in New York City with a recipe for something as mundane as meatloaf in the 1980s, a far cry from her days as "Tania."

...

The third in the suite of four 1974 letters attributed to the killer came on May 8, 1974. Called the *Badlands*, or Citizen, Letter, the anonymous author expressed his "consternation" with the depiction of violence in the movie *Badlands*, which starred Martin Sheen and was then in theaters. Based on hand printing, the author was once again identified as Zodiac. His concern is ironic, given that he had murdered five people and claimed to have killed even more victims. The author railed that "murder-glorification" was "deplorable" and was never "justifiable." He then pleaded that the paper yield to "public sensibilities" and stop running ads for the movie. Aside from the laugh Zodiac must have gotten from the irony dripping from this letter, there is something even more remarkable about its content.

In his perfect grammar and by using and correctly spelling the four- and five-syllable words contained in this letter, Zodiac seemed to be thumbing his nose at anyone who assumed he was the semiliterate slob many felt he was based on the misspellings in his previous letters. The same person who couldn't spell simple words like *front* and who also made such egregious misspellings as "raceing," "nead," "nineth," "butons," "buss" (for *bus*), and "loose" (for *lose*) could handle *consternation, sensibilities,* and *glorification*? In fact, as an exercise for fellow

Zodiac researchers, I have proposed in the past that if you were to read the Zodiac letters in *reverse* chronological order, and if you accepted the *Badlands* Letter as being genuine, then you'd have no choice but to conclude that Zodiac was an extremely well-educated and well-written individual who was *intentionally* misspelling words in his early letters. After all, you can only be as illiterate as your *very best* letter demonstrates you to be.

In short, had the *Badlands* Letter been the killer's *first* letter to the press, we would have had a much different view of him in 1969. I don't believe that the full impact of this letter in evaluating Zodiac's true nature is appreciated to the extent it should be. It appears to demonstrate an individual who is light years better educated than the person who penned the early letters.

As an interesting sidenote, I once put all of Zodiac's misspellings in the site www.gutenberg.org, which in the mid-2000s allowed one to search literature dating back hundreds of years, to see if Zodiac may have been influenced by or had culled his misspellings from some book he had read. A surprisingly large percentage of Zodiac's misspellings can be found in *The Journals of Lewis and Clark*, the team that explored the land the US obtained in the 1803 Louisiana Purchase. I have often wondered if Zodiac read that book, had it on his bookshelf, and adopted the types of spelling errors Meriwether Lewis made. Or did he simply coincidentally make the same type of spelling errors that Lewis did?

It is therefore possible that nearly five and a half years after his first murders Zodiac was feeling so superior to his pursuers that in the February "Sla" letter he gave us an in-your-face clue to his nationality (at which he had only been hinting before), as someone with a Norse background. And in the *Badlands* Letter, he may have been telling the police that, in essence, they were chasing their tails if they thought he was some "discretionary illiterate," as he had been called several years earlier. Certainly, after reading the *Badlands* Letter, it is difficult to imagine Zodiac as a resident of the seedier areas of San Francisco.

The final letter in the 1974 series is the July 8, 1974, Count Marco letter posted from San Rafael. The Count was a sort of curmudgeonly antifeminist columnist for the *San Francisco Chronicle* who battled against the inroads being made by the early women's liberation movement. There was a condescending air about his columns, and apparently Zodiac didn't appreciate his tone, which may have hit a bit too close to home.

This letter seems to represent a classic example of the psychological phenomenon of *projection*, whereby Zodiac took exception to a trait in Count Marco that was, in fact, one of Zodiac's most prominent ones. In this letter, Zodiac used a disguised and more elaborate, florid form of handwriting. He indignantly said that the editor should send Count Marco back to the "hell hole" from which he had come, due probably to his overbearing nature. He suggested that they cancel the column Count Marco wrote and have him see a "shrink." As for the Count getting psychological help for his superiority complex, Zodiac could have undoubtedly benefited from taking his own advice!

The letter was signed with a pseudonym, the "Red Phantom, Red with Rage." This led movie buffs once again to claim Zodiac as one of their own. An old movie from 1907, *El Spectre Rojo* by the Pathe Studios, had recently been rediscovered after having gone missing for many years. The movie may have hit close to home with someone like Zodiac, in that it showed a demon in his lair toying with the souls of several captive women along the lines of their being his "slaves in the afterlife." Along with the presence of the character Dr. Zodiac in the 1939 movie *Charlie Chan at Treasure Island* and Zodiac's reference to "The Most Dangerous Game" in his Three-Part Cipher, a case was made anew for Zodiac being interested in classic films. This once again implied that he may have been an older individual than many believed at the time.

PART EIGHT
INTO THE VORTEX: A NEW SUSPECT
EMERGES

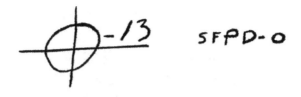

THE MOST UNLIKELY SUSPECT OF
ALL: EARLY EVIDENCE

I WAS BORN INTO a blue-collar family in Queens, New York, in the winter of 1956. Both my grandfather and father were lithographers. They were also baseball players. In fact, my grandfather had an opportunity to try out for the New York Yankees as a catcher in the days of Babe Ruth and Lou Gehrig. But in those days baseball players had a reputation of being hard-drinking rowdies, so my great-grandmother wouldn't allow him to do it. Instead, she made him stay home and work in our family's Italian store near the intersection of Sixty-Ninth Street and Queens Boulevard in Woodside, opposite a family-owned Mobil gas station and garage.

My father was a crack windmill softball pitcher and was, at one point, a prospect as a shortstop in the Pittsburgh Pirates organization. Like my grandfather, he was also an excellent bowler. But his bad knees ended his baseball aspirations. I, on the other hand, was a schoolyard kid who disappeared every summer to play softball, stickball, basketball, and whiffle ball in the PS 12 schoolyard up the street from my home on Forty-Third Avenue. I did well academically but never really took an interest in any one subject.

For many years, I lived the life of a professional student. I had been told by my friends that I was given a mind that was like a high-powered sports car. When I was in school I got lots of As, sat in the "smart row" in fourth grade, skipped a year in junior high school, and earned a 3.9 GPA in college. My continued involvement in higher education was essentially an effort to "test drive" various fields to see if I could find a career that interested me. Despite the almost infinite range of possible career paths from which one can choose in life, I never did find one that truly held my attention.

In 1979, I had been accepted to one of the most prestigious science programs in the country, the University of Rhode Island's Graduate School of Oceanography. I was immediately sent on a six-month junket outside the continental US. My first stop was an all-expenses-paid course in coral reef biology at the University of Hawaii field station on Coconut Island in Kaneohe Bay. There I studied with some of the most brilliant minds in the field, Dr. Len Muscatine and Dr. Bob Trench, along with a class full of gifted students. As I studied alongside them, I quickly knew how lucky I was to have access to all these brilliant minds. From there, I was sent to Kuala Lumpur, Malaysia, to conduct sampling of animals and plants in a mangrove swamp environment, which would lead me to my master's degree. Out of my thesis came a professional, peer-reviewed scientific paper on food chain analysis in a Malaysian mangrove swamp that was cited for many years afterward in other works on the subject.

However, there was one seemingly inconsequential but none-theless crucial thing that happened to me in Malaysia that years later would change my life forever. While there, I stayed with an expatriate Australian couple, Glenn and Miriam. One lazy Saturday morning, I was looking through their bookshelf selections when I came across a very thin work called *Lateral Thinking* by Edward de Bono. The book caused me to approach both thinking and problem-solving in an entirely new way.

In the first chapters of the book, de Bono makes the following observations: When most people approach a problem they do the mental equivalent of digging a hole, and if they don't find the answer, they keep digging deeper and deeper in the same hole. In lateral thinking, you begin by digging a shallow hole, but if you don't find the answer you're looking for, you begin digging other holes in different places. Little did I know that this innocent analogy would one day help me conceive of an idea to identify the Zodiac.

When I was fifteen or sixteen years old, I had seen a TV show about Jack the Ripper. This documentary lit an ember that smoldered silently deep inside me and imbued me with a fascination for serial killers. I never imagined in my wildest dreams that I would one day attempt to solve such a case, but it did mean that as I would stumble onto books about these killers in libraries or bookstores over the years, I would grab them up and read them voraciously.

In 1987, I had read Robert Graysmith's new paperback edition of *Zodiac*[49] and found myself completely absorbed in the case. What attracted me most to the story was the cold, sterile appearance of the meticulous rows and columns of eerie symbols that comprised his coded messages. This neatness whispered to me of the killer's fanatical obsession with detail that, combined with his obvious intelligence and more than a bit of luck, had allowed him to escape detection for many years. Graysmith's book was one of the few that I kept at my bedside and reread from time to time, when I was looking for a frightening story.

In that summer of 1998, Graysmith's account once again beckoned me, so I picked it up and relived the captivating story of the case. But by 1998 things were different because I was different. By that time, I had also read a book by the behavioral profiler John Douglas, who was made

---

49   Robert Graysmith, *Zodiac* (paperback edition) (New York: Berkley Books, 1987).

famous by the movie *The Silence of the Lambs*. In that book, *Journey into Darkness*, I learned about the *homicidal triad*, a series of behaviors that, according to Douglas, would allow one to predict if a youth may someday become a serial killer—bedwetting, cruelty to animals, and fire starting.[50]

I immediately wondered if Douglas's ideas—or behavioral profiling in general—had ever been applied retrospectively to the Zodiac case. My sense at the time was that it must have been: the case was too important and there was too much at stake for someone not to have done so. My mind went back to what I believed at the time (as most people did) to have been Zodiac's first crime—the 1966 murder of Cheri Jo Bates, which had always intrigued me. And it was then that I had my first original idea about the Zodiac case: Might someone be able to look in 1960s' Riverside newspaper "police blotter" columns to find the name of a youth from the late 1950s or early 1960s who was well known as a fire starter or who was unusually cruel to animals? This idea ultimately didn't pan out. I learned quickly through an email exchange with a San Diego college juvenile law professor that the names of juvenile offenders have been protected from publication by newspapers since the early 1900s. Regardless, this idea represented my first probing foray into the world of the Zodiac and a first attempt to devise a strategy for identifying a new suspect.

The other, even more important lesson I learned from this exercise was the power of the internet. Before the advent of this miraculous tool, I would have had to go to a library and find the name of this juvenile law expert and then send him a letter. Then I might have had to wait weeks for a reply, if I even got one. And if I didn't, I'd have to start the whole process all over again. More waiting. Nothing would have stifled my interest in the case more quickly. However, the internet gave me instant access to the names and email addresses of experts such as this (and many, many others), copious information, and lightning-fast

---

50   John Douglas and Mark Olshaker, *Journey into Darkness* (New York: Scribner, 1997), p. 36

correspondence. These facets were invaluable in doing my research on the case.

An original observation I made around that time was in the manner in which Zodiac encoded the letter *E* in his solved Three-Part Cipher. That letter was encoded by *seven* different characters: *Z, P, W* + *O, N, E*. I decided to add the numerical value of these letters; to wit, *Z* = 26, *P* = 16, and *W* = 23. That totals 65. I then added 1 (i.e., "+ (plus) *O-N-E*"). This gave 66. I wondered if this was not a veiled reference to the murder of Cheri Jo Bates in 1966. It is obviously impossible to draw any firm conclusions as to whether this is what Zodiac intended or not. However, the killer would later at least imply that he had murdered Ms. Bates when he mentioned his "Riverside activity" in his March 1971 *L.A. Times* letter. And once again the fact that *ZPW* + *ONE* totaled 66 was a potential clue that nobody had noticed before. Such being the case, it bolstered my confidence that, even though this evidence was old and had been picked over for a generation by thousands of people, including members of Mensa, the high-IQ society, there were still new discoveries to be made.

Beginning in August 1998, I was frequenting all the Zodiac websites I could find. One of the earliest I could find had been put up by a California student named Jackson Garland. I also began reading the discussion threads on the case that were available on the Net. They were mesmerizing to me, and I eagerly devoured each new topic that popped up. I eventually began to correspond with a behavioral profiler and author, Dr. Mike Kelleher, who took an interest in me and my work. We talked mainly about the Bates murder, given the interest I had in what I believed to be Zodiac's first crime. Around that time the notion of developing my own suspect in the Zodiac case first crept into my thinking. But from a distance of three thousand miles from where the crimes had taken place and nearly thirty years removed from them, I considered my situation as being all but hopeless. The very notion of developing a new suspect seemed a mere fantasy. In addition, as stated above, the case had been scrutinized worldwide for a generation by untold numbers of police detectives, retired detectives, and amateurs from across the country and now, with the advent of the Net, around the world. What chance did I stand against them? How was I going to even begin to figure out a way to solve a complex case like this?

Little did I know it at the time that the answer would be *lateral thinking*.

In early 1999, a Zodiac researcher named "Jonathan Zychowski Jr." (real name Denis Pettee)[51] introduced me to a fellow researcher from Northern California who lived near the Zodiac murder sites. This researcher posted on the Zodiac message boards and was a wealth of information. He and I immediately clicked. We exchanged many fascinating emails touching on all different aspects of the case, including a discussion of the lead suspect at the time, Arthur Leigh Allen. The researcher's name was Ed Neil.

Throughout late 1998 and early 1999, Dr. Mike Kelleher and I also continued to exchange emails. We talked and talked, mostly about the Bates murder and how it related to the Zodiac case. Then one day in late June 1999, I asked Mike one more question, and he wrote back with a fateful answer. In reply to my question, he reminded me that Zodiac didn't write his first Northern California letters until *after his second attack*. This caused me to stop and consider his response for a moment. My exposure to Edward de Bono's little book in 1979 was about to lead me to explore a "hole" that nobody had ever thought to look in before.

The very first letters Zodiac wrote are believed (based on hand printing) to have been the "Bates Had to Die" letters in Riverside. These letters were postmarked April 30, 1967, exactly *six months* to the day after the murder of Cheri Jo Bates. This realization gave birth to what I felt at the time was a silly and naïve idea that wouldn't amount to anything, but which I felt I had to explore. I asked myself: If the man who would later become Zodiac followed this pattern in 1966–67,

---

51 "Jonathan" authored the first internet site on the Zodiac case. It was about a suspect named Peter O.

might he also have written his first letter as Zodiac exactly *six months after his own first Northern California murders*—those of Jensen and Faraday on December 20, 1968? This would place the first Northern California letter as having been postmarked June 20, 1969.

I immediately realized there was a serious problem with this idea: "the Zodiac" did not yet exist as a named entity in the eyes of the public on that date. He didn't write his first letters to the press until July 31 of that year. That was over a month after June 20. He also didn't name himself "the Zodiac" until his August 1969 letter. I therefore considered a new possibility: that Zodiac may have written his first letter to the Bay Area newspapers in order to commemorate the six-month mark of his first murders *under his own name* or a pseudonym.

I decided that if he had written under his own name, I was going to take a stab at locating that letter and in turn identify the Zodiac.

Not knowing how to access microfilm of the *San Francisco Chronicle* in my area, I enlisted someone to assist me with my research in San Francisco, someone who shared my passion for the case. Someone like Ed. I explained my idea and he agreed to look at the newspapers on microfilm. I told him to use his best judgment as to what the letter from Zodiac might sound like, since I could offer no specifics about its potential content. I just advised him to try to locate one that was "different" and which contained themes that might have relevance to the case.

A few days later, on June 24, 1999, a date that is forever seared into my memory, I received a single letter in my email; it was the only one Ed thought was strange enough to send to me. He told me he only sent it because it mentioned Adolph Hitler. I opened it, and in doing so was about to raise the lid on a secret world that had lain hidden just below the surface of the Zodiac case for a generation. I can still recall the feeling of exhilaration that overtook me as I read this letter, which was about much more than just Hitler. As I have gained new insight into the case, my interpretation of this letter has evolved over the past twenty years. My understanding of the behavior of the Zodiac has also evolved through my interactions with forensic psychologist Richard Walter. However, even in 1999, I was able to quickly see elements in the letter that jumped off the page at me as being relevant to the Zodiac case.

The letter Ed sent me from June 26, 1969, (Exhibit 12)[52] opened by stating that the author had an issue with the direction in which society was heading and that a "bloody confrontation" was imminent. His was clearly a sociological problem. He railed against the *San Francisco Chronicle* for supporting the "militants and lawbreakers" of the time, which of course were the hippies and the student protesters from such places as Haight-Ashbury and Berkeley. His issue was therefore with the same age group you'd expect to find making out on the remote lovers' lanes where Zodiac was already stalking his young victims. The writer spoke of young people lying "dead or wounded in the streets." This had quite literally already come to pass at Zodiac's first crime scene, the crime that took place six months before this letter appeared, when Betty Lou Jensen was found dead on the ground near Lake Herman Road and David Faraday was barely alive. It intrigued me that both Zodiac and the letter writer seemed to have issues with the *same* demographic—young people in the Bay Area: the man's sociological problem clearly involved the same group that Zodiac had generally targeted in his attacks.

The author then displaced blame for any violence that might occur in the future and laid that responsibility at the feet of the *San Francisco Chronicle* and its columnists. Zodiac would later single out one columnist, Paul Avery, as a target for some of his letters, including the 1970 Halloween card and the 1971 Peek through the Pines Card.

He proceeded to speak of a concept that was surely not lost on the killer: the writer accused the editor of being willing to publish anything that would help to sell more newspapers. The Zodiac sent his taunting letters to the papers with the knowledge that the editor would publish

---

52   Kjell Qvale, "Who's to Blame," Letters to the Editor, *San Francisco Chronicle*, June 26, 1969, p. 42.

them as a news story and as a way to warn the public of this new danger. He also knew they would publish it because, in carrying out that "public service," they would sell newspapers like hotcakes. He then warned that if the *Chronicle* didn't change its course, it would be "rather expensive" for all the people of Northern California. This proved to be true, as Northern Californians suffered greatly when Zodiac was committing seemingly random murders and later revealed his plan to shoot or blow up school children. The use of *rather* mimicked Zodiac's manner of minimizing things in a distinctly British way.

The author ended the letter with a warning that the prevailing social climate in the Bay Area was possibly paving the way for the coming of a new Hitler. There is tremendous irony in this statement (something Zodiac clearly loved based on the droll greeting cards he sent to the press) given the person who was making it. However, at the time, I didn't appreciate the full scope of that irony. I will have more to say on the subject of Hitler and irony later.

The most important aspect of this letter, though, and the one that was most telling in making the connection between the letter writer and the Zodiac, is one that would continue to elude me for years. It wasn't until I had gained a better understanding of the case through the education I received from Richard Walter in behavioral profiling that I would come to appreciate the true reason the author wrote this letter. He actually clearly states this reason in plain English in the last paragraph, and also reveals the underlying issue he had with the editor of the *San Francisco Chronicle*. Nevertheless, this odd letter had suddenly set me on the path that was about to lead to a myriad of intriguing and completely unexpected discoveries about its author.

When I reached the end of this letter, my mouth surely must have dropped to the floor. I had gone back through the mists of thirty years and used Ed as my proxy to select the letter. He therefore had possessed none of the biases that someone might attribute to me based on the name of the person who had penned the letter that Ed ultimately selected. Ed had looked at this odd name and assumed it was a pseudonym. When I saw it, however, I knew that such was decidedly not the case. When I saw the strange name of the author of the letter, Kjell Qvale of San Francisco, I immediately recognized it as being one that I had seen somewhere before. But where? After a few minutes of reflection, I figured out that I had seen it several times in the *Daily Racing Form*. Being a horse racing fan, like any other horseplayer, I had a stack of old *Forms* in my basement. And I knew that this man with the unusual name was somewhere in that stack. After all, once you see that name, as Qvale himself would assert years later, you never forget it.

My journey into the vortex of the Zodiac case began when I then put the name Kjell Qvale into an internet search engine within minutes of reading Qvale's 1969 letter to the editor of the *Chronicle*. The most exciting and exasperating twenty years of my life were about to begin. I didn't appreciate it at the time, but when the first web hit came onto my computer screen, I was on my way to developing the most fascinating, controversial, and seemingly unlikely suspect in the hunt for a serial killer that had already spanned a generation. Once I entered the event horizon of the case, everything around me ground to a halt and my life became frozen in time, like an insect trapped in amber. I simply could not move forward until I knew if my simple idea had at long last identified the Zodiac.

In that first search, I learned many intriguing things about Mr. Qvale. He was an extremely wealthy, high-powered British-import car dealer and entrepreneur. For years, researchers had identified Zodiac as someone having ties to the UK due to some of his usage. He was of Norwegian descent, which immediately got my attention because of the 1974 Sla Letter from the Zodiac, which had mentioned the Old Norse language. (As my involvement in the case grew, I'd learn that there were, as I have pointed out previously, many other potential Norse references in the case.) Qvale had once owned the world-famous racehorse Silky Sullivan, whose name I had invoked many times at the track when talking about a horse that comes from dead last in the field to win a race. And I learned something else that immediately riveted my attention: I came

upon a website called A Universe of Spies. [53] My immediate thought
was that Qvale had been involved in espionage or intrigue of some sort.
But as I started to read, I realized that the site was about something
completely different—flying saucers! How did a man like this become
associated with something as bizarre as flying saucers? As it turned out,
he had inserted himself into the discussion of UFOs over twenty years
before the first Zodiac murders took place. He did it in such a way as
to show that he apparently craved front-page publicity in the Bay Area
newspapers much as Zodiac would years later. *This represented the first
key behavioral link I would make between Qvale and Zodiac.*

In June 1947, a pilot in Washington State coined the term *flying
saucers.* He used it to describe some disc-shaped crafts he saw flying at
what he determined to be otherworldly speeds. This set off a firestorm
of sightings from across the country over the next several weeks.
Newspapers were filled with descriptions of these crafts—they were disc
shaped, they were flat, they were round like balls, they were hundreds
of feet wide, or they were the size of a teacup. People thought they
were experimental aircrafts our government was testing. Some thought
they were crafts developed by the Nazis, the Japanese, or the Russians.
Scientists discounted them as mass hysteria or "floaters" in the beholder's
eyeball. The odd thing is that nobody was saying they were actually what
most people today believe them to be: *crafts from outer space.* That is, not
until Kjell Qvale came along and changed the discussion.

On July 5, 1947, the same date on which Zodiac would attack
two of his victims in 1969, Qvale stated that he saw a group of flying
discs over Auburn, California. He used his experience as a naval pilot in
World War II to say that what he saw were "space ships," and he even
went so far as to say that he wished they would land and tell us where
they came from.[54] His sighting was carried on the front page of the

53   Martin Kottmeyer, "A Universe of Spies," http://aliens.greyfalcon.us/A%20
UNIVERSE%20OF%20SPIES.htm.

54   The timing of his report is very interesting. Sightings of these saucers had
been building since June 24 and reached its crescendo on July 4. This means that

Alameda Times-Star[55] on July 7 and was picked up on July 8 on the front page of the *San Francisco Examiner*[56] and the interior pages of the *San Francisco Call-Bulletin.*[57] In a book published twenty years after this first UFO flap across the US, Qvale is cited as the *only* credible person in 853 reported cases summarized from coast to coast to state that flying saucers were indeed from outer space.[58] While believing that flying saucers are from outer space is no big deal today, the situation was apparently *very* different in 1947.

I had been exposed to flying saucers and the people who report them in a 1970s' undergraduate sociology course. And the one thing I knew was that most people who reported flying saucers in a manner that was elevated above what the average person was saying were seeking one thing, the same thing that Zodiac demanded: *widespread front-page public attention.* Here was an early behavioral Rosetta stone of sorts that translated the attention-seeking of Kjell Qvale in 1947 to that of the Zodiac of 1969. The roots of Zodiac's need to see his name on the front pages of the Bay Area newspapers has rarely, if ever, been more convincingly demonstrated than by Qvale in 1947.[59]

When I got home that evening, I went to my basement and searched through my pile of old *Daily Racing Forms.* Sure enough, I located Qvale's name as an owner of a horse. Its name was Skystalker.

---

the newspapers of July 5 were filled with stories about flying saucers. Although a few days later naysayers and skeptics would begin to give believers a run for their money, on July 5 people were still captivated by this phenomenon and eagerly consumed each new sighting. Dr. James E. McDonald, *Report on the UFO Wave of 1947* (Washington, D.C.: Privately Published, 1967), pp. I-7 to I-8.

55   "Nation Intrigued by 'Saucer' Mystery," *Alameda Times-Star*, 7 July 1947, p. 1.

56   Dick Pearce, "Skeptical Experts Call Disc Reports Mass Illusion," *San Francisco Examiner*, 8 July 1947, pp. 1–2.

57   "Discs Abound in S.F. Skies," *San Francisco Call-Bulletin*, July 8, 1947 p. 4.

58   Dr. James E. McDonald, p. II-5.

59   In 2006 Qvale would try to downplay both the significance and timing of his sighting. I discuss this in chapter 22.

Due to a reference to the sky and the intimation of stalking, I found the name very intriguing with respect to the Zodiac case.

I immediately told Ed about my discoveries and can still recall the excitement that coursed through me that day. It would remain with me as I made more discoveries in the months to come. It was admittedly extremely early in our research on Qvale, but we had already located a Norwegian letter writer to the *San Francisco Chronicle* with British ties who had sought widespread attention on the front pages of the Bay Area newspapers long before Zodiac existed.

I emailed Ed on July 2, 1999, and said, "Wouldn't it be something if Qvale lived in the Heights in 1969?" referring to Presidio Heights. When I said this, it was more of a facetious musing than anything else. I fully expected that I would be quickly dispossessed of this unlikely notion once we did the requisite research. However, a few days later Ed wrote to me and excitedly told me that a friend of his had gone to the *Polk's Guide*, a local San Francisco phone directory from 1969. He learned that at the time of the Zodiac crimes Qvale did in fact live in Presidio Heights, at 3636 Jackson Street—just a couple of blocks from where cabbie Paul Stine had been murdered! His home was just down the street and around the corner from the original destination Stine had written on his trip sheet—Washington Street and Maple Street. It also overlooked the police search area near the Julius Kahn Playground. Now things were starting to get very eerie. Of all the places in San Francisco he could have resided, Qvale lived within two blocks of the Stine murder scene. What were we truly onto here? As we learned in chapter 9, the killer had last been spotted by SFPD officer Fouke walking in the general direction of Qvale's home, on the same side of Jackson Street as that home and a little over a block away from it. While I obviously can't say that Qvale's home was Zodiac's destination after he murdered Stine, what I do know is that the killer *had at least not walked past Qvale's home* when he was spotted that night, a fact which would have quickly ended our inquiries.

Now things were heating up, and I was extremely eager to know what Kjell Qvale looked like in the 1960s. I found a website advertising a magazine for sale called *Turf and Sport Digest*. It was a publication about thoroughbred racing from August 1970 and advertised a photo of Qvale and Silky Sullivan. Did he resemble the 1969 SFPD wanted poster of Zodiac? Was he short, overweight, and bald? I quickly wrote out a check and sent away for the magazine and waited. About ten days later, a package in brown paper arrived at my door. I knew immediately what it was. I raced to get the wanted poster sketches of the killer. I tore open the package, thumbed through the magazine, and located the photo, which was there as advertised.

There it was as plain as day: there was no denying that Qvale closely resembled the SFPD "Amended" wanted poster sketch! (See Exhibit 13.)[60]

Anyone who would question my objectivity with respect to Mr. Qvale (since I knew who he was prior to seeing the June 26, 1969, letter that Ed sent me in 1999) and say that I simply decided to somehow "make" him into Zodiac should consider this: had it turned out that Kjell Qvale lived on Nob Hill and bore absolutely no resemblance to the 1969 SFPD wanted poster, it is highly likely that I would have immediately dropped him as a potential suspect. My research was evidence driven, and that research suggested a link between the facts I was learning about Qvale and those surrounding the Zodiac. These facts, not anything personal or the notion that I had recognized his name on the June 26, 1969, letter, kept pushing me further down the road of researching his past.

It was like someone somewhere had suddenly pushed the ON button and my brain began to boot up and race like never before. Almost instantly, I was consumed with a passion for doing research on both Qvale and the case. This level of commitment to any one research topic was a completely new and unique experience. I went from going

60   Jim Scott, "The Man Who Owns Silky Sullivan," *Turf and Sport Digest*, (Baltimore: Montee Publishing, August 1970), pp. 30–34.

through the motions of every day at my job to literally not being able to wait to get out of bed in the morning to see what new discoveries awaited me.

The final two pieces of the puzzle for my early research had to do with dates. On December 3, 1999, I decided to do a search in the SSDI—the Social Security Death Index. This is where the names of all deceased people who had possessed Social Security numbers are located. In 1999, before identity theft became such a hot-button issue, there was tremendous access to information on this type of website. Dr. Mike Kelleher had mentioned to me that when someone found the right suspect they might find a relationship between important dates in that suspect's life and the case. Specifically, I wanted to try to find birth and death dates related to Qvale's parents to see if they had any relevance to the case. I started at "QVALE, A" and intended to keep going through the alphabet to "QVALE, Z" to find someone whose birth date seemed right knowing that their son, Kjell, had been born in 1919, as per other research I had done on the internet.

It took me only two letters of the alphabet to locate Bjarne Qvale. He had been born in Trondheim, Norway (the lone "sister city" to Vallejo when Zodiac struck at Lake Herman in 1968), on September 27, 1887. I was floored. September 27 was the same date on which Zodiac had attacked Hartnell and Shepard at Lake Berryessa in 1969! I instantly sensed that this had to be Kjell's father. But my foray into that index failed to yield information about anyone who could have been Kjell's mother. Where were her records? Were they in the SSDI at all?

Research I did via fax with the Statsarkivet i Trondheim, an agency that had publicly available genealogy data on people who had lived in that area of Norway, showed that the Qvale clan had left there sometime before 1932.[61] From inquiries I had made with the *statsarkivet*, I knew that Qvale's mother's name was Signe and that she had been born in March, 1893. I also had learned from reading articles on Qvale's college

---

61   Tor-Ingar Nordsetronnningen, "Statsarkivet i Norway," letter dated 4 January 2000.

career that they lived in Seattle. So I tried contacting the Washington State Library in early January 2000 and asked them about any obituary information they may have had.

On January 21, 2000, I received a stunning email message. The librarian quite simply said, "I found your gal." An obituary showed that Signe Qvale had died on December 20, 1939. She apparently had never received a Social Security number. That was why she wasn't in the SSDI. *December 20 was the same date as Zodiac's first murders in 1968, the ones on Lake Herman Road.* The sheer unlikeliness of birth and death dates related to *both* of Qvale's parents also being Zodiac murder dates intrigued me like no other facts I had learned about him up to this point.

As soon as I learned that Signe Qvale's date of death matched yet another Zodiac date, I felt deep down inside myself that I had solved the case. I also knew then and there that the Zodiac story was going to set the course of my life for the foreseeable future. I just did not realize how long into the future that would turn out to be. How did I know I was right even with such little evidence? Because I had spent forty-three years of my life knowing what *wrong* felt like and this felt completely different from anything I had experienced before.

A few days later, something hit me like a ton of bricks about Bjarne Qvale's birth date. I knew it was September 27, but I felt that I could pretty much solve the case flat out if I could determine that he was born on that date at exactly **6:30 PM**, the time that the Zodiac had written on the door of Hartnell's Karmann-Ghia. Was this common knowledge within the family? Was it researchable? I went to the Family History Center run by the Mormon Church in New York City. As I indicated before, in the late 1990s it was easy to request and obtain genealogical information on people, since identity theft had not yet become a major societal issue. I could barely contain my excitement as I requested the microfilm that contained the birth records data for the Nidaros Domkirke in Trondheim for 1887. What might I find? Was the solution to the case now within my grasp?

On the film I found a page that was out of a birth register from that era. The page was divided into ledger columns containing information about each baby that had been born, including birth date, parents' names, and baptism date. Entered in 1800s' script near the top I found the name Bjarne Qvale. His birth date was confirmed as September 27, 1887. I eagerly scanned through the columns labeled in Norwegian searching for the one that had the time of birth. However, there was none. I laughed quietly to myself because I knew deep down that it could not possibly be as easy as this to bring this difficult and complex case to a solution. But at least I had given it a try.

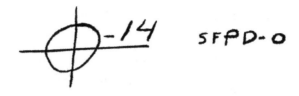

MY SUSPECT'S BACKGROUND

KJELL QVALE WAS BORN JULY 17, 1919, in Trondheim, Norway. His father was a sea captain whose career eventually required him to leave his family and move to Buenos Aires, Argentina, and then to the west coast of the United States. The family of seven was reunited after mother Signe and her children came to North America through Nova Scotia in the year of the stock market crash of 1929. They eventually settled in Washington State.

The family was athletic and Kjell skied for West Seattle High School, where he won a few championships. While playing sandlot baseball, he also found that he could run faster than other boys in his age group. A lot faster. He eventually became a track athlete competing in the 100-yard dash. In 1938, he competed for Norway in the Europe Games, which were held in his hometown of Trondheim that year, and made the finals of the 100-yard dash. He went on to become a star athlete for the University of Washington. He won the Pacific Coast Championship among college sprinters in 1941 in Los Angeles. He was slated to be the captain of the track team the next season before being drafted into the navy prior to the beginning of that season. Qvale was no vanilla-bland runner. In 1941, he unofficially tied, or maybe even unofficially broke, a record in the 100-yard dash that was held by no less than Jesse Owens, the star of the 1936 Berlin Olympics.[62]

Qvale was described several times as being very aloof and had been so all his life. This trait began to manifest itself in the sports he chose—skiing, golf, and as a sprinter in track, all of which are individual endeavors. Even though one technically belongs to a track *team*, the event Qvale specialized in was an individual event, not a relay.

Before the next track season came around, Qvale was drafted and went to Corpus Christi, Texas, to attend a naval training facility to eventually become a transport pilot in World War II. When he got out of the service, he opened a Willys dealership in Alameda, California. He met with limited success. One day in 1946, he was in New Orleans to look at some motorcycles when he first laid eyes on an MG-TC sports car from England. This chance encounter would determine the course of his career and his life for the next sixty-plus years. He later opened his dealership on Auto Row on Van Ness Avenue and became the biggest imported-sports-car dealer on the West Coast. Eventually, in the early 1950s, he added Volkswagens to his line of British marques and sold untold thousands of Beetles and other VW models, like the Karmann-Ghia.

An entrepreneur, he diversified into such things as making jeans, banking, and women's tennis. He even produced a movie in the 1970s. In the 1950s he started the San Francisco Auto Show for imported cars, which were shunned at other auto shows. He also founded the Pebble Beach Concours d'Elegance luxury car show. In the early 1960s, he got seriously interested in thoroughbred horse racing and eventually purchased Green Oaks Farm in Oakville, California. He became the president of Golden Gate Fields in Albany, California, and purchased

---

62 Anonymous, "Qvale Nears World Record: Once Ran for Norway," *Seattle Times*, May 2, 1940.

the world-famous horse Silky Sullivan after his racing days were over. He also purchased a horse named The Scoundrel for the unheard-of sum of $500,000 in 1964 and owned other successful horses, such as Silveyville and Variety Road.

In the late 1950s, Qvale began racing cars, and in the 1960s he built a competition department at his dealership, which produced three liquid-suspension cars for the 1964 Indy 500. It also designed and produced the "Genie" car that was scheduled to run in the 1966 *Los Angeles Times* Grand Prix in Riverside on October 30, 1966, the same date of the murder of Cheri Jo Bates.

Qvale purchased Jensen Motors in England in 1970 as a way of building a supply of British sports cars to sell in the US. He ran it until labor and regulatory red tape forced it into bankruptcy in the mid-1970s. He later purchased a plant in Modena, Italy, where he designed and built the Qvale Mangusta for a company he named Qvale Modena, which also quickly failed.

Qvale became extremely wealthy and powerful as a result of his many endeavors. He belonged to such exclusive organizations as the San Francisco Country Club, the Pacific Union Club, Cypress Point Golf Club, and the Olympic Club. His was an amazing rags-to-riches story, since he had come to this country in the year of the great stock market crash and risen through his business acumen and wits to be the biggest imported-car dealer on the West Coast. Bentley, Jaguar, Rolls Royce, MG, Austin-Healey, Jensen-Healey, and Land Rover were among the marques he sold. He purchased a home at 3636 Jackson Street in Presidio Heights in 1965.

But Qvale's most interesting association was his membership in the ultraexclusive Bohemian Club.[63] This is a secret society that meets once per year at what is known as Bohemian Grove on the Russian River, some seventy or so miles north of San Francisco. It is comprised of only the most powerful and influential businessmen and politicians in the country, and many presidents, including Richard Nixon, have attended

---

63   Nelson, p. 180.

meetings there over the years. Originally formed by newspaper men in the late 1870s, this is where someone like Qvale would rub elbows with and get to know such people as the hierarchy of the *San Francisco Chronicle*. Unless you are extremely wealthy and powerful, you are not invited to join this influential group.

In early 2012, Qvale was featured in a television commercial for Bank of the West. In the commercial,[64] it indicated that at the age of ninety-two, he still went to the office every day. He estimated he had sold "two to three million cars" in his lifetime. But as we'll see later, the same traits that made him a successful businessman also put him on the radar as a candidate to have been the Zodiac.

In the 1990s, Qvale, who was described as a risk-taker, took a stake in and ultimately took over the First National Bank of Marin in San Rafael, California. He then moved the operation to Las Vegas and made a small fortune in the subprime credit card market, despite several regulatory run-ins based on business practices I'll examine in a later chapter. He sold the bank to other investors in 2005.

He stayed active until his death in November 2013, remaining busy in the car industry, horse racing, travel, and even a new comedy club that he opened briefly in 2010. He was called at various times "a business icon" and a "legendary powerhouse in the international motor industry" who was "instrumental in popularizing English sports cars." According to probate court records, he left behind a fortune of approximately $100 million. Needless to say, the above description is not the usual résumé or life history of a serial killer. Ted Bundy comes to mind as someone vaguely similar to Qvale in that regard. He was accepted to two law schools and outwardly at least led a respectable life. However, of the two, Qvale is by far more unlikely given the scope and degree of success he enjoyed over the course of his lifetime.

---

64 https://www.bankofthewest.com/static_files/botw2/home/campaigns/go-west/kjell-qvale.html

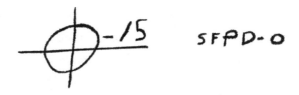

Bus Bomb I

IN THE SUMMER OF 1999, I learned that Kjell Qvale lived at 3636 Jackson Street in Presidio Heights at the time of the Zodiac murders. As a result, I became very interested in what his view would have been of the area of West Pacific Avenue in the vicinity of the Julius Kahn Playground. That was where the police search for the Zodiac took place on the night of the murder of Yellow Cab driver Paul Stine. I surmised that the view must have been ideal, given that both areas were directly behind—that is, north of—Qvale's back yard (Exhibit 14). In fact, if Zodiac lived at 3636 Jackson Street and had wanted to watch a police search after the murder of Paul Stine, he couldn't have chosen a better area for this search than the Kahn Playground and its environs. This area lay directly north of Zodiac's original destination for the cab of Washington Street and Maple Street. My main goal for examining the area had nothing to do with Qvale himself. Rather, I wanted to gauge the amount of foliage present on the ground to determine how Zodiac could have possibly eluded the massive police and dog search in the area of the playground that followed the cabbie's murder, as he stated he did. While doing so, I kept in mind that it may have been much different in 1999 from what it was in 1969. I learned from Ed Neil about a website called Terraserver.com that featured satellite photographs of the United States, so I turned to that resource for assistance. By today's standards, these images were quite primitive. As I recall, the satellite shots were called SPIN-1 and SPIN-2. There were different degrees of magnification for these photographs, and I remember not being able to see the highest magnification view of the neighborhood for technical reasons of some kind. So my research was limited to literally squinting at a very low-resolution overview of the area from what felt like the moon with houses looking like small dots.

As I examined these photos day after day, I appreciated more and more just how good a view one would have had of the police search area from Qvale's home. I quickly learned that the view of the Kahn Playground was completely unobstructed. Using Yahoo Maps, which was also very rudimentary in the days before such things as Google Earth, I was able to narrow down the location of Qvale's residence at 3636 Jackson Street to one of three that loomed like sentinels over the playground/tennis court area from the north side of Jackson Street. On my subsequent trips to the Bay Area, I noted the following observation: as you moved from the playground up West Pacific Avenue toward Cherry Street, Qvale's view of the park from 3636 Jackson Street would have become very limited since the ground slopes sharply uphill as you move west of Maple Street. I concluded that Qvale would have had a very poor view of the park at West Pacific Avenue and Cherry Street. This was not something that could be appreciated on a flat, two-dimensional satellite photograph.

One day in August 1999, I made a discovery that was to play on my mind for many months to come. It wasn't something I was consciously looking for when I started out examining the satellite photos, nor was it anything about which I had theorized prior to looking at these photographs. It was simply an *observation*. This observation came from nothing more than repeatedly staring at these satellite images of Presidio Heights. What I noticed was completely serendipitous and of extraordinary interest to me. Nobody to my knowledge had ever made this precise connection before. It ultimately led me to a conclusion that, if it could somehow be verified, would ultimately bring the Zodiac crimes right to Qvale's doorstep.

As I familiarized myself with the layout of the streets in Presidio Heights, I came to realize that the most salient feature of the neighborhood, the one that distinguished Presidio Heights from any other in the city of San Francisco, was a group of luxury homes at its westernmost end. The mansions that comprised this extremely wealthy enclave were arranged in a unique manner, specifically an oval formation with a street coursing through the center of the oval and homes placed both on the inner and outer perimeters of that street like spokes coming off a bicycle wheel. It is called Presidio Terrace.

I also noticed that there appeared to be five large east–west streets through Presidio Heights. These five streets filtered down toward Presidio Terrace from east to west. I searched the Net for "Presidio Heights," and, sure enough, a map of the neighborhood showed that it was defined by precisely five streets—California, Sacramento, Clay, Washington, and Jackson—from south to north, with Presidio Terrace lying at their western end. West Pacific Avenue runs north of Jackson Street but is on the north side of the wall separating the residential neighborhood from the park area. On the map, Presidio Terrace was located at the end of Washington Street, which essentially ran directly into its heart (see pattern of five east–west streets running toward Presidio Terrace in Exhibit 4).

When I saw the pattern of the *five* streets and the oval structure at the west end, I immediately recognized something startling: *There was a definite analogy between the five main east–west streets of Presidio Heights plus Presidio Terrace and the basic structure of Zodiac's first bus-bomb diagram* (Exhibit 15a) *with its five bags of fertilizer and circular timer.* I immediately developed a working hypothesis: **I theorized that Zodiac's bus bomb was not a bomb at all but a map of the Presidio Heights neighborhood, where the killer had murdered Paul Stine. This made sense because the November 9 letter was written about the Stine murder, so including a possible map of that neighborhood disguised as a bomb diagram fit contextually with the subject matter of the letter.**

But what did the map mean? What was its purpose? Was there more to this analogy than just what appeared on the surface? What was the killer trying to say? Did this map hold a clue of some kind? I pondered this for a few days.

I decided to take the bomb diagram and extend the "streets" out from each of the "bags of fertilizer." I copied the bomb diagram and whited out all the confusing circuitry wires. I then held it so that, as on an actual map of the city, Presidio Terrace was to my left, that is, west, and the bags of fertilizer were to my right, that is, east. I drew in five lines, one from each "bag of fertilizer," that ran toward the "Timer" and labeled them starting from south to north beginning at the bottom: California, Sacramento, Clay, Washington, and Jackson. I now noticed that, unlike the actual map of the neighborhood, it was not the "street" corresponding to Washington but the one corresponding to Clay that ran into the center of the "Timer" that represented Presidio Terrace. I also noted that, in proportion to the rest of the streets, Presidio Terrace was much larger in the bomb diagram than in real life (compare Exhibit 15b to Exhibit 4). Furthermore, it was round, not oval, as it appears on a map. However, this didn't deter me from making the analogy: the bus bomb was not a literal but possibly a *diagrammatic* representation of a map of Presidio Heights that may have been made from memory and didn't show the neighborhood literally or to scale.

After I drew in the "streets," something completely unexpected jumped off the page at me: The "circuit box" that lay just "north" of the five streets devoid of wiring now seemed to resemble a "house" that lay to the "north" of Jackson Street, the last "street" in the series to the north. I also noticed something else: in two places, Zodiac indicated that he was using six-volt batteries to power the device. In his written recipe for the bomb contained on page 6 of the November 9, 1969, letter, the killer stated that these were *car* batteries. I recalled, probably from getting my own cars repaired over the years, that US cars did not use six-volt batteries. As stated earlier, six-volt batteries were not characteristic of American cars but of imported cars—**like the British cars Qvale had been importing to the US since 1947.** I used the internet to verify these facts.

The next observation I made about the diagram is that the circle that comprises the "Timer" opens and closes at the one o'clock position, just like the crossed circles that Zodiac used to sign his letters. This match occurs *only* when the diagram is held so that the "Timer" is closest to the reader and the "bags of fertilizer" are away from the reader. This is the equivalent on a real map of having "west" near you and looking "east" from Presidio Terrace toward the "bags of fertilizer." This seemed significant to me. When you look at the diagram in this manner, the words "Mirror," "bus," and "Bombs (1 bag each)" are all oriented so as to be read by a person looking at the diagram from this perspective. This served as proof that the diagram should be viewed in this manner.

Since the diagram/map is an aerial view, the only practical way Zodiac would have gotten to see his neighborhood in this manner was to fly over it, and the best way to orient yourself in Presidio Heights and locate 3636 Jackson Street would be to fly in from the west. In this way, you could easily recognize the unusual landmark of Presidio Terrace. Then, by using both that and the aforementioned Le Petit Trianon at Washington and Maple Streets, with its distinctive white roof, you could zero in on the area you are searching for on Jackson Street, a block to the north.

Kjell Qvale was a pilot in World War II and owned a plane in the 1960s. He either flew it or at least had access to it and therefore had ample opportunity to overfly his Presidio Heights home at 3636 Jackson

Street on a recreational flight. This appears to be the perspective from which Zodiac made the diagram of this neighborhood.

From staring at the satellite photographs of the neighborhood for so long, I knew almost without looking that the north–south streets in Presidio Heights (such as Cherry, Maple, and Spruce) ran from slightly east of south to slightly west of north. Since the motorcycles traveling from "south to north west" in the November 9, 1969, letter were presumably on the street, not riding through the brush of the park area in the middle of the night, the killer was apparently aware of the orientation of the cross streets in Presidio Heights as well and that the motorcycles he had heard were traveling on one of these north–south streets.

The paramount question now became this: Was there a greater purpose to the diagram? Did the bus-bomb map single out any house in particular? For this answer, I began to study the diagram once again, focusing on the "street" with the ill-fated "bus" traveling down it. I swung the diagram around so the "street" with the "bus" that was supposedly about to be blown up was at the bottom, that is, south, with the "circuitry box" above it at the top, that is, north. I had concluded from my initial analysis of the diagram that the "circuitry box" was a depiction of a home that sat *north* of Jackson Street, the northernmost of the main thoroughfares in Presidio Heights along which a school bus might run. All of these streets—California, Sacramento, Washington—run east–west. By looking at this portion of the diagram in this manner, I had placed the "house" north of the "street." *But which house was it?*

As I stared at the bomb diagram, I noticed that, in this view of the "house," it seemed to be separated from the street with the "bus" heading along it by *two parallel structures* (Exhibit 16). I didn't know what to make of this, so I went to the low-resolution satellite photographs. Though many homes in Presidio Heights are separated from the street in the fashion suggested in the diagram, I could make out one home in particular on the north side of Jackson Street between Maple Street and Spruce Street that stood out not only because it had the two parallel structures separating it from the street, *but also because the home itself seemed to be set back off Jackson Street so far that the front of this home was even with the back of the home directly to its west. It also happened to be one of the three houses that I had singled out as possibly being Qvale's home.* This appeared to be what the killer was getting at in the bomb diagram.

With its confusing changes of orientation and because it seemed to be comprised of two interlocking diagrams at right angles to one another, I came to view the bus bomb like a painting by M. C. Escher. The diagrams were linked by one common element as its pivot point: the "circuitry box"/"house" that was shared by *both* of the smaller diagrams comprising the larger one. The larger of the interlocking diagrams answered the question, Which neighborhood is this? And the other answered the question, Which home in that neighborhood is being singled out?

I knew that Qvale's home was at 3636 Jackson Street. I had previously identified three homes on the north side of Jackson Street as possibly being Qvale's home. However, I was unsure if the home that was separated from Jackson Street by the two parallel structures, and which therefore matched the home pointed out by the bomb diagram/map, was actually 3636 Jackson Street. Nor was there any way for me to determine this without flying to San Francisco and looking at the houses on Jackson Street for myself.

The hallmark of any valid theory is that it must be able to correctly predict certain facts. So I crawled out on a limb and made a bold prediction that I conveyed to retired Napa County Sheriff's captain and detective Ken Narlow in the form of a challenge: I stated that if he could make it into Presidio Heights and take a close look at the addresses of the homes on the north side of Jackson Street between Maple and Spruce Streets, 3636 Jackson Street, the home of Kjell Qvale would be the one that matched the home set back off the street in the bus bomb diagram/map.

On what is now a very memorable and ironic day, Ken told me he was going into San Francisco for the day with his wife, Marie. It was

September 11, 1999. Ken said he simply wanted to spend some time in the city and take Marie to lunch at a restaurant there. He promised me that while he was in the city, he would stop by Qvale's neighborhood and take photos of the homes on the north side of Jackson near the center of the block and toward Spruce Street to the east. So I sat back and waited with great anticipation.

A few days later, Ken sent me copies by mail of the photos he had taken. He zeroed in on the home that was set back off the street on the north side of Jackson Street. He told me that the two parallel things I was seeing were a walkway that led from a small gate at the sidewalk up to the front door and a driveway that led to a garage that was set down a ramp below the level of the street. He had taken a photo of the house number on that particular home: **the address clearly read 3636 Jackson Street.**

My "bus-bomb map" interpretation had therefore correctly predicted that the home on the north side of Jackson Street that was set back off the street relative to its neighbors and separated from Jackson Street by two parallel structures was indeed that of Kjell Qvale.

There are, of course, other homes in Presidio Heights that could fit the "home set in off the street separated by two parallel structures" paradigm. One of them is the home on Jackson Street where SFPD officer Don Fouke says he saw the man who may have been the Zodiac disappear on the night of the Stine murder. Given that fact, was the killer singling out the house near Maple Street in order to taunt Fouke and SFPD? So I decided to look at the letter that accompanied the bus bomb for more clues as to which house it might be.

As stated earlier, on page 2 of the November 9, 1969, letter, Zodiac makes reference to motorcycles that passed by 150 feet from his position going from "south to north west." I took this reference to mean that he was standing about 150 feet from a street on which motorcycles were traveling from the southeast to the northwest—in which direction one would find the Kahn Playground, where the search was taking place on the night of the Stine murder.

At the ends of both Cherry Street and Maple Street, there is a three- or four-foot drop-off from the wall separating the park from the neighborhood. This would make it impossible for a motorcycle to enter the park via either of these two streets without suffering considerable damage. That made the location of 3712 Jackson Street, where Officer Fouke last saw Zodiac, an unlikely reference due to its position west of a street that doesn't allow motorcycles access to the park. Also, 3712 Jackson is only about one hundred feet from Maple Street, not "one hundred and fifty feet." In addition, it isn't set back off the street compared to the homes adjacent to it. The unique thing about 3636 Jackson Street that seals its resemblance to the house in the bomb diagram is that the front of 3636 is even with the *rear* portion of the home directly to its west. So it is *literally* set in off the street.

So which street would these motorcycles likely have been on? As stated earlier, at the end of Spruce Street, there is an opening in the wall that is big enough to have permitted a motorcycle to have entered the park. Again, this was the likely destination of these motorcycles at the time of the search for Stine's killer. After the main entrance to the Presidio at Arguello Boulevard, Spruce is the next street to the east that would have allowed access to the immediate area of the police search by motorcycle.

As per Qvale's quitclaim deed, if you were to walk *exactly 150 feet* west along the north side of Jackson Street from the northwest corner of its intersection with Spruce Street, you would end up right in front of 3636 Jackson Street, where SFPD officer Armond Pelissetti may have first spotted Qvale that night. So when Zodiac said that "motor cicles [*sic*] went by about one hundred and fifty feet away going from south to north west," this could have been tantamount to Qvale saying, "I was standing in my property at 3636 Jackson Street [the home that matches the one singled out in the bus-bomb diagram] when motorcycles went by on Spruce Street heading toward the park."

We know from the killer's own words in his letters that Zodiac was allegedly sending the police and public clues to his identity. But it was one thing to imagine that he may have sent nuanced bits of information that may have vaguely hinted around his identity to make people chase their tails. It's another thing entirely to imagine that he had sent everyone a map to his front door! The implications of this were staggering.

The problem was that there was no way to objectively prove I was right. Even so, for many years the bus bomb would remain in the back of my mind as an intriguing clue that pointed directly at Kjell Qvale's Jackson Street home and supplemented my objective, factual research on the case.

When I stumbled onto the solution to Zodiac's first bus-bomb diagram in August 1999, I felt deep down that I was right about my interpretation. I had brought the Zodiac crimes right to Qvale's doorstep and in doing so had solved the case. But I also knew that my interpretation was too subjective to stand alone as evidence. So I realized that I had to keep digging to put together more concrete, nuts-and-bolts evidence. And my solution to the bus bomb allowed me to work with more confidence. I knew I was heading in the right direction and that the evidence I needed to prove my case was out there to find.

In December 1999, I showed my bus-bomb solution to Dr. Mike Kelleher. He was floored by it and said it was the best solution to that diagram he had ever seen. He could find no flaws in my reasoning. He said that it gave him a "gnawing" sensation that I was onto something shocking. But with that compliment came a challenge. He pointed out that in April of the next year, Zodiac sent a second version of the bomb diagram with a different arrangement of the A and B reflector tubes. He asked if I had a solution for that diagram. I did not. Dr. Kelleher challenged me to come up with something equally significant and symbolic, like another map, for that second diagram. It would be over five years before I would stumble onto information that would lead me to take a closer look at the second bus-bomb diagram.

What that diagram revealed about the Zodiac was as equally shocking as what the first one revealed about the killer, if not more so. But this time, while a different map reference was involved, the solution was one that went way beyond singling out someone's house.

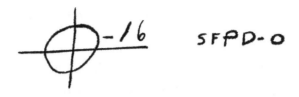

A Tale of Two Witnesses

ON THE NIGHT OF THE MURDER of cabbie Paul Stine, there were several people who were to become key eyewitnesses and figures in the Zodiac case. One of the things of which I am most proud is that over the course of my many years of research into the crimes, working with retired VPD detective Jim Dean, I was able to obtain their stories.

Of all the research I did talking to people about the case, the most crucial was that which Jim Dean and I did in our 2003 interviews with the extremely reclusive teenaged (but by then middle-aged) Stine eyewitnesses. The first day we made contact with them was by complete and utter chance, and the details of that fateful day are forever etched in my memory. It was as exhilarating a ride on the Zodiac case as one could get, and like a roller coaster, that ride was full of ups and downs and twists and turns. At first it left me thinking that my investigation had come to an abrupt end. But then, the entire direction of things suddenly and unexpectedly changed 180 degrees, like a roller coaster dipping sharply at first and then soaring again to even greater heights.

Lindsey and Rebecca Robbins

The morning of Wednesday, September 17, 2003, was a beautiful one in the Bay Area. I was out visiting Jim Dean and his wife, Chris, and he and I planned to go into San Francisco from his home in Martinez to canvass Qvale's Presidio Heights neighborhood. We wanted to determine if anyone who may have lived there some thirty-four years prior might remember interacting with Mr. Qvale the night police had turned their exclusive neighborhood upside down in search of what they thought was a cab robber and murderer. Little did we know that this day was going to turn out to be a very memorable one for both of us and have a profound impact on the case.

After driving from Martinez to Presidio Heights, we made what turned out to be a fateful decision to park at the corner of Washington and Cherry Streets before heading to Jackson Street to begin our canvass. Stopping right at the spot where cab driver Paul Stine was murdered, we got out so I could explain to Jim what had happened on the night of October 11, 1969. Jim and I were standing on the curb opposite the home from which the kids had watched the killer in and around the cab that night. I was explaining the sequence of events when suddenly there was movement in the gated alcove on the left side of the house where Officer Armond Pelissetti had herded the teenaged eyewitnesses to safety in 1969. Someone was out watering her plants. We looked at each other and shrugged, almost as if we instinctively knew what we had to do. We proceeded to cross the street, and when we got to the house, I asked the woman if she was Rebecca Robbins. She said no, she was her mother. Jim and I introduced ourselves and explained what we were doing in the neighborhood. Jim showed her his badge indicating that he was a retired detective from VPD, and I believe this opened the door to having a conversation with Mrs. Robbins.

I explained that we wanted to speak to her youngest son. She quickly countered that he probably wouldn't speak to us but that her older son, Lindsey, might. She was reluctant to give us his phone number but asked for ours, saying that if he was interested in talking to us, he'd call. Jim handed her a business card with his contact information. I seem to recall writing my name on the back so Lindsey would know that an amateur researcher was working with Jim. At that moment, I didn't have very high hopes that he would contact us. To my knowledge, he had never spoken to anyone outside of law enforcement about the night of the Stine murder. But at least we had tried.

But I had another question for her. I asked if her children believed that the police sketches made from their descriptions in 1969 were accurate. She said yes. I found that interesting in light of the comments Insp. Dave Toschi had made over the years. Jim and I thanked her and set off on our mission on Jackson Street.

When I drove the rental car around the block to the area near Qvale's home, it became clear that there were renovation jobs going on at the two mansions to the immediate east of his home at 3636 Jackson Street. There were sawhorses up with No Parking signs everywhere. Spaces were at a premium in this normally quiet neighborhood. So I went east to the next block, Spruce Street, to park. No luck there either. The only parking place I'd seen was directly in front of Qvale's home. I told Jim I didn't want to park there. I feared Qvale would see me and there might be some uncomfortable confrontation, which was definitely not my goal. Jim got a bit impatient with all my hand wringing and said, "Just park the damn car!" So I obliged him by easing it directly in front of Qvale's residence next to a curbside tree. I concealed my face as I hurried out the driver's side and walked quickly toward Spruce Street to get to our first house.

Jim and I went to the home on the northwest corner of Jackson and Spruce and rang the bell. A lady answered the door and patiently listened as we rambled on about what had happened there in October 1969. She said that they couldn't help us because they'd only moved into the neighborhood four or five years earlier. We thanked her for her time and made our way west. The next two mansions were the ones under construction. We peeked in the door of each, and it was obvious that they were unoccupied. As Jim and I plotted our course to traverse the distance west across the sidewalk in front of Qvale's home to get to the home next to his, we spotted a man with a cane walking hurriedly toward us. He was coming from the direction of Spruce Street and flagged us down in front of the mansion directly east of Qvale's home. We soon found he had a lot to tell us.

The man was the husband of the lady who had answered the door. He proved to be very knowledgeable about the local color of Presidio Heights. He told us that on the south side of Jackson had lived an attorney who had a son that had tongues in the neighborhood wagging in the 1960s. He was apparently prone to some violence and had once allegedly punched a hole in the wall of his bedroom. The neighbors felt he might have been Zodiac. The man also griped to us about a famous author from the neighborhood whose daytime help took up all the good parking spaces.

As we spoke, Jim's cell phone rang and he excused himself and walked to the tree next to our car to talk. I thought that this was a fine time for his wife, Chris, to call and leave me alone with the neighborhood gossip. The man went on to say that only two families on the block were living there in the 1960s. One of them was an old San Francisco family, whose fame had come from the time of the 1906 earthquake. The other lived at 3636 Jackson Street—the Qvales. Sure enough, as we spoke, a Jaguar came from the east and turned into Qvale's driveway, which was about fifteen or twenty feet from us. The man said, "Oh, there are Mr. and Mrs. Qvale now." Given how well this man knew the neighborhood and presumably the people who lived there, I immediately panicked, thinking he was going to introduce me to them so we could ask them about the night of the Stine murder! I formulated a hasty and unsophisticated plan: if the man made any such move, I was going to excuse myself and take off walking very briskly (that is, sprinting) toward Spruce Street. I couldn't think for the moment and didn't know what else to do! Luckily, that introduction did not happen and the man turned and walked back toward his home. The Qvales retreated into theirs.

After the Qvales were out of sight, I carefully joined Jim at the tree next to our car and directly in front of their home. From the gist of the conversation, I could tell he wasn't speaking to Chris or to one of his daughters; he was speaking to Stine eyewitness Lindsey Robbins. Able to hear Jim's side of the conversation, I stood there soaking up every detail I could, my back to Qvale's home. Then suddenly, the Jaguar that had just driven up pulled out of the Qvales' driveway and headed east. Mr. Qvale was at the wheel. I found it incredibly ironic that we were standing in front of the home of the very man I had identified as the Zodiac while having a conversation with one of the key eyewitnesses about the night of the Stine murder. In fact, given his love of irony and his odd sense of humor, I think it's something Zodiac himself might have appreciated.

After the call ended, Jim was nearly tripping over himself to tell me what had transpired. Lindsey Robbins had called and was at first very angry that Jim and I had bothered his mother. He said that the night of October 11, 1969, had happened "a long time ago" and that it had changed his life—and not for the better. The Zodiac story "followed [him] everywhere." As his mother had also indicated to us, he stated that newsmen from as far away as Japan had hounded him for interviews over the years. He and his family had refused them all. He didn't want to talk about "that stuff." Jim then identified himself as a retired detective who had worked on the case, and his agenda was to get to the truth about a suspect he was investigating. Suddenly, Lindsey relented and changed gears, saying, "Well, let me tell you this . . . I've never told anyone any of this before." And just like that, the floodgates opened. He said that the one person who never asked him and his siblings for an interview for either of his two books on the case was Robert Graysmith. Lindsey didn't understand why he had never approached them. However, I put forth a theory earlier as to why Graysmith never tried to speak to the Robbins kids or to SFPD officer Don Fouke.

Lindsey Robbins started by saying that the information contained in Graysmith's book about the night of the Stine murder was, in his words, "complete BS." He told Jim that he wanted to set the record straight and tell him what had happened "straight from the horse's mouth." For a hardened Zodiac researcher, this was about as good as it gets. Jim was then made privy to a treasure trove of details that researchers had been clamoring to hear for a generation. And what he had to say ended up being very supportive of my research, but not before some scary moments.

Lindsey felt the wanted poster sketches were extremely accurate, since the two versions essentially matched. He then got to the point in his narrative (described in chapter 9) where the killer got to the corner of Cherry and Jackson Streets as Lindsey watched him flee the crime scene. Jim interrupted to ask Lindsey if it was possible that Zodiac turned east: that is, in the direction of Qvale's home at Jackson Street. Though he didn't hint at why he wanted to know the answer, Lindsey suddenly got upset and blindsided Jim with a question from out of the blue: "Is this about the Qvale BS?"

Jim, taken completely off guard, meekly mumbled that it was. He was surprised by the tone of Lindsey's heretofore calm voice.

Lindsey grew very agitated. "It didn't happen, OK? No way!" he said. "I grew up with that family. We grew up playing together. I looked the guy right in the face. Don't you think I would have known if it was my friends' father?"

Jim, now completely on his heels, said, "Well, you certainly seem to know exactly what you are talking about. That pretty much wraps up our case, I guess. Your candor and conviction are unimpeachable."

When Jim related this to me, I immediately felt that my investigation was sunk—and, ironically, by someone whom I had hoped to talk to for four years. I am 100 percent certain that this is where it all would have ended for me, after all of my research and hard work, were it not for one little thing: Lindsey Robbins had a final question for Jim.

"What is it that makes you think that Qvale had something to do with it?"

"Well, for one thing, Qvale looks exactly like the SFPD sketches that you just said were so accurate!" Jim asserted, regaining his footing and taking advantage of the opening.

Shocked, Lindsey replied, "No, he didn't! He never wore those heavy, horn-rimmed glasses that Zodiac wore."

"The hell he didn't!" Jim quickly retorted. "Every photo we have of him from the 1960s shows him wearing the same type of glasses Zodiac wore!"

Now it was Lindsey's turn to be stunned. "No shit!" he said.

At this point, something extremely strange and a bit disconcerting happened. Lindsey seemed to dissociate himself from the conversation with Jim and started mumbling to himself. I call it a *rhetorical loop*. He said five or six times to himself that he had grown up with that family. He had played in their house. They played in his house. Wouldn't he have recognized their father? How could he think his friends' father was a serial killer? How could he face them again if he told them he thought that Mr. Qvale was the man he had seen that night? It was an extraordinary and eerie moment.

In a later conversation with Jim, Lindsey made it very clear that, while he knew some members of the family in 1969, he had never met Mr. Qvale until the 1970s. *He therefore had no idea what Kjell Qvale looked like in the 1960s.* By the 1970s, styles had changed, and Qvale was seen in a 1972 photo with long hair, sideburns, and no glasses. This is the Kjell Qvale Lindsey apparently had in mind when he initially said to Jim that there was "no way" it was he whom Lindsey had seen on the night of the Stine murder.

We sent Lindsey the photo of Qvale with Silky Sullivan the next day via fax. Lindsey had a remarkable reaction to it. I go into his reaction in more depth in the next chapter. When Lindsey had been shown a photo of Arthur Leigh Allen in the 1980s, he had laughed at the possibility that it was Allen he had seen that night.

He described Qvale as being "aloof as hell." This reference immediately matched one of the key traits of the profile by forensic psychologist Richard Walter, which is discussed in chapter 17, and one that had been used to describe the killer since the 1960s. Lindsey said that all he really knew about Qvale was that he "sold cars and raced horses and that's it." He also told Jim that he was scared to death of the man. He said that he was not easily intimidated, but that Qvale was wealthy and powerful. While not physically imposing, he was someone with whom you would not want to cross swords. He asked Jim if he knew who we were messing with, since Qvale had plenty of power and wasn't afraid to throw his weight around. Lindsey spoke in hushed tones about him: you could practically hear the fear and intimidation seeping out of his voice.

Eyewitness testimony is notoriously unreliable. They are often under duress because they are being threatened by the criminal and are staring at his weapon, not his face. They may only get a brief glimpse of the perpetrator as he commits the crime, then runs away. The viewing conditions may be anything but ideal. However, in this case, the cab was bathed in light. The witnesses were detached from the crime, since they were in the safety of their own home. And Lindsey thought the man had stabbed, not shot, Stine, so Lindsey didn't even think about the threat of a gun. Therefore, they weren't in fear for their own lives. The man they saw was methodical and moved slowly, so they were able to watch him for a protracted period of time. They were youthful, focused, and had 20/20 vision. They studied the man and consciously tried to retain details. One was on an upper floor and one was at eye level, so they both had unique perspectives. When the killer came around to the driver's side of the car, he approached even closer to their vantage point. In short, they were the *ideal* eyewitnesses because *every condition that usually makes for a poor eyewitness was absent in their case.*

Lindsey Robbins passed away in October 2015. I was very sad to hear that he had died long before his time and am eternally grateful for everything he shared with Jim and me beginning in 2003. We could tell that the things he related to us he did at great personal risk because of his close relationship to one member of my suspect's family. From listening to the taped conversations Jim had with Lindsey, it's pretty clear to me that, all things being equal, he would've liked to have said much more incriminating things about Kjell Qvale. However, he was clearly torn between what his head and his heart were telling him to do. He was extremely intimidated by KQ's power and political influence, the type of power a power-assertive individual might have wielded. Lindsey was hoping to gain entry into the Bohemian Club at the time and didn't want to say anything negative about a current member to jeopardize that possibility. While it was frustrating to me that Lindsey was unable to express what Jim and I believe he actually wanted to say, we had to respect his boundaries and the limits he had to observe in speaking about so wealthy and powerful a man.

Don Fouke

My "white whale" from 1999 to 2004 was retired SFPD officer Don Fouke, based on the belief that Fouke had stopped and spoken to the Zodiac as he fled the Stine murder scene. Fouke proved difficult to find, mainly because in *Zodiac* Graysmith calls him "Donald *Foukes*." This misled everyone looking for the man.

The first person to locate Fouke was producer Harry Phillips of ABC News in October 2001. However, Harry didn't provide me with any contact information for Fouke, so by the end of 2003, I was searching for him on my own. I eventually located him in 2004 with the help of the late San Francisco private investigator David Fechheimer, who graciously assisted me several times behind the scenes over the years. I always felt that Jim Dean's badge was like a Disneyland e-ticket that opened all the doors and got people like Lindsey Robbins to speak to us, so I left it to Jim to break the ice with Don Fouke.

Imagine if something that took place over the course of five seconds of your life, virtually the blink of an eye, was analyzed endlessly on the internet by people worldwide who would spill millions of words about it and parse every hundredth of those five seconds. And although you would tell your story pretty consistently time and time again, every time you tried to defend yourself, people would split those few seconds more and more and continue to assert that you were not telling the truth. This is the unfortunate story of Sgt. Don Fouke (Ret.) of SFPD.

On the evening of October 11, 1969, Fouke was paired with rookie officer Eric Zelms. They were to patrol the eastern portion of San Francisco's Richmond District in the western part of the city that night. This placed the pair on Presidio Avenue around 10:00 PM, when a call came over the radio of a "211" (a robbery) and a possible man with a gun. The description they heard from Dispatch was of an NMA—a Negro Male Adult. Fouke didn't know that Officer Pelissetti had already gotten to the crime scene and had just put out a new description of the killer as a white male.

Although he has received much criticism on message boards over the years for his actions that night, Fouke explained why he headed west toward the Arguello Boulevard gate into the Presidio instead of backtracking east to Maple Street, where he'd spotted the man walking down the sidewalk on the north side of Jackson Street, after hearing the corrected description of a white male at Jackson and Cherry Streets. He felt that the man wanted to get to the Presidio in order to lose himself among the trees there. Fouke then reasoned that this man was likely the killer, not simply a resident of Presidio Heights casually walking home from a night out, and was just making believe he was going to walk up the steps to the home at 3712 Jackson Street. In Fouke's own words, he was "faking [him] out." Fouke felt it was likely the man had doubled back down the steps after the patrol car had passed so that he could go north on Maple Street to get to the Julius Kahn Playground and the cover it offered. After his brief conversation with Pelissetti at Jackson and Cherry Streets, Fouke therefore decided to "head the killer off at the pass" by driving through the park on West Pacific Avenue, which runs inside the Presidio wall behind the houses on the north side of Jackson Street. To do that he had to head west, thus driving *away* from the location where he had seen the man a few moments before, to Arguello Boulevard in order to get inside the wall of the Presidio and pick up West Pacific Avenue. Many amateur researchers seem to fail to grasp Fouke's reasoning and wonder why he didn't drive back to 3712 Jackson Street, where he had last seen the possible suspect.

Based on what Fouke told us in his interviews, it's difficult to understand SFPD's investigation into Stine's death. It had been widely believed, and logically so, that SFPD had made great use of the fact that one of its officers had spotted the killer as he left the scene. For years, it was pretty much taken for granted that Officer Fouke and/or Officer Zelms was responsible for the second, or "Amended," police sketch of the killer. But when you speak to Fouke, he is adamant that he never even sat down with sketch artist Juan Morales. How it is possible that SFPD had such a resource as Fouke available to them but never utilized him by having him sit down and make his own sketch?[65] Fouke was a trained observer who obviously had a keen eye for detail, based on how much he recalled from the brief sighting he had of the man.

Equally disturbing is the fact that Fouke told me that his department never once showed him a photo of Arthur Leigh Allen, whom SFPD was aggressively pursuing in the early 1970s! Fouke always maintained a cool and detached, if at times defiant, demeanor whenever I spoke to him. However, when Jim and I showed Officer Fouke Arthur Leigh Allen's photo, he got quite angry and agitated for the only time during our many interviews. He stated that there was "no way" that Allen was the man he saw that night. He said that Allen was "not even close" and was "way out of proportion" compared to that individual. Likewise, when George Bawart of the Vallejo Police Department showed Lindsey Robbins a photo of Arthur Leigh Allen, as discussed

---

65 Officer Don Fouke told me in a 2003 interview as regards the wanted poster sketch that the killer was older than 25–35 years of age, had hair that was "flat" on top, was heavier than the kids thought, and that there was "something about the chin."

earlier, Lindsey said he completely laughed off the possibility that Allen was the man he had seen that night.

Why not let the officer who had spotted the killer weigh in on the department's main suspect? It's virtually inexplicable. But Fouke says that when he was shown a photo of Allen in the 1980s, it was also by George Bawart of VPD, not by his own department! Why didn't SFPD ever show Lindsey Robbins Allen's photo? It is mind-boggling to imagine that SFPD did so much work on Allen but never even bothered to ask Fouke and the Robbins kids if Allen looked anything like the man they had seen that night! Where might the investigation have gone if they had showed Allen's picture to both and they each repudiated Allen as the killer?

Amateur investigators often accuse Fouke of covering up the truth about his encounter; that he spoke to Zodiac but is covering it up. There are "3.8 seconds" unaccounted for in his description of the events, so he must have spoken to the man. However, of Fouke and Officer Armond Pelissetti, one of the first officers to arrive on the scene of the murder of Paul Stine that night, it is Fouke who consistently tells the essence of his story about slowing down, seeing the man, not stopping or speaking to him, hearing the description change, and heading into the park to try to intercept the suspect. He never has to catch himself or correct what he says. He feels he did nothing wrong because they were looking for a black male at the time he spotted the Zodiac. Ironically, it is actually Armond Pelissetti whose story seems to have changed and evolved over time, as we will see.

PART NINE
Evolving Profile and Emerging Evidence

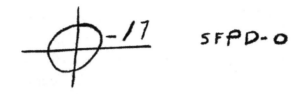

REDEFINING THE ZODIAC KILLER: BEHAVIORAL PROFILING

"In my experience, once you identify the motive you can identify the responsible."
—Pierre Bidou, *Zodiac: The Director's Cut* DVD, *This Is the Zodiac Speaking*: "Lake Herman Road," 2008

"There was something about this case that was different."
—Robert Graysmith, *Crimes of the Century* TV show, 1989

"We are interested only in power. Not wealth or luxury or long life or happiness: only power, pure power."
—George Orwell, *1984*

"I assumed he didn't live in the neighborhood [Presidio Heights], *a* [sic] *upper-middle-class neighborhood."*
—SFPD officer Don Fouke on the man he saw near Maple and Jackson Streets on the night of the murder of Paul Stine, *This Is the Zodiac Speaking*: "Presidio Heights," 2008

IN LATE 2004, even though the Zodiac case was "closed" by SFPD according to Charlie Goodyear's April article in the *San Francisco Chronicle*,[66] I remained determined to find out if Kjell Qvale truly was, according to his statement in the October 2, 2000, *Chronicle* article by Tom Zoellner about my research,[67] the "very last person in San Francisco" who could have been the Zodiac. I decided to send an email to forensic sculptor Frank Bender. Bender was a member of the prestigious Philadelphia-based cold-case-solving organization, the Vidocq Society. In the email I asked the society to take on the Zodiac case, and fortunately they referred me to Mr. Richard Walter.

Richard Walter is a forensic psychologist, or what the average person would more commonly call a behavioral profiler. But he is not just *any* behavioral profiler. He doesn't just practice the usual type of profiling that we see on television and in books. Mr. Walter's business card says that he specializes in "crime scene assessment," which differs from the traditional behavioral profiling done by the FBI in Quantico. As it sounds, crime scene assessment means that you develop a profile based *exclusively on the evidence a serial killer leaves behind at the scene of a crime*. Different types of killers leave behind different types of crime scene "calling cards" depending on what they derive from their murders. These include the type of victim killed, the weapon used, whether or not there was bondage or torture, and whether the crime scene is pre-planned and organized or spontaneous and disorganized.

Mr. Walter is one of the three cofounders of the Vidocq Society, of which he is now a former member. The society is an assemblage of over eighty of the most elite police detectives, psychologists, and forensic scientists from around the world, including experts in every conceivable discipline of crime detection, such as blood spatter analysis, forensic entomology, polygraph analysis, forensic odontology, and forensic

66   Charlie Goodyear, "Files Shut on Deadly Trail/SFPD Caseload Renders 35-Year Mystery Inactive," *San Francisco Chronicle*, April 7, 2004.

67   Tom Zoellner, "Amateurs Stir Embers of Notorious Zodiac Case," *San Francisco Chronicle*, October 2, 2000, p. A17.

anthropology, who fly to Philadelphia once a month to review an extremely difficult cold case over a gourmet lunch. This often requires the group to review gory crime scene photos while negotiating their portion of duck à l'orange. These experts are singled out for exemplary work in their respective fields and are then offered lifetime membership in the group. At their monthly meetings, the society invites one police department from across the US to present its most intractable cold case. The society then uses its collective expertise to analyze the investigation to date and brainstorms new potential avenues of inquiry the officers can use when they return to their home base.

The baseline work Mr. Walter did in the field of forensic psychology while in the Michigan state prison system, where he interviewed tens of thousands of inmates and used those interviews to develop patterns of criminal behavior, helped to form the basis of modern-day criminal profiling. In other words, when Richard Walter speaks about profiling, people listen.

In addition to specializing in crime scene assessment, Mr. Walter also uses a different classification of serial killers than does the usual profiler. In 1999, he described his methods in a journal article he coauthored with Dr. Robert Keppel, "Profiling Killers: A Revised Classification Model for Understanding Sexual Murder."[68] In this article, he and Dr. Keppel took murder classifications previously used to profile rapists and adapted them for use in serial killer cases. The advantage to the combination of crime scene assessment and Mr. Walter's revised classification system for serial killers is that it makes for profiles that are more useful to homicide detectives, who often don't find traditional profiles to be of great practical assistance in solving real-world crimes.

One of the biggest obstacles I had encountered since day one in trying to prove that Kjell Qvale was the Zodiac is that, from a behavioral standpoint, Zodiac has been probably the most misunderstood

---

68   Robert D. Keppel and Richard Walter, "Profiling Killers: A Revised Classification Model for Understanding Sexual Murder," *International Journal of Offender Therapy and Comparative Criminology* 43 (4), pp. 417–37.

serial killer in history. Anyone who has read Robert Graysmith's *Zodiac* is assured in the introduction that Zodiac was a "sexual sadist." This is a completely laughable notion, based on the primer I received in profiling from Richard Walter, whom I first met at the Warwick Hotel in Philadelphia on December 27, 2004. Zodiac was clearly neither a sadist nor a sexual killer to those who, like Mr. Walter, are schooled in recognizing the differences between the various types of killers. In an interview some years after his book came out, Graysmith corrected himself and said that Zodiac was a "sexual killer without the sex." Unfortunately for him, that is not accurate either. The irony of a political cartoonist getting in over his head and using profiling terms he didn't understand is that Zodiac was about as nonsexual a killer as you can ever find! Zodiac wasn't about sex. Nor was he about sadism. He was all about the same thing that Mr. Qvale was about for all his life—something which I will discuss below.

Zodiac was not a sadist. While he was a violent criminal, his violence wasn't structured in the way a sadist's violence against his victims would be. In his 1997 book, *Signature Killers,* Dr. Robert Keppel states, "Contrary to expectation in most murders, the sadist is excited by the process of killing, not the death itself."[69] For example, Mr. Walter once told me that some sadists will actually learn CPR so they can choke the life out of a victim and then bring that person back so they can choke them again and again. With a killer like Zodiac, who generally struck quickly and dispatched his victims clinically, there *was* no "process" of killing.[70]

Zodiac, like Kjell Qvale, was an aloof individual, not the type of personality who wanted to spend significant time with his victims. The glaring exception of this was at Lake Berryessa, where he probably spent time with Shepard and Hartnell in order to reassure them that it was

---

69   Robert Keppel, *Signature Killers,* (New York: Pocket Books, 1997), p. 79.

70   When I think about the "process" of killing, someone like BTK comes to mind.

"just a robbery" and make them more compliant before tying them up. It is of paramount importance when considering the notion of sadism that when Zodiac had Bryan Hartnell and Cecilia Shepard hogtied and completely helpless, he didn't linger with them for any great amount of time *after* he tied them up; he simply stabbed them and left. A sadist would have just begun to have his way with his victims after he had them bound and completely at his mercy.

In addition to the above facts, Mr. Walter pointed out that absent from the Zodiac attacks are the types of injuries typical of sexual crimes—beating, strangulation, recreational cutting/picquerism (i.e., probing knife play that is not needed to effect death), and percussive injury. This once again points away from a sexual killer.

The "other" profile of the Zodiac was that he was a "nobody who lacked control in his life," a "loser" who created the Zodiac persona in order to assuage some deep-seated feelings of inadequacy and then boasted of his crimes in his letters as a way of "compensating" for those feelings. He lacked power and control in his life, so he pursued these things as Zodiac. He had a rich fantasy life, et cetera. This profile was produced using more traditional profiling methodologies—that is, before crime scene assessment was developed—and was proposed by more recent profilers, including John Douglas[71] and Dr. Mike Kelleher.[72] Mr. Walter explained to me that with the advent of crime scene assessment, misconceptions such as this have now been corrected.

An "organized" killer like Zodiac is a planner, as evidenced by him taping a flashlight to his gun at Lake Herman Road, the precut lengths of rope he brought with him at Lake Berryessa, his clear intent to take a piece of Stine's shirt with him after that murder, and also his choice of Washington and Maple Streets for the Stine murder. As Zodiac also did, an organized killer takes quick control over his victims, using lethal force or the threat of lethal force. He shows adaptability in his behavior,

---

71 John Douglas and Mark Olshaker, *The Cases that Haunt Us*, (New York: Scribner, 2000), pp. 187–234.

72 Kelleher and Van Nuys, pp. 219–28.

as the killer did at Lake Berryessa. While he used a gun at his first two crime scenes, he realizes that gunshots may echo across the water and draw undue attention. He therefore uses a knife. He brings his weapon to the crime scene with him and takes it away when he leaves. He can take trophies or personal items from his crime scenes, such as Zodiac apparently tried to do with Faraday's ring and by taking the shirt and other items from Stine's cab. He will alter or stage a crime scene to give himself time to get away, which the eyewitnesses said happened at the Stine murder scene. Zodiac reportedly sat Stine up behind the wheel of his cab to make him look like he was alive. But the most important trait of an organized killer is that he is careful not to leave behind evidence at his crime scenes *and will make a concerted effort to remove evidence from his crime scenes.* Finally, if he is aware of the need to take such precautions, he *will not leave evidence on his letters, on cabs, in phone booths where he made calls to the police, et cetera.* This fact will be crucial when considering the physical evidence in the Zodiac case, particularly the highly controversial DNA from Zodiac's letters.

Given the misconceptions as to what type of killer Zodiac was, it's no wonder that when I came along in June 1999 and dared to say that one of the wealthiest and most powerful entrepreneurs in San Francisco (whom *San Francisco Chronicle* reporter Tom Zoellner later described to me as being "presidential" in demeanor) was the Zodiac, they looked at me as if I were crazy. Fellow amateurs were quick to try to get me back in line with conventional thinking by saying that Qvale "did not fit the profile" of the Zodiac. They assured me that "people like him" did not become serial killers. Why would he "risk it all" and "throw it all away" to become Zodiac? He "already had power and control over his life," so why become a serial killer to gain power and control? I had no answers for them at that time, only my circumstantial evidence that seemed to point directly at Qvale.

As it turns out, I was not in any way off base with my suspicions about Qvale. Rather, it was the profile that needed to be reviewed and brought up to date through crime scene assessment, as I learned when

I eventually met Richard Walter. And that profile was off by a full 180 degrees: **Zodiac was the exact opposite of the "loser" who was "compensating for his feelings of inadequacy" that most people seemed to think he was. Far from seeking power to overcome feelings of powerlessness, Zodiac sought power because he was** *already intoxicated by it and wanted more.*

Therefore, a generation of investigators, both police and amateur, had been looking for Zodiac in all the wrong places and among the wrong segment of the population. This notion of Zodiac being a person of power obviously had an immediate and drastic effect on the list of suspects. In fact, it flipped that list on its ear and placed wealthy, powerful people like Qvale at the very *top* of the list. At the same time, it relegated the known criminals, murderers, mental patients, and dregs of society, who had been 99 percent of the suspects up until 2004, to the very bottom.

Before our meeting, Mr. Walter had read over the facts about Zodiac's four canonical crime scenes and had come up with a profile of the killer based on his actions at those scenes. There are four basic types of killers in Walter's profiling paradigm: the "power-assertive (P-A)," the "power-reassurance (P-R)," the "anger-retaliatory (A-R)" and the most intelligent of the group, the "anger-excitation (A-E)" killer, or sexual sadist.

Because he does his profiling based on the crime scene and not the paradigms used by such entities as the FBI's Behavioral Sciences Unit, Mr. Walter viewed Zodiac's letters as being extraneous in determining his profile, even though other profilers have used them as the basis for their own profiles. This is because the letters Zodiac wrote taking credit for his murders represented the killer's *postcrime* behavior and were therefore irrelevant to Walter's method of using *only* the evidence left behind at the crime scene. And while a letter is characteristic of the boasting this type of criminal does, there is also the possibility of deception in the letters from a serial killer. He may provide misleading information to confound investigators (while still subconsciously

204 • MIKE RODELLI

revealing things about his true background). Such deception would be unlikely in the unspoken "language" of the evidence the killer leaves behind at the crime scene, which lays bare his behavioral soul. In fact, Mr. Walter said that one of the primary goals of a profile is to help investigators understand and interpret the crime scene evidence.

The unifying theme of all of Zodiac's crime scenes is that they show a killer who used overwhelming force to take quick and decisive control of his victims and then generally dispatched them with equal rapidity. At Blue Rock Springs, we know that Zodiac accomplished his attack without uttering a single syllable. He never sexually assaulted any of his victims. Mr. Walter therefore concluded that the Zodiac's crimes were consistent with what is known as an "organized, nonsexual, power-assertive (P-A) killer with sociopathic traits." The main goal of such killers is the usurpation of power from their victims. *Power* is defined here as the ability to control events in one's life and to influence what happens in the lives of others. Zodiac was able to transform the deaths of five people into a platform for writing his letters to the press in a wildly successful effort to exert control over all the citizens of the Bay Area. Had he simply begun to send bizarre letters, codes, and bomb diagrams to the press without a verifiable body count, these letters would have had little impact other than being a curiosity. In fact, they most likely would've been completely ignored as having come from a crank. **Therefore, the power that Zodiac initially derived from his victims was that of his own credibility.**

Mr. Walter explained that a P-A is aloof, condescending, and superior. He has an exaggerated ego. This type of killer already has power and control in his own life and has an insatiable need for more power and control over both people and things—a desire that is *limited only by the bounds of the killer's imagination*. A P-A is grandiose with an inflated sense of self-worth. He is arrogant. He is narcissistic. He has an unlimited need for stimulation in his life and bores easily. A P-A hates any display of tender emotions because emotions are signs of vulnerability and weakness and undermine power. He has a need for glory and recognition. He is deathly afraid of not being important. He is jealous of intimacy and must eradicate intimacy where he sees it. He is self-indulgent, needs to assert his virility, and has a winner-take-all attitude toward life. He may wish to convey the image of a military warrior in order to overpower his victims, as Zodiac did when he dressed as an executioner at Lake Berryessa.[73] The crimes are also not over until he says they are over, which means he can relive them for years after they take place. With a P-A killer, the attack is preplanned, not spontaneous. He uses forceful aggression to control his victims, such as the threat of immediate death via a handgun. His crimes are a search for virility, mastery, and dominance: he is "the man" and wants to prove it. Injuries to victims are purposeful, not recreational. His language is direct and commanding.

In addition, a power-assertive killer is very conscious of image. For that reason, there is no mutilation of his victims, because mutilation is perverse and would undermine his feelings of power. Mr. Walter also explained that this image consciousness may be why Zodiac may have initially abducted Kathleen Johns but ultimately rejected her as a victim and allowed her to escape—she fell well under the killer's target socioeconomic level and had a baby in the car. She admittedly was driving a car that she called "junky."

And of course, the defining trait of a P-A is that a crime *does not count unless someone knows about it.* And in the case of the Zodiac, that "someone" was the entire populace of the Bay Area. Therefore, the power-assertive profile would actually have *predicted* Zodiac's need to write his letters, even though the sheer scope of Zodiac's boasting was a unique and grandiose gesture that was unrivaled by other similar killers and by which we remember the killer to this day. The run-of-the-mill P-A might typically boast about his crimes to a family member, an associate, or to a stranger over a beer at some dive bar. Zodiac's need to boast, in contrast, was obviously on such a scale that it encompassed the entire Bay Area. In other words, Zodiac wanted to let all the residents

---

73   Keppel and Walter, p. 421.

of the Bay Area know who had committed the crimes—postcrime behavior that was consistent with Mr. Walter's profile of a P-A killer.

The power-assertive profile, in its ability to explain things about the Zodiac and even predict his boastful letter-writing behavior, was obviously much more descriptive of him than the nebulous notion of a killer with "low self-esteem compensating for his feelings of inadequacy." And the P-A profile was ascribed to Zodiac by Mr. Walter, whose only job is to solve cold cases.

On the HLN show *Very Scary People*, former FBI behavioral profiler Mary Ellen O'Toole said, "When you think about the definition of the zodiac, it implies somebody who is omnipotent, and so I think this is an individual who is very *arrogant*, loves that *power*, loves that *control*" (italics mine). These are all traits of a power-assertive personality type.

In contrast, when amateur investigators try their hand at profiling, the results are usually misleading. Mark Hewitt, a Zodiac researcher and author, stated on *Very Scary People* that Zodiac was "somebody who, in their [*sic*] own life, feels very powerless and only feels important and significant if they [*sic*] can go out and kill somebody." Hewitt, who trained in theology, not forensic psychology, was, in fact, reiterating the working profile of the killer beginning in 1969. However, Mr. Walter feels that this is an incorrect profile that has led both the police and amateur researchers down dead-end trails for many years.

There was only one Zodiac and therefore only one person who demonstrated all of the above-mentioned behavioral traits of this killer. This includes traits common to power-assertive killers in general and also *traits that were unique and specific to Zodiac himself*. For instance, according to Mr. Walter, the use of ironic humor in the Zodiac's letters is not usually behavior that is exhibited by a P-A perpetrator.

Mr. Walter feels that Zodiac was a recreational or "luxury" killer who killed by choice for fun and did so because he *could*. Zodiac was therefore telling the truth when he said, "I like killing people because it is so much *fun*," in his first coded message from July 1969. This type of killer is by definition not killing to satisfy some compulsion or fantasy.

For that reason, some, but not all, P-As can stop killing if they can sat-isfy their power needs through other means. Walter went on to say that, based on his years of experience, the police are more adept at capturing those killers who are killing compulsively. Conversely, law enforcement is not as adept at catching those killers who do so by choice. Therefore, many of this type of killer, like Zodiac, go uncaught. Geographic profil-ing, which usually places Zodiac's likely residence somewhere in or near Vallejo, is also of no use against noncompulsive killers, since they are, according to Walter, "too smart" to be caught by such means. What Mr. Walter means by this is that, even though geographical profiling didn't yet exist as a discipline in the 1960s, it was created because profilers noticed that some criminals had distinct patterns of behavior that could be used to make inferences as to where they lived. Zodiac was too intelligent to create such a pattern, however, and so his crimes have led investigators to believe he was from Solano County when, in fact, he was not.

Since geographic profiling looks at murder sites alone, it fails to take into account that in the Zodiac case there is another entire set of data points: *up until 1971, every Zodiac letter was sent from San Francisco.* Also, while the murders initially took place far afield from that city, the last one occurred in San Francisco proper. Giving due consideration to where the letters were mailed, Zodiac may have started killing far from his home base and then "brought the crimes home" as he got more comfortable with killing and in his knowledge that he could outsmart the police. This ultimately led him to kill close to his residence in Presidio Heights.

The BTK Killer of Wichita, Kansas, for example, killed one of his last victims down the street from his own home after initially claiming victims who lived miles away from it. Apparently, brazenness comes with experience and the confidence of outsmarting the police. However, in the case of BTK, it took decades for him to bring the crimes near his home. With Zodiac, it took less than one year.

Due to arrogance and the need to necessarily increase the risk of the crimes in order to increase the power derived from them, Zodiac had first progressed from executions on dark back roads to dressing up in a gaudy outfit on an exposed peninsula for any passer-by to see. This increased the risk at Lake Berryessa. He then upped the ante on his last execution-style murder, making it the riskiest one of all. He committed the crime in a residential neighborhood near his own home at an intersection that may not have been his one of choice, since Zodiac originally told Stine to stop one block east of where he eventually shot the cabbie. He then casually walked back to his home without any facial disguise.

Behavioral profiler O'Toole also said on *Very Scary People* that Zodiac thrived on taking risks as a way of increasing the thrill of his crimes. So killing someone in his own neighborhood with no facial disguise and then calmly walking away from the crime scene with the supreme (if false) confidence that he had not been seen by anyone would perfectly fit this need for upping the risk level of the Zodiac's crimes. Far from being risk averse, the Zodiac seemed to have *thrived* on taking risks in the commission of his crimes and by taunting the police through his phone calls and letters.

As Mr. Walter explained to me, the different categories of serial killers are like families. And like families, there can be variations on theme within those groups. Not every member of your family or mine is exactly the same: we are not all simply clones of one another. So, too, is the situation with serial killers. In Zodiac's case, one thing that set him apart from other power-assertive killers is that he was able to stop killing. Walter attributed this fact to the notion that, in contrast to a serial killer such as Washington, D.C., sniper John Muhammad, a P-A killer whose *sole* source of power in life was murder, Zodiac must have had an alternative source of power and control in his life that enabled him to stop his killings as readily as he did. An entrepreneurial business empire like Qvale's would qualify as such a source.

A typical power-assertive rapist might be someone who expresses his power by being extremely muscular and tattooed, with a shaved head and an intimidating gaze, and by utilizing other trappings of male power, such as riding a big motorcycle. However, since power-assertives are part of a "family," there is also a type of P-A who possesses a different kind of power—political connections, personal influence, or financial clout. In the case of Kjell Qvale, eyewitness Lindsey Robbins was clearly afraid of Qvale's financial power and political connections to the point of apparent intimidation.

As mentioned above, another thing that was unique to Zodiac as a power-assertive killer was his use of ironic humor as evidenced by his droll greeting cards. Ironic humor is usually the realm of the cunning, sexually sadistic killer, not a power-assertive, who is more direct in his thinking and not into the complex twists and turns of irony and the ironic humor that may attract a sadist. This set Zodiac apart from other P-A killers.

The final unique aspect of Zodiac's personality that Walter discussed is the "luxury of sophistication." Specifically, this refers to luxury of thought: someone who is *intellectually* at leisure and has the capability to dream up such nontraditional evidence as letters, cryptograms, and "bus bomb" diagrams. Mr. Walter feels that Zodiac was a man of considerable means due to the amount of time he was able to devote to the conceptualization and execution of his letters, meticulously laid-out codes, and bomb diagrams. As we'll see, there are other things to suggest that Zodiac was well-to-do, rather than an unemployed person with "time on his hands" who was just scraping by in life.

Zodiac killed because he was powerful and arrogant. He killed for fun, because he felt he had the right to do so—and because he *could*. Based on the P-A profile, he committed murder in order to increase pre-existing feelings of power, not to ease feelings of powerlessness. The investigation into the Zodiac crimes therefore needs to focus its efforts on wealthy people who were intoxicated with power, as opposed to those who were devoid of it.

The Zodiac stopped killing after the murder of Paul Stine while trying to convince the police that he had merely changed his murderous patterns and was "disguising" his crimes as "routine robberies, killings of anger and a few fake accidents." He then satisfied himself with writing his taunting letters for several more years. But how can this be? The image most people have of a serial killer is that they cannot stop killing and don't do so unless arrested, institutionalized, killed, or otherwise incapacitated. But not so for Zodiac.

When a layperson like me considers why Zodiac stopped killing, he tends to think that Zodiac did so because he "almost got caught" on the night of the Stine murder and that he was somehow "scared" out of killing. He then came to realize that since he was a wealthy person with seemingly everything to live for, writing letters was a much safer avocation at that point. However, when I put that hypothesis to Mr. Walter, expecting a nod of approval, I was surprised when he quickly chafed at that notion and took the exact opposite point of view. Zodiac, he said, stopped killing because the main thing he was deriving from his crimes was, as discussed above, power. He reminded me that Zodiac was also a recreational killer and was killing for fun. So, unlike a sexual killer, who is generally compulsive and therefore can't stop killing, Zodiac was apparently able to stop killing after the Stine murder for this reason: he not only eluded SFPD officers Don Fouke and Eric Zelms on the evening of the Stine murder by pretending to walk into one of the homes on the north side of Jackson Street, he was also accosted and spoken to by Officer Armond Pelissetti and escaped that second encounter with SFPD unscathed. Thus, he received a double dose of extreme power by being able to dupe his nemesis, the police, not once but *twice* in the same evening. Mr. Walter feels that this double triumph over his pursuers gave him such a power rush that he was able to stop killing and then satisfied his future power needs through his various business interests and the letters he wrote.

Up to that point, I was quite skeptical about using profiles based on criminals who had been apprehended to identify one who had successfully eluded capture for so many years. After hearing Mr. Walter's profile of the killer, however, I was convinced that any skepticism I had harbored about behavioral profiling had been unfounded. The reason was simple: under the two-word umbrella term *power-assertive*, Mr. Walter had captured many of the individual traits that *had been discussed by Zodiac researchers for many years as describing the killer, as well as predicting his need to boast about his crimes*. I sensed that the new profile represented a major advancement and paradigm shift in the investigation. The fact that a power-assertive has a pathological need to boast about his crimes perfectly fit Zodiac's most unique trait—the long series of letters by which we remember him to this day. I became convinced by Mr. Walter's profile that Zodiac was a power-assertive killer and that I was on the right track.

Richard Walter's profile also shows that Zodiac demonstrated traits that are characteristic of a sociopath:

- a lack of empathy
- proneness to boredom
- glibness/superficial charm
- grandiose sense of self-worth
- conning, and manipulative nature
- habitual lying
- risk-taking

...

One of the things about profiles is that sometimes we need a real life examples in order to fully understand them. In the fall of 2014, something happened that would give Mr. Walter's power-assertive profile real-world context in a most unexpected way. At that time, a small number of women's voices began to be heard. By the spring and sum-

212 · MIKE RODELLI

mer of 2015, this small group of women had become a large chorus of people accusing one of America's most cherished comics, Bill Cosby, of having committed acts so horrific that they stunned the nation. Cosby was another man who, like Qvale, would fall into the category "the last person anyone would suspect." Cosby was known for generations as the "Jell-O pudding guy" and more famously for his role as the affable Dr. Clifford Huxtable on *The Cosby Show*. He denied their charges of being a serial rapist who had drugged untold numbers of women before taking advantage of them. And, of course, Americans knew these charges simply could not be true.

Cosby was famous, he was wealthy beyond measure, he was powerful, and he had accomplished many incredible things in his lifetime. Many of his accusers had approached him for career advice or to ask that he mentor them, both of which, incidentally, would have put him in a position of power in their lives. At the time of some of these alleged crimes, he was at the zenith of his popularity. Why, people asked, would he have resorted to drugging women just to get them to have sex with them? Why would Cosby "throw it all away" just to have sex (or in Qvale's case, commit murder)? It didn't make sense, and Cosby's supporters sniffed at the air indignantly at the mere mention of such an absurd notion. People like Cosby, who had everything going for him, simply did not commit crimes like this. His accusers were mocked, ridiculed, and ignored. Even though they were leveling serious charges, it was *they* who became the subjects of scrutiny, not the man they had dared to accuse. They were liars. They were, for some unknown reason, conspiring to ruin Cosby's reputation. Or worst of all, they were gold diggers hoping to make money off of their sordid and unfounded allegations.

But then, in July 2015, a judge released a court transcript of Cosby's testimony in a lawsuit that had been filed years earlier in Pennsylvania. It showed that Cosby had testified under oath to trying to obtain quaaludes in order to "have sex with women." And just like that, the worst fears of the public came true: Cosby was essentially admitting to having done something that was central to the theme of the charges his accusers were leveling at him.

But this book is about a man who murdered people in the 1960s, not a rapist. What in the world could Bill Cosby have to do with the Zodiac? The answer is that the Zodiac and Bill Cosby are both the same type of offender—power-assertives,[74] one of whom was allegedly a power-assertive rapist and the other a power-assertive killer.

Power is a funny thing. People who don't have it neither understand nor crave it. But for criminals like Zodiac and Bill Cosby, power is an intoxicant. A power-assertive offender rapes or kills because he already has power and wants more of it. When I heard the allegations against Bill Cosby, I immediately thought about what behavioral profiler Richard Walter had told me about power-assertive killers in the winter of 2004, and I realized from the descriptions that his victims were providing of Cosby's alleged MO that he fit that profile. Power-assertives like to take immediate control over a situation. Cosby allegedly did this by drugging his victims into submission. Zodiac did so by the actual use of overwhelming lethal force or the immediate threat of such force.

Cosby put a public face to the wealthy power-assertive offender. It is something that people can relate to when I explain why the evidence says that Qvale could have been a serial killer. The same people who said in 1999 that it was impossible that Qvale was the Zodiac would also probably have said that it was equally absurd that Bill Cosby was, according to one of his victims, one of America's most prolific serial rapists.

However, the evidence that continues to accumulate seems to indicate that Cosby could have been exactly that. Both Cosby and Zodiac did what they did for power; it is just that they derived such power from committing different crimes. The one thing they did have in common was that both Qvale and Cosby, because of their respective stations in life as wealthy, successful, and "powerful" people, were completely and seemingly irrevocably above suspicion.

---

74 The original context for serial killer categories was the crime of rape.

There is one more key component of Mr. Walter's profile of the Zodiac, which I will discuss in the final chapter.

Profiling the 1966 Bates Case from Riverside

I want to take a brief look at how profiling shows that Zodiac is likely *not* responsible for the 1966 murder of Cheri Jo Bates. One of the most interesting things about the Bates case is the profile of her killer. I've spoken to Richard Walter about the case informally. He is unwilling to go on the record on this profile, since there are ambiguities in the crime scene evidence that would require him to have access to the actual police files in order to form a definitive opinion. He feels that the evidence that's available to the public in the Bates case, in contrast to the police report descriptions of the Zodiac's attacks, is insufficient. In his eyes, the evidence is also contradictory, since it seems to point in two different behavioral directions. However, even these two different possible profiles are useful to the discussion of Zodiac as her killer.

I have discussed some aspects of the *possible* profile with Mr. Walter, and here is what I've come up with based on those talks. Due to the complexity of the details, I'm not at liberty to go into the specifics of the case. Suffice it to say, they suggest the crime may have been committed by one of two subtypes of killers, *neither of which is a power-assertive like Zodiac was.* Therefore, crime scene assessment seems to rule out the Zodiac as having murdered Cheri Jo.

In other words, the more likely someone was to have murdered Cheri Jo Bates, the less likely he is to have been the Zodiac. Yet this doesn't mean the Bates case is not of importance to my research. First, it was this case that initially sparked my serious interest in the Zodiac mystery in 1998. Second, even if Zodiac didn't commit this murder, it seems extremely likely that he wrote at least the 1967 "Bates Had to Die" letters. Third, Zodiac may have imitated certain aspects of this crime in his own career—writing letters about his own murders, using an automotive ruse to approach Kathleen Johns, and so on. Fourth, he would later seem to claim credit for this murder in his March 1971 *Los Angeles Times* letter.

...

Based on all the advancements of my research, including Mr. Walter's input, in 2005 I decided to try reaching out to the media once again. I tried writing to Tony Valdez, a man I knew from newscasts while having lived in Los Angeles in the 1980s. Valdez had moved to Fox News after having been on the KNBC Channel 4 news. He passed along my information to a senior producer named Pete Noyes. Noyes shocked me by saying that mine was the "best research" and the "biggest investigative story" he had ever seen in his entire career. And what a career it had been to that point! I learned that he had been in the news business since the early 1960s and had actually teamed up with reporter Dan Rather on November 22, 1963. They both were at CBS and were trying to secure the rights to the world-famous Zapruder film after the assassination of President Kennedy. Here was a grizzled veteran of the news business who had seen untold thousands of stories come and go over the course of forty years essentially saying that my story was even bigger than the Kennedy assassination! I was highly impressed and my confidence in what I had accomplished was greatly bolstered. Unfortunately, Noyes was toying with retirement at the time and there was the ever-present specter of Fox News being sued if we revealed too much of my evidence, so the story never came to fruition.

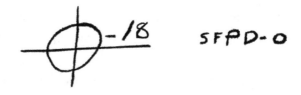

THE CIRCUMSTANTIAL CASE

"There are . . . cases where you have to build this wall brick by brick and when you get the wall built you push it over on them."
—Det. Steve Ainsworth, Boulder, Colorado, Sheriff's Office, *Forensic Files*, "Unholy Alliance," 2005

"Kenneth Bianchi's name was in the LAPD files. The guy they got for Green River, Gary Ridgeway? Name's in the file. BTK? Name's in the file."
—author James Ellroy, *Zodiac* commentary DVD, 2008

WHY IS KJELL QVALE a strong suspect in the case of the Zodiac? Forensic psychologist Richard Walter feels that the way you solve a case is to develop a profile of the perpetrator and then find the person who fits that profile and also can be tied into the facts of the case. The search for Zodiac begins with the profile of a wealthy power-assertive (P-A) individual with sociopathic tendencies, as described in chapter 17. But a profile can only identify a *group* of individuals; it cannot in and of itself identify the killer. There were probably thousands of power-assertive individuals—businessmen, politicians, police officers, security guards, et cetera—living in San Francisco in 1969. What singles Qvale out as being the P-A from the Bay Area who actually was the Zodiac?

Now that the reader has learned the facts of the case, details from the Zodiac letters, Richard Walter's profile, and the observations of the key eyewitnesses, it's time to see how Qvale measures up to what we have come to learn about the Zodiac:

1. Kjell Qvale was a dead ringer for the SFPD "Amended" wanted poster sketch from October 1969. His circa-1965 photo elicited a very strong reaction from Stine eyewitness Lindsey Robbins. Nobody can possibly fit all the various descriptions of the Zodiac—from short to tall and 160 to 230 pounds—but Qvale fits what is arguably *the most reliable sketch*: the one from the night of the Stine murder. The only one created by witnesses who were definitely looking at the Zodiac Killer under nearly ideal conditions and who also weren't under threat of physical harm. In addition, the wanted poster sketches are the only ones that were reviewed by a trained observer in SFPD officer Don Fouke. He essentially rubber-stamped the sketches with a few changes.

A photo of Qvale with the famous racehorse Silky Sullivan from circa 1965 proves his striking similarity to the "Amended" wanted poster sketch (Exhibit 13). The photo of him from a 1971 *Allers* magazine article[75] shows that he had reddish-brown hair (Exhibit 17). Zodiac was described as having that same hair color by the Stine eyewitnesses, and a hair found behind one of the stamps on the October 13, 1969, Stine letter was also reddish brown in color.

More importantly, in 1969 Lindsey Robbins knew only other Qvale family members, not Kjell. As stated earlier, he told retired VPD detective Jim Dean in 2003 that, while he knew of the Qvales in the 1960s, he didn't meet Mr. Qvale until the 1970s. *Therefore, Lindsey didn't know what Kjell Qvale looked like in the 1960s.* When Jim faxed Lindsey the Silky Sullivan photo, in which Qvale has short hair, no sideburns, and the same sort of eyeglasses Zodiac wore on the night

---

75   Lennart Cedrup, "De Fantastiske Qvale-SØsknene," *Allers* 26/71, 1971.

of the Stine murder, *Lindsey had a very strong, visceral reaction to it.*[76] Lindsey looked at it and told Jim he was "shocked" and "stunned." He also used the words *extraordinary, disturbing,* and *remarkable* to describe the resemblance. He asked Jim, "Are you sure this is him? Could there be some kind of mistake?" Jim assured him it was Kjell Qvale. Lindsey said, "You'd have to be an idiot to say it is not striking." He stated that Qvale was the closest to the man he saw that night of anyone he had ever been shown over the years. He reiterated that, before seeing the 1960s' photo of Qvale with Silky Sullivan, he was unaware that Qvale had ever worn heavy, horn-rimmed glasses.[77]

So a credible eyewitness to the murder of Paul Stine who knew Mr. Qvale personally had a very strong reaction to his photo. From Lindsey's interactions with Jim described earlier, it was clear that he was deathly afraid of Kjell Qvale. Therefore, admitting there was such an eerie resemblance between Qvale and the man he had seen on October 11, 1969, was absolutely the last thing Lindsey would have wanted to do. He clearly wanted anything *but* that to be the case. (In fact, in conversations with Jim, Lindsey went so far as to postulate based on no evidence at all that it may have been one of Kjell's siblings, not Kjell himself, who was the Zodiac. I believe he did this in order not to have to confront and accept what his eyes were telling him.)

Retired SFPD inspector Gus Coreris, who closely interacted with the Stine eyewitnesses and was responsible for getting them together with SFPD's sketch artist Juan Morales, felt that the sketches would

---

76 Many people have said that you could make "anyone" into a Zodiac suspect simply by placing a pair of horn-rimmed glasses on him. However, Lindsey's reaction was to the *overall* changes in Qvale's appearance from the 1960s into the '70s, including his hair and sideburns. These changes were therefore not limited to simply placing glasses on the Qvale Lindsey knew from the '70s.

77 It should be noted that Mr. Robbins never stated outright that he felt that Mr. Qvale was the Zodiac Killer or that he was definitely the man he saw around the cab that night. He indicated to Jim Dean that, because of his long-standing relationship with Qvale, such an opinion would never cross his lips.

have been accurate. He told me in a 2000 conversation that the kids were "damn sharp." In a conversation with me, a friend of SFPD officer Armond Pelissetti told me that Pelissetti had indicated to him that he was always "highly impressed" with the teen witnesses, and because the scene was brightly lit and they had an "unusual vantage point," he has always felt that the sketches were quite accurate.

We showed Officer Don Fouke two photos of Qvale, one the Silky Sullivan photo (Exhibit 13) and the other the color photo of Qvale standing next to a car in front of his home from the 1971 article in *Allers* (Exhibit 17). Even though I made it clear to Fouke that he was looking at the same man in both photos, he said that "the man in the Silky Sullivan photo" had "the right chin" and that "the man in the photo with the car" had "the right hairline."[78] He also said that the man he saw on the night of the Stine murder had a "distinctive chin," as discussed in footnote 65. He called Qvale a "possible" for the man he saw that night, which was as strong an endorsement as he could give in 2003.[79]

In his November 9, 1969, letter, Zodiac said that he was wearing a "descise" on the night of the Stine murder. If so, what did his disguise consist of? It's unlikely that it was a facial disguise, since that would've been easily seen through by police had he been stopped for any reason. That he had also not dyed his hair was proven by the fact that the reddish-brown body hair was found under the stamp on the Stine letter, which matched the color of the killer's scalp hair as described by the eyewitnesses just a few days before that letter was mailed. A good reason Qvale in particular as Zodiac would *not* have dyed his hair and/ or worn a facial disguise is that his face and "who he was" were his tickets to getting out of trouble if the police had happened to stop him.

---

78 Fouke indicated at one point that the man he saw had a "widow's peak." I contacted him and determined that what he actually meant by "widow's peak" was that the man had a receding hairline. Qvale also had a receding hairline in 1969.

79 He has apparently also said this about at least one other suspect over the years—Larry Kane.

Kjell Qvale looked just like the Zodiac.

2. In the 1960s, Kjell Qvale had an unusual way of speaking, just like the Zodiac. After the attack at Lake Berryessa, Bryan Hartnell, who never saw the killer without his hood but who spoke to Zodiac for a period of time, stated that the man had an unusual cadence to his voice that Hartnell couldn't reproduce but that he would recognize if he ever heard it again. It was not so much an accent per se as a manner of speaking that caught Hartnell's attention. Although Hartnell had difficulty verbalizing its characteristics, the voice was striking enough that he found it something he needed to report to the police.[80]

In a November 20, 1958, article in the *Daily Commercial News*, the author described Qvale's conversational pace as being *leisurely—almost slow.*[81]

In an April 1984 article in *Car and Driver*,[82] the author described Qvale's voice in this manner: "The mode of speech is refined, articulate, well-modulated, like an announcer on a classical music radio station." Such announcers aren't known for being fast talkers. They're known for a soothing, slow manner of speaking. To reinforce the fact that Zodiac had an unusually slow manner of speaking, as discussed earlier, there is that report in the Napa SO files about a man who was actually eliminated as a suspect because, in stark contrast to the killer, he simply spoke too fast.

Retired Superior Court judge Eric Uldall suggested to me that since Qvale didn't speak any English when he came to this country,[83]

---

80 "Napa County SO Supplemental Crime Report," p. 18.

81 Hugh Russell Fraser, "Bay Area Profile," *Daily Commercial News*, November 20, 1958, p. 5.

82 Pete Lyons, "Kjell Qvale: Two Million Imports and Counting," *Car and Driver*, April 1984, p. 64.

83 Kjell Qvale, *I Never Look Back: My Story*, (China: 2005 C&C Offset Print-

he may have learned to speak the new language slowly, so as to be understood and not made fun of due to his Norwegian accent. This may provide the roots of Zodiac's slow manner of speaking as an adult.

Note: The 2012 Bank of the West commercial showcased Qvale's slow manner of speaking. In 2003, I received a tape from the BBC of an interview Qvale did about Jensen Motors in the 1970s. In it, Qvale laments that they attempted to design "such a cheap car" in the Jensen-Healey. He pronounced the word *car* as "caaaaar," in a distinctive, drawn-out manner. He also said "requiiiiired" and "airers" in a distinctive manner for *required* and *errors*, respectively. Of interest is that Qvale's manner of saying *car* is not similar to a Boston accent, which is more like "kah" and not as drawn-out as Qvale's "caaaaar," nor is the way in which Qvale spoke similar to a Southern drawl. Hartnell had a difficult time putting his finger on the Zodiac's distinctive manner of speaking, suggesting it was not a readily identifiable speech pattern, such as the aforementioned Boston accent or Southern drawl.

Kjell Qvale had a distinctive, slow manner of speaking like the Zodiac Killer.

3. Qvale wrote to me twice in 1999 on monarch-sized paper, which he used as his business stationery (Exhibit 18). Judge Uldall remarked to me on how he had read thousands of parole letters from convicted criminals during his time on the bench yet he had never once seen a criminal write a letter making a parole request on monarch-sized paper. He also stated that no criminal he had ever known through their parole letters could have written the *Badlands* Letter, with all of its multisyllabic words, since most criminals he encountered were illiterate.[84] He called monarch-sized paper "rich

ing, 2005), pp. 7–8.

84   Within the pages of the Solano County police reports I received from Det.

man's stationery," since it generally has to be specially ordered and is used for writing letters with an elegant touch to them. I had personally never heard of such stationery before I came to the Zodiac case (which is a remark I have often seen from other researchers in message-board posts over the years). While it's true that many wealthy and successful individuals use monarch-sized stationery, the question is, *How many Zodiac suspects used it?* As stated earlier, of the three thousand or so that have been developed since 1969, Qvale is the *only* one I know of who wrote even *one* letter on this type of stationery.

Zodiac's use of monarch-sized paper (the very name of which, likely not by sheer coincidence, suggests the lofty status of the user, as befit Zodiac's ego) for nearly all of his taunting letters is one of his signature behaviors. A *signature behavior* is something a perpetrator does that is unique, a calling card of sorts, and that is not something that is necessary to the completion of his crimes.

Kjell Qvale shared Zodiac's signature behavior of writing on monarch-sized paper.

4. Qvale's highly unusual habit of autographing cars. There is yet another unique behavior that immediately singles Zodiac out from all other criminals: he autographed the door of Bryan Hartnell's Karmann-Ghia at Lake Berryessa with his crossed-circle symbol and then wrote a note to the police on the car claiming credit for his crimes. This act represents yet another of Zodiac's signature (i.e., unique) behaviors.

In 2011, Canadian researcher Chris MacRae indicated to me that Qvale, like Zodiac, had autographed at least two cars in his lifetime. One he autographed in black felt-tip pen on the sun visor (Exhibit 19), and another vehicle, an MG, he autographed in

---

Patrick Grate in 2001, there are many letters written by the "usual suspects" from the area. The level of illiteracy in them is obvious and few, if any, of them could have written the Zodiac letters.

white artist's ink on the dashboard.[85] [86] MacRae stated that this type of behavior was supposedly common at high-end car shows, like the Concours d'Elegance shows that Qvale used to organize. He said that the winners of these shows would often autograph the winning vehicle.

That same year I wrote to the Pebble Beach Concours d'Elegance and asked one of its officials, Sean Jacobs, about the possibility of winners of the competition at the Concours autographing cars. He seemed perplexed. He indicated that, in his experience, it was a rare occurrence and that he had never seen a winner write on a car at one of his shows.[87] Subsequent research on the internet revealed no evidence of people routinely signing automobiles at Concours d'Elegance shows. In fact, I could find no examples of *anyone* signing a car at a Concours d'Elegance. Other than a handful of cars that were signed by celebrities over the years, such as Steve McQueen, Jay Leno, Justin Bieber, Warren Buffet, and some famous sports car drivers, like Carroll Shelby, this behavior is exceptionally rare. *Therefore, this act virtually serves to identify Kjell Qvale as a strong suspect given his proven history of having duplicated yet another of the killer's unique signature behaviors.*

Note: When I discuss "autographing" an automobile, I'm not referring to the act of writing on a windshield to say, for instance, "For Sale," "Just Married," or "Class of 2017," or at a car dealership to show model year, financing terms, and price. I'm talking here about someone actually writing his name or otherwise *personalizing* a car.

When I examined the entire suite of photos related to Qvale signing the sun visor area of a car, it appeared that the car he autographed was a red Jensen-brand automobile. This is the auto manufacturer that Qvale

---

85   Zodiac wrote on Hartnell's car in black felt-tip pen. He also drew on and signed the October 27, 1970, Avery Halloween card in white artist's ink.

86   After my book first came out, my good friend Eduard Versluijs reminded me that he had also told me that Qvale autographed cars. Eduard told me this in the early 2000s. So I want to thank both him and Chris MacRae.

87   Sean Jacobs, Pebble Beach Concours d'Elegance, personal communication, May 24, 2011.

purchased in 1970 that bore the name of one of Zodiac's victims from 1968, Betty Lou Jensen. **Therefore, Qvale had not only autographed a car, he autographed a make of car that he had manufactured himself and that bore the name of one of Zodiac's victims.**

Autographing a car is an idiosyncratic behavior shared by both Zodiac and Qvale *to the exclusion (I am sure) of all other suspects in the Zodiac case and to the exclusion of likely 99.9 percent of the population of the Bay Area at the time.* While it's difficult to quantify the exact percentage of the population that autographs a car, I'm sure the average reader can intuit the improbability of this behavior based on his or her own experience. This is yet another of Zodiac's unique behaviors that finds an analogy in Qvale's personal life. Put another way, it's fair to say that since 1969 *virtually* nobody, as compared to the number of people who were alive in the US in 1969 and have been born since 1969, has autographed an automobile. Nobody, that is, *except the two glaring exceptions of the Zodiac and Kjell Qvale.*

Qvale shared Zodiac's signature behavior of autographing cars. In signing an MG and a Jensen, Qvale autographed two brands that held a special significance to his automotive career. Zodiac autographed a Volkswagen Karmann-Ghia at Lake Berryessa, a brand of car that also had a special significance to Qvale's automotive career.

5. 1947 flying-saucer sighting. When looking for a suspect whose behavior in his youth was analogous to yet another of the Zodiac's signature behaviors, his desire for widespread public attention on the front pages of the Bay Area newspapers, one need look no further than Qvale's flying-saucer incident of 1947, which predates the killer's own need for widespread public attention by some twenty years.

As discussed in chapter 13, on July 7, 1947, Kjell Qvale was featured in a front-page article in the *Alameda Times-Star*. This report was then picked up on the front page of the *San Francisco Examiner* and by one other newspaper, the *San Francisco Call-Bulletin* the next day. In the *Times-Star* article, Qvale established his credibility as an "authority" on different types of conventional airplanes by stating that he was an experienced pilot who had flown in World War II. He was the only credible person in the 853 cases from across the country summarized in *Report on the UFO Wave of 1947* to say that flying saucers were "space ships." In the *Alameda Times-Star* version, the basis for the other two articles, Qvale went even further by stating that he wished that the saucers would land and the occupants would tell us where they had come from. Both the *San Francisco Examiner* and *San Francisco Call-Bulletin* apparently thought this statement was so outlandish that they failed to mention it in their articles. Qvale's overall statement was so fantastic and far out of line with what anyone else was saying about flying saucers in 1947 that it virtually assured him front-page coverage.

This publicity-grabbing act serves to link the behavior of Kjell Qvale in 1947 to the innermost behavioral workings of the Zodiac in 1969. Not only that, what Qvale said about flying saucers may have served to terrorize the general public over the possibility of an alien invasion, just as Zodiac used his letters to terrorize the general public with his bus-bomb threat.

Once again, as was the case with writing on/autographing cars and using monarch-sized paper, I know of no other suspect who demonstrated such a strong desire for publicity—and did so over twenty years *before* there was a Zodiac. This was Qvale's first success at manipulating the media to get front-page coverage for his message. Over time he would continue to hone that skill, as per the statements in *Lunches with Mr. Q* regarding Qvale's use of the media to promote his business endeavors (see point 8 below). This may have later manifested itself in the ease with which Zodiac got the media to dance to his music.

The flying-saucer explanation is also a very unusual event that demonstrates that beneath the facade of wealth, normalcy, and utter respectability, Qvale was capable of strange behavior that would have undoubtedly shocked his wealthy peers. One can venture a guess that few, if any, of his fellow millionaires in Presidio Heights had flying-saucer entries on their résumés.

Kjell Qvale demonstrated yet another of Zodiac's signature behaviors by seeking attention on the front pages of the Bay Area newspapers some twenty years before there was a Zodiac Killer.

"We can learn if there is any significance as far as the Zodiac is concerned in the dates of these killings. It might be possible that he follows some certain pattern."
—SFPD chief of inspectors Martin Lee in October 1969 news conference

6. Dates. The Zodiac murders, which appear at first glance to have been committed on completely random dates, take on a shocking pattern when viewed through the prism of Qvale's life. The first murder took place on **December 20**, 1968, the anniversary of the death of Qvale's mother, Signe, which had occurred on **December 20**, 1939. Zodiac later emphasized the significance of this date by commemorating it a year after the Lake Herman Road murders with a letter to San Francisco attorney Melvin Belli that was postmarked **December 20**, 1969. The Blue Rock Springs attack took place just after midnight on **July 5**, 1969, which was twenty-two years to the day after Qvale's flying-saucer sighting of **July 5**, 1947. The attack at Lake Berryessa on **September 27**, 1969, took place on the birthday of his father, Bjarne Qvale, which was **September 27**, 1887.

Qvale's letter to the editor appeared in the *San Francisco Chronicle* on **June 26**, 1969 (Exhibit 12). On **June 26**, 1970, precisely a year later, Zodiac postmarked his Mt. Diablo letter, thus "just happening" to commemorate the date of Qvale's own rare letter to the editor of that newspaper. A year to the day after Zodiac's Mt. Diablo letter, Qvale held a news conference in England, on June 25, 1971, during which he announced that the company he had purchased in April 1970 (one which incredibly bore the name of one of Zodiac's early victims, Betty Lou Jensen), *Jensen* Motors, had become profitable. *Qvale himself* *controlled the date of the resulting articles by choosing to fly to England and holding the news conference on June 25.* As one would expect, on **June 26,** 1971, the day after the news conference, articles appeared in *The Times* of London[88] and the *Financial Times.89 Therefore, both Qvale and Zodiac alternated the commemoration of the same date during a three year period (i.e., 1969 to 1971).*

Another date that seemed to hold significance to Qvale is November 20, although he denied this possibility to me in our 2006 meeting. The first commemoration of this date that I located was on **November 20,** 1958, when the article about his business appeared in the *Daily Commercial News.* The next iteration was on **November 20,** 1964, when Qvale once again controlled the timing of two articles. One was on the front page of the *San Francisco Examiner,*[90] and the other was in the *San Francisco Chronicle.*[91] Qvale held a news conference on November 19 (similar to what he would later do in England with June 26, as discussed above) announcing that he was "the biggest" import auto dealer on the West Coast. On **November 20,** 1968, Qvale made a crucial business merger. On November 20, 1998, Qvale filed papers to start a joint venture based on golf course development.

When I saw **November 20** recurring time and time again in Qvale's life, I immediately wondered if there was some significance to that date with respect to the Zodiac case. It would be a while before I got to the bottom of this mystery, but when I did, it would be with an unexpected find. It was of an eerie symbol that surely would have

---

88   Clifford Webb, "Jensen Ends Year with a Profit: Staff to be Bigger," *The Times* (London), June 26, 1971, p. 16.

89   James Ensor, "Jensen Profit Attributed to Higher Production," *The Financial Times* (London), June 26, 1971, p. 13.

90   Jerry Diamond, "Qvale's Auto Coup—He's the Biggest," *San Francisco Examiner,* November 20, 1964, p. 1.

91   Josh Hogue, "Qvale Dealership Now Nationwide," *San Francisco Chronicle,* November 20, 1964, p. 6.

attracted a younger Zodiac's attention in an article in the *San Francisco Examiner* from 1955 (see chapter 21).

Zodiac claimed to have abducted Kathleen Johns and her daughter on **March 22**, 1970, and taken them on a "rather intresting *[sic]* ride" through the area around Tracy, Patterson, and Modesto.[92] On **March 22**, 1971, Zodiac commemorated this date by sending the Peek through the Pines postcard to "Paul Averly" of the *San Francisco Chronicle*. On **March 22**, 1974, after a gap of *over two and half years* of not personally orchestrating any articles in *The Times* of London, Qvale suddenly orchestrated an article in that paper by once again using his familiar method of personally issuing a statement to the press the day before.[93] And again he used the company he owned in England bearing the name of one of Zodiac's first victims, Jensen Motors, as the basis of the article.

In the 2012 book *Lunches with Mr. Q*, on page 55, author Kevin Nelson states that he was looking through a binder of clippings that Qvale kept on his career as an auto dealer. The very first article in the scrapbook was dated **August 1**, 1948, and was from the *San Francisco Chronicle*.[94] This was the first major article ever written on the arrival of British import cars at local dealerships. In a photo accompanying the article, Qvale is seen driving an MG on a dirt road near Millbrae, California.[95]

In 1969 Zodiac sent his initial letters to the *San Francisco Chronicle*, the *San Francisco Examiner*, and the *Vallejo Times-Herald*. These letters were postmarked July 31, 1969. The killer specifically demanded that the three papers print the ciphers by the afternoon of **August 1**, 1969, or the killer would go on a murderous rampage and kill a dozen people. *Therefore, Zodiac wanted his first public exposure in the three local papers*

---

92   Zodiac letter, July 24, 1970.

93   "Jensen Warning," *The Times* (London), March 22, 1974.

94   Nelson, p. 55.

95   Barney Clark, "A Bay Area Invasion—On Wheels," *San Francisco Chronicle*, August 1, 1948, p. 5L.

to take place on the anniversary of the first major public exposure that Kjell Qvale received for his import auto business in 1948.

The Zodiac is closely associated with the murder of Cheri Jo Bates in Riverside, California. This is true even if Zodiac did not actually commit the murder but merely commemorated it with the three 1967 "Bates Had to Die" letters. The date of this murder coincided with the running of the *Los Angeles Times* Grand Prix, in which Qvale had entered a car.

The *Los Angeles Times* Grand Prix had started years earlier as the Riverside Grand Prix. Qvale had entered his first car in that race on **October 11**, 1959. Therefore, the murder of cabbie Paul Stine on **October 11**, 1969, took place on the tenth anniversary of Qvale's first entry into the Riverside Grand Prix.[96] This race would become associated with the 1966 murder of Cheri Jo Bates after the event had evolved into the *Los Angeles Times* Grand Prix. As if to emphasize the relationship between the 1959 race and the date in the Stine murder, in the killer's October 13, 1969, letter written immediately after this crime took place, Zodiac makes a reference to *road races,* a term that would describe the Riverside Grand Prix auto race that took place ten years earlier.

Kjell Qvale's important dates are also Zodiac's important dates. The dates of the Zodiac murders appear to be completely random until they are viewed from the perspective of Qvale's life and import-ant dates related to his parents.

7. Qvale's homes/geography. The murder of Paul Stine took place just two and a half blocks from Qvale's Presidio Heights home, which he had purchased in 1965. The home is located at 3636 Jackson Street, in the middle of the north side of Jackson between Maple and Spruce. This definitely ties Qvale very intimately to that murder scene. Qvale's

96 http://www.racingsportscars.com/photo/Riverside-1959-10-11.html (Qvale entered car #266.)

mansion on Jackson Street would not only have been a safe haven for the killer, but it also would have provided a commanding view of the park and the Julius Kahn Playground, where the police/dog search the Zodiac described in his subsequent letters centered that night (Exhibit 14).

Recall from chapter 11 that in his November 9, 1969, letter Zodiac went out of his way to state not once but *three times* that he had disappeared "into the park." When Zodiac was last seen by Officer Fouke, he was on the north side of Jackson Street—the same side as Qvale's home—and headed east, in the direction of that home and about a block away. He was not headed in the direction of the park at that time, and had that been his destination, he had already passed up an opportunity to enter it at the end of Cherry Street.

If you had lived at 3636 Jackson Street and been spotted by Officer Fouke walking within one block of that home and on the same side of the street, I believe that you would also have been eager to plant the seed in the mind of the police that you had "disappeared into the park" and that your destination was not a home in the Presidio Heights neighborhood. Zodiac even asked that a passage in his November 9, 1969, letter in which he states *twice* that he went into the park be printed in the newspapers. This would then have painted a picture in the mind of the public, as well, that he had disappeared into the park. And if everyone believed that you had gone into the park, nobody would ask inconvenient questions as to your *actual* destination that night.

Qvale also had strong ties to Solano County. He raced horses for years on the California fair circuit, which includes the track in Vallejo. In fact, in 1968 in particular, the summer prior to the Lake Herman Road attack, Qvale was actively racing horses in Vallejo, as per the records from *Daily Racing Form* results charts. That's when he ran the aforementioned horse named Gun Barrel. In 1972, Qvale purchased waterfront property in Benicia, which he never apparently developed. As Dr. Mike Kelleher stated to me in 2000, the act of purchasing property also speaks to a strong familiarity with Solano County.

Qvale owned a horse ranch on Money Road near the Silverado Trail in Oakville in the 1960s.[97] This ranch was about halfway between Napa and Lake Berryessa. The elapsed time between when Zodiac wrote on Hartnell's door (6:30 PM) and the phone call to Napa PD was an hour and ten minutes. This would have allowed Qvale to drive to his ranch (approximately thirty-eight minutes), change clothes and possibly cars (about seven minutes), and then drive to the phone booth in Napa (approximately twenty-three minutes) in time to make that call in the required hour and ten minutes.

A sports car enthusiast living in Oakville would have found himself in an area with plenty of winding, hilly back roads on which to put one of his high-powered vehicles through its paces. Qvale was also an admitted "speed addict," who had also owned fast boats in the past, one in particular on Lake Tahoe. So he may well have been familiar with Lake Berryessa, despite denying so to me in 2006.

Qvale also hosted a "hill climb" race that was held at Mt. Diablo in the 1950s.[98] This was reportedly the first MG race in America. Therefore, Qvale has demonstrable personal ties to that geographic landmark, one that figures prominently to the "radian" reference in the case. And his link to Mt. Diablo had to do with cars.

In his November 9, 1969, letter, Zodiac stated that the motorcycles went by 150 feet from his position on the night of the Stine murder, traveling from south to northwest.[99] As stated earlier, a map of the neighborhood shows that all of the cross streets in Presidio Heights go in a slight but perceptible southeast-to-northwest direction. So in using that directional term, Zodiac may have been cryptically referring to these cross streets (Exhibit 4). There's no access to the Presidio by car or motorcycle at the end of either Cherry Street or Maple Street due to the three foot drop-off at the boundary of the park at the end of each

97   Ed Neil, personal communication, 1999.

98   Qvale, pp. 66–67.

99   Letter from Zodiac Killer dated 9 November 1969.

of those streets. However, at the north end of Spruce Street, the next block east of Qvale's home, there is an opening in the wall that would have allowed a motorcycle, but not a car, to access the park. Spruce Street, therefore, qualifies both as being a street that runs from south to northwest and one that would have allowed access to the park via motorcycle. If you measure from the northwest corner of Spruce Street exactly 150 feet to the west, you end up in Qvale's front yard. Therefore, when Zodiac tells us he saw motorcycles going by 150 feet away from his vantage point heading from "south to north west," he could just as easily have been saying, *I was standing in my front yard and saw/heard motorcycles going up Spruce Street into the park.* Qvale's property at 3636 Jackson Street started 137 feet west of the western line of Spruce Street and continued west for another 52 feet, thus placing a point 150 feet west of Spruce Street within his property boundaries. And as we'll see later, according to SFPD officer Pelissetti, Qvale may well have been standing in his front yard during the early part of the police search that night.[100]

From my research and the knowledge I gained by visiting Presidio Heights over the years, I believe that more than just a minimal amount of planning went into Zodiac's choice for the original site of the Stine murder. His selection of Washington Street and Maple Street, which he provided to the cabbie for his fare-book entry, suggests that Zodiac was someone who was not simply casually acquainted with this neighborhood (Exhibit 4). (Some of this discussion is based on research that Ed Neil posted to www.zodiackiller.com in 2003.)

As I indicated earlier, the mansion occupying the northwest corner of Washington and Maple Streets is called Le Petit Trianon. Assuming

---

100 There is a second reference to Zodiac's location in the November 9 letter. Zodiac stated that the dogs never came within "two blocks" of his location. In a March 2003 conversation I had with Insp. Dave Toschi of SFPD, he stated that some of the search dogs went to Arguello Blvd. after leaving the cab. Arguello is over two blocks from 3636 Jackson Street. Had Zodiac said that the dogs (those that went to Maple Street) came within a half block of his location, that may have been a clue that hit too close to home for the killer's comfort.

234 • MIKE RODELLI

that Zodiac would have asked Stine to stop at the analogous corner of Washington and Maple Streets as the northeast corner he chose at Washington and Cherry Streets, it's important to note that Le Petit Trianon is set about forty feet back from the northwest corner at Maple Street. This means that the line of sight from that mansion to a potential crime scene on the northeast corner of Washington and Maple Streets would have been extremely limited; not only because the mansion was set in off the street, but also because of the intervening trees on the northwest corner of Maple. *This served to eliminate a potential source of witnesses watching from that vantage point.*

The home on the northeast corner of Washington and Maple Streets in front of which the cab would have parked is L shaped and the part nearest the corner is set back off the street about fifty-four feet. An iron fence separates it from the street, with many trees intervening between the house and the fence. *This once again would have served to limit the ability of someone inside the home to see what was going on at the northeast corner.*

The home directly across the street, on the southeast corner of Washington Street and Maple Street, has an interesting history. It had been owned by a lady named Mignon Augsbury. Mrs. Augsbury died in 1968. This home also had servants' quarters that extended up the Maple Street side. Those quarters had a separate address and entrance on Maple Street. When she died, for whatever reason, she left $50,000 and a Jaguar automobile to her gardener. In the 1970 Polk's Guide, this gardener is listed as living in the mansion. But is that accurate, or might they simply have used his name as a placeholder of sorts for the guide, while the gardener's family actually still occupied the servants' quarters on Maple? Of note is that the biggest Jaguar dealer in the San Francisco Bay Area (and on the West Coast, for that matter) was Kjell Qvale. He may therefore have been well acquainted with Mignon Augsbury because she was a Presidio Heights neighbor and also owned a Jaguar, which she may have purchased from and/or had serviced by his dealership. It seems logical that if you lived in Presidio Heights and owned a Jaguar, you took it to Qvale's dealership for servicing. And Qvale may also have been aware that by October 1969 she was deceased. The main activity in that mansion after her death may well have been in those servants' quarters on Maple, and the mansion was essentially unoccupied and dark at night. If so, then anyone walking by it on a regular basis, such as someone out walking a dog every night, may have made due note of this fact. Repeated efforts I have made over the years to reach a member of the gardener's family to ask what they remember about the situation at 3799 Washington Street at that time have been unsuccessful.

Therefore, it's entirely possible that the home on the southwest corner of Washington and Maple Streets, diagonally across from a vehicle parked at the northeast corner of that intersection, would have been the *only one of the four* homes at that intersection that posed a real threat to the killer if he chose to murder someone at that location. In other words, Zodiac may have calculated through his intimate knowledge of the neighborhood that *three of the four homes* on that corner posed little to no threat to him. This may be why he chose that particular corner. Once he continued on to Cherry Street, however, all bets were off and he left himself exposed to being seen by the kids at the party.

The other interesting aspect of this corner is that Maple Street between Jackson to the north and Washington to the south comprises a surprisingly steep hill compared to the same stretch on Cherry Street. It is, in fact, a fairly taxing uphill walk from Jackson to Washington. This may have had the effect of limiting the number of dog walkers and joggers rounding the northeast corner of Maple and Washington Streets who might happen onto a crime taking place on that corner. In contrast, walking from Jackson to Washington Street on Cherry Street was actually a slight *downhill* walk, making the walk south on Cherry Street to Washington Street a much less arduous task. At the time, people apparently did even the most mundane or leisurely of tasks, such as going to a movie or baseball game or even walking the dog, while wearing a shirt and tie. Many people also smoked in the 1960s, making an uphill walk with the dog even more of an exhausting task. This may have made Zodiac feel confident that he was less likely to be interrupted at the northeast corner of Washington and Maple Streets than at Washington and Cherry Streets, given the number of people who would likely choose the path of least resistance in their activities.

In contrast to the situation at Washington and Maple Streets, there are homes in close proximity to the northeast corner on both the north *and* south sides of Washington Street and Cherry Street, where the crime was committed. This makes it a much riskier and less favorable place to commit a crime such as the one Zodiac undertook. And, as stated above, it's a much more likely place for a dog walker or jogger to turn the corner coming south to Washington Street than was Maple Street. So in murdering Stine at that intersection, Zodiac was actually subjecting himself to significantly *greater risk* than he would have at Maple Street. For this reason we can be fairly confident that Zodiac planned to murder the cabbie at Maple Street, but that somehow his plans were foiled by something that cropped up unexpectedly when they arrived at that intersection, such as a jogger unexpectedly turning the corner onto Maple Street from Jackson Street to head east on Washington Street, thus happening on the cab as it pulled up.[101]

While none of this proves anything for certain, we can use it to draw inferences. Former San Francisco City Attorney's Office investigator Tim Armistead pointed out that Zodiac seemed to know that the fastest way to the west side of town from downtown San Francisco was to hail a cab in the theater district. Add to that the fact that retired SFPD inspector Vince Repetto was of the opinion that "97 percent" of people living in San Francisco couldn't find the intersection of Washington and Maple Streets on a map. He was implying that the killer didn't happen upon this neighborhood by chance. Both Capt. Martin Lee of SFPD and Rebecca Robbins felt that Zodiac knew the

---

101 Some researchers have said that Zodiac actually shot Stine at the corner of Maple Street and that the out-of-control cab then rolled to Cherry before the killer could get it under control. There is absolutely no evidence for this assertion.

site in which he chose to kill, the Presidio Heights neighborhood, well, and the geography of the area suggests that Zodiac may have had a fairly intimate knowledge of the corner at which he intended to kill Stine. All of this implies that he was more than just a casual visitor to San Francisco or Presidio Heights from the North Bay or even from another part of the city. In fact, it argues in favor of someone who knew Presidio Heights very well.

One final advantage to killing at the corner of Washington Street and Maple Street: this location was just up a very dark, tree-lined hill and around the corner from Qvale's home. Had the crime occurred here, Qvale, a former track star, could have run or walked briskly down that dark hill and been home long before anyone even knew Stine had been murdered. He also would never have been seen by the Robbins kids nor had his famous encounter with Officer Fouke. Due to the kids and their wanted poster sketches and the testimony of Officer Don Fouke, the fact that Zodiac was unable to carry out his original dark plan that evening may consequently contribute to his ultimate downfall.

Critics have stated with great certainty that Qvale would not have killed someone in his own neighborhood without wearing something to disguise his face. Therefore, he cannot be the Zodiac. But those who assert this don't understand Qvale, the behavior profile of the Zodiac, or the dynamics of the neighborhood. Kjell Qvale was a very aloof individual. He was not the guy out throwing a football around with the kids on Jackson Street. So it's absurd to imply that someone who lived on the next block would have known him on sight just because he lived in the neighborhood. I certainly wouldn't recognize the people who live around the corner from my home in New Jersey. Also, both Qvale and Zodiac were risk-takers, with Qvale being, as we will see, an admitted risk-taker in business. And Qvale's knowledge of Presidio Heights, as described above, may have allowed him to limit his risks on October 11, 1969. By his knowing of the death of Mignon Augsbury in 1968, *there may have been nobody living at the corner of Washington and Maple Streets who knew who he was.*

Mr. Walter stated that, in order to up the thrill of his crimes to prevent boredom from setting in, someone like Zodiac would have had to increase either the *frequency* of the attacks or the *risk* associated with his attacks. If, as I believe, Zodiac was killing on a rigid schedule based on important dates in his life, the only way for him to increase the thrill *was to increase the risk.* Thus we see the progression from two execution-style attacks to the bizarre outfit on the exposed peninsula at Lake Berryessa to murdering Paul Stine in his own neighborhood. Therefore, Qvale killing down the street from his own home perfectly fits these parameters.

Speaking of who Qvale was, what may have happened had Don Fouke stopped Zodiac and called him over to the car and things went beyond, "Have you seen anything unusual in the last few minutes?" Remember that Fouke stated his reluctance to interact with residents of that wealthy community. He may have been easily intimidated by those residents. Qvale would likely have indignantly asked Fouke if he knew who he (Qvale) was and threatened to go directly to the mayor and have Fouke's job. Were he later approached by the police, he undoubtedly would have threatened legal action against anyone who said he was the Zodiac or even looked like him, thus intimidating the youthful eyewitnesses to the Stine murder. Then, as was the case from 1999 to 2013, Qvale would have made it very difficult politically and legally for the police to investigate him. And before the advent of modern-day behavioral profiling, the police wouldn't have even remotely considered someone like Qvale to be a viable suspect due to his immense wealth and status in the community. None of that would've been possible if Qvale had disguised his face in any way.

With respect to Vallejo and Solano County, Judge Uldall pointed out to me that the shortest distance between the Solano County racetrack (where Qvale raced horses in the 1960s) and the track at Pleasanton was to go out Lake Herman Road from Columbus Parkway and then continue south. This route would have taken him past both the Blue Rock Springs attack site and the Lake Herman Road site. The judge surmised that Qvale may have committed the Zodiac crimes on weekends under the ruse of going to his ranch in Oakville to tend to his horses. He then used the ranch, where he kept various junker cars, as a secluded base of his operations for the Zodiac crimes.

Qvale admitted to loving fast cars and sold sports cars beginning in 1947. You can't "open up" a fast car on Market Street in downtown San Francisco. So a logical place for a sports car enthusiast to go for a joy ride would be to cross the Bay Bridge and then head northeast toward Vallejo and Napa, where there are lightly used back roads with dips, hills, and turns that make driving interesting and challenging. Lake Herman Road, the site of Zodiac's initial attack, would definitely have qualified in this regard. And we know from the August 1, 1948, *Chronicle* article, Qvale definitely drove the back roads of the Bay Area.

An article in a 1963 *Sports Car* magazine describes a road rally event that was essentially a five-hundred-mile trek through the Bay Area.[102] Qvale was involved in planning the event, at least to the extent that he contributed the use of his dealership for the awards dinner. Participating in this type of event, which Qvale may have done at some point in his life, may have exposed him to the back roads of Solano County. Thus, when you're looking for someone who felt completely at home on the back roads of an area where he doesn't necessarily live, one candidate would be sports car enthusiasts like Qvale and their wide meanderings on obscure byways.

In his autobiography *I Never Look Back*,[103] Qvale states that he was "very active" in the Northern California MG club and that he participated in many "rallies, tours, hill climbs, etc." He was also involved in organizing the racing events.

Kjell Qvale lived just down the street from the Stine murder scene, was intimately familiar with Presidio Heights, and had strong

102 Ed Simons, "Sparks in the Golden West," *Sports Car* December 1963, pp. 18–19.

103 Qvale, p. 98.

ties to both Napa County and Solano County through his horse ranch in Oakville, the horses he raced in Vallejo, and his involvement with and love of sports cars.

8. Stine Letter/"Over by." The October 1969 Stine letter is the only one in which the author gives any hint as to his location relative to any of the murder scenes when he states that he killed the cab driver "*over by* Washington Street and Maple Street." The phrase *over by* is understood to mean that some location is close to you. In contrast, in his first letters, he speaks about killing people in "Vallejo" or at "Lake Herman" or "by the golf course in Vallejo." In the *Times-Herald* letter in particular, he doesn't say that he killed the two kids "over by Lake Herman" or that he killed Darlene Ferrin "over by the golf course."

This suggests that Zodiac was writing from a position that was close to the Stine murder scene and that he made a subconscious error when he couched his position relative to that crime scene in that manner. In contrast, the other attacks had taken place in the "North Bay."

Zodiac may have subconsciously given away the location of his residence as being close to Washington Street and Maple Street, and far from Vallejo. As indicated earlier, Qvale lived near the Stine murder scene.

"By today's standards, Zodiac was quite the media genius."
—Dr. Mike Kelleher on October 17, 2002, ABC's *Primetime Thursday* show on the Zodiac

9. Manipulation of the media. Qvale's 1947 flying-saucer sighting was the first example of his using the newspapers to get his message out. Qvale showed that he knew how to get the media to feature both himself and his business endeavors in the pages of the local newspapers as far back as the August 1, 1948, article in the *San Francisco Chronicle*. He then proceeded to show tremendous agility with the media, both in

San Francisco and overseas.

In 1949 Qvale needed some big-time publicity to jump-start the British car business into which he had ventured. So he participated in a stunt to demonstrate just how small and sporty these cars were by having one of them driven under a vehicle that was known as a lumber carrier.[104] This P. T. Barnum–type act got the attention of *Life* magazine, which ran a story along with the photo of someone else driving the MG under the carrier. In his autobiography, Qvale shows a photo of himself duplicating the feat, as well as discussing his role in organizing the demonstration, thus proving his involvement in the story even though his photo was not the one featured in the *Life* story.[105] In this manner, Qvale was able to pique the interest of the press in order to get nationwide free publicity for the midget sports car craze. This free advertising is credited with putting British sports cars on the map in the minds of American consumers.

As mentioned earlier, on November 20, 1964, Qvale put out the news that he was "the biggest" import car dealer on the West Coast and got the media to write stories about him in two newspapers (footnotes 90, 91). And on June 26, 1971, Qvale personally orchestrated articles in *The Times* of London and the *Financial Times* about Jensen Motors (footnotes 88, 89).

In Lunches with Mr. Q, author Nelson states, "Mr. Q's success was due, in part, to a *flair for promotion and publicity* [emphasis mine]." This precisely describes the Zodiac and his letters, which represented, in essence, a twisted marketing scheme. He then lists thirteen different publicity stunts and events that Qvale staged over the years in order to promote the import car business in the Bay Area.[106] In a heading within the chapter titled "The Care and Feeding of the Media," the author states that Qvale provided British cars for *San Francisco Chronicle*

---

104 "MG Midget Craze," *Life,* January 10, 1949, pp. 63–66.

105 Qvale, p. 65.

106 Nelson, pp. 58–67.

columnist Herb Caen,[107] thus establishing that Qvale had provable ties to the *San Francisco Chronicle*, Zodiac's paper of choice.

One thing is very clear from all of this: Qvale surely knew how to get the media to dance to his music long before there was a Zodiac. In summary, Qvale's long relationship with the local media prior to 1969 demonstrates that Zodiac didn't have to be a member of the press in order to know how to manipulate the media.

Qvale possessed the requisite skills to manipulate the media and had years of experience doing so. This may explain why Zodiac showed no learning curve in attracting widespread attention to himself when he first came onto the scene with his first letters in July 1969.

10. Sister Cities. In 1968 the City of Vallejo participated in the sister-city program I mentioned briefly in chapter 2.[108] This program, established in 1960, promotes goodwill between Vallejo and other, similar seafaring cities located around the world. Several such cities spread across Europe and Asia are now in the program. As stated earlier, the very first sister city—and the *only* one in the program at the time of Zodiac's initial attack—was the coastal city of Trondheim, Norway (footnote 5).

Trondheim, Norway, is where Kjell Qvale was born in 1919.

Zodiac was a killer who strongly hinted that he was planting clues to his true identity in his letters. But few have imagined that he may have also been planting clues to his place of birth in the locales where he attacked his victims. He always emphasized that both of his early attacks took place in "Vallejo," even though he clearly was someone who read the newspapers and would've known that the Lake Herman attack took place in unincorporated Solano County, not Vallejo proper.

---

107 Qvale, p. 61.

108 "Vallejo's Sister Cities 1960–1980," compiled by John Buchanan, date unknown.

Needless to say, if this is correct, then trying to apply geographic profiling (which appears to point to the Vallejo area as Zodiac's most likely place of residence) to the Zodiac's murders is an exercise in abject futility, since his choice of murder scenes may have been extremely personal and esoteric and may well have had *absolutely nothing to do with the area where he lived.* Geographic profiling can't possibly account for a killer choosing a location to commit a crime because of its sister-city relationship with his place of birth, which is why Richard Walter has said that geographic profiling is virtually useless for recreational murderers like Zodiac, who kill for fun or sport and who are too smart to fall prey to capture via analysis of the geography of their crimes.

One example of a killer who defied capture via geographic profiling was the Golden State Killer, Joseph Deangelo. Despite the fact that his entire career of scores of rapes and multiple murders from 1976 to 1986 predated the creation of the technique, making it impossible that he was aware of it, efforts to identify the city where he lived failed. Such profiling suggested that he would have lived in Rancho Cordova or Carmichael, California. In fact, he lived in Citrus Heights, California, a nearby city. Rancho Cordova is ten miles from Citrus Heights, and Carmichael seven miles from Citrus Heights.

The stated site of Zodiac's first two attacks, Vallejo, was the sister city to Kjell Qvale's birth city of Trondheim, Norway.

11. Reddish-brown hair. On ABC's October 17, 2002, episode of *Primetime Thursday* about the Zodiac Killer, it was revealed that a small reddish-brown hair had been found beneath one of the stamps on the October 1969 Stine letter. Kjell Qvale also had reddish-brown hair.

Both Kjell Qvale and the Zodiac Killer had reddish-brown hair.

12. Branding. Zodiac is widely credited with having created his own "brand" of murder complete with a logo, the crossed circle, and a catch-

244 · MIKE RODELLI

phrase, "This is the Zodiac speaking." The crossed circle contains all the letters of the name Qvale—Q-V-A-L-E—and serves as the signature of the Zodiac letters (Exhibit 20). Since the crossed circle is known as Odin's cross in Norwegian culture, this symbol serves to link Qvale's name to the highest god in the Norse pantheon. Qvale created his own company and brand names for selling cars (British Motor Car Distributors and Qvale Modena). He also created a logo for Qvale Modena that consisted of the head of a dragon, which clearly harkened back to his Norse roots. On April 28, 1970, Zodiac sent a droll greeting card on which there appeared a miner riding on a dragon.

Zodiac's "logo" contained all the letters of Qvale's name, and the logo for Qvale Modena featured a dragon, a typical Norse symbol which was the theme of Zodiac's April 28, 1970, greeting card.

13. Qvale's Modena building. In 2003, my friend Eduard Versluijs told me something of interest. He said that Qvale owned a car manufacturing building in Modena, Italy, which he had purchased in 1999. On the facade of this building was a giant crossed-circle symbol, the same symbol Zodiac used to sign his letters. The photo on the website was cropped so that you could see only two things: the name Qvale and the crossed circle beneath it (Exhibit 21)—almost as if the site was emphasizing the relationship between the two.

As indicated above, all the letters in the name Qvale can be obtained from a crossed circle. Qvale then placed a giant Q around the crossed circle, thus marrying his initial to that symbol.[109] While it's true that nearly every letter of the alphabet can be derived from the crossed-circle symbol, what suggests a relationship between the crossed circle on the Modena building and the last name Qvale is that the massive Q on the facade of the building surrounding the crossed circle, with its line that comes straight down from the circle to the six o'clock position, is identical in form to the type of Q that one would derive from a crossed-circle

---

109 John Lamm, "The All-New DeTomaso Mangusta," *Road and Track*, November 1999, p. 70.

symbol. In other words, the facade of the building hinted at the first letter and the others could be derived from the circle within the giant *Q*. This would mean there were essentially two iterations of the name Qvale on the facade, an overt one on the sign and a cryptic one that was contained within the crossed circle, making the name above the crossed circle a key of sorts to revealing the meaning of the symbol to Zodiac.

Kjell Qvale purchased a building in 1999 that had a giant crossed circle on the facade and then associated his last initial with the crossed-circle symbol that spells out his last name.

14. British references. It clearly appears that Zodiac, whoever he was, was strongly influenced by British culture. This is widely accepted by students of the Zodiac case, so I won't enumerate those references here. I've discussed those ties throughout this book.

Qvale's ties to England were unquestionable and dated back to 1947. He therefore had an *over sixty-year association* with that country. There is evidence that he was deeply immersed in British culture, which was undoubtedly essential in his business dealings with British car manufacturers and in owning a British car manufacturer in Jensen Motors (located in West Bromwich, Midlands). He began importing British cars in 1947. In an interview he did in a British newspaper during his tenure as the owner of Jensen Motors, he stated, "Lotus [the British sports car company] *are* not going to do that."[110] This is a quintessential British way of referring to a company or a sports team, etc., in the plural instead of the singular. Qvale didn't speak this way in interviews he did in the US, so it shows a dichotomy in his speech patterns and indicates that he could turn British usage on and off depending on the audience. Qvale once said of his life that it "has all been rather exciting," as well as stating in his 1969 letter to the *San Francisco Chronicle* that the paper's failure to act would be "rather expensive for all the people of Northern California" (Exhibit 12). These are examples of typical

---

110 Giles Smith, "More Joint Projects Likely from Jensen-Lotus Talks," *The Times* (London), October 26, 1971, p. 5.

British understatement. Qvale's step-mother, Florence Jacobson, was born in England.[111] This leaves open the question: Did Qvale learn anything about British culture, such as *The Mikado*, from her?

Kjell Qvale had a sixty-year relationship with England and was exposed to British culture during that time.

15. Norse references. The most obvious reference to Norse/Norwegian culture in the Zodiac case is, of course, the 1974 Sla Letter (Exhibit 22). In this letter, Zodiac points out that the initialism SLA, which was prominent in the news at the time after the Symbionese Liberation Army (SLA) had kidnapped newspaper heiress Patricia Hearst, actually has a hidden meaning. As indicated earlier, there has been some quibbling as to what this word actually means in Old Norse. However, Zodiac stated that, in his mind, it meant "kill," and as we'll see, in our 2006 meeting detailed in chapter 22, Qvale also told me that the word meant "kill." Therefore, if Zodiac had a misunderstanding about the meaning of the word, then Qvale interestingly had the *same* misconception.

As noted, the Sla Letter is by far not the only possible Norse reference in the Zodiac case. The envelope of the October 1970 Halloween card to reporter Paul Avery had that strange "return address" (Exhibit 23) consisting of what appear to be two Norse runes, as first pointed out by Eduard Versluijs in the 1990s. As described in chapter 11, these two runes along with the four associated dots appear to comprise a bumerke, the symbol used in Norse countries to identify someone as the source or maker of a given item, or to denote ownership of a piece of land, et cetera (Exhibits 10a–d).

The first of these runes is Ansuz, known as the Rune of Communication. The significance of communication with the public in the Zodiac case is self-evident.

111 Washington State Dept. of Social and Health Services, Certificate of Death #21334.

The second Norse rune in the "return address" is a reversed Laguz, which is the Rune of Water. The possible significance of water in the Zodiac case has been debated for many years. But here potentially is a rune that appears on a Zodiac letter that actually lends credence to the notion of water playing a role in the case. In Norway, water has a dual meaning. It is, of course, the essence of life, since it sustains all living things on Earth. But since Norway is a seafaring country, there is also a darker aspect of water. It can also signify death on the open seas, since water can be treacherous and can take human life through powerful storms or unexpected waves. So, to Norwegians, water represents both life and the specter of sudden death. This is what is meant to be conveyed by the rune Laguz.

There are also *secondary* meanings associated with Ansuz and Laguz. Individual runes, for example, are associated with specific Norse gods. Taken together, the secondary meanings of these two particular runes *essentially define wealthy power-assertive individuals like Zodiac and Qvale.* Ansuz is not only the Rune of Communication; it also represents the highest, most powerful Norse god in its pantheon, Odin. Odin is a cynical god, the god of both wisdom and war, who is distant and emotionally removed from the people he rules. He sits above the world looking down on it but lacks the emotion needed to be a great ruler. He enjoys stirring up strife among his people. He is, in short, aloof and distant, like Zodiac, and just as Qvale was described as being in a 1964 article on him by Tony Hogg. In this article, Hogg devotes a long paragraph to describing how aloof and unapproachable Qvale was. He makes it clear that Qvale had been aloof all of his life, not just since becoming wealthy.[112] Recall that Lindsey Robbins had also stated that Qvale was "aloof as hell." Aloofness is also part of Mr. Walter's power-assertive profile. If Zodiac were going to associate himself with any Norse god, there is no other one with which he could ever identify but the most powerful and exalted—and aloof—god in the Norse pantheon.

---

112 Tony Hogg, "Kjell Qvale," *Road and Track*, February 1964, p. 75.

Laguz is also the rune that represents the Norse god Njord, the god of wealth. In the 1960s, Qvale was obviously extremely wealthy, lived in an exclusive neighborhood, and wrote to me on monarch-sized stationery in 1999. Ultimately, in 2013 he left an estate worth $100 million.

It is significant to note again that Zodiac uses this composite runic symbol/bumerke as both the "return address" on the Avery Halloween card *and* in the place on the inside of the card where his signature should have been. In both places, we'd expect to see the *name* of the person who actually sent the letter. Therefore, the runic symbol is being used quite literally as a cryptic representation of the *identity* of the person who sent the card to Avery.

So who was the Zodiac Killer? Based on the meanings associated with Ansuz and Laguz, what Zodiac may in essence have been saying was that the author of the letter was (a) of Norwegian origin, (b) a wealthy individual, (c) someone who liked to communicate with the public, (d) someone who had a relationship with water (Qvale's father, Bjarne, was a sea captain, and Norway's national identity is that of a seafaring country), (e) someone who was aloof and who viewed himself as being superior to others, and (f) someone who didn't allow emotion to cloud his judgment, as befits both the aloof god Odin, a power-assertive killer, and the imperturbable Zodiac, who slowly and casually strolled away from the Stine murder scene.

In short, these runes encapsulate and embody the salient characteristics of *both* Kjell Qvale and the Zodiac in a symbol that closely resembles a Norse bumerke in both appearance and function.

Yet another Norse reference is the fact that there is a relationship between the god Odin and the concept of the *zodiac*.

In the ancient poem of Grimnismál there are twelve celestial abodes enumerated by way of preeminence, and in the Later Edda, twelve names by which Odin was especially designated. This preference shown in the Mythology for the number twelve has appeared to several interpreters to refer to the divisions of the year among the heathen Northmen, and their reckoning of the sun's course. According to their theory, each of the twelve Æsir was the director of his respective month; the twelve names of Odin were names of the months; *and the twelve celestial abodes denoted the twelve signs of the zodiac [italics mine], which the sun passes through annually.*[113]

As stated in chapter 5, there is also a link between Odin and the crossed-circle symbol. A crossed-circle symbol in Norse mythology, as we have seen, is called Odin's cross (Exhibit 2). This symbol signifies the "highest power" and "the king." Clearly, it's a symbol with which, like the rune Ansuz, a narcissist and egotist like Zodiac would identify. It once again evokes the relationship between Zodiac and Odin.

Just as the composite runic symbol takes the place of the return address and is part of the signature on the Avery Halloween card, so the crossed circle on Zodiac's letters takes the place of a true signature on these letters. Recalling that a crossed circle contains the letters *Q*, *V*, *A*, *L*, and *E*, by applying the crossed circle to the letters as he did, Zodiac *may have in reality been signing a name to the letters*. This again is suggested by his building in Modena, as described above. Some Norse bumerker even resemble a crossed circle, which is in keeping with the concept that Zodiac was actually signing his letters with such symbols (Exhibits 10a–d).

In chapter 5, I discussed the concept of "slaves in the afterlife" as having deep roots in Norse culture. When a wealthy or prominent Viking died, one of his slaves was often chosen to be executed and accompany him to continue his role as a slave who would serve him after death (footnote 12).

As discussed in chapter 11, the word *Thing*, to which Zodiac called our attention by how heavily he wrote it on the November 8, 1969,

---

113 http://www.northvegr.org/secondary%20sources/religion%20culture%20 history/the%20religion%20of%20the%20northmen/011_02.html

Dripping Pen Card, is also a Norse/Viking concept. It is capitalized in this context, as it was on the card.

I have examined Norwegian–English dictionaries over the years. The only words I could find that are derived from the name Kjell are the Norwegian words *kjeller* (cellar) and *kjelleretasje* (basement floor). In his November 9, 1969, letter, Zodiac stated that he was storing his bus bomb in his *basement*. Therefore, even in relating something as seemingly mundane as where he was supposedly storing his bomb, Zodiac may have been providing us with a clue to his identity.

Some researchers have argued that the crossed-circle symbol could be a gun sight, the leader on a movie trailer, a symbol purloined from the face of a Zodiac-brand watch, or any number of other things. They will argue that the symbol on the Avery card is Graysmith's "wide flange beam" symbol, the cattle brand for the Red Ryder or the Vincent Fontana/Big Dipper Ranch, a clue to a suspect's initials in a Freemason's/pigpen cipher,[114] or a clue to that intersection in Vallejo. All of this is certainly possible. Taken in a vacuum and looked at individually, these words, concepts, and symbols may represent virtually *anything*. However, given the *collective* number of apparent references to Norse culture in the letters, as well as the fact that the Sla Letter is essentially a giant neon finger, it calls our attention to the fact that the writer has some connection to Norway. I believe that it's reasonable to argue that the various Norse interpretations I describe above are the correct interpretations of these symbols and references and that they were what the author of the Zodiac letters intended.

Other than the references to popular American culture in the Zodiac letters, such as lapel buttons, and "Blue Meannies," the strongest influences seen in the Zodiac literature are those from *both* England and Norway. There may not be another suspect in the case whose life was impacted as strongly by both of these cultural influences as was Kjell Qvale. And when you add in Zodiac's obsession with power to the

---

114 Lafferty, p. 400.

British and Norse influences in the case, you now begin to see a picture of Kjell Qvale slowly emerging from the shadows of the case.

Kjell Qvale was born and raised for his first ten years in Norway.

16. Ties to automobiles. (See discussion in chapter 24.)
Kjell Qvale was closely associated with cars.

17. Qvale served in the military as a naval flier in World War II.
One thing that most Zodiac researchers agree on is the influence of the military in the Zodiac case, due in part to Zodiac's naval look at Lake Berryessa. Semaphore symbols, which are used on flags to wave planes onto the decks of carriers, are used in Zodiac's coded messages and may provide a hidden clue about the author's military background. In addition, the killer used some military phrases in his letters, like "come out of cover," "wipe out a school bus," and "pick off the kiddies." As a World War II pilot, Qvale would have learned at least some combination of the following: Morse code, navigation and navigational terms, and semaphore flags. He would have been familiar with such Zodiac-related items as flight shoes (wing walkers), and he was also exposed to sidearms and marksmanship.

It should be noted that there is no proof that Zodiac was very proficient with weapons; he was certainly, it seems, no marksman. As discussed earlier, he was unable to kill Mike Mageau despite having a free head shot from a foot or two away at a stationary and unsuspecting target. He then blamed Mageau for "spoiling his aim" on his initial shot at Mike's head, saying Mageau had "leapt backwards" at the precise moment of the shot. According to Mageau's account, this didn't happen; the killer had simply missed. He barely hit the lower part of the long cargo compartment window of the Faraday station wagon and apparently missed the rear passenger's-side window entirely. Zodiac himself later admitted to "spraying" his bullets like a "water hose," something, as stated earlier, a proud and skilled marksman would never admit to doing. Therefore, a minimum of training with a gun in the military, such as that which a noncombat transport pilot like Qvale might receive, would be consistent with what we know about the killer's level of marksmanship.

The shoes Zodiac wore at Lake Berryessa were wing walkers. These are used by flight crews to walk safely on the wings of aircraft, thus pointing directly at not only a military man, but more precisely at a pilot clad in naval-type clothes. Qvale was exactly that, a World War II naval pilot as per the yearbook detailing his military training.[115] In Qvale's 1942 military yearbook, there is mention of a cadet becoming a "wing walker" at the end of a bombing run in order to assist preparing the plan for return to the hangar. So this terminology was being used in the era of Qvale's training.[116]

Kjell Qvale was in the navy, and his military service in World War II proves he had sidearm and semaphore training and exposure to the notion of wing walkers, which is relevant to the Zodiac case.

18. Road races. In his October 13, 1969, Stine letter, Zodiac made the observation that the police could have apprehended him after he killed the cab driver if they had "searched the park properly instead of holding *road races* with their motor cicles [*sic*]" (italics mine). This unusual terminology is suggestive of someone associated with auto racing. At the very least, this seems to reveal Zodiac as someone who was familiar with racing terminology. The average person would probably have said something more to the effect of the cops being able to catch him if they had not been "racing each other," or "racing around the park."

In November 2008, I received an email from a Zodiac researcher named Nick R., who stated that he had spoken to Qvale earlier that year about business-related matters. During the course of their conversation,

---

115 USNAS, *Mark II of the Slipstream* (Montgomery, AL: The Paragon Press, 1942), p. 54.

116 USNAS, *op. cit.*, numberless page in section "Squadrons 18-A and 18-B Main Station Field."

Qvale used a phrase that stuck out in his mind: he said that he used to be involved with the "road races" at Laguna Seca.

To further reinforce that Qvale used such terminology, in his autobiography he states, "In 1950, a true road race was planned in our region."[117] Qvale goes on to state that he was the chairman for those races and helped to organize them. The poster for that event states at the top "ROAD RACE" (Exhibit 24). As the event chairman, Qvale may well have worded, or at least approved, the poster.

Kjell Qvale used the unusual phrase "road races," just as Zodiac used that phrase in writing about the night of the Stine murder. Qvale actually organized road races in the 1950s.

19. Stine Letter/November 9 letter references. With the October 13, 1969, letter that Zodiac wrote after the murder of Paul Stine, he immediately began to feed his pursuers proof that he had never left the search area that night. Many amateur researchers have tried to say that the killer was lying and that he had quickly fled the area via car or on foot and simply provided details in his letters that he had gleaned from the local newspaper accounts of that night. However, to an attentive reader, Zodiac seems to provide subtle, but definite, evidence to the contrary.

The auditory clues Zodiac describes in both this letter and his November 9, 1969, Bus Bomb Letter (see discussion in chapter 11)—such as motorcycles and cars racing around to see "who could make the most noise," dogs barking, and fire trucks being used to mask the sounds of the patrol cars—seem to bolster Zodiac's claim that, despite the large manhunt that took place that night, he had remained in the area. He was there. He was not only watching but he was within earshot and *listening* to the search as it evolved. A newspaper reporter likely would have described the things he or she had seen. Zodiac, on the other hand, gave himself away as having been in the area by describing what he *heard*.

---

117 Qvale, p. 99.

For someone who didn't have a safe haven in the area in which to hide—or a valid reason to be on the streets of that neighborhood at the time—remaining in the park area and subject to capture would have been extraordinarily foolhardy behavior. That was especially true if Zodiac were captured and still had any of Stine's blood on his clothing or person and had the large piece of bloodstained shirt in his possession. But for someone who lived in the neighborhood and was simply outside in his yard 150 feet from Spruce Street, or on the streets walking his dog, or watching and listening from his living room after the murder, the sounds of that night would have been essentially all around him.

In a 2010 conversation I had with SFPD inspector Vince Repetto, he expressed the opinion that Zodiac did not leave the search area that evening.

Qvale not only lived directly adjacent to the search area across the street from the Kahn Playground, but an SFPD officer spoke to him shortly after the crime took place on the streets of Presidio Heights, precisely where all of the action of the search that Zodiac described took place.

Given the proximity of his home to the police search area and his presence on the streets, Kjell Qvale would have been able to describe the sounds of the police search following the murder of Paul Stine as mentioned in Zodiac's subsequent letters.

20. Attention-seeking behavior. Qvale's 1947 flying-saucer sighting was clearly an attention-seeking event in his life that put him on the front pages of two Bay Area newspapers. However, there are other examples of what appear to be attention seeking by Qvale, a trait that makes him a behavioral match for the Zodiac.

In 1964 Qvale purchased the world-renowned racehorse Silky Sullivan. He acquired the horse after its racing days were over and claimed that he bought it for "stud duty," even though an article in *Sports Illustrated* printed just prior to the 1955 Kentucky Derby pointed out just how undistinguished a pedigree Silky had compared to some of the other horses in the race.[118] Silky was a freakish horse because of his running style, and there was nothing in its pedigree to indicate it would be a useful sire.

What did happen after Qvale purchased Silky Sullivan is that the horse made his owner somewhat of a celebrity. To be perfectly clear, the horse was already a huge attraction when Qvale purchased it: Kjell Qvale did not make Silky Sullivan a star. Rather, it was Silky Sullivan that helped promote Qvale and Golden Gate Fields and who made Kjell Qvale a minor luminary simply by virtue of the fact that he owned the horse. Qvale would parade Silky Sullivan through Golden Gate Fields every St. Patrick's Day to the adulation of the crowd. In the photo I obtained of Qvale from 1999, there is a lady in the background reaching out to the horse in what almost looks like religious adoration (Exhibit 13). Since it was Qvale who held the reins of the horse, by extension he must have also felt the adoration of the crowd. Qvale had accomplished nothing other than to purchase the fame that accompanied this horse. In fact, the *Turf and Sport Digest* article that included the photo of Qvale and the horse was titled "The Man Who Owns Silky Sullivan." It was not called "Silky Sullivan and His Owner" (footnote 60). The article is predominantly about Qvale, his exploits at the track and his business endeavors. Only about 10 percent of the article is about the horse. Thus the title, which uses the horse as a reason to speak about its owner.

In 1964, Qvale used the purchase of a racehorse to draw circus-like attention to himself, attention that this time was both immediate and nationwide. In May of that year, he purchased a horse named The Scoundrel from a man named Rex Ellsworth for $500,000, an exorbitant price that was all but unheard of in those days, especially since the horse was virtually unproven.[119] The Scoundrel had not yet even completed his three-year-old season and was therefore extraordinarily light

---

118 "Kentucky Derby," *Sports Illustrated*, April 28, 1958, p. 10.

119 Anonymous, "Scoundrel Sold to S.F. Auto Dealer—$500,000," *San Francisco Chronicle*, May 23, 1964, p. 37.

on accomplishments and thus seemingly not anywhere near worth the type of money Qvale put out to own it.[120] It had already run in two legs of the Triple Crown (the Kentucky Derby and the Preakness) before Qvale purchased it, winning neither, so it wasn't even distinguishing itself against horses its own age, like Northern Dancer, nor against older, more seasoned horses of the time, like Kelso, to warrant such an exorbitant purchase price. But what did happen is that newspapers from coast to coast picked up the story of the whopping purchase price. When the horse went lame less than a week after Qvale purchased it, he again shocked people when he simply brushed off the lost investment of half a million dollars as "bad luck."[121] But the horse had already bought Qvale widespread publicity in the sports pages of many newspapers, especially since its first race was to coincide with Qvale entering the three cars in the 1964 Indy 500. Both horse and cars were to race on the same weekend. Just as Qvale's 1947 flying-saucer description was way above the norm and served to make Qvale stand out from other faces in the crowd, so too did his purchase of The Scoundrel.

Like the 1949 spectacle of driving an MG under a lumber carrier, the 1964 purchase of The Scoundrel was a stunt P. T. Barnum himself would likely have been proud of.

Kjell Qvale liked to attract attention to himself through proxies.

21. Lapel buttons. Might there possibly be a connection between Kjell Qvale and lapel buttons? Interestingly, in the photo of Qvale with Silky Sullivan, Qvale is shown wearing two lapel buttons on his suit jacket (Exhibit 13). The article appeared in *Turf and Sport Digest* in August of 1970.[122] The one reference in the article that allows us to pinpoint

---

120 $500,000 in 1964 was the equivalent of approximately $3.1 million in 2017.

121 Gil Lyons, "Remember Kjell Qvale? He Still Runs First," *Seattle Times*, December 17, 1964, p. 55.

122 Jim Scott, "The Man Who Owns Silky Sullivan," Turf and Sport Digest, (Baltimore: Montee Publishing, August 1970), pp. 30–34.

the date of the interview that formed the basis of the article is Qvale's reference to a horse of his, named Mirror Time, winning a race after losing for a period of time. Mirror Time won the sixth race at Golden Gate Fields on March 4, 1970. The racing meet had only started a week earlier. Zodiac's Dragon Card requesting the people of the Bay Area to wear Zodiac lapel buttons was written April 28 of that year. All that can be concluded from this photo is that Qvale was aware of and not averse to wearing such buttons, despite his lofty socioeconomic status. However, the timing of the article just a few months *after* Zodiac's April letter piques one's interest: magazine articles are generally prepared several months in advance. It's possible that, in finding the right photograph to accompany the August article, Qvale chose one sometime just *prior to* April 28, 1970, the date of Zodiac's Dragon Card that references lapel buttons. Could the photo have been the inspiration for Zodiac writing about lapel buttons seemingly out of the blue?

In a March 17, 1970, St. Patrick's Day article in the *Chronicle*,[123] the *same* photo, of Qvale wearing lapel buttons and standing next to Silky Sullivan, was included that would later appear in the August 1970 *Turf and Sport Digest* article. Due to the horse's late-February birthday and his English sire, as well as his Irish-sounding name, Qvale used to show him off to the crowd at Golden Gate Fields every St. Patrick's Day, thus the article. This photo therefore appeared to be Qvale's go-to photo for such stories. It's possible that toward the end of April 1970 the author of the *Turf and Sport Digest* piece, Jim Scott, asked Qvale for a photo to submit to the publisher with the article. In looking at this photo once again, Qvale may have been reminded of lapel buttons just in time to include such a reference in the April 28 greeting card that he sent as Zodiac.

The fact that Qvale wore lapel buttons also demonstrates that, even though he wasn't part of the youth culture, like Zodiac, he was

---

123 Anonymous, "Silky Leaves the Harem," *San Francisco Chronicle*, March 17, 1970, p. 50.

attuned to the pop culture references of the time, such as the reference to "Blue Meannies" in Zodiac's 1971 *Los Angeles Times* letter.

Qvale can be shown to have worn lapel buttons in the 1960s.

22. Riverside. As stated earlier, the first crime with which Zodiac has been associated is the October 30, 1966, murder of Cheri Jo Bates in Riverside, California. Amazingly, Qvale was very likely present in that city on the very weekend she was murdered, because he had entered one of his "Genie" race cars into that year's running of the *Los Angeles Times* Grand Prix.[124] Although his car got taken out of the race the day before due to mechanical problems, Qvale was present in Riverside that weekend.

While it's a matter of debate as to whether or not Zodiac killed Cheri Jo Bates, he has been linked to the case for nearly fifty years through the three "Bates Had to Die" letters he sent (as per analysis of the hand printing on the envelopes) exactly six months after the murder, on April 30, 1967. This coincided with yet another major automobile race at the Riverside track.[125] It's possible that, although he had no car entered, Qvale went south from San Francisco to watch the April 1967 race as a fan and member of that industry and mailed the three "Bates Had to Die" letters when he was down there. He also had friends, such as Pedro Rodriguez, driving cars in that event.

Thus, a man who lived just down the street from Zodiac's last murder scene can also be logically tied through auto racing to the site of the 1966 murder of Cheri Jo Bates in Riverside *on the very weekend on which she was murdered*, as well as to the weekend on which Zodiac sent the "Bates Had to Die" letters.

Kjell Qvale lived in San Francisco close to where cabbie Paul Stine was murdered but also had valid reasons to be in Riverside

---

124 Times Grand Prix program, October 30, 1966, car #11.

125 United States Road Racing program, April 29–30, 1967.

both on the weekend that Cheri Jo Bates was murdered and when the "Bates Had to Die" letters were mailed six months later.

23. Meticulousness. As noted in chapter 5, Zodiac's coded messages were constructed by an extremely meticulous writer. In a 1964 article in the *Daily Racing Form*, Qvale is described as "as meticulous a man one is likely to come across."[126]

Kjell Qvale demonstrated the type of attention to detail necessary to construct Zodiac's obsessively neat blocks of code.

24. Melvin Belli Connection. In a 1952 article about a high-class dinner party that was being held in the Bay Area, both Kjell Qvale and Melvin Belli are named as invited guests.[127] Belli was the brunt of a Zodiac prank with the October 22, 1969, run-around on the Jim Dunbar show and a target for one of Zodiac's letters in December 1969, and Zodiac mocked Belli in his April 28, 1970, letter with the "Melvin eats bluber" lapel button.

Kjell Qvale and Melvin Belli, whom Zodiac needled in his letters and to whom he also sent a letter in December 1969, moved in the same circles and more than likely were acquainted with one another.

25. William "Peek-a-Boo" Pennington. In early 2015, a message-board poster with the screen name Blind Bat posted an ad from a 1946 Oakland, California, yellow pages for a private investigator named William V. Pennington. Mr. Pennington specialized in divorce cases, and the photo on the internet proved that he had worked closely

---

126 Leon Rasmussen, "Fast Horses Add Up to Success for 'Mr. K. Q.'," *Daily Racing Form,* June 4, 1964. Thanks to Chris MacRae.

127 Anonymous, "Charles Jones' Plan Large Cocktail Party," *Daily Independent Journal,* October 6, 1952. Thanks to "Coffee Time," a poster on zodiackillersite.com.

with Melvin Belli (Exhibit 8). Belli figures prominently into the Zodiac case from the October 1969 incident on Jim Dunbar's show and the December 20, 1969, letter that the Zodiac addressed to him.

Mr. Pennington's nickname in the ad was Peek-a-Boo. This nickname immediately jumped off the page as having a strong possibility of being the inspiration for one of Zodiac's most unusual pieces of correspondence. In place of the two letter Os in the word BOO in Pennington's ad, there were little eyes complete with eyelashes. These eyes exclusively look down and to the right. And in the word PEEK, there was a three-stroke K, the uniquely formed letter that is most associated with Zodiac's hand printing.

In October 1970, Zodiac sent his strange Halloween card to reporter Paul Avery. Inside the card was a cryptic statement: "PEEK-A-BOO YOU ARE DOOMED!" For over forty years, this was widely perceived as being a threat on Avery's life. Also on the Halloween card are the little eyes complete with eyelashes that, like the ones on the Pennington ad, look exclusively down and to the right. It's difficult to imagine another explanation for these similarities other than the Pennington ad being their basis. Next: Might the three-stroke K in PEEK in the Pennington ad have been the impetus for Zodiac making his Ks in that manner? If so, those handwriting experts who preached that Zodiac's printing could be identified via this unusual alphabetic character alone were led off on a tangent. Conversely, these experts felt that any suspect who didn't make a three-stroke K could be ruled out based solely on this character. Given the possibility that this letter mimicked the K in the ad and was not part of the writer's normal letter formations, eliminating suspects in this manner would potentially be catastrophic and play right into Zodiac's hands. Finally, there is the name Peek-a-Boo. The wording on the Avery Halloween card was "PEEK-A-BOO YOU ARE DOOMED!" As discussed earlier, in light of this extraordinary ad, is it possible that the 1970 Halloween card was actually meant to be a veiled threat against William Pennington masquerading as an apparent threat against Paul Avery?

But why a threat against Peek-a-Boo Pennington?

William Pennington's specific role in divorce cases was spying on married men, specifically *wealthy* married men. He would attempt to surprise his targets while in the midst of a tryst and photograph them in flagrante delicto. He would then apparently turn over his incriminating photos to Belli for litigation and hopefully a big settlement for the married man's wife. Of all the known Zodiac suspects, there are undoubtedly very few who were both **wealthy enough *and* old enough** in the late 1940s or early 1950s, and who lived in the Bay Area, to have drawn Pennington's attention. (The tail therefore wagged the dog, as evidence like the Pennington ad was dismissed when it didn't fit certain suspects.) And one of that minute handful would have been someone like Kjell Qvale.

If Zodiac had it in for Pennington, and the issue was a professional one, then Zodiac might have been much older than most people believe. This is based on the years during which Pennington was active. In fact, when the Pennington ad was first uncovered, its importance was minimized and even dismissed by most researchers because their favorite suspects weren't old enough to have seen the Pennington ad in the late 1940s. Plus they weren't wealthy enough or even married in the 1940s to have come to Pennington's attention during that time period. Not so with Qvale.

Given that Belli and Pennington can now be linked together, this begins to explain some of the previously inexplicable things in the case. The Zodiac appears to have targeted *both* of these men at various times in his letters—one overtly (Belli) and one cryptically (Pennington). Linking the two men through their work on divorce cases makes sense out of seemingly unrelated events.

One fascinating possibility about how Pennington came to receive a threat from the Zodiac comes from a statement by Cesar Romero playing the magician, the Great Rhadini, in the 1939 movie *Charlie Chan at Treasure Island*. Rhadini is in the business of exposing charlatan fortune tellers. In response to a comment by Charlie Chan about blackmail, Rhadini states that the sham fortune tellers (like a character in the movie, known as Dr. Zodiac) often dig up dirt on people and then use that information to blackmail and extort money from them. This might be viewed as being analogous to Pennington's role as a private investigator in his partnership with Melvin Belli, where they targeted married men with roving eyes, caught them in the act, and then extracted, that is, extorted, handsome settlements from them. In short, the Belli-Pennington team behaved just like Dr. Zodiac.

At the end of the movie, Rhadini himself is exposed as being the phony psychic, Dr. Zodiac, who is the one digging up the dirt on wealthy people in San Francisco. Therefore, the person who was crusading against the "dirt diggers" (Rhadini) was also named Zodiac. The movie plot's analogy to the role Pennington played and the presence of the name Zodiac in the movie provide food for thought as to the origin of the Zodiac's self-ascribed name. We will see in chapter 23 that a **Dr. Z** would crop up in Qvale's life in 2010 in a context similar to the plot of the Charlie Chan movie.

The Peek-a-Boo Pennington revelation has added a fascinating new dimension to an already complex case. Are Pennington's investigative records still extant in some storage facility? Might they contain the name of the Zodiac? My efforts to locate one of Pennington's descendants in 2015 were unsuccessful.

Qvale is one of the few suspects ever developed in the Zodiac case who was both old enough and wealthy enough to have possibly come to the attention of William "Peek-a-Boo" Pennington, whose 1940s' ad appears to be the basis for Zodiac's 1970 Halloween card to Paul Avery.

26. SFPD officer Armond Pelissetti/The night of the Stine murder.
The murder of Paul Stine took place just over two city blocks from Qvale's home. The original destination of the cab was Washington and Maple Streets, to which Zodiac alluded in his October 13, 1969, letter. That location was a shorter and therefore much faster and less perilous

walk from Qvale's home than the actual murder site at Cherry Street. But there is much more to the night of the Stine murder than meets the eye with respect to Qvale.

As indicated in chapter 9, shortly after Stine's murder was called in to SFPD, Officers Frank Peda and Armond Pelissetti arrived on the scene. After getting the eyewitnesses to the safety of their home, inspecting the cab, and changing the description of the perpetrator to a white male, Pelissetti took off on foot in the direction in which the killer was last seen heading by eyewitness Lindsey Robbins. Pelissetti said on the DVD that accompanied the director's cut of the movie *Zodiac* that he began walking slowly north on Cherry Street, carefully searching for the perpetrator. As Pelissetti approached Jackson Street, Officers Don Fouke and Eric Zelms drove around the corner of Cherry from Jackson. Fouke spoke briefly with Pelissetti, and Pelissetti informed him that they were looking for a white male. Pelissetti then walked north to the corner of Cherry and Jackson Streets and had to make a decision: Should he go right or left? He stated in 2006[128] and on the *Zodiac* DVD in 2008[129] that *he made a decision* to turn right and head east on Jackson Street. The fact that he had to make any decision at all proves that whatever the conversation was or was not with Don Fouke, *Pelissetti did not know that Fouke had seen a white male near the corner of Maple and Jackson Streets.* Otherwise, he would immediately have known to go east, toward Maple Street, where Fouke had just spotted the man walking down Jackson Street, without his having to make any decision as to which direction to walk. But even if Fouke had unequivocally informed him of his sighting, there was no actual proof that the man Fouke had seen was Stine's killer, even though the man was clearly worth checking out. Therefore, Pelissetti would have been wise to proceed slowly and carefully down Jackson east to Maple *regardless* so that he didn't pass by a gunman hiding in one of the short sets of stairs that lead up to the homes on the south side of Jackson, or

128 Michael Butterfield, personal communication, June 2006.

129 Fincher, *This Is the Zodiac Speaking,* "San Francisco," 2008.

one who was hiding under or behind a car, and get shot in the back as he passed. Pelissetti was without vest, communications, or backup in 1969. However, he stated in 2006 that he walked *very quickly* and got to the corner of Jackson and Maple Streets in what he described as being a very small amount of time, the significance of which will become evident shortly. He said that when he arrived at the corner of Maple and Jackson Streets, he had to make yet another decision: Should he turn left and take a chance searching by the Presidio wall, where it was dark and where a gunman could easily find concealment, or should he turn right and head back south on Maple Street toward Washington? He decided to turn right at the corner at Maple Street and head south to Washington Street.

Officer Pelissetti stated that after turning the corner to walk up the hill to Washington Street, he ran into a man who was out with his dog. Who was this man? For the answer, I want to go back to January 2004.

In late 2003, I was searching for a way to contact Officer Don Fouke. I decided to try to do so through Officer Pelissetti, who had worked out of the same station house as Fouke. I called people in the San Francisco Bay Area white pages with the name Pelissetti and eventually found a relative of his, who asked him to contact me.

On January 12, 2004, I was heading out the door for my father's birthday. The phone rang and I decided to answer it. On the other end was Armond Pelissetti. He didn't provide me with any information whatsoever on how to reach Officer Fouke, but that clearly wasn't the purpose of his call. Rather, he said to me that my suspect (whom he did not mention by name) "[had] an alibi" and had been "eliminated." When I asked him what that alibi was, he refused to tell me, but he sarcastically advised me that if I "[had] any friends" at SFPD, they could fill me in on the details. He then wished me good luck in a manner I viewed as taunting, and he ended the call. I sensed that he enjoyed holding whatever information he had over my head and was left to wonder, for what would be over two years, what the alibi was. Needless to say, Pelissetti must have known who my suspect was in order to know that he'd allegedly been cleared. After all, unlike some other Zodiac researchers, I have only had one.

In 2006, Zodiac researcher Mike Butterfield and I were discussing the case. As part of the work he was doing, he had spoken to retired inspector Pelissetti. He told Butterfield that after he rounded the corner on Maple Street, he ran into a man with a dog on a leash who was apparently behaving oddly enough to attract his attention (Exhibit 25). The man was, according to Butterfield's account, not actually walking his dog but standing still, presumably on Maple Street. He was wearing very casual clothing—either a robe or a smoking jacket. Pelissetti stated that he spoke to the man, who said he hadn't seen anything unusual. But according to Butterfield's recounting of the story, the contact between the man and Pelissetti didn't end there, as one might have expected for a potential witness who hadn't seen anything. Pelissetti indicated that as he saw different people walk by, he would temporarily leave the man and then, after speaking to the other person, come back to the man with the dog and speak with him some more. Why? He appeared to have no investigative leads to give the officer, who was at that time in hot pursuit of a killer. If this had been just some random man who was innocently walking a dog and had absolutely nothing to do with the case, why did Pelissetti waste precious time and make a point of continually coming back to him? He made the man identify himself and account for his time.

He identified the man as being Kjell Qvale.[130]

---

130 Many people have asked why Qvale would have been out on the streets so quickly after his encounter with Fouke and Zelms. Put yourself in his place. He presumably thought he had fooled Fouke into thinking he was "just a resident of 3712 Jackson Street walking home." He fit seamlessly into that neighborhood. How could he have known that Fouke felt that the man had "faked him out"? Qvale must have felt that the police search was going to take place at or near the crime scene. He needed details of that search for his subsequent letters. So he may have felt that there was no danger in him being out walking his dog. He apparently had no fear that he had been seen by the kids or anyone else at the crime scene due to how slowly he had walked away from it.

Almost unimaginably, Pelissetti told Butterfield that it was actually he who was providing Qvale with the alibi he had mentioned to me in 2004! His doing so is based on something as subjective as the speed with which Pelissetti got from the crime scene to the encounter point with Qvale near Jackson and Maple. Pelissetti said he walked there "too quickly" for Qvale to have been Zodiac. Qvale wouldn't have had time, according to Pelissetti, to make it home, change clothes, make it back onto the streets, and get to the spot where Pelissetti had encountered him.

Pelissetti made it clear to Butterfield that he didn't want me to know this information. But since Butterfield had to verify part of the story against facts about that night that only I possessed from the Jim Dean interviews with the Stine eyewitnesses, he immediately called me and told me what Pelissetti had said. Why would Pelissetti not want me to know that he had spoken to Qvale on the night of the Stine murder, especially if this served as an official police alibi to clear him as a suspect and give me reason to end my own inquiries? Why all the secrecy surrounding this alibi? In 2011 things would become even stranger, as Pelissetti would change his story and undermine his own credibility.

Shortly after speaking to Officer Pelissetti, Butterfield called Qvale to get his side of the story of the night of the Stine murder. Qvale added even more confusion to the story by stating that it was not he to whom Pelissetti spoke that night. Qvale made the odd, noncommittal statement to Butterfield that he *"should have been"* in England" that night. But recall that ABC News has previously said that it couldn't place Qvale outside the country at any of his "usual haunts" for any of the Zodiac murders. This conversation between Qvale and Butterfield would lead directly to my decision to go to San Francisco to speak to Qvale face-to-face that fall.

Presumably, Officer Pelissetti would have worked his way just as slowly and cautiously down Jackson to Maple as he said he had worked his way up Cherry to Jackson, *since he never learned that the potential suspect had made it all the way to Maple Street and that Officer Fouke had spotted him.* So how much time was *really* involved in Pelissetti's trek? In addition, unless Pelissetti knew Qvale prior to their encounter, which seems unlikely given that Pelissetti said he made Qvale identify himself, he could not have known that Qvale was a track champion in his youth who had unofficially tied the record held by Jesse Owens, and that he was most likely still very quick on his feet even at the age of fifty. How quickly could Qvale have gotten home after encountering Fouke? A lot faster than Pelissetti might have imagined.

After encountering Officers Fouke and Zelms, Qvale could have entered the park at Maple Street and then sprinted back to his property under the cover of darkness. Of interest is that when Ed Neil and I first visited Presidio Heights in 1999 and walked on West Pacific Avenue behind the row of homes on the north side of Jackson Street that included Qvale's, he showed me that, in the yard immediately east of Qvale's residence, there was a gate in the wall that separates the back yard of that home from the Presidio (Exhibit 26). If that gate was in fact there in 1969, Qvale could have planned to run home on West Pacific, enter his neighbor's yard through that gate, and then make it safely onto his own property adjacent to that neighbor's back yard. That gate has since been removed.

When Officer Pelissetti wrote up the official police report of the night of the Stine murder that is available online today, he failed to include one word of the encounter with Qvale or even of a dog walker in general. Why is that the case if he not only encountered Qvale but is now providing him with his alibi? Is there a report on this encounter somewhere in SFPD's files? Pelissetti has indicated to me and others several times that there is; however, prying it loose from the department is an exercise in futility.

I believe it is all but unprecedented for a person of interest in a major serial killer case to get his alibi directly from a member of the very police department that is supposed to be investigating him. With retired inspector Pelissetti giving Qvale his alibi, I at least understood why I hadn't gotten anywhere with SFPD in the first place.

Since I never take anything for granted, I wanted to follow up as vigorously as possible with Pelissetti to make sure he was dead certain about what he said to Butterfield in 2006. I felt I couldn't follow up with him myself, so I asked Jim Dean to once again be the point man in this quest to establish that Pelissetti was 100 percent certain that he had spoken to Qvale.

I had Jim call Pelissetti at a work number I had gotten for him. Over the course of about a year, starting in 2007, Pelissetti, who seemed to be quite cagey when speaking about the events of the night of October 11, 1969, identified Qvale three times in three different ways as being the man to whom he had spoken. In the initial call, he stated to Jim, "If that clown from New Jersey is right, he'll sure make an ass out of me." To me, this indicated that Pelissetti's underlying motive in all of this was to protect his image for posterity, not to assist in solving the Zodiac case regardless of where that solution may have led. Now, there were not many "clowns from New Jersey" who had a suspect in the case in 2007, so I have to assume he was speaking about me. He refused to refer to Qvale by his actual name at that time. In a subsequent call from Jim several months later, Pelissetti stated the name of the man he had spoken to as being Qvale. Finally, in a letter that Pelissetti sent to Jim on November 24, 2007, he wrote out the name of the man to whom he had spoken that night. Qvale is the name he clearly printed in the letter.[131]

There would've been little reason in 1969 for Officer Pelissetti to have considered Qvale a suspect in an eight-dollar cab robbery. In fact, when Zodiac later took credit for the Stine murder, there would've been even *less* reason for someone in 1969 to have considered someone with a reputation in the community like Qvale possessed to be a possible suspect. That would have to wait for crime scene assessment to establish what type of individual the killer actually was, but this was obviously long in the future. Pelissetti indicated to Jim that he doubted Qvale was responsible for the Stine murder based on these criteria: his age,

---

131 Jim Dean, personal communication, 2007.

since he was older than the described age of the suspect; his dress that evening, which was different from that described for the suspect; the fact that he had no blood on his clothing; that he was a resident of the wealthy Presidio Heights neighborhood; and the circumstances of their meeting (i.e., how quickly Pelissetti got around the block).

In March 2011, a different amateur researcher, whom I will call Mark, spoke to Pelissetti. Pelissetti changed his story and now stated that "the man [Qvale] was on his own property,"[132] which was located at 3636 Jackson Street. That address is east of Maple Street. This was completely new information that doesn't jibe with anything Pelissetti had been saying both publicly and privately since 2006. Pelissetti had never even indicated that he ventured farther east on Jackson Street than Maple Street that night. Now he was placing himself a half block east of Maple Street at (or opposite) 3636 Jackson and placing Qvale in his own front yard, as opposed to on Maple Street near Jackson Street (Exhibit 25).

In 2006 Pelissetti had stated that he was providing Qvale an alibi based on how quickly he (Pelissetti) had walked from the crime scene to their meeting place near Maple Street and Jackson Street. But now Pelissetti was changing his story. Was he now saying that Qvale didn't have enough time to get home, change his clothes, grab his dog, and *make it into his own front yard?* Remember: in the new version of the story, Qvale doesn't have to walk from his home to Maple Street, and Pelissetti now has to walk the *additional* distance from Maple Street to Qvale's home. So the timeline has changed considerably and seems to destroy Pelissetti's alibi based on time.[133]

---

132 "Mark," personal communication, March 2011.

133 Zodiac stated in his November 9, 1969, letter that motorcycles went by 150 feet from his position going from south to northwest. This would be true if you consider the northwest corner of Spruce Street and imagine Qvale standing in the eastern part of his front yard, which is *almost exactly* 150 feet west of Spruce Street and Jackson Street. See wording on quitclaim deed for exact distance of Qvale's home from Spruce Street.

Mark informed Pelissetti that he had personally spoken to Qvale and that Qvale had contested Pelissetti's version of events, stating that he "should have been in England" that evening. In reality, this was a bluff based on what Qvale had actually told Mike Butterfield, and later me[134] in 2006; Mark had never spoken to Qvale. Instead of asking what Qvale might be hiding with his misdirection with regard to where he was that night, Pelissetti doubled down on his version of events and even told Mark that Qvale's strategy with amateur investigators was *to intentionally provide untruthful answers in order to get them to go away.* He told Mark, "The man is telling you something to get rid of you."[135] And this is apparently fine with Pelissetti.

Pelissetti is very matter of fact about the notion that he encountered Qvale that night. So what Qvale was telling Butterfield in 2006, Jim and me the same year, and then Mark in 2011 was *clearly a lie regarding the events of that evening.* Put another way, Qvale was implicitly acknowledging that by telling the truth about the night of the Stine murder, people would tend to be *more* interested, not *less* interested, in him as a suspect. What I would have asked Pelissetti had I been part of the 2011 conversation with Mark is this: *Why wouldn't the truth make someone like me go away and leave Qvale alone? Conversely, why did Qvale find the truth as to his whereabouts that evening to be so distasteful if he had nothing to hide? Why didn't Qvale's outright lying bother Pelissetti in any way?*

The odd relationship between Qvale and SFPD through Armond Pelissetti, who later became a homicide inspector, seems to be, to say the least, disturbing. Sadly, Armond Pelissetti appears to have lost his objectivity and therefore appears to have a stake in my case. When he said to Jim that I would "make an ass out of him" if I am right, he tips his hand to what that stake apparently is. But is there more at stake than just Pelissetti's image?

---

134 See chapter 18.

135 "Mark," personal communication, March 2011.

What is the reason for Pelissetti's ever-shifting story? The passage of time and the clouding of memories is certainly one possibility. However, Pelissetti seems extremely lucid when he's interviewed for various shows dedicated to the case and when people like Jim and Mike Butterfield speak to him. Yet his story about Qvale is continually evolving—and becoming more damning for Qvale over time.

Regardless of Armond Pelissetti's opinion of Qvale's guilt or innocence, his evolving account of that night does three things: (1) Given how adamant he is that he spoke to Qvale somewhere in Presidio Heights on the night of the Stine murder, he proves conclusively (along with the statements made by ABC News producer Harry Phillips in 2001 about Phillips not being able to place Qvale outside the country at any of his "usual haunts" for any of the Zodiac murders) that Qvale was clearly not telling the truth when he said he was out of the country that night. (2) Given that his story has changed over the years and also taking into consideration Qvale's history as a championship sprinter who could have run home very quickly after his encounter with Officer Fouke, it is impossible for Pelissetti to give Qvale an alibi for the Stine murder based on how quickly he encountered Qvale that night. (3) Pelissetti would have no credibility on the witness stand with respect to any alibi due to the changes to his story, first placing Qvale on the streets of Presidio Heights and then in his front yard.

Kjell Qvale was spoken to by SFPD officer Armond Pelissetti on the streets of Presidio Heights shortly after the Stine murder. He is therefore the _only_ person who later became a suspect in the case who was spoken to by the police for any reason after any of the Zodiac crimes. Qvale would later try to say he was in England that night, thus contradicting both Pelissetti's account and information gathered by ABC News in 2001 indicating that Qvale was not in England on the night Stine was killed.

27. Interest in movies. The Zodiac seems to have possibly been influenced by the movie *The Most Dangerous Game*. There was a Dr. Zodiac character in *Charlie Chan at Treasure Island*. It is also possible that he referenced *El Spectre Rojo* in the Count Marco letter. In 1975 Qvale produced his own movie, *Assault on Agathon*, thus demonstrating an interest in that business.

Several aspects of the Zodiac case may be derived from old movies, and Qvale himself once produced a movie.

28. Zodiac was likely an older individual in 1969. Many people view Zodiac as having been a "crazy hippie." However, there are hints throughout the letters and crimes that Zodiac may not have been a young man in 1969. At the time, people who were familiar with the slang of that era noticed that the term "getting your rocks off with a girl" from the Three-Part Cipher was apparently an outdated phrase. Zodiac wore old-fashioned pleated pants at Lake Berryessa and in Presidio Heights, which were commented on by *both* Bryan Hartnell and Officer Fouke. He also used the word *clew* in his November 9, 1969, letter. This word had its peak use frequency in the late 1800s and had declined in usage significantly since then.[136] Zodiac also appears to have used a yellow pages ad from the 1940s as the basis for his October 1970 Halloween card to reporter Paul Avery. This makes his references to pop culture, such as "Blue Meannies" and lapel buttons in his letters (either of which anyone of any age group could have picked up from TV, radio, or newspaper stories in the 1960s) apparent efforts at deception to make himself appear younger while he was subtly giving his true age away in other ways.

Kjell Qvale was fifty years old on the night of the Stine murder.

29. Vallejo crime scene descriptions. In his first letters to the newspapers on July 31, 1969, Zodiac says he killed the two kids at "Lake Herman." However, he doesn't mention the name Blue Rock Springs

---

136 Google search "etymology of the word clew," September 2015.

to describe the July crime scene. Rather, he says "near the golf course in Vallejo." Anyone going to Blue Rock Springs, even someone who wasn't from Vallejo, could have seen the sign with the name of the park. In other words, Zodiac seemed to go out of his way not to call the park by its name but rather to *describe it according to its proximity to the golf course.*

Kjell Qvale was an avid golfer all his life.

With all the evidence I had amassed against Qvale, I felt that upon handing off this information to the local authorities the case would quickly be solved. In reality, I had some extremely painful and time-consuming lessons to learn about money, politics, and the treatment of the wealthy by the police.

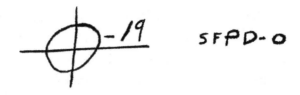

ROUGH SEAS: DEALING WITH THE POLICE

"He will receive a fair trial, whoever he is, and he will receive the consideration that any criminal who is brought to our attention does in the administration of justice."
—San Francisco DA John J. Ferdon on the Zodiac, October 1969, *Zodiac* DVD, 2008

"Maybe it was the Skakel money. Maybe it was their position. But I believe I was intimidated by them."
—Martha Moxley case det. Steve Carroll in "Skakel's Tossed Conviction Just Another Case of Kennedy Privilege," Maureen Callahan, nypost.com, May 8, 2018

THE FIRST POLICE DEPARTMENT I went to was SFPD, since Qvale lived in their city and they were the most prominent one associated with the case. The person in charge of the Zodiac case when I approached the department in 1999 was Lt. Tom Bruton, who has since retired. In my opinion, Lt. Bruton didn't seem to have a full understanding of the case. That made it exceedingly difficult to impress him with any of the evidence Ed and I had amassed. For example, in late 1999, Bruton appeared on the television documentary *Case Reopened*. As part of the re-enactment of the Stine murder, he stated in a voice-over that the original destination of the cab was Washington Street and Maple Street. He stated that the cab actually stopped at Washington Street and Cherry Street, which was, according to Bruton, "about four blocks away." In reality, Cherry is the next block west of Maple. You need know little more than this to understand just how obscure the intersection of Washington Street and Maple Street actually is: even an SFPD officer who had worked in the city for years and was in charge of the Zodiac case for the department had no idea as to the geography of Presidio Heights.

When I spoke with Lt. Bruton in July 1999, he indicated that he would like to see some fingerprints and handwriting from Qvale. He did not say that he would get them, so I assumed he was telling me that I had to do so for him.

So Ed and I devised a strategy.

We needed an excuse to write to Qvale. Ed suggested I use the 1947 flying-saucer incident as the basis for doing so. I readily agreed with his idea, so I took out a post office box in a town several miles away from my own so that I wouldn't to have to use my actual address or name when writing to him. I invented a pen name and hand printed a letter, hoping it would inspire Qvale to hand print his reply. That part didn't work out, because I received a typed reply that bore only his signature. Ed and I had already seen his signature by that time, and, at any rate, it couldn't be compared to Zodiac's hand-printed scrawl.

When I received the response from Qvale on small, rectangular stationery that had been personalized with his business name, I carefully opened it using plastic gloves I obtained from the cafeteria at work. I copied it for my records, then forwarded the original directly to SFPD for fingerprint analysis, and never heard anything about the matter again. A full year later, when I was working out in my basement,

I literally leapt off my stair-climbing machine in the middle of a workout, grabbed the letter, and rushed to find a ruler. I had an idea. I measured the paper and found that it was seven and a quarter by ten and a half inches. I called a stationery store and quickly confirmed that the paper Qvale had used to write to me in 1999 was monarch-sized paper—*the same odd-sized stationery that Zodiac had used for the majority of his taunting letters.*

I scheduled my first trip to San Francisco in October 1999. Ed and I met with Lt. Bruton personally while I was out there. At that time, Bruton intriguingly mentioned that he was interested in seeing fingerprints, handwriting, *and* DNA evidence. Ed caught Bruton's reference to DNA, which I had missed. We wondered where the DNA had come from, since we were unaware that any existed. We didn't get the impression that Bruton was going to investigate Qvale above and beyond any evidence we provided to him, so we decided to move on to another department that would.

In November 1999, at the suggestion of Dr. Mike Kelleher, I reached out to The Lamplighters of San Francisco. This organization stages Gilbert and Sullivan productions, such as *The Mikado*, in the Bay Area. I asked for copies of their programs from as far back as they were willing to go to see if Qvale was a financial supporter of these productions. When I received the photocopies from them, I scanned them for his name under the acknowledgments. It was not there. An interesting idea but ultimately a dead end.

In March 2000, Ed suggested I go to the Napa DA's Office and speak to investigator Bill White Jr., since his father had been a park ranger at Lake Berryessa in 1969 on the day of the Zodiac attack. I felt this was an excellent idea because White's family had ties to the case and probably had a strong interest in seeing it solved. White looked over the report I had written in early 2000 and seemed very impressed. He asked me not to provide the information to any other jurisdiction because they wanted to work on it "exclusively." After a few weeks, White said that the DA's office and the sheriff's office were going to "take the case off the back burner" and "reopen the Zodiac investigation" based on the report I had sent him. He said that he was forming a "task force" with the Napa County Sheriff's Office to investigate Qvale. Upon hearing this welcome and exciting news, I immediately decided to fly out to the Bay Area once again to supply White with more information and learn more about his plans. I was offered a meeting with the Napa County SO and DA's Office.

Ed and I went to the Napa SO in April 2000 and were taken to a basement meeting room. There we met with White and Det. Joe Steiner, who was presumably going to take the lead for the SO. The first thing Steiner said to Ed and me was, "I'm not going to investigate your suspect. I don't want to lose my job." Stunned, I sort of looked around to see if I was actually in the sheriff's office. I knew one thing: Steiner's statement had just completely sucked the air out of the room and sent my mind reeling. I was quite naturally speechless for a moment after all the talk of a task force by Bill White Jr. I looked over at White for some support. He simply looked away. What I heard was frankly the *very* last thing I had expected to hear from Steiner's lips that day. I felt that I had spent my money on airfare for nothing. I recovered enough poise to protest meekly to Steiner that I thought it *was* his job to investigate suspects. How do you lose your job by simply doing it? His response was something I'll never forget: he said that if I thought Qvale was Zodiac, I should "go into San Francisco, knock on the door of his mansion, and ask him [myself]." I simply could not believe my ears.

I left the SO very, very frustrated and extremely disillusioned. What caused the abrupt about-face to their disposition toward what I had sent them in such a short time? Or were they playing mind games with Ed and me? Whatever the case, I had seen and heard enough of local law enforcement for a while. Perplexed, Ed and I went to San Francisco and had lunch at a restaurant on one of the many piers of the Bay. We then drove straight to the place where so many of Zodiac's original letters had arrived—the offices of the *San Francisco Chronicle*.

Disheartened by the sudden change of events with the police, I knew it was time to try a different tack.

When we arrived at the paper we asked for reporter Tom Zoellner. Dr. Mike Kelleher had told me about him just a few months earlier. We knew he was very interested in our theory, having previously been shown my research. We were escorted into a conference room, and after speaking to us for about half an hour, Zoellner ended the discussion and said he would keep in touch with us. Then we left. After that, I returned to New Jersey to continue the research Ed and I needed to do on Qvale. And I waited.

I always viewed Ed's and my research like a football game. We had developed Qvale's name and had run the ball down to the ten-yard line. I'd now come to the realization that thus far nobody in law enforcement was willing to take the handoff and run the ball into the end zone for us. So I told Ed that it was just he and I in this investigation and that we ourselves had to do the research we needed, wherever that road would ultimately lead. Ed affirmed his commitment to researching Qvale and promised that, although his work schedule made things difficult, he was 100 percent on board and committed to getting things done. After all, he lived in Northern California, where all the resources we needed to do the requisite research were located.

I began to discreetly post bits and pieces of the evidence I had amassed to various Zodiac message boards. These sites were places where you develop a suspect by allowing people to discuss and dissect your evidence. They attempt to prove you wrong and that *they* are right and have solved the case. Ultimately, they were unable to convince me I was wrong, but I did find this exercise to be quite educational. I eventually understood that if I were going to solve the case, it would not be with the assistance of the posters on these boards.

In the summer of 2000, Ed decided to walk away from our research. This upset me greatly since I valued his assistance. Doing research on a suspect you really can't talk about publicly can be a frustrating thing, so I have to wonder if this is what informed his decision. After all, at the time, Ed enjoyed a very public presence on the main Zodiac message board. Luckily, around the time Ed's research stopped, I learned that the New York City Public Library on Fifth Avenue and Forty-Second Street had the *San Francisco Chronicle* on microfilm. I would therefore be able to do my own research, at least in this newspaper—an exciting prospect. I began driving my car close to the city and taking the train into Manhattan. I'd walk from Thirty-Third Street up to the majestic marble edifice where my grandfather, a self-taught engraver, had worked in the 1930s, and go to the microfilm reading room. I'd order six months' worth of the *San Francisco Chronicle* and get to work. My goal was to locate as many letters to the editor from Qvale in the Zodiac era as I could. I was hoping that, in one of them, Qvale might have used a unique Zodiac phrase, like "fiddle and fart around" to describe, say, doddering politicians.

The results ended up being the precise opposite of what I had expected and told quite a different story.

As it turned out, other than the June 26, 1969, letter that Ed had found, Qvale apparently rarely wrote letters to the *San Francisco Chronicle*. And this made sense because it was the liberal mouthpiece of the Bay Area, and Qvale was a staunchly conservative Republican. This meant the *Chronicle* was an unlikely paper to which Qvale would write in the first place. I quickly realized that if I ever found myself in court over my research, one of Qvale's attorneys couldn't simply dismiss Ed's and my discovery of the letter written around six months after the Lake Herman Road murders. The attorney couldn't say that it was a case of us having done nothing more than "stumble over one of Qvale's many letters to the editor of the *Chronicle*." My research had shown that it simply wasn't that way. By *not* locating other letters from Qvale, it actually served to strengthen my position considerably.

Qvale's June 26, 1969, letter therefore seemed to be significant in its uniqueness.

One of the ideas I had while combing through editions of the *Chronicle* in the summer of 2000 concerned the names of Qvale's horses. After discovering his name in the 1969 letter to the editor, the horse I found on that first day in the pile of *Racing Forms* stored in my basement was Skystalker, a name clearly laden with possible symbolism related to the Zodiac case. I definitely made a note of this. But were there others? I decided to look through the results charts of the races from Golden Gate Fields and other tracks on the Northern California circuit of the late 1960s for others. I also wrote to the *Daily Racing Form* and asked if they could send me charts of races from that era. They did, and I recall one very strange experience as I looked through the results of those long-ago races.

In the spring of 1968, some nine months before the Lake Herman Road murders, one of the offspring of Silky Sullivan won a race for Qvale at the track in Vallejo. The second-place horse was named Gun Barrel. It was owned by another barn, not by Qvale's Green Oak Stables. However, by July 1968, that other horse was running under Qvale's orange-and-green colors at the Solano County Fairgrounds in Vallejo.[137] Qvale had either claimed or privately purchased this horse between March and July. When Zodiac wrote his letter discussing the shooting of his victims in the darkness of Lake Herman Road that night, when talking about the attached flashlight, he used the awkward phrase "when taped to a *gun barrel*." Most people would have said, "when taped to the barrel of a gun." I found this statement intriguing given that Gun Barrel was also the name of the horse Qvale had acquired and was running in Solano County just miles from Gate #10 at Lake Herman Road in the summer of 1968.

Qvale also ran a horse in the early 1970s named Little Levee. At Lake Berryessa, there was, as I described earlier, a little levee that formed a spine that connected the peninsula where Hartnell and Shepard were attacked to the mainland. Were such things as Qvale's 1968 purchase of Gun Barrel and the fact that he named one of his horses Little Levee and another Skystalker tiny clues he was scattering around the

---

137 Thoroughbred Race Chart, 12th Race, Solano County Fairgrounds, *Daily Racing Form*, June 24, 1968.

landscape, or were they just maddening coincidences? I wasn't sure. I just kept stockpiling these odd names.

Another idea that struck me was to try to use horse racing as a way to possibly undermine any alibi that Qvale may have devised to place him outside the Bay Area on the dates of the murders. When you race thoroughbreds, you will at some point win races. And when you do, you pose for a photo in the winner's circle with the horse, jockey, trainer, and various handlers. Retired Superior Court judge Eric Uldall, who along with his father attended the races a lot at Golden Gate Fields in the 1960s, said that Qvale (who was also president of the track at that time) was almost always there when one of his horses ran. He also had a habit of rapidly rubbing his hands together in anticipation of the running of the race. So I went to the microfilm of the *Chronicle* and looked at the results charts for the four murder dates and the days immediately around them. I felt that if Qvale had won a race on one of those days and then tried to say he was out of the country, I might be able to pull off a Perry Mason moment by whipping out a photo of him posing with a horse in a winner's-circle photo with that day's date on it. Unfortunately, Qvale didn't have a high win percentage barn and didn't win any races with his homebred horses on any of the Zodiac murder dates or on dates immediately preceding or following them.

...

As part of Tom Zoellner's research on the article he was writing, he wanted to personally interview Qvale about my claims. When retired Napa Sheriff's Office captain Ken Narlow learned about this, he told me that he wanted to accompany Zoellner to the interview. But he would not do so unofficially. He said that, for the first time since he had retired, he wanted to get his badge back and investigate this new suspect. I felt this was a very powerful endorsement of the strength of my research on Qvale.

The one thing that made me think twice about going forward with the *Chronicle* article was that in August 2000 reporter Tom Zoellner suddenly told me that he wouldn't accuse Qvale anonymously. I was asked to provide the wealthy and powerful man I thought might be the Zodiac with my name and a way to contact me. This had never been part of the discussion before, and I found it quite unnerving. However, since the police, to my knowledge, had still not investigated Qvale as a suspect, I felt I had to comply. So I advised Zoellner to use my real name and the same post office box I had used to write the letters to Qvale about flying saucers. I wondered if I was putting myself in jeopardy by doing so.

The meeting between Qvale and Tom Zoellner ultimately led to the first article about my research in October 2000.[138] When Ken Narlow asked for his badge back, the Napa Sheriff's Office denied his request. So Tom Zoellner went on his own. Unfortunately, for legal reasons, the article did not name Qvale. Consequently, it didn't have the effect I had hoped for, although it did raise consciousness about my research. Ken Narlow had some positive (if cautious) things to say. Zoellner *also* went to Lt. Bruton of SFPD, whom I had not sent my most recent new developments. He was therefore in no position to comment in an informed manner on my latest research as of the summer of 2000. Narlow said, "Rodelli has raised a lot of good points—maybe they're coincidences, but maybe not. It frustrates me that there's *so much there* [emphasis mine], but nobody will go knock on the guy's door. I think the San Francisco police are shy of him [Qvale] because of his status, but if I was still working this case, I would sure go down and talk to the guy."

Narlow had hit the nail right on the head with respect to the reluctance of the police to investigate my claims despite expressing interest in them. His own department, after all, had told me to go knock on Qvale's door myself! Qvale stated in the article (which, again, did not

138 Tom Zoellner, "Amateurs Stir Embers of Notorious Zodiac Case," *San Francisco Chronicle*, October 2, 2000, p. A17.

name him) that there was "nobody in San Francisco" who was less likely to be the Zodiac than he was. And on the surface at least, that seemed true.

I had also hoped that the article might develop some new information or leads from the public, but that didn't happen.

In early 2001, I decided to try yet another police department with an interest in the case, the Solano County Sheriff's Office. I called the switchboard and asked whom I could speak to about the Zodiac Killer investigation. They gave me the name of a young detective, Patrick Grate. I sent my report to Grate, who read my report and expressed a great interest in it. However, he was upset with me for allowing Tom Zoellner to take away the element of surprise for any interview he might have done by confronting Qvale with my suspicions. I got angry and explained that I had gone this route *only* after trying to work with SFPD and the Napa SO. I told him that I did everything I could to work through those departments before going to the *Chronicle* reporter. Grate said that the case was so old that he didn't know the facts of it very well. He asked if he could send my report to a Superior Court judge who had followed the case since it began. I agreed, and he sent my report to the unnamed judge.

It didn't take long for the judge to contact me. On April 3, 2001, I received a call from someone who identified himself as Solano County Superior Court Judge Eric (Rick) Uldall. He was the nicest and most amicable man with whom I had ever spoken. He was truly a wonderful person and had many amusing anecdotes about law enforcement in the "old days." We had a memorable conversation. He said that he had been born in San Francisco and had been a student of the Zodiac case since he was a young prosecutor in Vallejo in the 1970s. For that reason, he was very familiar with Zodiac suspect Arthur Leigh Allen. He was also part of a group that met once a month at the International House of Pancakes on Tennessee Street, which was just up the street from Allen's old house on Fresno Street, in Vallejo to discuss the case. The main movers in this group were Lyndon Lafferty and Jerry Johnson, who had been pursuing their own suspect, William Grant, for thirty years. Lyndon later called this group the Mandamus Seven after a government official who is legally tasked with carrying out some function. Judge Uldall said that he didn't believe that Allen was Zodiac and that, while Grant was a strange guy, he didn't believe he was the Zodiac either.

The judge said that he'd begun reading my report at 11:00 PM the previous night and by the time he came up for air it was 2:00 AM. He said that, in his opinion, Qvale was the *only true prime suspect* ever developed during the course of the Zodiac investigation.

Judge Uldall and I became fast friends. I started calling him Judge Rick. He quickly evolved into an invaluable asset to me because he understood the politics of police investigations and of the city of San Francisco in particular. For example, he told me that the chief of police in San Francisco served at the pleasure of the mayor and could be let go at any time at the mayor's discretion. He felt that, due to his wealth and power, Qvale probably had a direct phone line to the mayor's desk. Since the chief was there only as long as the mayor wanted him to serve, Judge Uldall believed there was little chance that SFPD could investigate someone like Qvale. If he was right, this would explain a number of the obstacles I'd had (and would later encounter)with law enforcement in San Francisco.

Judge Uldall asked if one of his friends, retired Vallejo Police Department detective Jim Dean, who had worked on the Zodiac investigation in the 1970s, could read over my report. I said that any friend of Judge Uldall's was a friend of mine. Jim was immediately taken with my research and said he felt like he was back on the force working on the case again. This was to be the start of the long-term friendship and working relationship I was to forge with Jim, who was by my side for many of the important discoveries we were to make over the next several years.

The judge said he would have a talk with Det. Grate and try to get him interested in going out and questioning Qvale. At the time, I had no idea how difficult a task this would become thanks to Grate's own internal political problems.

Det. Grate did give the entire binder of police reports from the sheriff's office to Judge Uldall to copy for me. He said that I knew the case better than anyone and that I might be able to sift out some details from the reports that were of significance to my case. He cautioned me not to share them with anyone. It was a promise I tried very hard to keep; but, unfortunately, someone duped me out of some of the reports and made them public several years later.

Det. Grate ended up having his own sticky political problems to deal with. He wanted to go to San Francisco to interview Qvale, but he was prevented from doing so by his superior. At one point, that superior reportedly went to the city council to ask them if the city would be liable for damages if they knocked on Qvale's door, told him that they wanted to speak about the Zodiac case, and Qvale had a heart attack from the shock of the question. Over the years, upward of twenty-five hundred to three thousand suspects had been interviewed about the Zodiac case. I wondered if the police would have taken this extraordinary step if Qvale were an auto mechanic instead of an auto magnate and lived in a trailer park instead of a mansion. I believe the answer is obvious and that this was another example of "rich people's justice."

The final showdown between Det. Grate and his superior came in the form of a shouting match that, according to Judge Uldall, was one of those that "peeled the paint off the walls" of his office. Det. Grate persisted in his desire to go out to interview Qvale, but his superior, ever the political police official, would still not allow him to do so. Judge Uldall said that Pat and his boss nearly came to blows over the matter.

Det. Grate paid me a high compliment after reading my report. He asked if I would be willing to teach him how I did my research and indicated that he wanted to use some of my methods in his own investigations. He said that if he were a criminal, he would not have wanted me chasing after him! Both he and Judge Uldall made me feel that, even though I was an "amateur investigator," my research was anything but amateurish. Rather, it was completely objective, professional, and compelling, something an SFPD inspector would echo in 2012. After this request by Det. Grate, I was hit with the realization that if I had only decided to go into police work and become a detective when I was younger, that probably would have been a satisfying career choice for me. But when I was younger I had no inkling that detective work was the life for me because I had no idea what it entailed—or that I even had a talent for it.

The net result is that I had gone to three of the four police departments with an interest in the Zodiac case and each one had refused to even speak to Qvale for its own reasons.[139] I had tried to hand the ball off to all three departments, and they ended up handing it right back to me.

. . .

Meanwhile my research into Qvale continued. I was able to get a clipping file that the San Francisco Public Library kept on prominent people in the city. I was surprised at how thin the file on Qvale was. I immediately noticed that three of the articles had November 20 dates on them. One was an article by Hugh Russell Fraser in a local business newspaper, the *Daily Commercial News*, from November 20, 1958. The article described Qvale's auto business and showroom. And right in the middle of talking about Qvale's business, the author suddenly and without context digresses and mentions that Qvale's manner of speaking is "leisurely—almost slow." This reference jumped off the page at me because I knew that Zodiac was thought to have a slow, deliberate manner of speaking. As I indicated earlier, a suspect in Napa was ruled out as being Zodiac because of his fast manner of speaking (footnote 18).

---

139 I was discouraged from going to the Vallejo Police Department because they supposedly were focused on Arthur Leigh Allen as the Zodiac Killer.

The other two November 20 articles were from 1964. One was in the *San Francisco Chronicle* and one in the *San Francisco Examiner*. In them Qvale stated that he had become the biggest import car dealer on the West Coast. "He's the Biggest," one of them crowed. From my earlier research, I knew that Zodiac seemed to attack his victims on dates that were important to Qvale. I wondered to myself what significance to Qvale, and possibly to the Zodiac case, November 20 might have held. I stored this date in the back of my mind and made a mental note to look into it.

In 2001, I was introduced to a producer at ABC News named Harry Phillips. Over the course of the next year and a half, I cooperated with him as he put together a show on the Zodiac case. He was keenly interested in my research, which he called "spectacular" and told me that he felt I was "onto something."

One crucial thing I learned from ABC early on in our relationship was something Harry Phillips told me about Qvale's whereabouts on the night of the Stine murder. He said that ABC was unable to place Qvale out of the country at any of his usual haunts for any of the Zodiac crimes. Those "usual haunts" included England. Little did I know just how important this bit of information would become some five years in the future.

Maybe the most important piece of information to come out of the ABC Primetime Thursday show in October 2002 was the fact that SFPD's lab had uncovered a key piece of evidence while doing preliminary DNA research on the Zodiac letters. When they peeled back a stamp on the Stine letter of October 13, 1969, they found a small reddish-brown hair behind the stamp and embedded in the glue that held it to the envelope. From a color photo in an article in a Norwegian magazine that San Francisco city attorney Tim Armistead had located and provided to me, I knew that Qvale himself also had reddish-brown hair (Exhibit 17). The hair behind the stamp had no root bulb, which is where the nucleated cells that grow the hair are located. Therefore, it was impossible at that time to do the standard nuclear DNA testing on it, since such testing requires that those cells be present. However, based on a new technique developed by a paleogeneticist that permits the testing of rootless hair for nuclear DNA, such analysis may be possible today.[140]

Regardless, as we saw in the strands of hair found clutched in Cheri Jo Bates's hand, human hair contains mitochondrial DNA. Since mt-DNA is passed down from a mother to her children, all the children from the same maternal line would have the same mt-DNA. That meant that Qvale and all his siblings would have had the same mt-DNA in their reddish-brown hair as their mother. If mt-DNA were ever developed from that tiny hair, it could be compared to that of someone in Qvale's matrilineal family. If the letter writer were someone outside the family, while the mt-DNA might not have matched, that wouldn't mean that Qvale was not involved in the case; only that he wasn't the letter writer. Recall that Qvale did closely resemble the man who had murdered Paul Stine near Qvale's Presidio Heights home. In contrast, nobody had ever seen the letter writer as he penned the Zodiac letters.

The thing that struck me like a bolt of lightning was that the most likely way for a hair to get embedded in the glue of a stamp was presumably by someone licking it who had a moustache. And the day before this letter was sent the man seen by the Stine eyewitnesses and Officer Fouke did not have one! Were there two people at work? I contacted a forensic scientist from Ohio looking for an expert in human hair. He eventually sent a photo of the hair to an expert acquaintance of his. The expert said that the hair from the stamp was most likely a body hair, not a coarse hair from a moustache. The hair was also so short (being only a few millimeters in length) that it was too small to be analyzed for mt-DNA. As of the early winter of 2019, DNA technology did not exist that could successfully extract DNA from standard mt-DNA analysis of that short a length of hair.

---

140 https://www.dailymail.co.uk/sciencetech/article-7472631/Scientist-creates-ground-breaking-technique-crack-cold-cases.html#i-934ca24d8744c8cd

290 · MIKE RODELLI

Of all the fortunate breaks Zodiac may have received over the course of his lethal career, the combination of the missing root bulb and the extremely short length of the reddish-brown hair from the stamp certainly rate as his biggest: the absence of the root bulb makes it impossible to do nuclear DNA testing and the length of the hair precludes a mt-DNA analysis of the sample. Therefore, all we can do is stare at this tantalizing sample and wonder about what could have been. Zodiac had truly dodged a huge bullet with respect to this crucial piece of evidence.

...

In late 2001, I had an idea. Maybe Qvale's wedding anniversary was November 20 and therefore formed the basis of those articles I had received bearing that date: they were a commemoration of sorts. So I sent a request to the State of California for his marriage certificate. After a few weeks, I received a letter back stating that they could find no record of his being married in California. So I tried contacting the San Francisco Public Library to see if they could be of assistance. They sent me an article indicating that in December of 1950, Qvale and his new bride were honeymooning after being married in Chicago.

I wondered what had brought them all the way to the Midwest to get married. Neither Qvale nor his bride (who hailed from Alameda) had any family there. I wrote to the public records department of Cook County, Illinois. In January, I received a call stating that they had located the marriage certificate. Not being able to stand the wait for it to arrive by mail, I asked the gentleman to read me the date they were married. He said November 20, 1950.

There was the date! I now knew that all of these November 20 dates on articles were apparently linked to the date on which Qvale was married! There was yet another connection between Qvale and date commemoration that had nothing to do with the Zodiac case but with events in his own life.

A few days later, I received the certificate and wanted to look for myself to see the date on it. The copy was very light and difficult to read. I got a magnifying glass and looked carefully at the document. The date, although very faint, was clearly not November 20 but November 25, 1950. I couldn't believe that the man had not only read the wrong date over the phone but that the date he had erroneously provided also happened to be November 20! I was very disappointed and realized I was back at square one with respect to that date.

I next had an idea about what may have happened when Qvale was married in Chicago: Chicago is the headquarters of the Sears department store chain, and the flagship Sears store was located there. Zodiac's weapon at Lake Herman had been a .22-caliber High Standard weapon that was also sold by Sears under the name J. C. Higgins Model 80. Zodiac said in his November 9, 1969, letter that he had purchased at least one of his weapons "out of state," that is, outside of California. I wondered if Qvale might have purchased the .22 while in Chicago to get married. But I quickly learned to my dismay that the Model 80 was not yet being marketed by Sears in 1950. So Qvale couldn't have purchased such a weapon from Sears when he went to Chicago to get married.

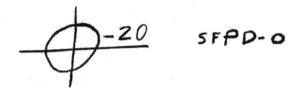

Bus Bomb II

IN THE SUMMER OF 2005, I was reviewing some of the documents in my files when I came across Bjarne Qvale's November 1970 death certificate. Bjarne Qvale was Kjell Qvale's father. As I scanned it for any information I may have missed since it first came into my possession over five years earlier, my eyes were suddenly drawn to something. Buried in the middle of the document was a portion that his doctor had filled out with the time period during which he had treated the decedent. Dr. Leslie Gould of Seattle, Washington, indicated that he had started treating Mr. Qvale on **April 20, 1970.**

I didn't know how I had previously missed this bit of information. It set my mind racing as to what it could possibly mean, and here is why: after a hiatus of exactly four months from the December 20, 1969, Belli letter the Zodiac Killer had gone ominously silent, sending absolutely no correspondence. However, Zodiac commenced writing to the *San Francisco Chronicle* again on April 20, 1970. In his letter he enclosed his thirteen-character "My Name Is" cipher as well as his second bus-bomb diagram. Most importantly, it was the exact same date that Dr. Gould had affixed to Bjarne Qvale's death certificate. Just like the dates of the murders, which to most people had seemed completely random, April 20, 1970, appeared to be taking on a totally new meaning when I viewed it through the filter of Kjell Qvale's life and, more specifically, the lives of his parents.

Why would this date have been of significance to both Zodiac and Qvale? I already knew that Zodiac had murdered on the date on which Bjarne Qvale was born—September 27. Bjarne would die on November 8, 1970, some six and a half months after the April 20 date on which he first consulted Dr. Gould. The idea hit me that maybe this April 20 appointment represented the onset of a serious final illness, the first sign of Bjarne Qvale's weakening condition. Did the April 20 letter secretly celebrate this potential release of the grip of whatever power Bjarne may have held over Kjell? I knew that Bjarne died while residing on Washington State's Mercer Island and that his address as listed on the certificate was 8 Meadow Lane. I quickly grabbed Zodiac's second bus bomb diagram (Exhibit 27) and went online to a Yahoo map of the area to compare that part of Mercer Island to the bomb diagram that accompanied the April 20 letter. What I discovered was extremely intriguing. (Exhibit 28 is a 2020 version of that 2005 map.)

As was the case in Presidio Heights with the first bus bomb, I kept in mind that the April 1970 sketch might not be a literal representation of the area. Looking at it, I quickly realized that Zodiac's second bomb diagram showed a number of features that appeared to be analogous to what I was seeing on the modern-day map. First, I needed to confirm orientation. Zodiac wrote on the right side of the bomb diagram that this side faced the east, as indicated by the "sun light in early morning." This told me to rotate the diagram so the *A* and *B* were at the top and the "String of Bombs" was on the right. I noted that, in respect to the other diagram, the small diagram above was showing the "Sun," a "Bus," and the slope of the land upside down for some reason. I had no idea why Zodiac didn't draw everything on the diagram so that it could all be viewed without having to rotate the page a full 180 degrees to understand part of it.

Looking at the bomb and the map, I quickly saw that there was a housing development of some kind to the east that closely resembled the north–south-running "String of Bombs." This immediately piqued my interest. This area is known today as The Lakes (Exhibit 29). West of The Lakes, although incomplete, was the hint of a circular road, Mercer Terrace Drive, going into Southeast Seventy-Third Place. Farther north lay 8 Meadow Lane, the home of Bjarne Qvale. In the diagram, this would have been the "photo electric switch" labeled "B." Was that *B* for "Bjarne"? Beginning not far from Bjarne's home was a road, West Mercer Way, that skirted the south shore of the island and that resembled the wire connecting "B" to the "String of Bombs." It wasn't literal, but once again there was an analogy between the features on the map and the diagram of the bomb.

I immediately sensed that I might be on the verge of answering Mike Kelleher's challenge from 1999 to explain the second bus bomb as I had the first one: it was yet another map!

Naturally, I asked myself if the area had actually looked like the current day map at the time that Zodiac created this diagram way back in 1970. So I contacted the King County, Washington, Assessor's Office. They sent me the only aerial photos they had of the area prior to 1970, which were from 1963 (Exhibit 30). When I took a look at them, I realized that in 1963 the area didn't look much like Zodiac's diagram at all. For one thing, The Lakes had not yet been carved out of the tree-filled parcel of land from which it would emerge. Also, Mercer Terrace Drive did not exist. Just as I was ready to put the idea of an analogy between a map of Mercer Island and Zodiac's second bomb diagram aside, I noticed a feature on the 1963 aerial photograph that made me think again.

In the lot directly east of the area where The Lakes would be constructed, there was what appeared to be a school. In fact, it was the Islander Middle School. Adjacent to the west side of this school were athletic playing fields. Just south of the school was an oval object—a running track! The presence of this running track hit me like a ton of bricks and transported me in a completely different direction from the diagram being merely a map of some location. When comparing the map of Mercer Island to the bomb diagram, the "street" with the "Bus" on it seems to represent Eighty-Fourth Avenue Southeast. This street runs north–south right next to the school and its running track, which parallels that road. A new interpretation of this diagram began to take root in my mind.

Long before I knew who Kjell Qvale was, when I had first laid eyes on the second bus-bomb diagram in one of my earliest readings of *Zodiac* in the 1980s, the "Timer" had instantly struck me as closely resembling something that seemed quite familiar—a rough representation of a golf green with the pin sticking out of the hole. It was like one you might see on a road map to denote the presence of a course in a given location! So now I had what looked like a running track, a golf green, and a representation of Bjarne Qvale's Mercer Island home. There was one other item on the diagram: the "Car Bat." Here was yet another obvious reference to automobiles, which were part of all the Zodiac crime scenes and which defined Kjell Qvale's business career.

Out of the jumble of working parts that constituted the "bus bomb," a picture was emerging of something I used to try to solve when I was a child in the 1960s watching the game show *Concentration*—a rebus puzzle! If someone had asked me to write down the various things that defined who Kjell Qvale was as an individual, I would've listed **cars, golf** (a sport to which he was absolutely devoted throughout his life), **track and field** (where he was a star in the 100-yard dash at the University of Washington in the 1940s), and a reference to one of his parents thrown in for good measure—the ***B*** representing Bjarne Qvale's Mercer Island home. But there was one more component to the rebus diagram in this letter that I had yet to discover.

I was still puzzling over why Zodiac didn't make the entire diagram readable while holding it in just one orientation. Why did he ask us to turn it 180 degrees in order to see how he was planting the bomb on a slope?[141] After all, he could have presented the upper diagram as in Exhibit 31. This would have preserved the position of the sun on the right side of the diagram, kept A to the right of B, and removed the need for the writer to turn the page around in order to draw the diagram. It also would have allowed the reader to see both diagrams while viewing the page in only one orientation. I suddenly realized that, by looking at the smaller diagram exactly as it is when viewing the rest of the diagram with the "sun" to the "east," there is a side benefit to orientating the two diagrams as he did, even though in the small inset the sun is actually shining up instead of down from the sky.

When viewed in this orientation, the "Bus" with the small hillside next to it takes on a completely new perspective. The *A* and *B* now appear to be on the side of a slope, or mountain, with point A being elevated in relation to point B. What activity takes place on the side of a mountain where you go from a higher point (A) to a lower point (B)? Skiing. This is yet another activity that would serve to define who Kjell Qvale was, since he was from Norway where skiing is a way of life for many people. His entire family was known for skiing in the Seattle area in the 1930s, and Kjell was a champion skier in high school and continued to ski avidly well into his old age. My conviction that this was indeed a rebus puzzle grew stronger now. But I also knew there was one prominent component of Qvale's life that was missing from the rebus puzzle, and try as I might, I could locate no hint to it in the diagram: thoroughbred horse racing.

Given his lifelong involvement in horse racing, I knew it was impossible to define Qvale without some reference to it. Conversely, I knew that if it were present, the rebus puzzle would then be complete in defining the major themes of Qvale's life. However, I found no such

---

141 The circle for the "sun" in the small diagram at the top only becomes a one o'clock circle (remember that Zodiac made either eleven o'clock or one o'clock circles) when you turn the page 180 degrees from the way you would view the main bomb diagram with the "sun light in early morning" in that diagram to the right, or east.

references in the April 20 letter. Nonetheless, I satisfied myself that this diagram appeared to be an ingeniously designed rebus puzzle that, just as the first bus-bomb diagram had told us the location of Qvale's Presidio Heights home, identified Qvale in terms of his unique set of lifelong interests. Except for that one thing.

A few days later, I happened to be looking at Zodiac's next letter, the April 28, 1970, Dragon Card (Exhibit 32). As I looked at the two prospectors sitting on their respective mounts, I remembered something I had also immediately noticed years earlier. The design of the "saddles" the miners were using represented a direct analogy to **jockeys sitting on horses.** Each saddle had a girth attaching it to the animal around its midsection, and there were the bridles on the dragon and donkey and "reins" that the small men held in their hands. So here was the missing piece of the rebus puzzle pointing at Qvale! Zodiac had to include it in his next letter because there was no conceivable way to incorporate such an analogy into the context of a diagram of the bus bomb!

You could do much worse than to describe Kjell Qvale as someone with interests in cars, skiing, track and field, golf, and thoroughbred horse racing (Exhibit 33). *And all of these are represented in the second bus-bomb diagram and ensuing Dragon Card.* Even without the reference to Bjarne Qvale's home and a map of Mercer Island, these elements are still present. Taken together, I believe they represent a stunning clue to the identity of the Zodiac Killer that has no equal in the history of crime.

There the matter lay until July 2014, when I decided to revisit this theory and endeavor to find out if the authorities in King County, Washington, had any maps or aerial photos of Mercer Island that spanned the gap between 1963 and Zodiac's 1970 letter.

A 1970 photo of Mercer Island that I was able to obtain, courtesy of Matthew Parsons of the University of Washington Libraries (Exhibit 34), shows that in the position of the circular "Timer" there is the hint of a circle that is Mercer Terrace Drive. The running track is still there, as is 8 Meadow Lane. This is what Zodiac would've seen if he'd flown over the southern part of Mercer Island at the time when the second bus bomb was created.

For those of you who doubt the analogy between the bomb diagram and the map of Mercer Island, remember that the southern end of Mercer Island was the *only* area I examined. It is, after all, the only area where 8 Meadow Lane is located. So I did not sift through hundreds or thousands of miles of maps to find an analogy to the diagram. And not only was the running track in the correct spot in the eastern part of the island, it was also oriented in the correct north–south direction. The semicircular street, Mercer Island Way, is located in the correct spot, too, between 8 Meadow Lane (i.e., providing the *B* for "Bjarne" in the diagram) and the running track, to form the analogy to the "Timer." That is truly an example of finding a tiny needle in a huge haystack. But even without the map analogy, the rebus-puzzle aspect of the second bus-bomb diagram remains fully intact.

Are my solutions to the two bus bombs subjective? Do they require interpretation? Could the bombs just be bombs? Might I be seeing patterns where there are none? In each case, the answer is yes. But the one thing I do know is this: I did not solve either of the two diagrams by first drawing a conclusion as to what each represented and then working backward to develop an explanation for that conclusion. And while it can be said that I solved the second bus bomb by having a preconceived idea that it was a map, in the end, that is not what I concluded the diagram represented. And I had absolutely no preconceptions that it might be an ingenious rebus puzzle.

As for the first diagram, that solution evolved step-by-step. I first used the scientific methodology of observation. I then formed the hypothesis that there was an analogy between that diagram and an aerial photo of Presidio Heights. Finally, I tested that hypothesis by having Ken Narlow determine if the home I'd singled out was actually 3636 Jackson Street. I certainly had no preconceived notion whatsoever that the original diagram might potentially be a map of anything: my map solution of the first diagram was anything but a conclusion looking for an explanation. In addition, the two bus-bomb solutions don't exist in a vacuum. Rather, they're part of an overall pattern of evidence against Kjell Qvale that includes more traditional documented, factual evidence and behavioral profiling.

...

Over the years, many people have debated whether Zodiac was an evil genius or just a guy who committed murders and got lucky, always somehow managing to stay one step ahead of his pursuers. With my solutions to the two bus-bomb diagrams, the Zodiac I have come to know is not only incredibly intelligent and darkly ingenious but also brazen beyond words. Imagine this: he sent the police a map to his house and, for good measure, a rebus puzzle that identified him through his primary interests. The maps were both disguised as bus bombs. You can just imagine him sitting back and laughing at everybody. I do indeed believe that the Zodiac Killer planted two different bus bombs. *But where he planted those bombs was in the minds of the populace of the Bay Area.*

Based on his early letters, with their gross misspellings and grammatical missteps, Zodiac has been portrayed as someone who was semiliterate or a discretionary illiterate. However, based on what I feel are the most daring clues ever sent by a serial killer to the police, Zodiac proved himself to indeed be the criminal genius who at times did get lucky breaks, as opposed to the "loser compensating for his feelings of inadequacy," whose luck by far outweighed his brilliance.

Let us not forget that within his early letters, the Zodiac was able to correctly spell words *after spelling the same word incorrectly earlier in the same letter.* He was also able to correctly use semi-colons, something many otherwise skilled writers have difficulty doing. And if you accept that the 1974 *Badlands* Letter is genuine, he threw it all in the faces of the police. It was sort of like "throwing down the mic" in today's parlance, by writing a letter that contained four- and five-syllable words that were correctly used and spelled. What he was saying in that letter is, "If you thought I was some illiterate idiot, think again!" The two bus bombs are simply manifestations of that same theme: Zodiac told us they were bus bombs. So while the police and society wildly wrung their hands protecting schoolchildren and scanning the horizon for one of these devices, he simply had a good chuckle at our expense and dared us first to correctly identify and then to solve them.

PART TEN
Left for Dead

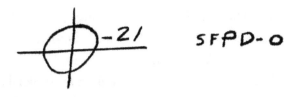

QUESTIONABLE DNA

"You're looking at the genetic identity of Zodiac."
—John Quinones, ABC News, to Insp. Kelly Carroll, SFPD, on
Primetime Thursday, October 17, 2002

*The problem with DNA is that if you have a science that is misunderstood,
that science becomes like magic. It gets the power of magic, and that is what
makes it very, very dangerous.*
—anonymous voice-over, *Exhibit A: Touch DNA*, Netflix, 2019

SINCE THE LATE 1980S, DNA has become the gold standard of evidence in the US justice system, and indeed around the world. To say that someone was "identified via DNA" is almost to say that a finger pointing down from the heavens has singled out this individual to the exclusion of the rest of humanity. In fact, DNA is believed to be so powerful and specific for one individual that the process is commonly referred to as *DNA fingerprinting*. DNA can identify parents in paternity cases, convict the guilty in cases that have gone cold for decades, and exonerate the innocent to probabilities of up to several billion to one. Those odds are so staggering that DNA has taken on an aura of magic in the mind of the public: DNA evidence can never be wrong. Or can it? As it seems to have been since the case began in 1968, the Zodiac case was once again poised to break all of the rules.

In the summer of 2002, ABC News, with which I was cooperating on a potential story at the time, provided funding earmarked by SFPD's cash-strapped forensics lab to analyze the Zodiac letters with the goal of obtaining a sample of the letter writer's DNA. That job fell to Dr. Cydne Holt, who was the head of the lab, and a few months later she developed a small fragment of DNA from what was alleged at the time to be just *one* of the Zodiac's envelopes. On the subsequent October 17, 2002, ABC *Primetime Thursday* show, a sample of Kjell Qvale's DNA, which he had *volunteered* to ABC News for analysis, was compared to the fragment that SFPD said it had developed with negative results. (However, as far as I know, the SFPD was never directly involved in obtaining a DNA sample from Qvale.)

As you can well imagine, this result essentially destroyed my credibility on national television.

The techniques used for DNA testing are extremely reliable and reproducible in the lab. The problem is that the technique must be performed by human beings. When lab technicians are unskilled or devise their own unproven and untested techniques, they may make errors. As a result, there can be serious consequences, such as a teenager in the UK who was unjustly accused of rape through contamination of the DNA sample used to convict him.[142]

SFPD's lab in particular has had many serious problems over the years. For example, in 2015 a lab tech and her supervisor both failed the DNA skill proficiency tests.[143] One prominent DNA expert, Dr. Ed

142 Pamela Owen, "Teenager wrongly accused of rape because of DNA contamination is released from prison," March 11, 2012, www.dailymail.co.uk/news/article-2113025/Teenager-wrongly-accused-rape-DNA-contamination-released-prison.html.

143 Jaxon Van Derbecken, "Technician, Boss in SFPD Lab Scandal Flunked DNA Skills Test," March 31, 2015, http://www.sfgate.com/bayarea/article/

Blake of Forensic Science Associates in Richmond, California, told me in 2007 that SFPD's lab was the "laughingstock" of forensics labs in the early 2000s.[144] At the time they developed what became the so-called Zodiac DNA in 2002, SFPD's crime lab was allegedly not even accredited, a serious deficiency for a forensics department.[145] Amazingly, none of the problems with SFPD's forensics lab were brought to light on the show ABC aired announcing the DNA results.

My friends also sensed that my circumstantial case was so strong that they urged me to keep moving forward with my research despite the questionable DNA results presented on the ABC show. And there was reason to be concerned about this particular sample: My friend and colleague Eduard Versluijs had worked in a DNA lab, and he was incredulous at the lab techniques he had seen Dr. Holt demonstrate on the ABC show. He called me to say that Dr. Holt had committed several glaring errors, such as not tying her hair back, resting her elbows on the work bench, and, most glaringly, handling an evidence envelope and then proceeding to extract the actual Zodiac letters from inside that envelope using the *same pair of gloves*. This can result in transferring any exogenous DNA from the evidence envelope (which is clearly exposed to the outside world) to the Zodiac letters contained within. And contamination of the old and overhandled Zodiac letters with exogenous DNA is the most worrisome problem in conducting this DNA analysis on them today.

I also received strong encouragement from two other European internet friends. But it was my colleague Jim Dean who really slapped me back to reality. He called me shortly after the ABC show aired and, in a lengthy conversation, told me I shouldn't give up. He said that, while my evidence was extremely compelling and thoroughly

---

Technician-boss-in-S-F-police-lab-scandal-6169230.php.

144 Dr. Ed Blake, personal communication, March 2007.

145 Jaxon Van Derbecken, "SFPD Withheld Doubts on Crime Lab from Auditors," April 25, 2010, http://www.sfgate.com/bayarea/article/SFPD-withheld-doubts-on-crime-lab-from-auditors-3191219.php.

documented, nobody knew where the DNA sample had actually come from. As it turned out, his words were much more prophetic than I dared to imagine at the time. Bolstered as I was by their support, I decided to keep moving forward.

Within days of the ABC show, the late Zodiac researcher Lyndon Lafferty had already begun to make inroads into questioning the viability of the new DNA sample. He contacted the late homicide inspector Mike Maloney of SFPD, who was investigating the Zodiac case at that time. Maloney stated to Mr. Lafferty that the DNA SFPD had in its possession was "premature." Lafferty asked if that meant the DNA results were invalid. Maloney paused for a few seconds to consider his response and probably also to consider the political ramifications of his answer and stated, "Yes."[146] And yet it was this "invalid" DNA that just days earlier on national television had been compared to three potential suspects, including my own!

In the 1990s, when DNA testing came into widespread use in law enforcement laboratories, one of the first things the San Francisco Police Department did was to begin analyzing the Zodiac letters for DNA. They were hoping it would be the magic bullet that would help identify the killer who had eluded them for so many years. The very basis of DNA testing of letters is the obvious assumption that a perpetrator has licked a stamp or the seal of an envelope and thereby deposited his DNA on the letter. Despite evidence suggesting that Zodiac had *not* licked his stamps and envelopes, which they had already developed in the 1990s and which the lab would allegedly reproduce in 2002, this basic principle was seemingly lost on the lab.

Since Zodiac wrote over twenty letters to the press, and the case took place many years before the advent of DNA testing, criminals at that time didn't realize they had to be careful when handling items that may be found by the police. For this reason alone, the Zodiac case seemed to scream out for a DNA-based solution. After all, there was no reason for anyone to imagine in 2002 any logical circumstances under

---

146 Lafferty, p. 323.

which Zodiac would *not* have licked his envelope flaps and stamps. This prejudiced, completely uninformed (and ultimately incorrect) assumption by amateur researchers on Zodiac message boards has proven to be a huge obstacle to getting people to understand the truth about the 2002 DNA sample.

Before analyzing a postage stamp or the flap of an envelope for DNA, the first thing SFPD's lab did was to test the letters for the presence of saliva. It is, after all, saliva that carries in it the cells that contain an individual's DNA. If there were no saliva on the letters, it follows there were likely no DNA-containing cells deposited on them, especially if the person applying the stamps wore gloves and therefore didn't deposit cells from either his mouth or his fingertips to the letters while applying the stamps and sealing the envelopes. In the 1990s, criminalist Alan Keel was the head of SFPD's crime lab. He began testing the Zodiac letters for saliva under the guidance of the aforementioned Dr. Blake. And what Mr. Keel found should have set off the alarm bells at SFPD as they looked for DNA on the Zodiac letters in 2002.

In order to test for the presence of saliva, the Zodiac letters were examined for two different components of saliva: amylase, an enzyme found in the oral cavity, and the DNA-bearing oral epithelial cells that are also present in great numbers in saliva.[147]

In March 2007, just before the David Fincher movie came out, I had an opportunity to speak to Mr. Keel. He told me, as he had also told Lyndon Lafferty as far back as 1999,[148] that the "true" Zodiac letters had so little amylase and so few cells on them that it would be fair to say that they had been sealed with "tap water." (Note: Keel did not assert outright that the letters were, in his opinion, sealed in that manner but allowed that it was a possibility.) This means that in 2002 SFPD had compared Qvale to DNA from a letter the killer had apparently not even been licked! This begged the question of how Zodiac had deposited his DNA on the envelope if his tongue had never even

147 Alan Keel, personal communication, February 2007.

148 Lafferty, pp. 318–19.

touched it! I found the notion that SFPD had allowed ABC to use this DNA evidence on national television to effectively eliminate Qvale to be completely incomprehensible.

Keel also revealed that there were two letters in the possession of the department that, in contrast to the "true" Zodiac letters, had abundant saliva and DNA-containing oral epithelial cells on them. He added that the DNA was easily extracted from these two letters and that *the DNA from those two letters matched between them.* These two letters were considered by the lab to be *forgeries,* since the "true," verifiable Zodiac letters had not been licked by the sender! Keel indicated that the letters were segregated in the lab based on the amount of saliva found on them, since the "true" Zodiac letters had *not* been licked and the forged letters *had* been licked! Once again I could not believe what I was hearing. Why is it that the two forged letters have DNA that matches across those letters but no matching DNA can be found across *over a dozen* Zodiac letters? I wondered why these facts weren't made public on the 2002 ABC show and why SFPD had even bothered to try to extract DNA from the Zodiac letters in the first place, given what the lab already knew about them from the saliva testing Alan Keel had done in the 1990s.

Keel went on to say that one of the forgeries was Zodiac's controversial April 24, 1978, letter, which had initially been declared an actual Zodiac letter based on handwriting, but which had later been deemed a forgery by many handwriting experts. The other forgery, Keel said, was one of the four 1974 letters attributed to the killer. However, Keel stated that he "could not recall" which 1974 letter was the second forgery. I'm sure I sighed audibly when he said that. I was literally salivating to know which one of the four 1974 letters was not authentic, since each of these letters had been used by various researchers at different times to point a finger of guilt at someone due to its specific content. Which one was a phony?!

Now there was DNA proof that whoever had penned the April 1978 letter had also penned one of the 1974 letters. And it apparently wasn't Zodiac. According to the chart of DNA testing results compiled by SFPD's lab in circa 2000, *the only one* of the 1974 letters that had been tested by Keel up to that time for DNA was the January *Exorcist* letter,[149] the letter with the swarm of palm prints on it. This created an interesting dilemma that lends credence to the possibility that this is a forged letter: Zodiac had penned over a dozen letters prior to writing the *Exorcist* letter and had never left even a single palm print on any of them. So why had he suddenly and carelessly taken off his glove(s) to write this one and leave a virtual montage of his palms all over it? From that standpoint alone, it makes sense that someone else may have written the *Exorcist* letter, its bizarre content notwithstanding.

While it's possible that one of the other three 1974 letters was tested for DNA subsequent to the compilation of the DNA summary chart that Keel had assembled, I believe that, until proven otherwise, the most likely candidate for being the 1974 forgery is the *Exorcist* letter. Although this is not noted in the chart, which does label the 1978 letter as not being authentic based on DNA testing, there may have been good reason to keep this information closely guarded. As a holdback, or a piece of evidence not known to the public, it could be used by police to rule out false confessions. If someone professing to have been Zodiac said that he had penned the *Exorcist* letter, the police would know he was an impostor: This means that the swarm of right-handed palm prints on the letter is from a forger, not from the Zodiac letter writer. And the actual letter writer would know that.

The interesting thing about the *Exorcist* letter is that, like the April 1978 known forgery, it came after a long gap in letters from the killer. In doing so, it also served to reinvigorate interest in the case, much like a letter sent by someone other than the Zodiac who had a vested interest in keeping the case alive in the mind of the public.

---

149 Robert Graysmith, *Zodiac Unmasked*, (New York: Berkley, 2002), p. 434. It's interesting to note that in this chart the 1978 letter is described as a "forgery" (which had been widely theorized for years). However, the 1974 forgery isn't labeled. This makes me think that SFPD is holding this information back from the public.

When I posted the information I had learned from Keel about the letters not having been licked on my website, I immediately received an email from a fellow Zodiac researcher who had close ties to Insp. Mike Maloney. He told me that, even though he personally thought that Arthur Leigh Allen was the Zodiac, he could back up everything I had said because Insp. Maloney had told him the same things. However, Maloney also said that in 2002 they had the lab re-analyze the letters for saliva, as Alan Keel had first done this during his tenure there a few years earlier. The report by Dr. Cydne Holt allegedly confirmed Keel's results by stating that there was essentially no amylase on the letters. The lab's conclusion? It reportedly felt, as Keel had earlier, that Zodiac had not licked his stamps and envelopes! And yet it seems that SFPD did not tell ABC about this inconvenient fact. *Therefore, before ABC News even aired the show in which I participated in 2002, SFPD must have known that the DNA that was to be used on that show was gravely flawed and essentially useless for eliminating suspects.* As confirmation of the essential absence of saliva on the "true" Zodiac letters, when I spoke to Keel in 2007, he described there being only a "background," that is, trace level, of saliva on these letters. This doesn't support the notion that the Zodiac letter writer licked his stamps and flaps.

The net result was that, whoever Zodiac was and for whatever reason, he apparently was not fond of licking his stamps and envelopes; or, even as far back as 1969, he knew that to do so might expose him to capture. And if he didn't lick them, then how did he allegedly leave his DNA on them? Something suddenly seemed very suspicious about the 2002 DNA sample that ABC had used to compare to Qvale on national television. And by now I was seeing red over it.

SFPD went ahead in 2002 and tested the Zodiac letters for DNA. *They knew all the while about their two or more rounds of negative tests for the presence of saliva and of the near absence of DNA-containing cells on the letters. Given their scarceness, any cells found could be contaminant cells from people who had handled the letters over the years.* Why was this allowed to happen? What was the rational, scientific basis for their doing tests for

DNA on envelopes and stamps that the lab's own analyses in the 1990s and in 2002 had shown not to have been licked by the sender? Whose DNA did the lab expect to find and why? These are questions the lab has kept silent about publicly since 2002.

In order to test letters that would presumably at best have only minute amounts of genetic material on them (an indicator of the paucity of cells on these letters), the lab had to resort to a technique called polymerase chain reaction, or PCR for short. PCR was, by inference from what Alan Keel had indicated about the ease of isolating DNA from the two forged letters, not required to get DNA profiles from the forged 1974 and 1978 letters. This created a second serious problem due to the inherent nature of the Zodiac evidence.

PCR acts like a chemical Xerox machine and copies minute amounts of DNA over and over so that DNA, which would otherwise be present in such infinitesimally small amounts as to be useless, can be analyzed. In the absence of such amplification of the molecule, the lab would simply be unable to analyze the DNA because there would be so little of it as to be below the limits of detection of its instrumentation. PCR, however, has one huge drawback: the technique should only be used with extreme caution in forensic settings *where there could be contamination of the samples with DNA from an outside source.* The reason is that amplified amounts of the small fragments of contaminant DNA can be mistaken for DNA from the perpetrator. After all, PCR doesn't know the difference between DNA from a criminal deposited in 1969 and DNA from a handwriting expert who may have sneezed on a sample in 1979. Herein lies the main problem with the Zodiac letters.

What exacerbated the issue of contamination is the technique SFPD's lab used to extract the DNA from the letters. In many photos of the Zodiac letters, you can see that small squares of the stamps have been cut out. These small swatches of stamp, which have the underlying envelope attached to them, are then placed in an extracting liquid and any cells that are on the back of the stamp are collected. However, there is a huge problem with this methodology.

Because the *front* of the stamp is still attached, material is extracted from it too. And the fronts of these stamps have been exposed for decades to the environment and to DNA from the untold number of people (handwriting experts, detectives, curious SFPD personnel, visitors who want to touch evidence in a high-profile case, etc.)! Why SFPD chose to use such a technique to extract their sample, one that virtually begs for contaminant DNA, is perplexing, given that there is an accepted alternative.

A 1998 episode of the *Forensic Files* TV series featured a case of a schoolteacher in Connecticut who started receiving threatening letters from what was believed to be a fellow teacher. As part of the investigation, the police lab analyzed these letters for DNA. The technique they used was to gently steam the stamp from the envelope and then use a cotton swab to extract DNA *exclusively from the side of the stamp that had been attached to the envelope.* This would prevent contamination on the outside of the stamp from injecting a possible contaminant DNA into the analysis.

Why was this technique not used on the Zodiac letters, which were decades older than the letters in the schoolteacher case and therefore much more likely to have been covered in contaminant DNA? Once it had been determined that the sender hadn't licked the stamps and flaps of the Zodiac envelopes, it seems that logic should have dictated that extracting the outside of the Zodiac stamps and flaps was a recipe for disaster. In fact, the condition of the letters with respect to the essential absence of saliva and cells from the letter writer under the stamps and within the seals of the flaps begs the question of why these letters were analyzed at all, especially given the high likelihood that they were contaminated on the *outside* with DNA that was *not* from the sender!

Conversations I had with Contra-Costa Forensic Crime Lab manager Debbie McKillop in the summer of 2017 provided interesting insights into this crucial sampling issue. She said that in normal forensics settings, when a perpetrator licks the glue side of an envelope, so much DNA is deposited that it *overwhelms* any contaminants that may be on the outside of the stamp. So you can therefore extract both sides and still feel confident that you have obtained DNA from the perpetrator. However, with the Zodiac letters, SFPD's own testing proved there was very little DNA on the glue side of the Zodiac stamps, which should have immediately led them to steam off the stamps and extract DNA from only the glue side. But instead, they inexplicably used the standard technique that seems to have been improper for evidence where the *amount of DNA on the glue side may have been so small that it was unable to overwhelm whatever contaminant DNA was on the front of the stamp.* In my opinion, this is a risk Dr. Holt should have been aware of and taken steps to prevent.

Therefore, despite their insider knowledge of there being very little saliva and very few cells on the letters, SFPD was unwilling to change its sampling methods. This ultimately resulted in the 2002 DNA sample that threw the case into chaos. SFPD refused to sample just the glue side of the stamps and flaps and just went on with "science as usual."

This reliance on an extraction technique that was inappropriate for the evidence at hand represents the fatal flaw in SFPD's early DNA work. Because they extracted both sides of the stamps, we don't know if even the few cells they obtained from each letter came from *the back or the front of the stamp!* For all anyone knows, there may be no cells on the glue side, with all the cells being contaminants on the *outside* of the stamp.

One thing that became apparent to everyone from the trial of O. J. Simpson in 1995 is that DNA samples are very easily contaminated. In that case, Simpson's defense team had a field day critiquing LAPD criminalists Dennis Fung and Andrea Mazzola, who were videotaped using improper collection techniques. Today, evidence that is to be tested for DNA has to be carefully collected under stringent protocols and then stored in special containers that will isolate it from potential sources of contamination from the external environment—the main one being the DNA of the person doing the collection and/or analysis of the samples! (Thus the shocking nature of the lab techniques that Dr. Holt

316 · MIKE RODELLI

demonstrated on the 2002 ABC show, as discussed earlier.) The isolation of the evidence being essential to protect it from being contaminated by any outside sources. *But in 1969, such protection of evidence simply did not exist because DNA testing itself did not exist, and the Zodiac letters were therefore casually handled and extremely prone to outside contamination for about two decades.*

In 2009, help in learning more about the 2002 "Zodiac DNA" would come, and it would come from a most unexpected source.

In April of that year, a woman named Deborah Perez came forward to claim that her stepfather was the Zodiac Killer. In stating this wild and implausible tale, which some people laughably touted at the time as being "the" solution to the Zodiac case, she inadvertently helped to bring down the 2002 so-called Zodiac DNA. Her story was that as a young girl she used to accompany her stepfather when he traveled from Southern California to commit crimes in the Bay Area as the Zodiac. She even claimed to have written some of the Zodiac letters. She insisted that her DNA be compared to the 2002 DNA sample (which the ABC show had clearly indicated came from a male contributor!).

It was the response from SFPD that raised my eyebrows. An anonymous police source stated to *San Francisco Chronicle* reporter Kevin Fagan that the DNA from the Zodiac evidence "may not be reliable," which seemed to confirm everything I was hearing about this DNA.[150] And when DNA evidence is unreliable, you clearly cannot rule anyone out with it. This constituted a huge admission on the part of law enforcement regarding the DNA, since they had remained silent on this issue for over six years and allowed my reputation to remain in tatters. I immediately called Mr. Fagan and asked him to follow up with his source for more information. Fagan told me that the reason the lab had doubts about the 2002 DNA is that, in order to scrape together enough cells to run PCR, they were forced to combine samples from three different sources within

---

150 Kevin Fagan, "Woman: Dad Was the Zodiac and I Can Prove It," *San Francisco Chronicle*, April 30, 2009.

the letters.[151] And in improvising this nonstandard lab protocol, SFPD apparently felt that it *may have introduced a fragment of contaminant DNA into the sample.* In Fagan's words to me, "They mixed them up and they [screwed] it up."[152] The fact that SFPD had to circumvent normal extraction procedures for stamps and envelopes by combining samples just to get enough cells to do PCR is tacit confirmation of what I've been saying all along. There are so few cells on the letters that in order to obtain even one sample that was suitable for amplification using PCR, they had to assay multiple areas of the letter(s) just to amass fifty or so cells. And the reason for this paucity of cells is what SFPD already knew from its saliva testing: the sender had not licked the letters!

The final nail in the coffin of SFPD's DNA came in 2012 when retired SFPD inspector Vince Repetto told me that Commander Mike Biel had asked the lead detective in the case at that time, Insp. Kevin Jones, to gather all the information on DNA analysis by the lab. Jones reported back that the DNA results from 2002 "could not be replicated" by the lab.

This is a significant admission.

Science is built on a principle that is in place to assure that one's laboratory results are a valid reflection of nature and not just a fluke or aberration. That principle, as referred to above, is called *replication of results.* A scientist must be able to reproduce his or her results under identical conditions to his or her original experiment in order to have them considered valid. And as any scientist knows, results that can't be replicated are called *nonscientific. And nonscientific results, like the 2002 DNA, cannot rule out anyone.*

These revelations made me livid and proved conclusively that Qvale had never been compared to DNA from the Zodiac because there was no known DNA from the Zodiac. My research had actually emerged from the ABC show unscathed. It's just that it took nearly seven years

---

151 It was unclear if they used samples from three different letters or samples from three different locations on one letter.

152 Kevin Fagan, personal communication, May 2009.

to prove it. The truth was that SFPD should have known in 2002 that their DNA was of questionable value.

There was one last issue to confront with regard to the DNA. Apparently, in 2002 Qvale had provided ABC News with a sample of his DNA. Surely Zodiac wouldn't be foolish enough to do something like that had he known that he had written letters and then licked the stamps and envelopes, since DNA was the most powerful evidence in the world.

Beginning in the early 1960s, Qvale was the president of Golden Gate Fields thoroughbred racetrack. In 2003, I spoke to equine veterinarian Dr. Ron Jensen. He told me something that put Qvale's willingness to donate a DNA sample in a whole different light. In the 1960s, postrace drug testing of horses was performed using saliva. Today it's done via urinalysis. In fact, Dr. Jensen told me that the name of the drug-testing area of the track was the "spit box." So of all the Zodiac suspects, Qvale is one of the very, very few who would've had an inkling that there were potential risks in licking stamps and envelopes in the 1960s via his close association with horse racing. Suddenly I found it quite intriguing that Qvale would have known about saliva testing in the 1960s and that the Zodiac letters had not been licked by the sender. Might this now have been a case of cause and effect? So what was SFPD's goal in allowing ABC to use the 2002 DNA on their show? We can assume it wasn't simply to "rule out" three suspects, since the DNA they had was not a scientific and reproducible sample. There were issues with the Zodiac letters, and they also knew that. One of the things that struck me was that at the end of the show, SFPD homicide inspector Kelly Carroll said that Zodiac should be very nervous knowing that there was now powerful DNA evidence that could be used to ID him. Carroll had a certain look of excitement in his eyes.

But think about this: If the killer didn't lick his stamps and envelopes, he would have *known* that he didn't lick them! So why would he worry about DNA from stamps and envelopes that had never touched his tongue? There was no inference that the DNA was mitochondrial

DNA from the reddish hair found behind the stamp on the October 1969 Stine letter. This would have been a better bluff to play if they wanted to scare the real Zodiac.

...

In recent years, I have literally rolled my eyes as amateur researchers in various public forums have suggested various ways to use DNA technology to solve the case. One of the most frequently mentioned of these is *touch DNA*. Touch DNA works on the premise that when you touch something with your bare hand you leave extremely small numbers of nucleated cells behind. These cells can be carefully collected at a crime scene and the DNA amplified to provide a DNA profile of the person who touched the surface in question.

Touch DNA, since it works with infinitesimally small amounts of genetic material, has extremely strict collection protocols associated with it. When you take fifty-year-old evidence, like the pieces of clothesline from Lake Berryessa, and first coat at least some of them with the victims' blood and then have either these same pieces of rope or others handled by (at least) the people at the scene of the murder in 1969, as well as (in a photo from the *Napa Register* in 1969) the two detectives who worked on the case, as well as who-knows-who else over the years, it makes looking for touch DNA an exercise in futility. But because the technique exists, some people think you can just casually say, "Let's try it on the clothesline to get the killer's DNA." I believe the reality of the situation to be much different.

This type of thinking goes back to the quote in the header of this chapter. This is one of the "magical" aspects of DNA technology. Since the average person doesn't understand how sensitive a technique touch DNA is and the rigors involved in using it, they ascribe magical powers to this type of DNA to transcend time, space, and exogenous contamination over the years to identify the Zodiac Killer.

Another piece of magical thinking involved with DNA technology is the notion of Zodiac having licked his stamps and envelopes. As stated earlier, former SFPD Forensics Lab director Alan Keel said there were so few cells on the "true" Zodiac letters that the sender may have used tap water to apply them. And yet, if you go to a Zodiac message board, you can routinely find people saying that Zodiac "licked his stamps and envelopes" and all we need to do to solve the case is develop DNA from these letters. It all sounds so simple!

Had Zodiac casually licked his stamps and envelopes, why has no verifiable DNA yet been obtained after twenty years of DNA research on these letters? The logical answer is that the killer did not lick his stamps and envelopes, as Alan Keel's research seems to have proven. This is what has made "Zodiac DNA" so elusive over the years.

Knowing how Zodiac applied the stamps to the letters using tap water, there is no reason he would not have offered up his DNA for comparison to DNA from the letters. After all, there was virtually no risk in doing so, and *not* doing so would, like the refusal of someone to take a polygraph test if he or she is innocent, raise a lot of eyebrows. This was especially true in 2002 for someone like Kjell Qvale.

Just one month after this book was published in December 2017 something amazing happened. In January 2018, on Tom Voigt's zodiackiller.com website, he interviewed an anonymous police source with knowledge of SFPD's DNA testing. This individual indicated that he/she had recently retired and was now willing to talk. What he or she said is that *"there is no Zodiac DNA and there never was."* The source went on to say that in 2002, after Dr. Cydne Holt had examined the glue side of the stamps and the seals of the envelope flaps for DNA and found no DNA from the letter writer, she had provided ABC News with *a DNA fragment that she had obtained from the front of a Zodiac stamp.*

While anonymous individuals are generally considered poor sources of factual information, this story seems to have a ring of truth to it because it serves to explain many of the facts I have learned over the years. Alan Keel had shown in the 1990s that the person sending the Zodiac letters hadn't licked the stamps and flaps. Therefore, it's not unexpected that Dr. Holt didn't find any DNA in the glue of the stamps and flaps. In order to fulfill her mandate to provide ABC News with DNA from *somewhere* on a Zodiac letter, the only logical thing to do was to obtain it from the front of a stamp, where all the contamination is located, as a last resort. Obviously, a solitary sample of DNA from the front side of a letter that had been handled by an untold number of people since it arrived in 1969 can hardly be assumed to have come from the Zodiac. In fact, given the absence of DNA anywhere else on the letter, it may well be assumed that, until otherwise proven, this DNA did NOT come from the Zodiac letter writer. But that was how it had been used by ABC News in October 2002 to throw my research under the proverbial bus and destroy my credibility. Finally, after sixteen years, the shackles of a "DNA exclusion" of my suspect had been removed, even if they should never have been applied in the first place.

...

Meanwhile, my research into Qvale continued on other fronts.

A few months after the ABC show, I was scrolling through microfilm of the *San Francisco Chronicle* and *San Francisco Examiner* for all the years starting in 1950, searching for a letter from Qvale to the editor of either paper that he had published on November 20 that, I hoped, formed the basis of his commemorations of that date. In the November 15–30 reel of the *San Francisco Examiner* from 1955, I had looked at November 20 and was scrolling to get to November 21 in case the letter had simply been postmarked by Qvale on November 20 and published later in the week. But I stopped my advance of the microfilm too quickly between editions and by complete and utter chance ended up in the sports pages for November 20. Since I was already there, I decided to look at the horse racing charts to see if Qvale was racing in those days. If so, I could find the names of his horses, et cetera. That decision turned out to be a fateful one.

I was going slowly through the sports pages when suddenly there it was right before my eyes. I couldn't believe what I was seeing! It was an article about hunting, of all things. In it, the author was explaining the proper method for placing the feet in order to be able to swivel your torso and shoot birds on the wing. Accompanying the article was a figure. The figure was something that, given who he was, would have made a youthful Zodiac's eyes pop out of his head, just as it had done to me that day. It consisted of a crossed circle—a perfect representation of Zodiac's signature. But it was what was inside the crossed circle that really got my attention. To show the shooter how to position his feet properly, there were two lines that came from the intersection of the *x* and *y* axes at the center of the crossed circle and went into the right upper quadrant of the circle. These lines had little feet drawn on them to demonstrate to the reader how to assume the correct stance for shooting. *To my eye these two lines formed a near-perfect radian!* (See Exhibit 35.)

Here was a figure that represented not one but *both* of the figures Zodiac would either use or refer to in his letters—the crossed circle of his signature *and* the radian he had proposed for Mt. Diablo! And it was in an article dated November 20.

When you connect the murders at Blue Rock Springs and in San Francisco to Mt. Diablo, they essentially, if not precisely, form a radian angle of approximately 57–58 degrees (Exhibit 36). (Note: A true radian is one degree more than the 56-degree angle in the hunting article diagram, but the 56-degree angle was virtually indistinguishable with the naked eye from a true radian.) Anyone whose mind was attuned to such things as radians, as the Zodiac clearly was, would have immediately seen the similarity between the angle in the illustration and a radian. Zodiac also mentioned *radians*, an exceptionally unusual word for a serial killer to know, in his July 26, 1970, letter. Therefore, illustrations of both of Zodiac's pet symbols, the crossed circle and the radian, were contained in this article. I felt that someone like Zodiac would have immediately identified with this composite symbol. He may then have come to view the date of November 20 as a lucky talisman of sorts and a significant one to him.

I felt I had at last found the connection between the November 20 date that Qvale commemorated several times beginning with the 1958 *Daily Commercial News* article (as discussed in chapter 18) and symbols the killer used or spoke of in his letters. And the way I had found it was by complete chance. Had I not happened to stop that reel of microfilm too soon that day, I would likely never have located this article.

...

I later made a stunning discovery that had escaped all Zodiac researchers who had come before me. Conspicuous by its absence in Zodiac's 57–58-degree radian angle (which connects Mt. Diablo at its vertex to Blue Rock Springs and Presidio Heights) is the spot marked by the Lake Herman Road murder site. Or was it? I asked myself why, in his taunting phone call after the Blue Rock Springs attack, the killer seemed to lead investigators to that obscure byway off Columbus Parkway, St. John's Mine Road,[153] which lies one mile north and west of Columbus Parkway. I then remembered the phone booth at Tuolumne Street and Springs Road in Vallejo. So I got a map and marked all three places. When I used the phone booth as the vertex and measured the angle between a line connecting the phone booth to St. John's Mine Road and a line connecting the phone booth to the Lake Herman Road site, I realized this was nearly a perfect radian angle, of about 56 degrees. That is too close to 57–58 degrees to be coincidental. So Zodiac seemingly had created not one but *two* radians as part of his crimes! If Zodiac intentionally chose the phone booth nearest the police station for his taunting phone call on the night of the Ferrin-Mageau attack, then I believe I know why he singled out the otherwise obscure location of St. John's Mine Road: when that point on the map is linked to the Lake Herman Road crime scene with the phone booth as the vertex of the

---

153 Ed Neil, personal communication, 1999.

angle, it formed his first radian (Exhibit 37).

In his July 26, 1970, Little List Letter, Zodiac used the plural "Radians," not the singular *radian*. Maybe this was a hint that went unnoticed for many years that there were, in fact, two iterations of the radian to be discovered. Though I don't know what he meant by "# inches along the radians," I will note that two of the legs of these radians cross either on or very close to Lake Herman. So I am left to wonder if Zodiac may have ditched his guns or other evidence in that lake. I have always felt that Zodiac chose the lovers' lane at Lake Herman for his first murders because of the clear view of Mt. Diablo at that site, so this location may have had tremendous symbolic importance to him.

Even though I didn't discover it until forty years after his first murders, this actually was Zodiac's *first* radian angle. The killer may have planted a clue to his second radian, the one with which the public is familiar, linking two of the other crime scenes to Mt. Diablo by killing exactly where he did on Lake Herman Road. When you look south from the roadside turnout where Jensen and Faraday were murdered, virtually all you see looming before you is Mt. Diablo—*the vertex of the second radian angle* (Exhibit 38).

PART ELEVEN
ENDGAME

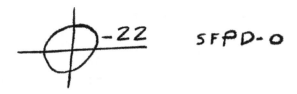

Coming Face-to-Face: The 2006 Interview

"I have to ignore threats from anybody, a politician or otherwise, who is not up to speed on his facts."
—Kjell Qvale, "Kopp, Burton Chime In on Bay Meadows Plan," by Mike Brunker, *San Francisco Examiner*, August 11, 1995

IN JUNE 2006, when I was speaking with Zodiac researcher Mike Butterfield about the case, he suddenly informed me that he was going to call Kjell Qvale and try to discuss the Zodiac murders with him. I was never very excited about other researchers calling Qvale to ask him questions, because I always feared that this might be the tipping point for a lawsuit against me. (Zodiac researcher Tom Voigt had also spoken to Qvale in about 2000.[154]) However, by 2006 I also knew I couldn't

---

154 One interesting point came out of Voigt's interview. While most people in 2000 would have pegged Zodiac as being in his sixties or seventies based on the age estimates of the killer provided in the 1960s, Qvale stated that he thought Zodiac would "be in his eighties" in 2000. This was out of line with those estimates. Mr. Qvale was in his eighties at the time.

talk a hardcore "Zodiac researcher" out of calling Qvale once he or she had decided to do so. So I went along with the plan and provided some questions to Butterfield in June 2006.

After the conversation he had with Qvale, Butterfield informed me that Qvale stated that if he could meet with me personally, he could convince me I was chasing after the wrong person. However, I had strong reservations about such a meeting. For one thing, I am neither a skilled police investigator nor a professional interrogator. Moreover, I also have never felt it was my place as an amateur investigator to take on the role that is normally reserved for the police. I had always hoped that someone from inside law enforcement would take on the challenge of questioning Qvale about the case. This had been my goal, as stated throughout this book, since 1999. Some of my critics said that I somehow "relished" the opportunity to play police interrogator and go to San Francisco to interview Qvale. However, the exact *opposite* is true: I actually felt betrayed by the police who had consistently run in fear every time I mentioned Qvale's name and were now forcing me into a role for which I was not at all suited or qualified.

In 2000, retired Napa County Sheriff's Office captain Ken Narlow told me something that I never forgot. **He said that what someone needed to do was to get a story out of Qvale and then try to poke holes in that story to see if it was the truth.** In the summer of 2006, Ken's words were still ringing in my ears, so I decided to take Qvale up on his offer. I informed him of my decision through Butterfield, who essentially brokered the deal. As part of my meeting with him, I felt that it was incumbent upon me to give Mr. Qvale every opportunity to refute my evidence and convince me that I was indeed researching the wrong person.

Six years earlier, Det. Joe Steiner of the Napa Sheriff's Office had told me that if I thought Qvale was the Zodiac I should go out to Presidio Heights, knock on his door, and ask him myself. At the time, I laughed out loud at his idea. Now it was actually coming to pass.

In 1999, the idea of interviewing Qvale about the Zodiac case had come up in my conversations with Dr. Mike Kelleher. At that time, he said it would probably take years of grueling research in order for anyone to be prepared for such an undertaking. Before the interview could take place, I would have to do plenty of research on Qvale's life, as well as on places, dates, and times relevant to the case. If you interviewed the man who was the Zodiac and he sensed that you weren't in command of all the facts about both him and the case, the interview would quickly become a disaster. This notion was foreshadowed by the quote from Qvale at the beginning of this chapter. Some six years and hundreds of hours of research later, I had fulfilled those preconditions and felt equipped for the role that was being thrust upon me.

I got out to the Bay Area in August 2006 and contacted Qvale through his dealership. Our conversations were oddly amicable, like old friends renewing their acquaintance. At first, we had decided to meet each other with "seconds," but then we changed our meeting to Friday. He and I would go to Golden Gate Fields for lunch and some races. There, and presumably in the car on the way to and from the track, we would talk about the case. I found it extremely odd that he would want to be seen with me in public discussing the possibility of his being the Zodiac, but I went along with his plan in order to make myself as accessible as possible: I didn't want to give him a reason to back out.

A few days before that meeting was to take place, I called him to finalize things. I really had no idea why he wanted to meet with me. Did he want to buy my silence and put me on a nondisclosure agreement? At the end of the conversation, I jokingly said that we were getting along so well that after the meeting he might want to give me a Bentley to drive. Now, I couldn't even afford the insurance for such a gas guzzler, and I wouldn't want one even if it were put in my driveway overnight. But I wanted to see how he would react. He called me back a day or so later to state that he was unable to make our appointed meeting on that Friday because he would be "out of town." He asked if we could meet in the initial format that we had discussed—with "seconds." Maybe he thought I was serious about the Bentley and wanted a witness at his side for the encounter. The day he picked out was the next Wednesday; the place, his office on Van Ness Avenue. I agreed to the meeting time and place and called Jim Dean, who was to be my second.

A friend of mine who follows horse racing sent me an email on Friday, the day of the now postponed meeting. He had learned that Qvale was not going to be out of town over the weekend. In fact, per the *Daily Racing Form*, he was going to be on a three-member panel at Golden Gate Fields racetrack on Saturday answering questions from prospective horse owners on how to get involved in racing. So the story about him being away for the weekend was clearly false. This was just the first of many things in my interactions with Qvale that would eventually turn out to be a fabrication.

I decided not to attend the seminar. In light of what eventually transpired at our meeting, this was a decision that I would come to regret. However, while I did go to Golden Gate Fields that day to bet on the races, I arrived in the afternoon for the first post. I'd decided not to attend Qvale's morning panel discussion because I felt it was inappropriate and even disrespectful for me to do so. In retrospect, I wish I had been there to see the facility, or lack thereof, with which Qvale fielded questions. Had I attended and he answered questions easily, that would have greatly changed my reaction to what his "second" was to tell me just before our meeting a few days later.

That Monday I had a doctor's appointment in downtown San Francisco. As I sat in the exam room waiting for the doctor to come in, I allowed myself to start thinking about the meeting that was set for Wednesday. I finally thought about the date. Monday was September 25. In two days, it would be the day of the meeting, which I suddenly realized would be on *September 27*: Qvale had rescheduled our meeting for the anniversary of the Lake Berryessa attack by the Zodiac Killer (which was also Qvale's father's birthday)! I shook my head and smiled at the irony of his date change, the same type of irony for which Zodiac had shown a penchant with his greeting cards and jokes.

In mid-September, I had mailed Qvale a copy of my entire report and its documentation. He therefore had access to everything I had learned about him up until that time. I did so out of respect for who he was and for everything he had accomplished in his life. I wanted to be as fair and evenhanded to him as possible, and to give him the opportunity he had requested to prove that I was on the wrong path by refuting any or all of my research.[155] After my meeting with Qvale, some message-board posters said I was ill-advised and even "stupid" to have sent him all my research beforehand. I then sat down with index cards and came up with a series of simple questions based on the material in my report. There were no trick questions among them. I played it straight up, just as my report is completely factual and documented.

Looking back, I don't believe the same thing can be said for the other side.

On the day of the meeting, which was scheduled for 10:00 AM, retired VPD detective Jim Dean was running late. Where was my second?! Ironically, even though he had grown up in the Mission District with Carlos Santana as one of his high school classmates, Jim had somehow gotten lost coming off the Bay Bridge and ended up on Cesar Chavez Boulevard, south of where he wanted to be![156]

I arrived promptly at the appointed hour and sat in Qvale's spacious marble showroom. As I walked in, I had seen him in his office on the upper floor peering out into the distance. He looked nervous and distracted to me. For some reason, I was completely at ease, probably since I was well prepared, considering the amount of research I had done since 1999: I felt like I had known Qvale for years. I hadn't been

---

155 I also did this in order to fire a proverbial shot over Qvale's legal bow and let him know what information would come out about him in open court if he ever sued me.

156 Ironically, I was living in Precita Heights right on Cesar Chavez Boulevard when I was in San Francisco. In fact, years later I finally watched the movie *Bullitt* and realized to my surprise that the house I was living in was right behind the gas station with the slanted, triangular roof where the two cars made U-turns before beginning the famous car chase scene!

there but a couple of minutes when Qvale's second came hustling down the stairs, took me aside, and said that at age eighty-seven Kjell's mind had begun to "wander" and that I should "take it easy on him." This came as a shock to me because I had seen no inkling of this discussed on the Net. I didn't even think of the horse racing seminar from a few days earlier. I immediately felt ashamed about having accepted the offer to ask questions of this man. I also felt badly that Qvale wanted in good faith to try to answer questions about the Zodiac case in an apparently weakened state. I cursed the detectives who had cowered and played politics since 1999, and that the interview hadn't taken place years earlier. I assured the man that this was to be a conversation, not an interrogation, and waited to be called upstairs. Finally, I was asked to go up.

I walked into Qvale's sizable office, which was lined with many books and also memorabilia from his long career as a car importer, horse owner and entrepreneur, and shook hands with him. I placed my stack of interview materials, including a copy of his 2005 autobiography, on the chair next to me. I felt the cold stare of the two secretaries as I had walked past them and gathered that they knew why I was there. I was immediately struck by the fact that Qvale was wearing a tie with tiny horses on it. Jim came along a few minutes later and the meeting was on. I soon forgot about the little horses.

Put yourself for a moment into Mr. Qvale's shoes. If someone from across the country had come to San Francisco to accuse you of being the Zodiac Killer, what would you have wanted to say to him? What would you have wanted him to know about you? I know that I would have stated that I was incapable of executing a teenager by shooting her in the back as she ran away or of shooting Faraday point-blank in the head. I would not be able to bring myself to pull the trigger. Likewise, I would be incapable of tying a young woman up and then stabbing her ten times while she pleaded and screamed for her life.

Qvale said no such things to me, although he did state several times that he "wouldn't hurt a fly." Somehow the more he repeated this mantra, the less convincing it sounded to Jim and me.

I first affirmed to Mr. Qvale that I was truly sorry that I was getting to meet a man of his accomplishments under the circumstances that had brought us together. I never lost track of who Qvale was and of what he had achieved in life. And although some people may find this bizarre and contradictory, throughout my research I never lost respect for Qvale the entrepreneur and horse owner; this was never personal for me.

I started off by saying to him what I had just said to his friend, "This will be a conversation, not an interrogation." I made it clear to Kjell that I was only going to ask him some questions. The first thing I commented on was the irony of meeting on September 27, the anniversary of the Berryessa attack and of his father's birthday. He turned to his second and shared a snicker with him. He indicated that it was purely a "scheduling conflict" that had necessitated the change of dates to that day.

With that point having been made and noted, I asked him where he was on the night of the Stine murder. After all, the Stine eyewitnesses said that Presidio Heights was a boring place and that "nothing ever happened" there. Surely nearly everyone who lived there in 1969 would remember what he or she was doing on the most thrilling night in the history of a neighborhood that seemed otherwise to lack any excitement. He told me, as he had told Butterfield in June, that he couldn't specifically recall where he was but he thought he *should have been* in England on October 11, 1969. He regretted that he couldn't locate his passport from that time period with the visa stamp as proof positive of his whereabouts. This despite the fact that Qvale apparently kept meticulous records, something I learned in the 2012 book *Lunches with Mr. Q*. Qvale attributed this quality to his wife at our 2006 meeting.

Qvale asked if I had received a copy of his autobiography in the mail recently. I was confused because I had a copy in front of me. Surprised by his statement, I said that I had not. However, after the meeting, I called my home in New Jersey and found that a book had indeed arrived via the mail. I believe that Qvale was clearly trying to unnerve or intimidate me by letting me know that he knew where I lived. I never felt threatened by him, either that day or at any time afterward, because I had plenty of friends in law enforcement. If anything untoward ever happened to me, they would've made a beeline directly to Qvale.

At some point, Jim tried to ask a question or follow up on a point I had made. Qvale's second immediately jumped in and stifled Jim's question, saying the conversation was to be between just "Mr. Q" and Mr. Rodelli. That was the first time I'd heard Qvale called Mr. Q. Jim wasn't permitted to speak again after that. Needless to say, this didn't make him at all happy.

I reminded Kjell that a retired SFPD inspector named Armond Pelissetti stated that he had run into him on Maple Street shortly after the Stine murder. He replied with another awkward statement—that he only walked a dog "twice in [his] life." I neglected to ask if the night of the Stine murder was one of those nights. He added that he "never" walked around his own neighborhood and that if he wanted to get exercise, he would "go to the gym." His answer seemed a bit odd. In his autobiography he explained how he doted on Silky Sullivan[157] and expressed a profound devotion on a dog that he owned named Jack. If Qvale's statement to me about only walking a dog twice in his life was accurate, then walking Jack or any other dog that night, as reported by Pelissetti, was a highly unusual event. One must then wonder *why* Qvale was out walking a dog on the night of the Stine murder if he did not normally do so. And if he wasn't out walking a dog, why does Pelissetti insist that he was? My feeling was that Qvale's reply represented a double-edged sword for him, given Pelissetti's statement.

---

157 In photos of Qvale in his autobiography standing with Silky Sullivan, Qvale is dressed in chestnut-colored chaps and clothes that match the color of the horse's coat. Given his well-documented aloofness, in addition to the almost human characteristics he described in the horse at various times, this suggests that he may have related better to Silky than he did to people.

I made a mental note of this response, since, in addition to Armond Pelissetti's statements, **recall that ABC News had told me in 2001 that they could not place Qvale outside the country at any of his "usual haunts" (which included England) on any of the Zodiac murder dates.**

The interesting thing is that Qvale could easily have said that he was out on the streets of Presidio Heights that evening and that it was nothing unusual. After all, he lived in the neighborhood and walked his dog every night at 10:00 PM. And how could I have contested his statement, since it would have made perfect sense? But instead, he told me an odd story that not only sounded unlikely but was, according to Pelissetti and ABC News, also untrue. Why did he choose to provide me with an account of his whereabouts that he knew was being contested by a member of SFPD? Recall that in 2011 Pelissetti would tell fellow Zodiac researcher Mark that Qvale apparently told amateurs who questioned him things that were false to make us go away. This would cast Qvale's answers to me in a much different light.

So, to summarize, Armond Pelissetti stated in 2006 and 2008 that he had encountered Qvale while walking a dog on Maple Street. Pelissetti then changed his story in 2011 and stated that he had first encountered Qvale and his dog while Qvale was standing in his front yard, not on Maple Street. For his part, Qvale says that this encounter never happened at all and that he was possibly out of the country. At any rate, he added that he essentially never walked a dog in his life. Pelissetti told Mark that Qvale lied to people to get them to leave him alone. It would seem to be a simple matter that these two men would tell the same story about a memorable event that happened for both of them on a very memorable night. But when you got down to interviewing them about that incident, they ended up telling false and/or contradictory stories. Why is this the case?

Pelissetti ties his arrival back at the crime scene to the arrival of SFPD inspectors Armstrong and Toschi. This would make his trek around the block a long one if it started around 10:00 PM. This is because

336 · MIKE RODELLI

Toschi and Armstrong were apparently much later in getting there than anyone had ever realized before; that is, probably not before 10:45 PM (footnote 33). So what is the timing of his encounter with Qvale, and why did it take Pelissetti so long to get back to the crime scene? How long after the murder did his encounter with Qvale actually take place? Pelissetti says it was very soon afterward. How long did it last? Why didn't Pelissetti tell anyone in his 2003, 2006, or 2008 interviews how far he'd actually walked to the east on Jackson Street? (In 2011 he would place himself near or opposite Qvale's property at 3636 Jackson Street.)

Why is it that neither of these two men could provide a straight answer when it came to detailing their supposedly simple, brief, innocent encounter on the night of the Stine murder? Why did Pelissetti call me in 2004 and try to discourage me from investigating Qvale any further, with his "alibi" claim? If Pelissetti is providing Qvale an alibi based on how quickly they met, why couldn't he keep his story straight as to where that encounter had taken place?

...

Qvale next volunteered that he did not follow the Zodiac case or any developments related to it at all except if a story happened to appear in the day's newspapers. I found this incredibly odd for someone who lived in the very neighborhood where one of the murders took place, a serene place where "nothing ever happened." This was especially true since an SFPD officer spoke to him right after the Stine murder, and his house was right down Maple Street from the killer's original destination in Stine's cab.

It's no exaggeration to say that seemingly *everyone* in the Bay Area was reading and talking about the Zodiac by mid-November 1969. That fact was confirmed on the *Zodiac* movie DVD when Robert Graysmith stated that the only topic of conversation by small groups of people at the paper was the Zodiac case.[158] It isn't difficult to imagine

---

158 Fincher, 2008.

that after Zodiac made his threat against schoolchildren, the story was in the forefront of everyone's mind all around the Bay Area. Everyone's, that is, except Kjell Qvale's.

I next asked Qvale what guns he had registered over time. He quickly protested that he'd "never so much as touched a gun" in his entire life. I reminded him that he had been drafted into World War II. He stated that this was true, but that he'd been a transport pilot. The only gun he had ever learned to shoot was the tail gun of the plane, in case the normal operator was shot or otherwise incapacitated.

Qvale then told a story to illustrate his point. He talked about a mare that was in foal at his ranch, but the baby was too big for the mother to deliver it. A decision was made to put the mare out of her misery. Qvale stated that it was his farmhand who wielded the gun to end the suffering of the poor animal. But for some reason, after he finished the story, Qvale started to go through the same story again. During that recounting he placed the gun very briefly in his *own* hand before once again asserting that the ranch hand had pulled the trigger. This minor alteration was noticed by both Jim and me, as we quickly looked at each other to make sure we had heard correctly.

I asked Qvale if he was aware that saliva was used to test for drugs in horses postrace in the 1960s and that this area of the track was known as a spit box. He denied any such knowledge. Recall that Dr. Ron Jensen had told me in 2003 that old-timers who had been around in the 1960s would have known about this term from the days of saliva testing of racehorses.

I then questioned Qvale about the crossed-circle symbol that appears on his building in Modena, Italy. Qvale bought this building in 1999 to house the manufacturing plant for his Qvale Mangusta sports car. Qvale chuckled indignantly and said that I was "seeing what [I wanted] to see." He assured me that the building was purchased "as is" from a locksmith company and that the crossed-circle symbol with a giant Q surrounding it was nothing more than a giant "key" that symbolized the locksmith business. He therefore implicitly denied any

338 • MIKE RODELLI

involvement in influencing what the symbol looked like, although there was a perceptible change in that symbol over time. This notion would turn out to be demonstrably false.

I asked Qvale if he had any in-depth knowledge of Norwegian/Norse culture and if he still celebrated his Norse roots. He denied knowing anything about Norse gods, runes, et cetera, and said he really didn't pay much attention to his cultural heritage.

I posed a question as to whether or not he attended the *Los Angeles Times* Grand Prix on the weekend of October 29–30, 1966. He said that he only went to Riverside "a couple of times." This answer did not preclude his being in Riverside that weekend. His reply was, in effect, a non sequitur.

I inquired if he knew what *sla* meant in Old Norse. He confirmed that it meant "kill" in that obscure language. He also corrected Zodiac's spelling of the word, adding a unique Norwegian character (å) to the end of the word in place of the Latin alphabetic character *a*. There has been much debate about the nuances of the meaning of *slå* in Old Norse based on definitions found in various academic dictionaries, but to Qvale it evidently meant "kill."

Qvale stated that, even though he owned a ranch in Oakville, he had never been to Lake Berryessa and didn't know anything about the layout of the city of Napa. He claimed that when he went to Oakville, a pilot would fly him to a small airport south of Napa. He would then take "back roads" to get to his ranch, thereby avoiding the town. Here is an implicit admission that he traveled the back roads of at least Napa County. Zodiac himself was also apparently familiar with these types of byways in the Bay Area. Qvale therefore didn't drive through the city of Napa itself to get to Oakville.

Qvale claimed that he had no knowledge of Vallejo or Lake Herman Road. He never played golf at Blue Rock Springs golf course. He claimed that he only played the two exclusive courses in San Francisco to which he belonged as a member—San Francisco Country Club and the Olympic Club. He said he only went to the horse races at the Solano County Fairgrounds in Vallejo "a few times." However, Judge Uldall had told me in 2001 that Qvale was frequently present at least at Golden Gate Fields, in San Francisco, when his horses ran.

The pattern of Qvale's answers shows that even in his own neighborhood and around the ranch that he owned for many years, he was portraying himself as a "stranger in a strange land." He doesn't really know anything about any of the areas where he lived or owned property. He never walked a dog, or only walked one "twice in [his] life." He knew nothing about Napa. This is either not the truth or clearly proves that Qvale was extraordinarily aloof and lived almost like a recluse in his home and at his ranch.

However, the truth is that Qvale was a globetrotting entrepreneur with a far-flung business empire that spanned several states and even Europe. He was a world traveler who had ties to England for many years. He even owned an auto manufacturing plant in England and later in Italy. He said to me in our meeting that he'd traveled about "half the year" in 1969. He had skied at all the major winter sports venues across the globe. He took a trip to the Galapagos in 2012 because he had been "so many places" that he'd run out of countries to visit.[159] He participated in many different public events, like car shows. He organized auto races and road rallies that made the drivers travel all over Northern California. He helped design a part of Laguna Seca race course. He owned and raced horses for years. All of this seems to contradict the reclusive, monastic, almost Howard Hughes–like existence that he seemed to describe when asked if he was familiar with the Zodiac crime scene areas. Despite being enamored of back roads, he apparently had little working knowledge of his own neighborhood and other areas he visited.

For no particular reason, Qvale volunteered that when he opened his car dealership, he was so young looking that people used to come in and ask if they could speak to his father, presuming that the man they were speaking to was too young to be the owner. He therefore

---

159 Nelson, p. 69.

took to wearing glasses *that he did not need* in order to look older. These glasses presumably had neutral lenses in them. This shows that Qvale was aware of things he could do to alter his appearance, as Zodiac may have done on the night he killed Paul Stine by wearing several sweaters to make himself look bigger and bulkier than he was. The man at Lake Berryessa was described by victim Cecelia Shepard to Dave Collins as being "bulky" looking. Might he have piled on sweaters under his windbreaker to make himself look heavier and done the same for the Stine murder?

Qvale stated that he had no knowledge of cryptography and that he only learned Morse code in the navy (although he couldn't think of the term *Morse code*).

He claimed he had no idea where he was on December 20, 1968, July 4–5, 1969, or September 27, 1969. I tried to jog his memory by asking if there were any annual family celebrations or gatherings he could recall on any of these dates, which are either on or near holidays, or on his father's birthday, September 27. He couldn't recall any that would have helped him place himself anywhere in particular.

He brushed off his flying-saucer sighting by saying that he only reported it because nobody else had. Clearly, he was minimizing this incident. His statements were so shocking and unusual that they got him on the front pages of two Bay Area newspapers at the time. They also made him the only credible person in over 850 reports from across the entire US at that time to say flying saucers were from outer space.

To prove that his statement to the press was not so casual, consider that Qvale's sighting reportedly took place at 2:30 PM on Saturday, July 5, 1947, in Auburn, California. The first account was in the *Alameda Times-Star* on *Monday, July 7, 1947*. So Qvale didn't even wait *one day* before calling in his report. In fact, he must have reported the incident to the *Times-Star* either on the evening of July 5 but too late to make the July 6 edition, or on July 6, since it was in that paper just two days after his sighting. He didn't just "casually glance at the papers for a few days" and then pick up the phone when he happened to notice that nobody else had reported the incident. In reality, he was right on top of the story, by the next day at the latest, in order to get his sighting into the July 7 newspaper.

In his autobiography, Qvale described how the members of his family all had to learn to do household chores after his mother died. In that account, he admits to being good at ironing, but he doesn't mention sewing.[160] However, it's clear that once his mother died the family had to collectively become skilled in domestic chores like sewing. Despite that, Qvale stated that he didn't have the sewing skills necessary to be Zodiac and sew the crossed circle into the hood at Lake Berryessa.

He denied being a fan of old movies, like *The Most Dangerous Game* or *Charlie Chan at Treasure Island*. He stated that his parents were "not the type of people" to be interested in light opera. He had no knowledge of *The Mikado*.

He claimed he'd had no major conflicts with his parents as a child. He described his mother as having been a "saint." Given that Qvale felt this way, I later wondered if the source of his possible anger at his father stemmed from the fact that he remarried to Florence Jacobson so quickly, that is, in March of 1942, just over two years after Signe's death.[161]

He seemed not to have any knowledge of astrology (although, there is no evidence that Zodiac did either).

He said that after reading over his letter to the editor of the *San Francisco Chronicle* from 1969 he could see nothing in it that would have any relevance to the Zodiac case.

In the book *Helter Skelter*, author/prosecutor Vincent Bugliosi states, "An innocent man protests his innocence."[162] Qvale didn't spend any time protesting his innocence to me in our meeting; in fact, neither

---

160 Qvale, p. 14.

161 Bjarne F. Qvale, *The Qvale Family* (Publisher Unknown: 1980), p. 52.

162 Vincent Bugliosi with Curt Gentry, *Helter Skelter: The True Story of the Manson Murders* (New York: Norton, 1974), p. 306.

342 · MIKE RODELLI

Jim nor I recall him saying it even once. As stated earlier, Qvale only reiterated that he "would not hurt a fly."

I asked Qvale if he knew of anyone who might have wanted to frame him for the Zodiac crimes. He said he did not.

When Zodiac needed a quiet neighborhood in which to kill a cab driver, he chose Qvale's own obscure Presidio Heights area. He was last seen walking on the same side of the street as Qvale's home and only a block away from reaching it. He also looked just like Qvale that night. When Zodiac needed a battery to power his "bus bomb," he chose a six-volt car battery, which he could well have taken out of one of the British cars that Qvale sold in 1969. When he needed to show us all how smart he was, he chose an obscure word in Old Norse. When he needed a symbol to sign his letters, he chose the crossed circle, which has all the letters of Qvale's name in it and which Qvale later had prominently displayed right under his name on his Modena building.

As Jim and I stood up to leave Qvale's office that day, Qvale nodded toward my report that I had mailed to him a week or so before our meeting. It was lying on his desk. He said that he had not read it, did not want it, and that I should take it away with me. I paused for a second. Then I looked him in the eye and said that I had prepared the report for him and he could do whatever he wanted with it. I didn't touch it or take it with me. Afterward, I sensed that I'd been given some sort of test. The tremendous symbolism in Qvale's request escaped me on a conscious level that day. I believe he was literally asking me to take back everything I had said. But I refused, and in doing so, I reinforced the fact that, to this day, I stand behind both my research and my conclusions.

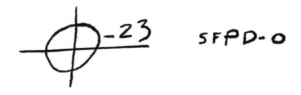

DECEPTION: 2006 AND BEYOND

"Dr. Zodiac man of great ego . . . enjoy using his power to dominate the lives of others. . . . To destroy false prophet must first unmask before eyes of believers."
—Charlie Chan, *Charlie Chan at Treasure Island*, 1939

"I shall appear on your stage tonight. Dr. Zodiac."
—note to Charlie Chan, *Charlie Chan at Treasure Island*, 1939

WHEN JIM DEAN AND I WALKED OUT of Kjell Qvale's dealership on September 27, 2006, my mind was reeling. Since we had not recorded the meeting, our first order of business was to retire to a 1950s'-style diner across Van Ness from Qvale's showroom to compare notes on the questions I had asked in order to make sure we had all of Qvale's responses to my questions straight. I was thinking about Qvale's answers and his motive for our meeting. Jim had moved from contemplation to anger. In fact, he was livid. He felt that we had been had. He called the meeting "Machiavellian" in nature. He felt that Qvale was being deceptive and that they had tried to throw us off our game by stating that Qvale's mind "wandered" and by silencing Jim.

As I left Qvale's dealership, I replayed the meeting in my mind. Qvale had been alert and answered our questions easily, without much hesitation, and no "wandering" of his mind had been apparent to Jim or me. I had expected that Qvale would be open and honest with me that day. At that point, I didn't know, as Armond Pelissetti would later reveal to Mark, that he *would lie* to get rid of people. I had rather naively assumed that the meeting would be run in a fair and aboveboard manner on both sides. However, my subsequent research would slowly piece together a story that proved otherwise.

My plan, when I had driven out to San Francisco that summer, was to stay in the area indefinitely and keep trying to prove that Qvale was Zodiac. But after the meeting ended I was conflicted and needed to get some answers to help plot the future course of my research. So I turned to the person who had brokered my meeting with Qvale: I called and emailed Mike Butterfield. I needed to hear once more from Pelissetti through Butterfield that it was unequivocally Kjell Qvale that he had spoken to on the night of the Stine murder. Qvale had contradicted Pelissetti's version of events by stating that he should have been in England, and I wanted to make sure that Pelissetti was 100 percent certain that he had spoken to Qvale. After hearing about our meeting with Qvale, Butterfield was confronted with the fact that Qvale may have given untruthful responses to some of my questions, and that there may be more to him than his completely respectable facade suggested. Butterfield never replied to my requests.

I knew that ABC News said it couldn't place Qvale in England that night. However, Pelissetti was a much more compelling witness because, while ABC was saying it could *not* place Qvale in England, Pelissetti was stating that he *could* assertively place Qvale on the streets of Presidio Heights. And that is a big difference.

Taking into account Jim's anger at what he thought of as a manipulated meeting and being told by his "second" that Qvale's mind "wandered," I looked into events in Qvale's life that might give credence to the "wandering mind" notion. I looked at the things that took place in the years *both leading up to and subsequent to* our meeting. This included items reported by the press and online media, as well as a book and a television commercial in which he participated. This research slowly but surely made me more cynical and suspicious of the statements Qvale's second made about Kjell having a "wandering mind" in 2006. It also began to convince me that Jim had been right about the level of deception that Qvale and his friend had "tag-teamed" us with that day. And if an innocent man has nothing to hide, what did that level of deception say about Qvale?

Continuing on my quest to track down additional discrepancies between what Qvale told me at our meeting and the truth, I first went to the San Francisco Public Library. I was trying to see if I could find a reference that said that small-arms instruction and cryptography were part of standard training for a World War II pilot. I found no definitive answers. However, in speaking to contacts of mine who had been in the military and learning of their own experiences with training, it seemed impossible, if not unimaginable, that someone going to war in any capacity would not receive any arms training at all. They pointed out that even the cooks, chaplains, and medics received such training in case they had to fight for their lives at some point. They also said that because Qvale was a transport pilot, he would have received survival training in case he were ever shot down over enemy territory. And part of survival in war is knowing how to shoot a gun.

In late October, I decided to drive back to New Jersey to do more research. As Ken Narlow had told me years earlier, I was trying to see if I could "poke holes" in Qvale's story.

The first thing that entered my mind was the panel discussion Qvale had on thoroughbred ownership at Golden Gate Fields just days before our meeting. I wondered how someone with a failing memory allowed himself to be subjected to the rigors of an open forum. He had to give a talk and then likely face questions from strangers on any subject related to racing and horse ownership that required an immediate and appropriate response. After all, he couldn't just sit on the panel and say nothing. Did people with such an affliction and as prominent as Qvale agree to participate in a session that may end up leaving them confused, at a loss for words, and completely embarrassed before potentially scores of people? This immediately made me think that there was something fishy about what Qvale's second had said about Kjell's "wandering mind." I kicked myself for not thinking of bringing up this panel forum as soon as he told me about Qvale's alleged affliction just before the start of our meeting.

The next thing I was able to learn was something that was staring me right in the face and that I should have known on the day of my meeting with Qvale. I kicked myself once again for not recalling the 1999 article from *Road and Track*[163] about Qvale's building in Modena, Italy. It was an article I already had in my possession and that I located in one of my folders weeks after the meeting. Here is a quote from the article, **"There is pride in his [Qvale's] voice as he takes you on a plant tour and explains how they'll convert the big circle on the building's front into a 'Giant *Q*"** (Exhibit 39). In his own words, Qvale tripped himself up. He had misled me at our meeting when he said that the building appeared as is when he purchased it, that the symbol on the building was nothing more than a previously existing giant key, and that I was seeing what I wanted to see. It was right there in black and white. He had left himself open to being contradicted on his 2006 statement to me with an interview he had done for this article. Since the article predated our interview by nearly seven years, Qvale had to know that proof to the contrary of what he told me in 2006 was out there and within my reach with research. However, I had missed an opportunity for a true Perry Mason moment at our meeting by producing a copy of this article. While it is correct that the building was once a locksmith's plant, it's also true that the "Giant *Q*" is there because Qvale *intentionally* placed it there—right around the crossed-circle symbol that contains the rest of the letters of his surname. He then tried to make me look

---

163 John Lamm, p. 70.

foolish in our meeting by chiding me about "seeing things" that only gave an illusion of supporting my case.

Lost in all of this discussion is the fact that Qvale didn't contest that there was actually a crossed-circle symbol within the large Q on the building he purchased. The bigger question is this: If I were truly "seeing things," and Qvale had absolutely nothing to hide with respect to his having placed the oversize Q on the facade of his plant in Modena, why didn't he just tell me that he had done precisely that in response to my question in 2006? And just as he could have given me a perfectly plausible story about walking his dog every night at 10:00 PM, Qvale chose to provide a more complex and patently untrue explanation. In other words, his evasive and misleading statements about the giant Q seem to suggest he had something to hide with respect to that symbol.

Qvale's compulsion to mislead me about something so seemingly innocent told me that my intuition was right. No matter how many names you can derive from a crossed circle, the one on that building was likely meant to spell out Q-V-A-L-E; thus the juxtaposition between the name Qvale on the sign and the crossed circle right below it on the building. By creating the huge Q with its line that extends straight down to the six o'clock position, he was giving us a clue. It seemed to me that, as was the case in Zodiac's two bus-bomb diagrams, Qvale had hidden a clue to his secret identity as Zodiac in plain sight—but this time it was on a different continent.

After I got back to New Jersey from San Francisco, I contacted a second thoroughbred veterinarian, Dr. Thomas Tobin of the University of Kentucky. Although I had already spoken to Dr. Jensen, I wanted to be as fair as possible to Qvale by getting a second opinion on the issue of saliva testing in racehorses. Dr. Tobin also felt that, given Qvale's close association with horse racing in the 1960s, he should have known about saliva testing for drugs at that time. While I can't get inside Qvale's mind and know exactly what he did or did not know, I can say what the probabilities are and what he *should* have known as both a horse owner and a track president from that era. Both Dr. Jensen and

Dr. Tobin agreed that postrace testing in thoroughbred horses for illegal medications was done via saliva in the early to mid-1960s.

Since Qvale was the president of the racetrack at that time, both of these veterinarians felt that he should have known that drug testing was being done on the grounds of his track and the methodology being employed. Drug testing is, after all, the backbone of the system that keeps the racing game honest. The president of a racetrack has to have his hand in every aspect of its operations, and while aloof with respect to people, Qvale appeared to be a hands-on type of person who controlled every aspect of his business empire. As president of the track, he may also have had to make or participate in disciplinary rulings against jockeys, trainers, or owners who violated the drug-testing policies. In addition, as an owner of racehorses, Qvale almost *had* to know the term *spit box*, which was a common term in the old days for the drug-testing area of the racetrack. In fact, the term is still in limited use today.

To equine veterinarians who know the racing game, Qvale's denial of knowing that saliva could be tested for at least drugs in the 1960s, like his denial of the giant *Q*, simply didn't have the ring of truth to it. And these veterinarians are the experts on the drug-testing aspect of the sport.

It seems virtually impossible for Qvale to have been both a horse owner *and* president of Golden Gate Fields and to move in the sport of horse racing at those rarefied levels and not be aware of saliva testing. His statement to me that he had never heard of a spit box was disingenuous. Therefore, from at least the perspective of drug testing and possibly A-B-O blood typing in secretors, I believe it's safe to say that Qvale would have known about the pitfalls of licking stamps and envelopes. This now puts the fact that Zodiac avoided licking his stamps and envelopes in a whole different light and provides a plausible, *scientific* reason for his not doing so that is much stronger than just the notion of someone "not liking the taste of glue."

The reality is that Qvale, due to his close relationship with a sport where saliva testing for medications was one of the rules, would've likely been one of the very few people in 1969 ever named as a Zodiac suspect to possess *specific knowledge* that licking stamps and envelopes could be potentially detrimental to his freedom. In light of this knowledge, the fact that Qvale volunteered a DNA sample in 2002 is not the proof positive that he had to be innocent of being the Zodiac that people believed it to be at the time. Zodiac was an organized killer. If he was aware of saliva testing for medications and blood type in the 1960s, he would have avoided licking his stamps and envelopes. Naturally, if Qvale knew that his tongue had never come into contact with the stamps and envelope flaps, then there is virtually no reason why he would not have offered a DNA sample for comparison in 2002—even if he *was* the Zodiac.

...

Meanwhile, other things were going on in my life.

In March 2007, there was no more coveted place to be for a Zodiac researcher than in the credits of the new David Fincher feature film about the case, *Zodiac*. Some of the most prominent amateur researchers active in the case didn't find their way into the credits of that movie. The story, which starred Robert Downey Jr., Mark Ruffalo, and Jake Gyllenhaal, was based on Graysmith's version of the Zodiac case. Nevertheless, when one of the producers of the film approached me in 2005 for assistance, I ended up getting SFPD officer Don Fouke to agree to help them with their research, since I was one of the few people who knew how to reach him. The net result was that Fouke appeared in person telling his side of the story on *This Is the Zodiac Speaking*, the DVD that accompanied the director's cut of the film that was released in 2008. In return for my assistance, I asked for no compensation other than to receive screen credit.

...

The next piece of information I came across about Qvale was from an article in the California Thoroughbred Breeders Association (CTBA) magazine from January 2008.[164] This article stated that Qvale had injured his hip skiing early in 2007, which was a few months *after* our September 2006 meeting. Did people with early-onset dementia expose themselves to the dangers of downhill skiing? Possibly, but this also made me wonder. A failing memory is usually associated with at least an implication of the onset of concomitant physical frailty, or at least diminished physical ability. In the article, Qvale is described as being "ever effervescent," which hardly seems a term one would use to describe someone with mentation that is slowing down in old age.

In response to Qvale's statement that he only went to Riverside "a couple of times" in 2000, I interviewed race car driver Bob Bondurant. Although I couldn't specifically state why I wanted to know the information for legal reasons, I asked him if he recalled Qvale being there the weekend of the *Los Angeles Times* Grand Prix in 1966. He said that Qvale was there that weekend and was present when they decided to scratch the Genie car that Bondurant was supposed to drive. That was on October 29, 1966. He said that Qvale would have flown down in his private plane.

Judge Rick Uldall told me in 2001 that Qvale was always at the racetrack when one of his horses was running. We know from the incident in 1964, when Qvale purchased The Scoundrel and also entered three cars at the Indy 500, that he liked to go and watch both his horses and his cars when they raced. After all, he loved speed. So it makes sense that he would have gone to Riverside on the weekend of the *Los Angeles Times* Grand Prix.

After much research calling experts on naval history in Washington, D.C., I was fortunate enough to be told about a yearbook of sorts that documented Qvale's training as a US Navy pilot in World War II. It was called *Mark II of the Slipstream*. I never would've imagined that

164 Larry Bortstein, "Kjell H. Qvale: Life in the Fast Lane," *California Thoroughbred Breeders Association Magazine,* January 2008, pp. 48–49.

a book detailing someone's military training even existed. On page 54 was a small photo of Qvale as a cadet from 1941, thus confirming that this yearbook was pertinent to what he would have experienced in the military at the time. In the section that detailed the training that cadets received that year in Corpus Christi, Texas, under "Gunnery" is a photo of a line of cadets taking target practice with sidearms. The caption reads, "Cadets take pride in a good target score"[165] (Exhibit 40). Although Qvale is not one of the cadets pictured, the training section was meant to be representative of the instruction received by *all of the cadets who went through that school*. That proved to me that Qvale had not been truthful when he said to Jim and me that he had "never so much as touched a gun" in his life. Once again, I was able to secure tangible proof that Qvale had likely given me an untruthful answer to a simple question in our 2006 meeting.

On July 6, 2009, there was an article by Richard Truett in *the Automotive News*[166] in which Qvale was interviewed about a deal between automakers DaimlerChrysler and Fiat. Qvale was able to provide insightful analysis of the future of the automobile business as well as to discuss recent downsizing he'd had to impose at his own dealership. This was nearly three years after his friend said that his mind had begun to "wander."

On July 17, 2009, Qvale turned ninety years old. To commemorate this occasion, Scott Ostler of the *San Francisco Chronicle* wrote an article about him.[167] In this article, he reinforced the notion that Qvale was a "risk-taker," which immediately stood out as being one trait of a power-assertive and a sociopath. He said that at the age of ninety Qvale was "still scanning the horizon, looking for the next adventure." Ostler said that "not in the picture" was retirement. Again, this hardly sounds

---

165 USNAS, p. 197.

166 Richard Truett, "Qvale, Nearing 90, Sees Life After Crash for US Industry," *Automotive News*, July 6, 2009, p. 10.

167 Scott Ostler, "Profile: Kjell Qvale, A Man for All Seasons, Ready for Any Race," *San Francisco Chronicle*, July 29, 2009, p. B3.

like what one would expect from someone who had suffered the onset of a "wandering mind" three years earlier. But the most damning thing in the article with regard to dementia that had supposedly begun to set in in 2006 is a statement about a musical instrument that Qvale was tackling.

Ostler stated that Qvale was just learning to play the piano for "the hell of it." This notion would be reinforced three years later in the book *Lunches with Mr. Q.*[168] The thing about dementia is that it's generally one's short-term memory that is the first thing affected. To someone who had an onset of this disease in 2006, a piano should have been an intimidating, if not impossible, venture. But here was Qvale in 2009, just starting to take lessons and learning to play a complex instrument. The notion of Qvale learning to play the piano with an impaired memory doesn't fit what one would imagine for the average person in his situation.

Ostler said that at his recent ninetieth birthday party, Qvale, who had told Jim and me that he didn't closely adhere to his Norse roots and didn't know much about Norse culture, had "danced the night away dressed as a Viking." In *Lunches with Mr. Q*, the author states that Qvale and his wife used to throw "Scandinavian-themed parties where hosts and guests dressed in traditional Norwegian *bunad* folk costumes."[169] This clearly contradicted what Qvale told me about his indifference toward his Scandinavian/Viking heritage in 2006. Nelson states, "Trondheim was the ancient capital of the Vikings and, [Qvale] noted proudly, his birthplace."[170] Nelson also reiterated Ostler's story about Qvale dressing up as a "Viking warrior" for his ninetieth birthday party.

---

168 Nelson, p. 15.

169 Nelson, p. 14.

170 Nelson, p. 133

Clearly Kjell Qvale was very much in tune with his Norse roots, despite his denials to Jim and me.[171] For the sake of argument, it may be conceivable that Qvale had forgotten that he had spoken to an SFPD officer on that memorable night in the quiet community of Presidio Heights, or that he had received small-arms training in the navy. But it is much more difficult to imagine that Qvale would have completely forgotten a lifetime of remaining true to his Norse heritage, that he and his wife had thrown a series of Norwegian-themed parties in the past, and that at those parties people went so far as to dress in traditional Norwegian garb.

The next piece of information I learned came from a 2010 article on www.thestarkinsider.com about a new business venture Qvale was embarking on at the age of ninety-one. He had decided to open a comedy club. In the article by Clinton Stark, Qvale was called "amazingly spry." Again, I wondered if someone who had a "wandering mind" in 2006 would still be considered "amazingly spry" and would be taking on a new business venture some four years later. As an added touch of irony, the author stated that the club had hired a comedian for opening night whose act was to sit in the audience and heckle the performers on stage. His name? **Dr. Z.**[172] (Recall that Dr. Zodiac was the character in the movie *Charlie Chan at Treasure Island* whose activities were analogous to a combination of Peek-a-Boo Pennington's dirt digging and Melvin Belli's extortion schemes.) It is also possible that the name "Dr. Z" was assumed by the performer just for that night. I searched the internet for a comedian with such a name in the Bay Area in 2010 and was unable to find one.[173]

---

171 Nelson, p. 15.

172 Clinton Stark, "Holly's Comedy Club a First-Class '70s Throwback," November 2010, www.thestarkinsider.com.

173 Mark spoke to the person after whom the club was named, and she said that she didn't recall any Dr. Z in the list of performers in the opening night lineup. Since Qvale owned the club, it's therefore possible that it was he who had hired the comedian without her knowledge.

354 · MIKE RODELLI

In 2011 Mark had his conversation with Armond Pelissetti to which I alluded in chapter 18. During that conversation, Pelissetti stated that Qvale's strategy in dealing with amateurs *was to be untruthful with them about such things as his encounter with Pelissetti in Presidio Heights.* This was done, as per Pelissetti, in order to "get rid of" Mark. Here was confirmation of the pattern that clearly suggested that Qvale wasn't suffering from any mental impairment that prevented him from answering my simple questions in 2006. Rather, when confronted with the facts I had amassed against him, Qvale was reduced to lying and obfuscating to Jim and me that day as part of a calculated strategy he had devised for dealing with amateurs who asked him inconvenient questions.

In early 2012, over five years after our meeting, Qvale appeared in a commercial for Bank of the West (footnote 64). Once again, his "wandering mind" didn't get in the way of his participating in this venture. The commercial was autobiographical and talked about Qvale's early life, coming to this country from Norway. To illustrate that storyline, there was a photo of his original passport from the 1920s. Although Qvale had presumably kept this eighty-year-old document from the time he was a child, he said in our 2006 meeting that he was regrettably "unable to locate" the much more recent passport from 1969. This passport would have had visa stamps proving that he was in England on the night of the Stine murder and contradicted both Armond Pelissetti (who said he spoke to Qvale shortly after cabbie Paul Stine was killed) *and* ABC News (which said they couldn't place Qvale out of the country at any of his "usual haunts" that night).

In 2012's *Lunches with Mr. Q,* the book saw Qvale going to work every day and still participating in the running of his business some five or more years after his mind started to "wander." As part of the book, Qvale was able to reminisce with anecdotes about his early life and provide a detailed accounting of his business philosophy. It detailed one trip he was taking with a friend to the Galapagos and then to England and India for business conferences with auto manufacturers like Jaguar. Another trip that year saw him going to England, Norway, and the French Riviera. On page 70, Qvale indicated that he was still thinking about long-term plans for his life and that, as of June 2011, he still wanted to manufacture a new sports car. Author Kevin Nelson marveled at how even the earliest articles about Qvale were neatly kept in a binder. The initial article was from the *San Francisco Chronicle* on August 1, 1948, and referenced Qvale's import car business. It showed Qvale driving the back roads of the Bay Area. And yet despite this apparently meticulous record keeping, Qvale had misplaced that key passport that would have served to alibi him for the night of October 11, 1969. (Recall that August 1 was also the date on which the Zodiac had demanded that he receive his first coverage in the *San Francisco Chronicle* in 1969 with his initial letter and the Three-Part Cipher.)

My father died in 2010, a day short of eighteen years after receiving a heart transplant. He had suffered from the ravages of Alzheimer's disease in his later years. I saw his memory steadily deteriorate from "wandering" and being slow to remember things at the beginning of his affliction to being much more debilitating within just a few years. His decline was steady. Dementia had no cure in 2006, just as it has none today, and is a steadily progressive affliction whose march is relentless. And yet here was Qvale supposedly suffering from the onset of dementia, or a "wandering mind," at our September 27, 2006, meeting, and his brand of this disease still allowed him to ski, open new business ventures, be featured in a commercial, participate in the writing of a book, travel to the Galapagos and other places, breed and race horses, be interviewed for articles, attend business meetings overseas, be called "spry" and "effervescent," and learn to play a demanding musical instrument.

The gist of *Lunches with Mr. Q* was that Qvale, even at the age of ninety-two, was still an active and vibrant man, a world voyager, a dreamer who still wanted to build cars, a man who was still living life to the fullest. He was able to learn to play the piano in 2009, not simply existing in the relentlessly contracting world of dementia. In short, it paints *anything but* a picture of a man whose mind had begun to "wander" as far back as 2006 and whose life was in any way winding down. By participating in the writing of that book and in such things as the Bank of the West commercial as late as 2012, Qvale seemed to contradict the picture his "second" had attempted to paint just before our meeting.

It certainly appeared on the surface like Jim was right, and that the 2006 meeting with Qvale was all about deception, outsmarting me, conning me into believing things that weren't true, and controlling the impressions of Qvale that I took away from the encounter. Now, in retrospect, after gathering the evidence that became available about Qvale after 2006, it appears that the "wandering mind" story was seemingly created out of whole cloth for one reason: to provide plausible deniability for the misleading answers Qvale gave to such questions as those regarding his whereabouts on the night Zodiac killed Paul Stine, his previous experience with guns, and the way in which he redesigned the facade of his building in Italy.

Can I state categorically that Mr. Qvale did not have a "wandering mind" in 2006? Of course not. However, I have presented documented evidence in this chapter that I believe would lead a reasonable person to conclude that, by all appearances, in the years subsequent to 2006, Mr. Qvale did not behave in the manner in which a man suffering from the onset of progressive memory loss in 2006 might be expected to behave. *In short, it seems that Qvale's memory was deficient only when it came to events relative to the Zodiac case.*

As I started pulling together all the information disputing Qvale's answers to many of my questions, I was reassured that I was on the right path to solving the Zodiac case. SFPD had renounced its own alleged "Zodiac DNA" in 2009, so that stumbling block had been removed. The question now was, What was Qvale hiding with his deception?

Some people have tried to minimize Qvale's lies and the overall impact of that meeting on my case by saying that when he met with me in 2006, he did not in any way owe me the truth. I disagree vehemently with this specious argument. After all, it was Qvale, not I, who requested the meeting after he said that its purpose was for him to convince me that I was wrong about him being the Zodiac Killer. When I accepted his offer and was willing to travel three thousand miles to hear him out, it was clearly up to him to be truthful with me.

I believe that Qvale didn't think I had the courage to accept his offer and meet with him face-to-face. Once I accepted his offer, he had three choices: he could take the Fifth Amendment (which he clearly couldn't do since this wasn't a court of law); or he could tell the truth and incriminate himself by placing himself on the streets of Presidio Heights shortly after the Stine murder, admit to his familiarity with guns, admit to his knowledge of saliva testing in the 1960s, and admit that he purchased a building with a huge crossed-circle on its facade and then wrapped his last initial around it; or, finally, he could choose to be untruthful. I believe he chose option number three with a twist: he decided to provide me with disinformation, but then to cover up that disinformation by having his "second" plant a seed to the effect that Qvale's mind was beginning to "wander." This immediately excused any response Qvale gave me during the course of our interview. However, the events that took place in his life both prior to and subsequent to September 27, 2006, clearly demonstrated that Qvale was not in any way mentally incapacitated at the time of our meeting.

There is one final reference in Lunches that is worth noting. Nelson describes a time when he and Qvale went to a meeting of the Pacific Union Club in August 2011. They parked across the street and had to traverse traffic in order to get to the club. Nelson described Qvale as going across the street like a "halfback on a breakaway run." He moved with "light-footed agility."[174] Once again, this is not the mental image one would have of a plodding, confused individual whose mind had begun to slow down and "wander" some five years earlier. In fact, it conveys just the opposite image.

---

174 Nelson, p. 172.

To summarize, after meeting with Qvale in 2006, his responses to my questions made me take a step back and do research to convince myself that I was still on the right track. But it was Qvale's own words, interviews he granted, and actions he took after 2006 that cast in serious doubt the notion that he had the onset of dementia. In addition, not only did statements by Armond Pelissetti and ABC News directly contradict Qvale's assertion that he "should have been" in England that evening but Pelissetti stated outright to Mark that Qvale's strategy was rooted in not telling people like me the truth. Qvale was also able to produce his original passport from 1929 for a television commercial but was unable to locate the one that would have proven conclusively he was out of the country on the night Paul Stine was murdered.

Qvale had told Butterfield as far back as June 2006, some three months *prior to* our meeting, about his impression that he "should have been in England" on the night of October 11, 1969. So even then, Qvale was apparently not providing truthful answers to simple questions. In other words, those types of responses weren't prompted by a strategy Qvale adopted after I jokingly made the statement about the Bentley just prior to our meeting.

In the end, I had to agree with Jim when he said that we were "had" at the 2006 face-to-face meeting. When in good faith I gave Mr. Qvale an opportunity to refute my entire case, he couldn't look me in the eye and tell me the truth in return. Mr. Walter later told me that when someone lies in an interview, it can constitute a confession of sorts, since telling the truth might implicate that person.

...

In July 2008, I was standing in my brother's front yard in Staten Island when my cell phone rang. It was Mr. Walter. He told me that an author named Mike Capuzzo was writing a book that was to include some of the famous cases on which Mr. Walter and the Vidocq Society had consulted over the years. He and Mike wanted to give my research on the Zodiac case some exposure in this book, hoping that when the book came out, people he knew in the media would read it and ask him who I was. My hope was that this might lead an investigative reporter to perform the job I had expected the police to have taken when I presented them with the facts. I was honored and anxiously awaited the publication of this book.

Finally, in the summer of 2010, Mr. Walter announced that Mr. Capuzzo's book, *The Murder Room*, was scheduled for release in August. When the book came out, I left work for a half hour to get a copy. As Mr. Walter and I had discussed, there it was in black and white on pages 407–408: "It was a night for stories, family stories. Walter was full of them. He had received a strange package from a man in New Jersey some years ago, Mike Rodelli, who claimed to have solved the most famous unsolved serial killer case in modern American history. He'd learned the name of the Zodiac Killer, the unknown assailant who had killed five Californians in 1968 and 1969, taunting the police with letters and cryptograms. Walter had been skeptical but he'd worked with the amateur sleuth for years, coaching him and now he was convinced the man was right—the Zodiac Killer was still alive, an elderly and quite wealthy man in California, still living off the pleasure of his iconic murders." In *The Murder Room*, Richard Walter had backed up publicly what he had told me privately—that I had solved the Zodiac case.[175]

I waited and waited, but nobody from the press approached me. Nor did they approach Mr. Walter. The ball once again remained in my hands.

...

In February 2010, I was doing research in the NYC Public Library, a place that always felt special to me because of all the amazing facts I had learned there about Qvale. Suddenly my cell phone began to vibrate,

---

175 However, because Qvale was still alive in 2010, author Mike Capuzzo was not able to name him in the book.

and I quickly made my way out of the microfilm reading room and into one of the spacious, tall white marble hallways. The person on the other end of the phone was Insp. Vince Repetto, who had been in charge of the Zodiac investigation in the mid- to late 1990s and who still worked at SFPD. He was calling me in response to an email I had sent him.

I had decided to give SFPD one more try. I hoped I wouldn't regret my decision.

Repetto and I spoke for several minutes as I looked out onto Fortieth Street traffic. It was to be the beginning of a friendship that has lasted to this day. Insp. Repetto was interested in my research on Qvale. Repetto had been on the force since about 1974, when he was used as a long-haired decoy on the streets of San Francisco for the Zebra Killers. He was currently in the Special Victims Unit and no longer assigned to Homicide or to handling the Zodiac case. However, former San Francisco City Attorney's Office investigator Tim Armistead told me that he had the connections within the department to get my report to the right people. Refreshingly, Repetto never even mentioned to me that Qvale had been "ruled out via DNA." Those days had thankfully passed due to the public discrediting of the 2002 SFPD DNA sample that had taken place a year earlier. His failure to mention the DNA was tacit proof that it was no longer a factor in the case.

Insp. Repetto and I spoke many times about the case. He pointed out that Qvale's links to both auto racing and horse racing would have put him in the places where the crimes took place and the letters were sent. This specifically applied to two auto races in Riverside, California: one on October 30, 1966, when Cheri Jo Bates was murdered, and the other on April 30, 1967, when the "Bates Had to Die" letters were mailed.

Insp. Repetto told me multiple times that SFPD didn't have a lot of confidence in the prints it had obtained from Stine's cab. He spoke about how crime scenes were contaminated in those days and admitted that there were "lots of people" around the cab. He also felt that Zodiac never left the search area. He made less than flattering comments about SFPD's forensics lab and told me that DNA samples were being farmed out in 2010 to a lab in Texas. He acknowledged that the Zodiac letters had been overhandled, thus possibly leading to contamination by exogenous DNA. He also said that in the 1960s ambulance drivers would often scavenge the pockets of deceased victims. Therefore, it's difficult to know how much money Stine actually had on him when he was killed. He said that it made sense that Officer Don Fouke made a written statement about his sighting of the man on Jackson Street, even though he waited about a month to submit it. This placed him on the record, and he would be able to testify in court as to what he had observed, if necessary.

Repetto also found the fact that in the Three-Part Cipher the letters *KQ* translated to *SF* when the code was solved, to be of great interest: *Qvale's initials in the code yielded his hometown.* This would represent a subtle and easily missed clue to the Zodiac's identity.

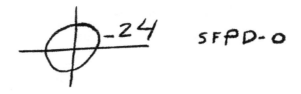

Why Was My Suspect the Zodiac Killer?

"The Zodiac Killer has identified himself to us."
—SFPD homicide insp. Kelly Carroll, voice-over on 2003 A&E *Cold Case Files*

"The wife, the brother, the mother, the friends of a serial killer never suspect that they could be a serial killer."
—Joseph Wambaugh, truTV "The Footpath Murders," *Forensic Files*, 2002

"The image of the Zodiac was this crew-cut, white-walled, horn-rimmed-glasses guy who looked like a postal clerk. And there was something about that that was intriguing to me: the notion that the Summer of Love was . . . squelched by this guy who couldn't have been a more conservative symbol. He was very 'fifties.'"
—David Fincher, *Zodiac* DVD, 2008

"As an inhabitant of the superior world, Michael Maybrick seems a most unlikely candidate for Jack the Ripper. 'A very handsome man' . . . he was talented, intelligent, successful and rich—not exactly the qualities one immediately associates with a serial killer."
—Bruce Robinson, *They All Love Jack*, 2015

SO NOW IT'S TIME for me to answer the ultimate question: Why was Kjell Qvale the Zodiac Killer? This will necessarily be a long process and will take us through discussions of behavioral profiling as it pertains to Qvale, a summary of my circumstantial evidence, the coded messages, the bus bombs, and a few other topics. We have much ground to cover and many threads to tie together, so let's begin.

In a voice-over on the 2003 A&E *Cold Case Files* show, a narrator said that the Zodiac "wanted to tell us who he was but couldn't." However, the reality may be that Zodiac not only wanted to tell us who he was *but that he did everything in his power to do so in his letters, bus-bomb diagrams, and cryptograms.* It's just that, until now, we have either misunderstood or quite simply turned a deaf ear to the things he was trying to tell us because of our innate reluctance to accept who the killer really was.

Zodiac was an evil person whose heartless, cold-blooded crimes caused unspeakable pain and suffering that has resonated not only throughout the Bay Area but around the world by virtue of books and the internet for nearly fifty years. But evil as he was, he was still a human being, a human being who demonstrated certain physical and behavioral characteristics. **And it is my contention that Kjell Qvale demonstrated all of these characteristics and that he provided us with ample, yet cryptic, clues to his identity.**

I sometimes have difficulty determining where Kjell Qvale ends and the Zodiac begins, so blurred are the lines separating the two. When people speak of Mr. Qvale, they naturally marvel at his wealth and all he did in business. However, it may just be that the most amazing thing he ever accomplished in his life was the one thing he never wanted anyone to discover.

Insp. Kelly Carroll of SFPD asked me in 2000 to tell him *why* Qvale would have become the Zodiac Killer. In those days before I met Richard Walter, I didn't have an answer for him. But now I do. That answer starts with Mr. Walter's profile, and how I perceived that Qvale fit the characteristics of a wealthy, nonsexual power-assertive killer with sociopathic traits, which I discuss at length below.

As I said earlier, when I first heard Mr. Walter's power-assertive (P-A) profile, I had an epiphany. The term *power-assertive* embodied many of the traits I had heard mentioned over the years to describe Zodiac—superior, egotistical, arrogant, condescending, aloof, and so on. I immediately felt confident that this was the profile that most accurately described the killer. The profile also specified that for such killers the "crime does not count unless someone knows about it." So, on top of perfectly describing the Zodiac Killer, the P-A profile also provided a simple and succinct explanation for Zodiac's need to write his letters and boast about his crimes: he was compelled to do so.

For over thirty years, the police, other profilers, and amateur researchers, with exceptions you can likely count on one hand, had concentrated their efforts on suspects with little to no money or power who came from the so-called dark underbelly and lower echelons of society—known criminals, drug dealers, sex offenders, the "usual suspects" from various towns, mental patients, military men who had spent time in mental hospitals, and, of course, the ubiquitous evil father or stepfather. They instinctively looked for people who were "compensating for their feelings of inadequacy" and grasping at power by becoming Zodiac. And before coming face-to-face with the circumstantial evidence I have amassed piece by piece over many years against Qvale and later Mr. Walter's profile, that is how I had also envisioned the killer. Certainly, I had never imagined anyone even remotely resembling Kjell Qvale as Zodiac. What normal person would?

...

I want to take a moment to clarify two crucial things about a behavioral profile: First, most people probably believe that behavioral profiles apply only to criminals, since they are used almost exclusively in that context in books or movies, on TV shows, and so on. However, such is not the case. In fact, to call someone a power-assertive is not to label him as a criminal at all. That's because, as discussed in chapter 17, profiling categories apply to all of us, and many people, from police officers to politicians, can be P-As and members of the P-A "family." Like your family or mine, this group is made up of many different types of individuals, both wealthy and not so wealthy, with varying traits. Most P-As make their living within the law. Others can wander outside of it. Interestingly, many successful, high-powered business people, like Kjell Qvale, are P-As. Although these people are not in any way criminals, it's their drive for wealth—and the power that accompanies wealth—that makes them the successful entrepreneurs that they are.

Second, a behavioral profile only identifies a *pool* of potential suspects who fit a given subtype (such as a P-A). That's the actual goal of a profile. It tells you where to look and, more importantly, where *not* to look, for a perpetrator by narrowing the search to a limited segment of the population. In other words, if the details of a given series of crimes cry out that they were committed by a sexual sadist (anger-excitation), you can rule out people who fit the nonsexual, wealthy, power-driven profile, because they are highly unlikely to have committed these anger-driven crimes. A profile, however, does *not* attempt to provide the name of the actual person who committed the crime in question; that is beyond the scope of any profile. In other words, taken in a vacuum, a profile alone does not solve a case.

So how is a profile used by the police?

Richard Walter told me years ago that the way you solve a case is to develop a profile and then find the person who fits that profile and who can be linked to the crimes in question through investigation.

Over the years, the Zodiac case has been "hijacked" in a way. Ironically, instead of being handled like a murder case and using profiling and investigation to solve it, the search has devolved into the type one would normally see in a fraud or blackmail case, where the primary focus is on handwriting, DNA, and palm prints, *all* of which come from the Zodiac letters, *not the actual crime scenes.* This has caused a huge distraction from the usual goal of a homicide case: finding the person who *behaved* like the Zodiac.

Mr. Walter feels that handwriting comparison is an art not a science and that one's writing can vary according to mood, intent, and desire to disguise. Handwriting can evolve over time too. There are also such unquantifiable variables as the possibility that Zodiac derived his three-stroke *K* from viewing the Peek-a-Boo Pennington yellow pages ad, which seems to have influenced the structure of the 1970 Avery Halloween card. Therefore, the presence of the three-stroke *K* may be an effort to disguise the killer's true handwriting. For these reasons, it can present problems for an investigation when handwriting is given too prominent a role in determining the ultimate guilt or innocence of a *murder* suspect. Mr. Walter stated that in a homicide inquiry such as this, handwriting can merely serve a confirmatory role, but *it should never be used to exclude someone who otherwise had the motive, means, and opportunity to have committed the crimes,* which is the premise of this book with respect to Kjell Qvale and the Zodiac's obsession with money and power.

In the Zodiac case, where the notoriety of the killer's letters overshadows all other considerations, handwriting is given much too prominent a role. What has unwittingly happened over time is that we have turned questioned-documents experts into de facto homicide inspectors with the power to rule out suspects in a murder case. These exclusions have nothing to do with whether or not the suspect matches the behavioral profile of the killer based on his behavior at his crime scenes, or what the circumstances are that tie him to the case. In granting this power, we make a potentially disastrous assumption: that

368 · MIKE RODELLI

the Zodiac Killer was not that rare individual who could successfully disguise his handwriting. Here's a quote about Jack the Ripper suspect Michael Maybrick in Bruce Robinson's 2015 book, *They All Love Jack,* "But maybe the author of the Jack the Ripper letters had a talent for disguising his handwriting. . . . It's worth a moment to quote an example of just such a man. . . . He could change his handwriting, or copy the handwriting of others, at will, and was described by authorities at Scotland Yard as 'the greatest forger they had ever known.' John George Haigh could write whole letters in the hand of a dozen or more people . . . and at a second's notice he could switch from one to another."[176]

So altering one's handwriting is not as impossible a task as questioned-document experts would have us believe. Maybe uncommon, maybe unlikely, but not *impossible.* The Zodiac has defied identification for nearly fifty years, so why be so quick to say that successfully altering his handwriting was beyond his capabilities? If John George Haigh could do it, why not Zodiac? *That is why you use a behavioral profile and circumstantial evidence, not handwriting to solve a case.*

The final word on handwriting in the Zodiac case is something that retired Napa County Sheriff's Office captain Ken Narlow told me in 1999, and which Mr. Walter echoed: even when you find the right person in a given investigation, *not every piece of evidence is going to fit.* There will always be an odd man out—a square piece of evidence that needs to go into a round hole. And in fact, Mr. Walter said that he is suspicious if *everything* about a suspect fits what's known about a crime, because that makes it look like the individual may have been "set up" in some way.

While a behavioral profile can't under normal circumstances determine exactly who the Zodiac was, it does tell us an important piece of information: that he belonged to the small pool of wealthy and powerful individuals who were living in the Bay Area at the time of the Zodiac murders, and that anyone who does *not* come from that

176 Bruce Robinson, *They All Love Jack,* (New York: HarperCollins, 2015), p. 364.

limited group, that is, most of the suspects named to date, is an *unlikely* suspect. As I indicated before, people who fit this profile might have lived in exclusive neighborhoods such as Presidio Heights. Right away, Qvale and many of his neighbors fall into that general pool of potential suspects. However, the profile in and of itself doesn't say, "Kjell Qvale was the Zodiac." It is therefore the job of the investigation to begin narrowing down the list of wealthy P-A suspects to see which one can be linked to the facts of the case. And when you find that one man from the pool of suspects whose own behavior mirrored the unique behavior of the Zodiac and whose life history fits the facts of the case, you have presumably found the man responsible for the Zodiac crimes.

Richard Walter's profile is important in several ways:

- It tells us to focus our investigative energy on the wealthy and the powerful and to *disregard* anyone who doesn't fit into that category.

- It flips the list of Zodiac suspects upside down, since those who were known criminals or "losers compensating for their feelings of inadequacy," have long had their place at the top of that list, while people like wealthy entrepreneurs were almost universally and immediately dismissed, as I learned when I came forward in 1999. Now the least likely suspects have suddenly become the *most* likely ones, and vice versa. The P-A profile made it more likely that Zodiac lived on Telegraph Hill or Russian Hill than in the seedy Tenderloin district, from which most people might have assumed the likes of him had slithered.

- As stated above, the profile of a killer in an average murder case will lead to a pool of potential suspects. This pool, depending on the profile, can sometimes be very large. However, the Zodiac case is no average case, and not unexpectedly, Mr. Walter's profile has led to a unique situation. Because of the faulty profile that was in place for many years, as well as the prejudices/expectations that people had for who the Zodiac was, the wealthy P-A pro-

370 • MIKE RODELLI

file ends up ruling out probably *all but a mere handful of the three thousand suspects who had come to the attention of the police over the years*. In other words, the P-A profile has created a *very small* pool of potential suspects. For that reason, it acts as a fine filter that allows us to greatly winnow the number of suspects to a very manageable number. And that number includes Kjell Qvale. (We will soon winnow that pool even more.)

On *Very Scary People*, profiler Mary Ellen O'Toole said that what was so interesting to her was that the Zodiac crimes were "devoid of emotion" and that you don't see any expression of anger, like battering of the victims. This comment serves to reinforce an observation that Richard Walter made to me years ago. He said that sexual crimes would be characterized by a beating, recreational cutting (i.e., piquerism), or percussive injuries, or a similar display to what Ms. O'Toole also noted as being absent. The absence of this anger and percussion proves that these are power murders, not anger-based or sexual murders.

Anyone who believes that these were sexual crimes or that the Zodiac was a sexual sadist is therefore way out in left field.

As discussed in chapter 17, Mr. Walter's profile is based strictly on what a killer leaves behind after he commits a murder. In short, Mr. Walter is an expert in reading the behavioral language inherent in crime scenes. And all of the Zodiac attacks reveal someone who consistently killed from a position of power already possessed, *not* that of a power-less "loser" who sought as it "compensation" for underlying feelings of powerlessness.

Mr. Walter read over my report in 2004 with its pages of circum-stantial evidence and said that I had "more than [I] think." The problem was that my raw facts lacked context due to the manner in which I had presented them. More precisely, I didn't correlate my evidence to the traits of a known behavioral subtype, like a power-assertive killer, to demonstrate to the police that Qvale fit an established behavioral model. For that reason, these facts weren't being provided to the authorities in a form they could easily digest, or to which they could give context via an accepted behavioral classification.

As stated earlier, a killer like Zodiac is very conscious of power and craves more and more of it. Qvale's entire life was a quest for wealth and power. He was a member of the Pacific Union Club, the San Francisco Country Club, the Olympic Club (another prestigious golf club), and an admitted member of the mysterious and ultraexclusive Bohemian Club. These are some of the biggest power organizations in the Bay Area. He organized the Pebble Beach Concours d'Elegance car show for expensive sports cars. He rubbed shoulders with the likes of Melvin Belli and Bing Crosby and even played golf in the singer's Pebble Beach Pro-Am Tournament many times with a professional golfer friend of his. These are all organizations and events that are populated by only the most financially and politically powerful men in the Bay Area. In addition, Qvale was a successful thoroughbred owner and breeder. Such a wildly expensive hobby is not generally one of the lower or middle classes, but rather one of the wealthy class.[177] As further proof that the concept of power was in the forefront of Qvale's consciousness, in the June 1969 letter to the editor of the *San Francisco Chronicle* that I used to identify him as a suspect, the last paragraph seems to demonstrate his true reason for writing the letter. This is something that had escaped me for many years until I finally recognized its significance in 2012.

In the final sentences of that June 26, 1969, letter (Exhibit 12), Qvale acknowledged the *power* that the editor held in shaping public opinion. This is the same power Zodiac would soon tap into and exploit for himself with his many letters to that newspaper that threatened and taunted the public. Qvale was issuing a warning to the *Chronicle*[178] that

---

177 Horse racing is called "the Sport of Kings" for precisely that reason: it was traditionally the province of the wealthy and powerful, who had deep enough pockets to be able to afford to build and maintain a stable of horses.

178 Some people may argue that since Qvale was a conservative, it would have made more sense for him to commandeer the *Examiner*, which was the more conservative paper in the city. However, I believe that Zodiac got more satisfaction out of using the liberal-leaning *Chronicle* to do his bidding and spread his

the editor was misusing and abusing that power by aligning himself with the "militants and lawbreakers" of that era—namely, young student protesters of the same age group that Zodiac knew he'd find on lovers' lanes. Based on Qvale's viewpoint as someone who proved himself to be an archconservative throughout his life, Qvale's issue was with *power* and how it should have been exercised by the left-leaning *San Francisco Chronicle*.

In fact, power and its use appears to have been the underlying theme of the entire letter, despite the fact that the word doesn't appear until the last paragraph. He also warned that if the editor of the *Chronicle* didn't change course, the people of the Bay Area would pay a steep price.

The letter Qvale sent in June 1969 served as a sort of blueprint of the yet-to-unfold Zodiac case. In it, he speaks about an impending "bloody confrontation," which would serve to describe the upcoming attacks as the killer "confronts" his victims and the police investigating these crimes. He describes the issue that disturbs him—young people and the responsibility that the *Chronicle* (as the liberal mouthpiece of Northern California) must take for any future bloodshed due to its implied support of their causes. He even states that "some" of the *Chronicle's* columnists must share part of the blame in the future, thus foreshadowing Zodiac's own later battle with reporter Paul Avery. All of this, in fact, might well describe in general terms the entire Zodiac episode itself, in which the archconservative Qvale pitted himself against young people. For example, three of the Zodiac's four attacks took place in lovers' lanes, where young people, to the virtual exclusion of middle-aged and older people, tend to congregate. He then essentially commandeered the *Chronicle* to both taunt the police and exert his own power over the citizens of the Bay Area through his many letters.

Qvale recognizes the tendency for newspapers to print any stories that will sell newspapers, as the Zodiac crimes and the letters later did. He states outright that the behavior of the *Chronicle* will "turn out to be rather expensive for all the people of northern California." This

---

message of terror throughout the city. It also had the larger circulation.

foreshadows not only the terror his murders caused in the region but also the fear engendered by his letters. This is particularly true in his overt threats to kill innocent schoolchildren. For anyone who knew him personally or professionally, Qvale then engages in a bit of humorous irony by warning about the potential advent of a new Hitler. This, coming from a man who was then lining his pockets by selling Hitler's own creation—the VW Beetle! Finally, he gets to the crux and reason for his letter—power. He does this by chiding the editor for misusing his opinion-making power, presumably by siding with the militant students to the detriment of the rest of the people of the Bay Area. The concept of *power* happens to dovetail nicely with Mr. Walter's profile of Zodiac as someone who was obsessed with power and who was willing to kill for it.

There it was, right in Qvale's letter, and yet it had taken me years to understand it: power was the underlying motive for Zodiac's crimes. And power was also the underlying motive behind Qvale's June 26, 1969, letter that started me down the road to investigating him as the Zodiac Killer. *Thus, the letter discovered on day one of my investigation serves to link Qvale directly to the P-A profile of the Zodiac.* Just imagine the sense of power Qvale must have felt to send a blueprint for his actions and their underlying reasons and not have anyone find or recognize it during the Zodiac era. The letter was his little secret.

What makes this letter of particular interest is that it represents the *only* letter to the editor of the *San Francisco Chronicle* Qvale had published in 1969 and the years immediately prior.[179] Suffice it to say, my research proved Qvale was anything but a frequent letter writer to that newspaper. *In fact, he was the complete opposite.*

Taking a step back, my idea to prospect within the letters to the editor of the Bay Area newspapers exactly six months after the murders

---

179 I determined from my research that this was the only letter Qvale had published in the *San Francisco Chronicle* from 1964–69. I have done additional research in the 1960s' archives of the *San Francisco Chronicle* without locating another letter from Qvale. However, I have misplaced my notes relative to the specific range of months/years prior to 1964 that I have completed.

at Lake Herman was objective in nature and could have led to literally *anyone* in the readership of those papers as the author. But it led to only *one letter and only one name*. He was the *only* person to later become a suspect in the Zodiac case who had been stopped and spoken to by the police in the vicinity of *any* of the Zodiac murders within minutes after it (the Stine murder) had occurred. And although he lived two and a half blocks from where Paul Stine was killed, he was also in Riverside on the weekend of the Cheri Jo Bates murder. This was tantamount to a laser strike on those letters that ended with my using Zodiac's own known behavior as a weapon to identify him.

...

Kjell Qvale was a study in contradictions. Like the moon, he had a very bright public side, but, as you will soon realize, he also had a side that nobody ever saw. He did things that he kept secret from even his closest associates. In 1946, Qvale drove his first MG-TC and thus began his career as a wildly successful entrepreneur. The next year he incredibly placed himself on the ground floor of the flying-saucer era by asserting that they were crafts from outer space. He nurtured the careers of many people who worked in his automobile plants and dealerships in his lifetime, but he was also capable of taking advantage of vulnerable subprime borrowers at a bank he owned. He was described as being charming, but on the other hand, he was also described as being extremely aloof.

Richard Walter once told me that people have three different personas: a public (or professional) one that you show your coworkers and the rest of the world every day, a private one that only your family sees behind closed doors, and a secret one, the one you never permit anyone to see. Mr. Qvale's friends and business associates saw the public persona: the charming, affable, highly successful entrepreneur. People like Lindsey Robbins, who knew Qvale for forty years, and Tony Hogg, the author of the 1964 *Road and Track* article, got a glimpse at Qvale's private persona: aloof, distant, and inscrutable. I believe that my research has uncovered the *secret* persona of Mr. Qvale, the one he kept hidden from the world. Those who knew only his public persona will find it extremely difficult to believe that the secret one even existed. That secret persona, the one that seems to have been in behavioral lockstep with the Zodiac, is the one I was able to slowly flesh out through years of research, as well as by way of my personal encounter with Mr. Qvale in 2006.

Earlier I discussed the traits of a power-assertive individual. But does Qvale truly fit the profile of a power-assertive? While ordinary people were going about their everyday lives in the 1940s, '50s and '60s, Kjell Qvale was quietly but unmistakably amassing an impressive portfolio of behaviors that exemplified the signal behavioral traits of *a power-assertive offender* like the Zodiac. These included aloofness, a sense of superiority, and the desire to garner the attention and control of the public while seeing his name on the front pages of the local newspapers.

Therefore, the first part of proving that Qvale was the Zodiac will be to enumerate the traits of a power-assertive killer and then to demonstrate that Qvale exemplified all of those traits and consequently fit the profile of the Zodiac Killer.

Aside from knowing and craving the taste of power, a power-assertive is also *grandiose* with an exaggerated sense of self-worth. Qvale's 1947 flying-saucer sighting/explanation was grandiose. Even though so many people from coast to coast across the United States were seeing the saucers at the time, only *he* knew what they truly were. He denied to me in 2006 that his 1947 statement had any significance other than just to "casually" report what he saw as a public service. However, the history of that era has long ago been written, and he stands out among the people reporting this phenomenon at that time both for what he said *and for how quickly he got his sighting into the local newspapers.* From our standpoint in 2020, it's amazing to think that virtually nobody in the US in 1947 was publicly voicing the opinion that whatever it was

376 · MIKE RODELLI

that they had seen in the skies over their part of the country was from outer space.[180] However, for reasons that were likely endemic to postwar society and possibly due to the aftereffects of the 1938 *War of the Worlds* radio show scare, they simply weren't.[181] Nobody, that is, except for Kjell Qvale. This demonstrated Qvale's burning desire to see his name on the front pages of the Bay Area newspaper. In other words, the root of the one behavior that separated Zodiac from all other criminals can be found in Kjell Qvale's past as far back as 1947.

Qvale's entering not one but *three* cars in the Indianapolis 500 in 1964 was also a grandiose gesture that was apparently not looked upon favorably by some in the race: Qvale's cars were allegedly sabotaged, likely by contamination of the engine oil.

In 1970, when Qvale was purchasing the British car manufacturer Jensen Motors, he grandiosely stated, "Well, I am the group; there isn't anybody else,"[182] to dispel rumors that a conglomerate was purchasing the company. He had so much financial clout that he alone constituted his own "group" of investors. Remembering his first encounter with an MG-TC in 1946, Qvale stated in a 1958 article, "If this MG can sell me in a matter of seconds, it can sell others in a matter of minutes."[183] In other words, he "gets" it much more quickly than the masses do.

Qvale's June 26, 1969, letter to the editor of the *Chronicle* (Exhibit 12) made a dire prediction for a tragedy that would affect "all the people of the Bay Area" if the paper didn't mend its ways. This is an example of a grandiose threat.

---

180 The famous Roswell Incident had to do with alleged physical evidence of a "flying disc," which of course led to a different type of speculation altogether. The 853 summaries in McDonald's 1967 book were about how people interpreted visual contacts they had made in their areas.

181 The impression one gets from reading contemporary articles is that in 1947 people were more fearful of flying saucers being weapons of either the Germans or Russians than of being visitors from outer space.

182 Business journal: "Sales Talk," *The Times* (London), October 19, 1970, p. 23.

183 Fraser, p. 5.

Another prominent characteristic of power-assertives is their aloofness. This is a trait that investigators have used to describe Zodiac for many, many years. Recall that one of the first things Stine eyewitness Lindsey Robbins mentioned in his initial conversation with retired VPD detective Jim Dean was that Qvale was "aloof as hell." He said that all he really knew about Qvale after knowing him for thirty years was that he "sold cars and raced horses." Lindsey was accustomed to being routinely shunned or barely acknowledged by Qvale on the occasions when they crossed paths, because he didn't move in Qvale's elite social circle. He accepted this as being the normal order of things.

In the 1964 Tony Hogg article in *Road and Track* (footnote 109), the author devotes a long paragraph to describing how aloof Qvale was and how he kept people at a distance. He added that Qvale had been aloof *all his life*, not just since becoming wealthy. This trait was prominent enough that Hogg felt the need to bring it to the attention of the reader. That this author felt compelled to devote part of his story to Qvale's aloofness was reminiscent of the aforementioned article in the *Daily Commercial News*, in which the author, also speaking of Qvale's car business, suddenly digresses from that story to point out Qvale's unusual and distinctive manner of speaking as being "leisurely—almost slow."[184] This matches an eyewitness description of the Zodiac's own unusual manner of speaking. Once again a distinctive trait of Qvale's that matched something about the Zodiac Killer was so prominent that the author included a reference to it that was completely out of context with the rest of the article.

Here are other characteristics of a power-assertive individual and how Qvale demonstrated them. Given that my knowledge of the things that Qvale did in his lifetime is limited to what is publicly available, some of these examples will inevitably be used to illustrate multiple traits.

• **The need for control.** When Qvale took over Golden Gate Fields

184 Fraser, p. 5.

racetrack in the early 1960s, Jensen Motors in the 1970s, and the First National Bank of Marin in the 1990s, he spoke of getting a "controlling interest" in these companies. For example, in his 2005 autobiography, he states, "By necessity I became the *controlling* partner in the bank."[185] Also, the organization that Qvale supported in the 2000s, the Parents Television Council, had as its goal controlling and limiting what people would and would not have been permitted to watch on television based on the application of the group's conservative principles to the medium. In 1950 Qvale married his secretary. This allowed him to take the power and control vested in the employer-employee relationship home with him at night.

- **Arrogance.** In a 1996 *San Francisco Chronicle* article about a contentious meeting at Bay Meadows, Qvale, as the chairman of the Jockey Club at the time, manhandles the crowd of board members by saying, "Shut up and sit down." He threatened not to allow the opposing side to even have a chance to speak. One participant called the meeting "the height of arrogance." Another said of Qvale's side, "You people are goddamn arrogant."[186]

- **An unlimited need for stimulation.** Qvale spontaneously stated in two interviews over the years that he "bored easily" and told the author in 2006 that he "loved speed"—fast cars, boats, and horses. In our 2006 meeting he told me that he only watched movies devoted to cars and speed. Also, the life of an entrepreneur, who involves himself with various business ventures, is one of endless stimulation.

- **Assertion of virility.** Paying $500,000 for a single unproven racehorse (The Scoundrel) in 1964, the equivalent of about $3.5 million today, was an expression of both power and financial viril-

---

185 Qvale, p. 199.

186 Jon Swartz, "A Rowdy Day at the Races," *San Francisco Chronicle*, August 31, 1996, pp. D1–2.

ity. And when this horse went lame a week after Qvale purchased it, he barely batted an eye, implying that there was plenty more money from whence that came. Qvale also stated/boasted that he lost tens of millions of dollars of his own money building the Mangusta. Yet he still managed to leave an estate of over $100 million when he died in 2013.

- **Self-indulgence.** Qvale owned a stable of horses and a horse ranch, fast cars, fast boats, and a Presidio Heights mansion. He was a member of the Bohemian Club, San Francisco Country Club, and Olympic Club. And he spent his leisure time playing golf at only the most exclusive country clubs, skiing at the capitals for this sport around the world, and taking expensive ocean cruises. He stated in *Lunches with Mr. Q* that he went to the Galapagos in 2012 because he had basically run out of places to visit.[187]

- **Narcissism.** Despite hardly being a household name, Qvale wrote and self-published an autobiography in 2005. By doing this he bypassed the scrutiny of a literary agent and publisher in determining if his book was of enough interest to the public to be published in a traditional manner. He also participated in *Lunches with Mr. Q* to further burnish his public image in 2012. This book was in essence a paean to his business prowess. Qvale was also virtually never seen unless he was dressed in the finest clothes. Richard Walter pointed out to me that self-image taken to the nth degree is narcissism. Qvale had a partiality to suits and white shirts. It should be noted that when SFPD officer Armond Pelissetti spoke to Qvale after the Stine murder, the officer stated that Qvale was dressed in a "smoking jacket or robe." This comment is of great interest, since in the 1960s many men, and likely Qvale in particular, would not be seen leaving the house to do anything without wearing a shirt and tie. The smoking jacket may indicate that Qvale had changed clothes quickly and just thrown

---

187 Nelson, p. 69.

something on so as to get back onto the streets as soon as possible after the Stine murder.[188]

- **Condescension.** Qvale's condescending attitude was evident in his 1958 statement about being able to be sold on an MG-TC in "seconds" while others required more time to catch up to his assessment. It was also apparent in his request to meet with him in 2006 on the premise of proving to me that he was not the Zodiac, and then he told me things that were easily proven to be untrue. Such was his condescending attitude toward me. He apparently never even considered the possibility that I was capable of doing the research necessary to see through his web of deception.

- **A need for glory and recognition.** Qvale entered not one but *three* cars at Indy in 1964 in order to try to win that race. He paid an exorbitant amount of money for The Scoundrel that same year in order to try to win a big horse race. His purchase of the world-renowned racehorse Silky Sullivan after its racing days were over brought Qvale much fame and recognition. He wanted to build a world-renowned sports car, even if both Jensen Motors and the Qvale Mangusta were failures.

- **Deathly afraid of not being important.** Qvale always kept the public informed of new business ventures with articles such as the ones from November 1964, and he wrote a 2005 autobiography and participated in another book about himself in 2012.

- **Crimes not over until he says they're over.** Qvale's purchase of Jensen Motors, with the name of one of Zodiac's victims, in 1970; purchasing the Modena plant with the crossed circle on it in 1999, some thirty years after Zodiac first emerged; and the presence of Dr. Z at the opening of his comedy club in 2010 all

---

188 In one of the crime scene photos from October 11, 1969, an onlooker in the background of Stine's cab can be seen dressed in a white shirt and sport jacket at 10 PM on a Saturday night. Judge Uldall's wife, Ellie, also advised me that men, especially those from Europe, would often not venture outside unless wearing a shirt and tie in that era.

served to keep the memories of the Zodiac crimes alive in the killer's mind.

- **Distance from emotions.** Aside from Qvale's lifelong aloofness, in his autobiography Qvale included a tribute at the end to his recently deceased wife of over fifty years. While I'm reluctant to use something so personal in this discussion, it nonetheless does illustrate an important point. Richard Walter told me that this statement is revealing in how many times the word *I* or *my* is mentioned, instead of *she* or *her*. This awkward and aloof tribute speaks more about his wife as an employee and seems to give equal value to her role as his wife and all the positions Mrs. Qvale held in their businesses, which are mentioned in the same sentence. In contrast, there is little that is personal or emotional in the statement.[189] The sad, inevitable conclusion is that Qvale had kinder words for his horse Silky Sullivan and for his dog, Jack, than he did for Mrs. Qvale.

The final trait is a winner-take-all attitude toward life. I doubt anyone who knew him would question that Qvale played every high-stakes business and sports venture he ever involved himself in to win the entire pot each time (even if it didn't always turn out that way).

Earlier I discussed the concept of *luxury of sophistication*. Given the killer's ability to conceive and execute such things as meticulously constructed codes and bus-bomb diagrams, Mr. Walter feels that Zodiac was a person of means who could make his own schedule. As stated earlier, one might argue that Zodiac was someone who was unemployed and who simply had "time on his hands" to create the coded messages. However, other aspects of the case strongly suggest that Zodiac was not part of the lower or middle classes. Those aspects that point out Zodiac as an individual of means are (1) his seemingly intimate familiarity with the wealthy enclave of Presidio Heights (discussed in detail in

---

189 Qvale, p. 212.

chapter 18); (2) his use of monarch-sized paper, which retired Superior Court judge Eric Uldall called "rich people's stationery"; (3) his likely use of multiple cars for his crimes; and (4) his use of multiple weapons, including two different 9 mm handguns. By the late 1960s, Qvale was extremely wealthy and was able to make his own schedule, although at our 2006 meeting he stated that in the late 1960s he was so busy that he "didn't have time" to be the Zodiac, which was clearly a baseless argument, especially since the Zodiac crimes were committed either at night or on weekends or holidays, or both.

Zodiac was also attracted to irony and ironic humor, which Mr. Walter says is unusual for a power-assertive killer. As stated in chapter 11, Zodiac's ironic greeting cards, such as the Dripping Pen Card, demonstrate this fact. In 1970 Qvale purchased a car company, Jensen Motors, that bore the name of one of Zodiac's first victims, Betty Lou Jensen. On the opening night of Holly's Comedy Club, in 2010, which Qvale owned, they hired a comedian with the incredibly ironic name Dr. Z to sit in the audience and heckle other performers as part of the act.[190] Qvale also imbued the scheduling of our September 2006 meeting with tremendous irony. Recall that after originally suggesting a date of September 22 for the meeting, he changed it to September 27—the date not only of his father's birth in 1887 but also of Zodiac's 1969 Lake Berryessa attack.

Qvale was also willing to throw his weight behind such causes as the aforementioned Parents Television Council, which lobbied the industry to cut down on violent and graphic content in TV shows geared for families and children. The goal of this organization echoed the theme of Zodiac's 1974 *Badlands* Letter, in which the author asked that the *Chronicle* stop running an ad for a movie that portrayed a large amount of violence. This would be the ultimate irony if he were

---

190 In July 2016 Jim Dean contacted a principal of the defunct club. She stated that "nothing" would have gone on in the club about which she would not have been aware and that there was "no heckler" in the audience on opening night. Clearly, the article by Clinton Stark says otherwise, and her assertions indicate that it was not she who had hired the performer.

also the Zodiac, who threatened to kill schoolchildren and became a modern-day boogeyman to an entire generation of young people from the Bay Area.

Last, but certainly not least, is Qvale's 1969 letter to the editor of the *San Francisco Chronicle*, in which he warns in grave terms of the possible coming of a "new Hitler." Beginning in 1952, Qvale did something that was not at all popular in the years just after World War II had ended: importing thousands of Volkswagen Beetles to the West Coast of the US. He continued to do so until the 1980s and made untold millions of dollars doing so. In *Lunches with Mr. Q*, he stated, "We put VWs [Beetles] all over the damn place."[191]

One reason Volkswagens were so unpopular around the world is that *they had been conceived of in part by none other than Adolf Hitler himself.* Here is a quote about this problem, "Its [VW's] ideological lineage as Hitler's prestige project . . . lent the vehicle a deeply compromised pedigree by 1943."[192] Therein lies the irony in Qvale's dire warning about the potential coming of a "new Hitler" in 1969: he had no moral issues whatsoever with lining his pockets with money by selling (according to *Lunches with Mr. Q*) "two thousand" of Hitler's creations per month."[193] While Qvale was railing about the "evils" that the coming of a "new Hitler" might bring upon the Bay Area, he was making a fortune in 1969 by selling cars that were designed in part by the worst mass murderer in history. The irony in Qvale's warning was actually quite delicious and says that, while he may have had grave misgivings about Hitler, he didn't mind building his fortune by selling Hitler's pet creation.

The final part of Richard Walter's profile is that Zodiac demonstrated traits that are characteristic of a sociopath. Even a casual reading

---

191 Nelson, p. 103.

192 Bernhard Rieger, *The People's Car* (Cambridge, Massachusetts: Harvard Press, 2013), p. 90.

193 Nelson, *ibid.*

of the literature on this subject shows that there are certain traits that are widely accepted as being associated with sociopathy.

A sociopath is, by definition, someone who lacks a conscience and who can't feel empathy; they're like human "robots," who for unknown reasons can't appropriately perceive and process normal human emotions. In fact, they must try to learn and imitate real emotions by mimicking displays of emotions they observe by others. The manner in which Zodiac was able to so coldly recite horrific facts from his crime scenes in his first letters and how he distanced himself from his victims by referring to them as "the boy" or "the girl" clearly demonstrates this lack of empathy. For this reason, sociopaths are capable of committing the most heinous of crimes free of the overwhelming guilt and remorse others would feel after doing such horrible things. Sociopaths have no moral compass or social conscience. On the surface, even intimating that Qvale could have been a sociopath may seem absurd, given that he was a cultured and successful businessman.

So what are the facts, and do they support the notion that a financially successful, personable, and charming businessman can also be a sociopath, despite his outward normalcy? Just as they can be P-As, politicians, police officers, Wall Street traders, and successful entrepreneurs can also exhibit sociopathic tendencies. Moreover, these traits can be huge positive factors in their successes. In the case of entrepreneurs, they are able to make objective and even ruthless business decisions that aren't clouded by emotion. On such difficult topics as downsizing companies, as Mr. Qvale did at the First National Bank of Marin in the 1990s, he stated that in order to transition the bank to cater to subprime borrowers he "eliminated" most of senior management.[194] (Note that the word *eliminated* has a more ruthless, mercenary tone to it than saying, for example, that management personnel were "downsized" or were simply "laid off.") Being a P-A or a sociopath, however, does not by definition mean that someone will necessarily commit crimes against humanity, even though sociopaths are reportedly responsible

---

194 Qvale, p. 200.

for much of the crime that is committed and reportedly constitute a disproportionately large percentage of our prison population. In fact, some extremely successful people, like prominent attorneys, can be sociopaths.

Did Mr. Qvale demonstrate sociopathic traits? Here are some signposts that point out the way with respect to Qvale and this condition.

In interviews Qvale did over the years, without any coaxing, he freely mentioned his proneness to *boredom*. Such a tendency is a prominent trait of a sociopath. In fact, in the opening sentence in an interview from November 1999, Qvale stated, "I get bored easily."[195] In yet another, Qvale states, "No one wants to lead a boring life."[196] [197] Qvale owned, bought and sold fast cars, fast horses and fast boats, all of which provide cures for boredom. The need for unlimited stimulation is itself symptomatic of a proneness to boredom. As stated earlier, an entrepreneurial life can be a cure for boredom, as it offers many different types of business-based stimulation. Qvale's aversion to boredom is a theme that runs consistently throughout his life.

Someone who is described as "personable" can also be considered to be *glib* if his charm is only superficial. Glibness is another trait of a sociopath. Qvale was unquestionably a man of great personal charm. But in stark counterpoint to that personal charm was the deep and longstanding aloofness and distance from other people that lay beneath its surface, as discussed throughout this book. In the 1964 Tony Hogg article, the author listed the reasons Qvale kept his distance from people, and why you had to go through "proper channels" just to speak with him. The justification the author cited for Qvale's aloofness is that because he was wealthy, people would reportedly ask him for handouts

---

195 Lamm, p. 68.

196 Ostler, p. B3.

197 This statement is clearly false, as many people are apparently content leading a monotonous, predictable life where everything happens by rote day in and day out. However, a sociopath might well think that everyone shares his views on this subject.

or loans, or they wanted to be placed on top of the list for some new sports car that was being released. Hogg also attributes the aloofness to "shyness" and a "disinclination to speak when he has nothing to say." However, as discussed earlier, he then indicates that *Qvale had been aloof all of his life, not just since becoming wealthy, thus negating the arguments suggesting that his aloofness was related to his success in business.* Recall that Qvale also chose to participate in individual sports—track and field, golf, and skiing, not team-oriented sports like football (which he only played for a short time), basketball, or baseball.

Another trait that Qvale demonstrated as far back as 1947 is *grandiosity*, which, as discussed earlier, is also a trait of a power-assertive. This is clearly evident in his flying-saucer explanation, as discussed earlier. Qvale's 1947 behavior finds an analogy in the Zodiac case in the killer's one-line Sla Letter, which is grandiose in the same way that Qvale's flying-saucer episode was. In 1974, everyone in the Bay Area was exposed to the Symbionese Liberation Army (SLA) and its exploits, just as in 1947 practically everyone was seeing flying saucers. However, apparently only the killer was in on the fact that *sla* meant "kill" in the hopelessly obscure language of Old Norse, and he made sure to inform the masses from his lofty position as Zodiac that only *he* knew its actual meaning in that arcane language. Extremely few people in the Bay Area at the time knew Old Norse, or that *sla* meant "to kill" in that language. In our 2006 meeting, Qvale stated that he was one of them.

Qvale made many efforts to become internationally known in his life, like entering the three cars at the Indy 500 in 1964. He also paid an outrageous amount of money to purchase The Scoundrel in 1964 and grandiosely stated that he was "trying to win the Kentucky Derby," even though it had already run in the Derby a few weeks before. At any rate, The Scoundrel hardly seemed to be a world beater. However, despite Qvale's statement about winning the Derby, the rules of horse racing prevented The Scoundrel from ever running again in that major race.[198]

---

198 The Derby is exclusively for three-year-old horses. A horse therefore only gets one shot at winning it.

This extravagant purchase along with his lofty goals for the horse got Qvale's name splashed across the sports pages of newspapers around the country at the time: paying half a million dollars for one unproven racehorse in 1964 was such an inconceivable business decision that it sent you straight onto the pages of newspapers.

To wit, in an article from May 1964, Qvale is seen getting coverage on the front page of the sports section of the *San Francisco Chronicle*. The article notes that Qvale had to "agonize" over making the "unenviable" decision of whether to go to Indianapolis to watch his three cars run in the "500" or to go to New Jersey to see his overpriced racehorse run in the Jersey Derby at Garden State Park.[199] This is a decision that the average person never has to make. Qvale was ultimately frustrated in his desires to win the "big race." But he clearly wanted the worldwide fame that would have been accorded to him by winning one of those events.

A sociopath is also *conning and manipulative*. These traits manifested themselves in Qvale's personality in 2006, when he invited me to come out to San Francisco to meet him and then provided demonstrably and objectively deceptive answers while his "second" said Qvale had a "wandering mind."

Finally, a sociopath is a *risk-taker*. While Qvale was not a daredevil in a physical sense, he stated in a 2004 article, "I am an eternal optimist who doesn't mind taking a risk—although that can be deadly." [200] The author states that after the 1940s, Qvale "spent the next sixty years taking risks. But they were business risks." This risk-taking and excitement inherent in entrepreneurship may have been something that eased Qvale's proneness to boredom by always presenting him with new challenges. In 1947, Qvale took the biggest risk of his life by eschewing the established Willys-brand vehicles for the totally unknown and unproven MGs. He also assumed enormous risk when, fewer than

---

199 Anonymous, "Scoundrel Hurts Foot," *San Francisco Chronicle*, May 28, 1964, p. 1 of sports section.

200 Mark Rechtin, "A Lion in Winter," *Automotive News*, January 26, 2004, pp. 86–88.

ten years after the end of World War II, he decided to sell cars that were in part designed by Adolf Hitler. Scott Ostler also referenced this tendency toward risk-taking in his 2009 article.

However, it's in the traits that most sociopaths do demonstrate that Qvale did *not* exhibit that we find where Qvale diverges from the average sociopath—and what made him the successful businessman that he was. Most sociopaths are shiftless and without goals. They often live their lives parasitically, by sponging off of their unwitting victims. Clearly this doesn't describe Kjell Qvale in any way. The brilliance of his accomplishments is what made his sociopathic tendencies so difficult to see. Keep in mind that both power-assertives and sociopaths are part of a "family." Their behavior can exist across a broad spectrum. Law-abiding, highly successful people can be both P-As and sociopaths; Qvale would not be unique in this regard. In fact, Richard Walter pointed out to me that a sociopath need not manifest *every* trait generally attributed to them (which simply represents variation within that "family"). This is what causes the variation on the theme within the sociopath "family" discussed in chapter 17.

Despite evidence that Qvale helped the careers of many individuals whom he took under his wing in business, he also was capable of enriching himself in ways that were cruel and opportunistic on the anonymous masses. This demonstrates a lack of empathy, which is *the* defining trait of a sociopath.

In 2004, when he ran the First National Bank of Marin, for example, Qvale was forced to sign Consent Decree #2004-45—a "Cease and Desist Order and Restitution" (Exhibit 41a and b) with respect to the fees he was charging subprime borrowers to get a credit card. On the surface, the bank was doing a good and noble deed for people who were trying to re-establish their credit after going through a rough financial period in their lives. In fact, issuing credit cards to subprime borrowers was apparently the bank's entire business model. But to establish an account to rebuild their credit, these borrowers were subjected to shockingly exorbitant fees.

When Qvale first got involved in the bank, it was headquartered in San Rafael, California. But the business climate in Nevada was more conducive to the plan Qvale had devised of concentrating on the subprime lending market. In order to move from San Rafael to Las Vegas to implement their plan, Qvale "eliminated" most of the workforce. He then started offering a startling secured credit card product to these struggling borrowers.

According to an article in the *Las Vegas Sun* from May 25, 2004,[201] borrowers had to pay $260 to establish their account, of which a full $200 was put toward a security deposit. Of the remaining $60, the bank took $57.50 in fees, leaving the card holder with a paltry *$2.50 in usable credit*. This put the customers behind the eight ball almost from the start and allowed the bank to place an unfair burden on the financially strapped borrowers it allegedly served. These customers had few options of where to do business, since they were dependent on a bank that was willing to accept them due to the high credit risks they represented.

In other words, Qvale's bank was profiting handsomely by charging exorbitant fees, including interest on their security deposit, to subprime borrowers who were trying to get a credit card in order to rebuild their lives. Qvale is listed as the president of the bank on the consent decree signature page, along with "other" bank officers who apparently endorsed this burdensome business model. Their names appeared below his on the signatory page, thus acknowledging their complicity in this scheme. What was supposed to be a symbiotic relationship between consumers in need of assistance and the institution looking to make a profit for its owners and shareholders was turned into an opportunistic one. The needs of the card holders were subjugated to the greed of the institution that Qvale ran. And unlike his auto dealership where he and his reputation were front and center, Qvale was able to assume some level of anonymity in exploiting the subprime market by offering this harsh deal to borrowers behind the name of a bank. The cease and desist

---

201 Kevin Rademacher, "LV-Based Bank Ordered to Pay Credit Card Patrons," *Las Vegas Sun*, May 25, 2004, online edition.

order/consent decree called for the bank to make restitution without having to admit any wrongdoing, which is another example of "rich people's justice" in action. Harm was caused but nobody goes to prison.

The 2012 book, *Lunches with Mr. Q*, by Kevin Nelson, is a thoroughly uncritical look at Mr. Qvale's life in business, which, in its lack of balance, is in essence like an autobiography written by a third party. In this book was a boast by Qvale of how astronomical a profit he made off the eventual sale of the bank in 2005—so much so that he wouldn't even discuss the numbers involved. There is no mention of, nor any remorse expressed for, how the bank's business practices prior to the consent decree may have financially injured the same subprime borrowers they were allegedly trying to help. It appears that Mr. Nelson didn't dig beneath the surface of the First National Bank of Marin story to see what else might have been lurking beneath.

This banking plan reveals a surprising lack of empathy for the subprime borrowers of which the First National Bank of Marin and President Kjell Qvale took advantage in order to enrich its owners. In addition, Qvale's actions at the First Bank of Marin highlight the notion that a sociopath only cares about satisfying his own needs without any care about who he hurts in the process. And this was not the first time Qvale got caught taking advantage of subprime borrowers. There was a prior consent decree the bank had to sign in 2001 when the bank was caught doing *the exact same thing it later did in 2004*—requiring a large sum to secure a credit card and leaving the consumer with virtually no available credit. The practices were deemed to be "unfair and deceptive."[202]

In his autobiography, Qvale blames the regulatory action on the Office of the Comptroller of the Currency (OCC) due to its "overzealousness" and for not working with the bank to improve the emerging market. But it wasn't the OCC that had devised the bank's oppressive business model. This was a way of displacing blame for his own business

---

202 Anonymous, "Feds Say Vegas Bank Deceived Customers," *Las Vegas Sun*, December 5, 2001, online edition.

plan from himself and his bank to the government regulators, whom Qvale believed should have kept him in check.[203]

It's the same lack of empathy and distance from his emotions that allowed Mr. Qvale to lay off so many workers at the Bank of Marin, to come up with his plan to make money on the backs of subprime borrowers, and to write such an emotionally distant tribute to his wife in his autobiography. In pointing out the Bank of Marin story, I'm not trying to say that Qvale was incapable of being supportive of other people or generous with his time and money. What I am saying is that, as the president of that bank, he was *also* capable of demonstrating a surprising predatory streak with a lack of empathy for his borrowers, which is one trait of a sociopath.

To summarize, evidence from the events of his life show that Kjell Qvale was a power-assertive personality. However, there's nothing criminal about being a P-A personality. Many successful businesspeople are. Nor is it a crime to be a sociopath or to have sociopathic tendencies. Many law-abiding people are both P-As *and* have sociopathic tendencies but never commit any crimes. In fact, both traits taken together can make for a highly successful entrepreneur capable of making ruthless business decisions. But as discussed earlier, these groups are like "families" with many different members across a broad spectrum. Like an iceberg floating at sea where only 10 percent of it is visible above the water, so too can 90 percent of power-assertives with a tendency toward sociopathy be law-abiding citizens drifting quietly beneath the waves of society. But do the facts say that Qvale was in the other 10 percent? Specifically, was he the power-assertive personality with sociopathic tendencies living in the Bay Area from 1968 to 1974 who became the Zodiac?

We will next examine and give context to the circumstantial evidence against Qvale.

...

---

203 Qvale, p. 203.

On September 28, 2013, I had a revealing conversation with Mr. Walter. We had been acquainted for almost nine years by this point, and I had spoken to him many times over the course of those years. As part of that conversation, I put the following question to him: Why did Mr. Walter feel that my case correctly identified the Zodiac, as he had stated in 2010 in *The Murder Room*? I indicated that there were literally thousands of suspects in the Zodiac case, each one of which had a circumstantial case swirling around him (with a handful of these cases being of more than just passing interest).

In reply, Mr. Walter said that the reason my conclusion that Qvale was the Zodiac, which is supported by the assertion that Walter made in *The Murder Room*, is plausible is this: my circumstantial case is logical, my facts about Qvale fit together, and collectively they also *tell a story*. And the story they tell is that of the Zodiac. He further indicated that Qvale's resorting to being untruthful with me in our 2006 meeting is highly indicative of the fact that he had something to hide.

In June 2010, I met with author Mike Capuzzo and Mr. Walter in Philadelphia in advance of the release of *The Murder Room*. After I related my circumstantial evidence to Mike, he indicated to me that, as a storyteller himself, he felt that in essence Qvale was telling his own life story through the facts of the Zodiac case. When I looked back on that conversation, I realized that some three years before I would have my conversation with Mr. Walter, Mike had also hit upon the precise reason my evidence against Qvale was so powerful.

My opinion/contention is that Kjell Qvale was a wealthy power-assertive individual *whose own life story is like the story of the Zodiac.* That story is one of a killer who, like Qvale, was wealthy and powerful; who, like Qvale, had extremely strong ties to cars (see below); who, like Qvale, wrote on the unusual monarch-sized paper; who killed on certain dates that were significant to Qvale; who, like Qvale, put his autograph on a car; who, like Qvale, spoke in a slow, distinctive manner; who, like Qvale, demonstrated ties to both England and Norway; who somehow evidently knew not to lick stamps and envelopes in the 1960s; who, like

Qvale, had a military background, possibly as a pilot. That is who the Zodiac demonstrated he was. Now we must compare the Zodiac's story to the evidence against Qvale to see how well they match up.

...

The first circumstantial link between Qvale and Zodiac is that the Zodiac is *absolutely and intimately* tied to cars and other vehicles. In fact, the Zodiac was completely obsessed with cars. He also apparently had intimate knowledge of the remote back roads of the Bay Area and the lovers' lanes on these roads. The Zodiac case was a series of crimes and letters that centered on cars, buses, motorcycles, road races, car batteries, and other references to vehicles. Evidence derived directly from the case demonstrates that Zodiac was completely consumed with these references, which are ubiquitous and which are the centerpieces not only of all the killer's crimes but also of his bomb threats and geographical references in his letters and phone calls. The crimes of the Zodiac can't be explained and would be unrecognizable without automobiles. The number of references is dizzying and leaves no doubt that cars were Zodiac's comfort zone.

In fact, cars and other vehicles appear to be the prism through which the Zodiac viewed the world.

At the risk of being accused of overkill, I wish to enumerate the many references to cars in the Zodiac case. There is an extremely important point to be made at the end of this exercise, so I ask for your patience here.

At Lake Herman, Jensen and Faraday were approached while sitting in a parked Rambler station wagon, and Zodiac pulled up to the crime scene in a car. Zodiac even shot into Faraday's car that night. He may also have chased a couple that was in an imported British sports car down Lake Herman road prior to shooting Jensen and Faraday. At Blue Rock Springs, Zodiac also pulled up to the crime scene in a car and shot victims who were themselves sitting in a parked car. At Lake

Berryessa, Zodiac stated that he was an escaped convict who had stolen a car, asked for the keys to Hartnell's car, and even wrote a message on the door of the Karmann-Ghia. When he described the location of the couple to Officer Slaight, unlike most people, who by convention would probably have struggled to give some account of the geography of the location where the couple could be found, Zodiac simply said the couple was driving a white Karmann-Ghia. In other words, the police had to find the couple by using the location of their car, *not* the physical location of the victims. Finally, in the murder of Paul Stine, Zodiac used a taxi cab in an unprecedented way as a "mobile crime scene" by having the driver go to a specific destination in Presidio Heights and then shooting him in the head. Zodiac also stole Stine's car keys. Zodiac's first phone call was made at a gas station, and his second at a car wash.

Zodiac also took credit for three crimes that were related to automobiles, even if he did not personally commit them. First, there was the 1966 murder of Cheri Jo Bates in Riverside that involved the killer disabling her Volkswagen Beetle (a brand of cars Qvale had been importing since 1952). Next, was the March 1970 abduction of Kathleen Johns. The killer loosened the lug nuts of her rear wheel, followed by a harrowing ride in a car around the area of Patterson and Modesto, which ended with the torching of her vehicle. Finally, there was the June 1970 murder of SFPD officer Richard Radetich, who was shot while sitting in his parked patrol car.

Furthermore, Zodiac's bombs had to do with blowing up a vehicle—a school bus—not a school building. These bombs were powered by *car batteries*. In his letters after the Blue Rock Springs attack, the killer spoke about "squealling [*sic*] tires" and a "raceing [*sic*] engine," as well as telling a story about how he was driving a brown car that night. In his letters subsequent to the Stine murder, he talked about motorcycles, police prowl cars, fire trucks, and "road races" as his way of proving he remained in the search area. In his initial letters, Zodiac threatened to "cruse [*sic*]" (drive) around all weekend picking off a dozen victims if his demands weren't met.

But we shouldn't be surprised at any of this given that cars were apparently Zodiac's frame of reference for *everything* in the world. Put another way, if you removed cars, school buses, motorcycles, and car batteries from the Zodiac case, there would be no Zodiac case. This also holds true for the Bates, Johns, and Radetich crimes.

Although he certainly had other business interests, were it not for imported cars, just as the Zodiac case would not have been the Zodiac case, *Kjell Qvale would not have been recognizable as Kjell Qvale*. Qvale's name, in fact, is synonymous with cars. After all, he sold several million of them over the course of his lifetime and was known as "the Father of British Imports" on the West Coast. Beginning shortly after World War II, Qvale's life began to revolve around cars, specifically imported British sports cars and Volkswagens. He drove his first British sports car, an MG-TC, in 1946. In the August 1, 1948, *Chronicle* article mentioned in chapter 18, Qvale is shown driving a recently introduced sports car in Millbrae on the same type of back roads of the Bay Area with which Zodiac would later show his familiarity. In 1949, he was able to convince *Life* magazine to write an influential article about the new British import car craze. In 1952 he became an exclusive importer of Volkswagens to the Pacific Northwest. Qvale hosted road rallies in the 1950s that placed drivers on hundreds of miles of back roads all over the Bay Area. As the *Chronicle* article suggested, he had most likely driven these very back roads of neighboring Solano Counties himself in search of challenging terrain for the various British sports cars he both personally enjoyed and sold. He probably had also driven many of the back roads of Napa County adjacent to his ranch in Oakville, where (in contrast to the streets of downtown San Francisco) you can open up a fast sports car to test its performance. He also hosted a hill-climb event at Mt. Diablo in the 1950s, proving his association with the landmark Zodiac cited in his June 26, 1970, letter. He founded the San Francisco Import Auto Show. Before it got removed the day before the race for mechanical reasons, Qvale had a car entered in the October 30, 1966, *Los Angeles Times* Grand Prix in Riverside, which took place on the very weekend that Cheri Jo Bates was murdered there. Zodiac is widely thought to have been influenced by the Bates murder. Being in Riverside would have been the perfect way to learn about this relatively obscure Southern California crime that didn't get much press coverage in Northern California.[204] There was yet another major auto race in Riverside on the weekend of April 30, 1967, which Qvale may well have attended. It was on this weekend that the "Bates Had to Die" letters were posted. *Therefore, Qvale, even though he lived two blocks or so from the Stine murder scene in San Francisco, would have had a valid reason to be in Riverside both when someone murdered Bates and when the three "Bates Had to Die" letters were mailed. That reason had to do with cars.*

In the 1950s, the Sports Car Club of America, of which Qvale was then an officer, held races at an airport in Tracy, California, near Highway 132 where Kathleen Johns was abducted by the Zodiac in 1970.[205] Qvale was a master mechanic in his youth and was also involved in the design and construction of race cars in the 1960s. Radians are used in the engineering of racing and other engines, especially as regards the calibration of cam shafts. Qvale suggested the course alteration at Laguna Seca that led to the famous corkscrew turn at that track. He founded the Pebble Beach Concours d'Elegance car show. Qvale organized "road races," a term that Zodiac used in his October 1969 letter. In April 1970, Qvale purchased a car manufacturing plant in England that bore the name Jensen Motors. A year and a half before, the Zodiac had killed Betty Lou *Jensen* on Lake Herman Road. Qvale later used Jensen Motors to insert articles in two British newspapers on the anniversary of two Zodiac letter dates. In the late 1990s, he manufactured the Qvale Mangusta in Modena, Italy.

---

204 Qvale sold VWs in Northern California, so it's unlikely that (as was the case with Bryan Hartnell's Karmann-Ghia) Qvale had sold the Beetle owned by Cheri Jo Bates.

205 Tom Wilson, "Tracy Airport Regional Races," *Sports Car,* October 1959, pp. 43–45.

Qvale can be shown to have autographed a car, a Jensen Healey, that held a special place in his career in the auto industry. This took place subsequent to the Zodiac era. He did so using a black felt-tip pen. The Zodiac autographed and wrote a message on a car at Lake Berryessa that had special significance to Qvale's career. He also used a black felt-tip pen to do so. Autographing cars with their name or initials is something only a miniscule percentage of the population ever does in their lifetime. In fact, it is one of the *signature*, or unique, behaviors of the Zodiac.

As a car dealer, Qvale would have had access to any number of nondescript trade-ins for use in his crimes, thus allowing him flexibility in never having to use the same car twice. In addition, he apparently kept junkers on his horse ranch in Oakville, possibly for use by the hired ranch hands in running errands. This is evidenced by a photo in his autobiography of his ranch. In that photo, an older white car is visible. This car is along the lines of the type of car Zodiac may have used in his crimes (Exhibit 42).

Since 2010, it has been strongly rumored by Zodiac researcher Tom Voigt of the website zodiackiller.com that the Zodiac sent a letter that is being held back by the California Department of Justice. The killer supposedly sent this letter to the director of a California governmental agency. Of all the possible governmental agencies to which the killer could have written, of all the ones with which he could have had a grievance or peeve, the one to which the letter was reportedly sent is the *California Department of Motor Vehicles.* This makes perfect sense and is in keeping with Zodiac's (and Qvale's) clear obsession with cars. In and of itself, Zodiac's obsession with cars lends strong credence in my own mind to the existence of the DMV letter.

As an automobile salesman who had to deal with exasperating governmental regulations and red tape throughout his career, Qvale is a suspect in the case that one can easily envision having had issues with the DMV. In fact, emissions regulations in the early 1970s severely damaged Qvale's efforts to build inexpensive sports cars at Jensen

Motors for export to the US and ultimately contributed to the demise of that company.[206]

One fact that had escaped me until April of 2011 is that the license plates on Bryan Hartnell's white Volkswagen Karmann-Ghia from Lake Berryessa were not California plates. They were actually from Oregon. This was pointed out to me by Canadian researcher Chris MacRae on the Napa PD impound report on the car, which is available on the Net (Exhibit 43). This revelation has opened up an entirely new line of investigation that seems to link Qvale intimately to the car on which Zodiac wrote his chilling message in 1969.

The other thing one can learn from the impound report is that in 1969, the owner of that white Karmann-Ghia was surprisingly not victim Bryan Hartnell himself, nor anyone from his family. I had only seen the impound report when it was partially redacted to show that the owner was a "Bruce" with the surname blacked out. I had assumed that it was "Bruce Hartnell," whom I presumed to be Bryan's father. I was wrong. When I finally saw the unredacted version from MacRae, I saw that the name of the owner was a "Bruce Christie" of Portland, Oregon. But who was Bruce Christie, and how did he come to be the owner of Hartnell's Karmann-Ghia?

I wrote to the Portland Public Library in April 2011 and learned that Mr. Christie was apparently involved in the used car business in Portland in the 1960s. What jumped out of the email at me was the fact that Bruce Christie was a control tower worker from 1961 to 1964 at *Riviera Motors* in Portland. In the 1960s, Qvale was the sole, the exclusive, the *only* importer of Volkswagens coming into the Pacific Northwest. Qvale's importing company was, in fact, named Riviera Motors. *Put another way, in 1969 Bryan Hartnell was driving a car that was actually owned by an ex-employee of Qvale's Oregon VW dealership/ importer. This all but proves the pedigree of Hartnell's car as having originated at Qvale's Portland, Oregon, dealership.*

---

206 Terry Dodsworth, "Jensen's Bumpy Road," *The Financial Times* (London), September 16, 1975, p. 8.

If you were Kjell Qvale and you were Zodiac, when you drove around Lake Berryessa that day, it would have taken you only an instant to recognize that a Volkswagen Karmann-Ghia with Oregon plates was a car that you were 99 percent likely to have imported. And while Qvale could not have known that Christie owned that particular car on September 27, 1969, the fact that it bore Oregon plates would have immediately linked Qvale's dealership to that car in any reasonable person's mind.

While Zodiac may just have come across Hartnell's car by sheer happenstance, not by specifically targeting or following it, it's entirely possible that the reason Zodiac wrote on the door of the Karmann-Ghia is the same reason Qvale would later autograph a Jensen Healey: **the car that Hartnell was driving that day had a tremendous significance to Kjell Qvale's career as an importer of foreign cars, since he made untold millions of dollars selling Volkswagens beginning in 1952.** In short, Zodiac may have been providing a clue to investigators about his strong personal relationship with this particular car by taking the extremely unusual step of autographing the vehicle. Of course, this potential clue was so hopelessly obscure and cryptic as to be completely unintelligible in 1969.

At Lake Herman, Zodiac seems to have driven past a British import, that is, an MG or a Triumph, done a double-take, and then turned around and taken off in the same direction as the car. Here is yet another example of a car, this time a British marque, attracting the killer's attention.

Now it can be proven that the same man who "just happens" to be the only person of interest ever developed who was spoken to by the police after any of the Zodiac crimes, who closely resembled the SFPD sketch, who had reddish-brown hair, who had an unusual and slow manner of speaking, and who wrote on monarch-sized paper had also imported Bryan Hartnell's car and may have sold the MG or Triumph that Zodiac chased at Lake Herman. *Qvale is the only suspect I know of who can be tied in any way to three vehicles (Hartnell's VW, the British*

*import at Lake Herman, and, as we will see, Stine's taxi) that were either
directly or indirectly involved in the Zodiac case.* To other researchers,
Zodiac's reason for chasing the MG/Triumph and writing on the car
seems completely inscrutable. The auto chase at Lake Herman involving a British import likewise appears to be a random and coincidental
event. But, like the dates of the murders, when viewed through the filter
of Qvale's life, these two incidents take on different meanings entirely.

Here is a rundown of the facts related to Hartnell's Karmann-Ghia:

- Kjell Qvale has autographed cars that had significance to his career, like a Jensen Motors vehicle, which he manufactured, and an
  MG, of which he sold many and which Zodiac may have chased
  at Lake Herman. He used a black felt-tip pen to sign the visor
  of one car.

- Zodiac wrote a message, also in black felt-tip pen, on Hartnell's
  Volkswagen Karmann-Ghia.

- Qvale was the sole importer of Volkswagens to the West Coast
  beginning in the early 1950s.

- Volkswagens, therefore, are cars that had a huge significance in
  the professional career of Kjell Qvale.

- Qvale had imported Bryan Hartnell's VW, as evidenced by the
  fact that it was actually owned by an ex-employee of Qvale's,
  Bruce Christie, and by the Oregon plates on the vehicle that day.

- Therefore, just as Qvale did over the years, Zodiac also wrote a
  message on a car that had great significance in the life and career
  of *Kjell Qvale.*

- The crossed-circle symbol that Zodiac wrote on the door of the
  car contains all the letters in Kjell Qvale's last name and is a bu-
  merke-like signature that also appeared in place of a signature on
  the Avery Halloween card and which would later appear underneath Qvale's name on his building in Modena, Italy. Therefore,
  the first thing Zodiac may have written on Hartnell's car was a

crossed-circle symbol that represented the name QVALE.

To summarize, Zodiac seemed to be obsessed with cars. Qvale's entire adult life also revolved around various types of cars. His exploits with auto racing and road rallies in the Bay Area, as well as his experiences as a horse owner and his residences, could have led Qvale to be familiar with all of the Zodiac crime scene areas. In addition, Qvale had strong ties to Bryan Hartnell's Karmann-Ghia, as well as to imported British cars like the one Zodiac chased at Lake Herman.

I have spent so much space discussing in great detail Zodiac's obsession with cars for the following reason: *this obsession is of paramount importance to laying the Zodiac crimes right at the doorstep of Kjell Qvale.*

In chapter 17, we learned that Richard Walter's profile of the Zodiac is that of a wealthy and powerful man. However, the final piece of Walter's crime scene assessment is that Zodiac's entire criminal career literally centered on cars. When you combine the killer's obsession with cars with the profile of a wealthy and powerful individual, you have already swung the needle way around to Kjell Qvale as someone who closely fits the extremely specific profile of the Zodiac. *In fact, the confluence of the wealthy power-assertive profile and Zodiac's obsession with cars nearly singles out Kjell Qvale (or someone virtually identical to him) as the prime suspect in the case without the need for any additional evidence. Conversely,* between Mr. Walter's profile and the "filtering" effect it has had in winnowing potential suspects, as well as Zodiac's obsession with cars, you have also ruled out over 99 percent of the other three thousand-plus suspects ever developed in the case. While it usually points to a large pool of potential suspects, the full behavioral profile in the case of the Zodiac has, in its specificity, powerful implications in identifying the man responsible for the crimes.

Mr. Walter indicated to me that cars, and in particular high-powered sports cars and race cars, are symbols of masculinity and power.

Therefore, the ubiquitous presence of motor vehicles in the Zodiac murders and letters actually serves to reinforce the P-A profile.

...

In June 1999, I started on this odyssey by using Zodiac's known behavior of sending letters to the editors of the local Bay Area newspapers as the basis for trying to identify him. I also examined the timing of what are believed to be the killer's very first letters and the "Bates Had to Die" letters sent exactly six months after the October 1966 murder of Cheri Jo Bates. By January of 2000, just a few months after learning Qvale's name, through determined factual research, I was able to prove these things about Mr. Qvale, which I discussed in chapter 13:

- Like Zodiac, he wrote a letter to the editor of the *Chronicle*, something I have seen from only one other named suspect in the case. This letter appeared just where I predicted it to appear based on Zodiac's previous letter-writing behavior in Riverside in 1966–67.

- In his letter, Qvale spoke about having a sociological issue with young people, the same demographic you'd expect to find sitting in parked cars on lovers' lanes.

- He was of Norwegian extraction, which therefore explained Zodiac's ability to pen the Sla Letter, as well as explaining the presence of many other Norse references in the Zodiac letters.

- He had strong ties to England, which would explain the many British references and usage in the Zodiac letters.

- He demonstrated a strong desire to see his name on the front pages of the Bay Area newspapers as far back as 1947 (i.e., flying-saucer sighting), which provides a peek at the very roots of Zodiac's need to demand that his own stories get "frunt"-page coverage. I have never seen this desire for publicity so clearly demonstrated by or proven for any other suspect.

- His flying-saucer sighting took place on July 5, the same date as the Blue Rock Springs attack.

- His father was born on September 27, the same date as the Lake Berryessa attack.

- His mother died on December 20, the same date as Zodiac's attack on Lake Herman Road.

- He was a dead ringer for the "Amended" SFPD wanted poster sketch.

- He lived within two blocks of the murder of Paul Stine and would therefore have been well acquainted with Presidio Heights, an obscure and isolated neighborhood, which explains why Zodiac felt a level of comfort killing there.

- His home overlooked the Stine search area around the Julius Kahn Playground, thus providing him with a perfect view of the police and dog search that took place that night.

- He owned a ranch in Oakville, which lies between Lake Berryessa and Napa. This ranch could have served as a stopping-off point for Zodiac after he left the lake and headed into Napa to make his phone call to the police.

- His name, Kjell Hammond Qvale, had exactly seventeen letters in it, the same number of columns as in Zodiac's coded messages, and the first letter of his last name was Q, the seventeenth letter of the alphabet. Also, his original name had eighteen letters in it, thus matching the number of characters of "gibberish" at the end of Zodiac's Three-Part Cipher.

- He had a car entered in the 1966 *Los Angeles Times* Grand Prix and he had been in Riverside for that race on the same weekend that Cheri Jo Bates was murdered.

- He had a reason to have been in Riverside yet again for a car race on April 30, 1967, when the three "Bates Had to Die" letters were mailed.

- He wrote two letters to me on monarch-sized paper, the same odd-sized stationery that Zodiac used for his own letters. I'm sure that very few readers have ever used monarch-sized paper, have received letters written on it, or even know what it is.

- Like Zodiac, his life was intimately associated with cars, which explains why all of Zodiac's crimes and many of his letter references, including the "bus bombs," involved vehicles.

- My interpretation of the first bus bomb was that it was in reality a map to his home at 3636 Jackson Street.

I submit to you, the reader, that this is quite an impressive and unexpected list. And as the items in this list demonstrate, the facts of Mr. Qvale's life explain many of the things we see in the Zodiac case in ways that other suspects simply do not. That is what riveted my attention the most, and why Qvale's life story is also the story of the Zodiac. And as you are aware after reading this book, the above list is just the tip of a very large iceberg of circumstantial evidence. My critics will call all of these things "mere coincidences" or "Zynchronicities."[207] I call them *troubling* coincidences that collectively comprise a strong beginning to a circumstantial case.

Of coincidences and circumstantial evidence, Richard Walter said that over 70 percent of major cases are solved on the basis of circumstantial evidence alone *with no physical evidence at all*. Again, we're talking about *major* cases. Over the years, posters on message boards have minimized the evidence against Qvale because it was "only circumstantial," as if the word *circumstantial* were somehow a pejorative term. Obviously, if a district attorney doesn't feel that he can win a case, he won't bring it to court in the first place, and they apparently win quite frequently on circumstantial evidence alone. So what Mr. Walter's pet statistic tells us is that circumstantial evidence is powerful enough

---

207 The word coined by Ed Neil to describe synchronicities or coincidences in the Zodiac case.

to win even major cases—and that it does so more often than people might imagine.

To briefly put before you once again what I covered in chapter 18, here is the other circumstantial evidence I amassed about Qvale subsequent to January 2000:

- He had a noticeably slow, measured manner of speaking just like Zodiac.

- He had been described, as had Zodiac, as being aloof and as being this way all his life, not just after amassing his fortune as an adult. There is no other suspect of which I am aware whose aloofness was so prominent a character trait that it was described in a magazine article.

- He had reddish-brown hair, the same color as was described for Zodiac and the same color as the small hair found behind the stamp by SFPD on one of the Zodiac letters.

- He had served in the US Navy, as was often theorized for Zodiac.

- He shared Zodiac's unique behavior of writing his signature on a car.

- He may have imported the British car that the young man and his date from Lake Herman were sitting in and that was involved in the chase the night of the Jensen-Faraday murders.

- He had definitely imported Bryan Hartnell's Volkswagen Karmann-Ghia, and this car was owned by an ex-employee of Qvale's. So in autographing the car as Zodiac, Qvale was actually autographing a vehicle that had strong significance to his career as an import car salesman. He later autographed a Jensen Motors car, which not only was significant to his career as a car dealer/manufacturer but which bore the name of one of Zodiac's earliest victims.

- He was on the streets of Presidio Heights shortly after the Stine

406 · MIKE RODELLI

murder took place and is the only person ever to become a suspect in the Zodiac case who was interviewed in any capacity—that is, as either a witness or a suspect by the police—after any of the Zodiac murders. This serves to explain how Zodiac obtained details of the search that night but was not subject to being captured. This can't be accounted for by simply stating that the killer "left the area" after the murder. Zodiac described the sounds of the police search, which means he had to have been close by.

- Due to his involvement in horse racing, where postrace saliva testing was used in the 1960s for possible drugging of racehorses, Qvale would have understood the possible drawbacks of licking stamps and envelopes even before the advent of DNA testing. This explains the essential or literal absence of saliva and cells on the Zodiac letters.

- In 1968, when Zodiac killed on Lake Herman Road and claimed the crime took place in "Vallejo," that city was the "sister city" of Qvale's hometown of Trondheim, Norway. In fact, as of December 20, 1968, Trondheim was the only sister city of Vallejo.

- Part of Qvale's business plan over the years was to manipulate members of the media for positive press for his business, and he knew at least Herb Caen, if not other members of the media and even the hierarchy of the *Chronicle*.

- He was a member of the prestigious Bohemian Club, where he could have rubbed shoulders with the management of the *Chronicle*.

- He can be proven via a 1952 newspaper article to have moved in the same circles as Melvin Belli in the early 1950s.

- He is one of the few suspects who was both old enough and wealthy enough to have come to the attention of Belli's partner, William "Peek-a-Boo" Pennington, whose 1940s' yellow pages ad appears to have inspired Zodiac's 1970 Halloween card to Paul Avery.

- Qvale's Norse heritage would have allowed him to know what a *bumerke* is, such as the one apparently comprised of two Norse runes that appears on the Halloween card.

- He admitted in 2006 that *sla* meant "kill" to him in Old Norse.

- He was obsessed with dates and anniversaries: June 26, November 20, and March 22.

- He raced horses, like Gun Barrel, in Vallejo in the 1960s, thus proving his relationship with that city, which he tried to minimize at our 2006 meeting. Zodiac used the phrase *gun barrel* in his August 1969 letter, which was written after Qvale had purchased this horse.

- Qvale was fifty in 1969, older than most people believed the Zodiac to be. This might explain the old-fashioned pleated pants the killer wore at two crime scenes, as well as his use of "getting your rocks off" in the first coded message.

- Finally, Zodiac, who looked just like Qvale, was last seen walking in the general direction of Qvale's home on Jackson Street, on the same side of the street as that home, and about a block away from it.

I have read other books on various suspects, and nowhere have I seen a list of circumstances this comprehensive that involves all aspects of Mr. Qvale's life. It is one thing to put forth a laundry list of circumstantial evidence. But what does the list really mean? What context can it provide to the facts of the Zodiac case? What unique aspects of the story of the Zodiac are actually explained by Qvale's life history?

When you view the Zodiac case through the filter of Qvale's life, such things as the seeming randomness of the dates of the murders take on an unexpected order. Qvale explains the Sla Letter and all the Norse references made by the Zodiac. He explains the British references in the letters. He explains Zodiac's use of monarch-sized paper, which Qvale also used, probably to the exclusion of all the other suspects ever named. He explains why Zodiac killed in Presidio Heights. He explains how Zodiac was able to gather all the details of the police search for his letters on the night of the Stine murder and yet was not subject to capture. He explains (by having raced horses there) Zodiac's familiarity with Solano County. His Oakville ranch explains how Zodiac could have familiarized himself with both Napa and Lake Berryessa. He explains why the Zodiac letters were not licked by the sender. He explains the reddish-brown hair behind the stamp. He explains Zodiac's knowledge of the back roads of the Bay Area. He explains Zodiac's need for widespread public attention on the front pages of newspapers. He explains why Zodiac wrote his signature on Hartnell's car. He explains Zodiac's seeming familiarity with attorney Melvin Belli. He explains Zodiac's "naval look" and his use of wing walkers. He explains Zodiac's presence in Riverside in October 1966 and April 1967. More importantly, his wealth and position in life explain why Zodiac was never identified prior to 1999, since he was the last person anyone would suspect!

This is why I feel that the life story of Kjell Qvale, as told by my circumstantial evidence, also tells the story of the Zodiac. Conversely, if someone else was, in fact, the Zodiac, then by definition their life history would have to tell the story of the Zodiac even better than does Qvale's.

···

Killers such as Zodiac sometimes have difficulty separating their private lives from their lives as serial killers. And it appears to me that Qvale's life as Zodiac life "bled over" into his private life. Here are examples of this phenomenon: Zodiac wrote a message on the door of a car that Qvale had imported (a Volkswagen Karmann-Ghia). Qvale purchased a car company bearing one of the names of Zodiac's early victims (Jensen Motors). **Qvale's letter to the editor appeared on June 26, 1969. Zodiac marked that same date a year later with his June 26, 1970, Mt.**

Diablo Letter. Then Qvale used the car company named after one of Zodiac's victims to commemorate the date again on June 26, 1971, in both *The Times* of London and the *Financial Times*. Qvale later autographed a Jensen-Healey automobile. He purchased a building in Italy that bore a crossed circle on its facade. He joined the Parents Television Council that demanded less violent content on television, similar to the content of Zodiac's *Badlands* Letter. Finally, he had a comedian named Dr. Z in his opening-night audience at Holly's Comedy Club. Thus, both personalities "acknowledged" the existence of each other.

My twenty years of research have proven that Qvale is the *only* suspect ever named in the investigation by either the police or amateur investigators who

- **was spoken to by the police near the scene of *any* of the Zodiac murders shortly after that crime took place;**

- **demonstrated Zodiac's signature behavioral need for widespread publicity over twenty years before the crimes took place;**

- **wrote even *one* letter in his life on monarch-sized paper; and**

- **can be shown to have ever autographed even one car in his life, which is another signature behavior of the killer.**

There may possibly be one other suspect about whom just *one* of these things is true. But there is no other suspect that anyone has ever named since 1969 about whom *all* of these things are true. As unlikely as it may seem given who he was and his many accomplishments, it is inarguable that in this regard Kjell Qvale stands alone among the suspects in the Zodiac investigation. As indicated earlier, when you find someone who looks, speaks, and behaves like the Zodiac, you have presumably found the man responsible for the Zodiac crimes. In addition, it is often said that in a long investigation, the name of the person responsible for the crimes is often already in the police files. Qvale's name has reportedly been in SFPD's files since he encountered Officer Pelissetti *on the very first night of their investigation into the Stine murder.*

When we think of serial killers and rapists, and especially a serial killer whose behavior was both as cruel and bizarre as Zodiac's was, it is counterintuitive to conceive of someone like Kjell Qvale as a suspect. This is an obstacle that I encountered time and time again in trying to explain my evidence to both other amateur investigators and the police. However, as evidence in this book has shown, when you describe Zodiac in terms of a man who was obsessed with power and then take a step back and recognize the killer's obsession with cars, Qvale quickly goes to the very front of the line in terms of suspects in the case.

There is another aspect to this dilemma: deep down inside ourselves, we may secretly not want people like Qvale to be criminals, since at a very fundamental level the possibility destroys our notion of the order of how things *should* be and leaves us wondering just who we can and cannot trust. It is unsettling to imagine that crimes such as the Zodiac murders can be committed by a man who might justifiably be considered a pillar of the community and who would never raise an alarm with anyone. The same can be said of Bill Cosby. However, the hard reality is that literally anyone can commit crimes; criminals don't have to come from what we may perceive as the "criminal element."

In short, despite various people having described Qvale over the years as being a true gentleman and even "presidential" in bearing, the undeniable truth is that the evidence presented here shows that Qvale's life story tells the story of the Zodiac in very fundamental ways. I'm aware of how people who knew him perceived Mr. Qvale based on his long career as a successful entrepreneur, horse owner, and his many other endeavors. I also recognize that the people who knew him best, from their business and social dealings with him, will undoubtedly have the most difficulty reconciling the man they knew with the picture the facts contained in this book paint. This is what makes Qvale's identity as the Zodiac so very shocking, unexpected, and, on the surface at least, nearly impossible to fathom.

In his 2018 book, *The Man from the Train*,[208] author Bill James talks about one phenomenon that causes people to have difficulty accepting realities that aren't a normal part of their everyday lives. He calls it *irrational resistance.* James says that experience can sometimes be our *worst* teacher. When something comes along that just "shouldn't be" based on our prior life experiences, we tend to reject that notion out of hand as being impossible. Such seems to have been the case with Mr. Qvale ever since I came forward in 1999. However, as we have seen with Bill Cosby, wealthy, powerful—*even famous*—people can also commit major crimes.

To wit, when I first proposed Qvale as Zodiac, my fellow amateurs quickly assured me that "people like that" don't become serial killers, because they already have power and control in their lives. So why kill for it? The idea that someone like Qvale was Zodiac seemed ludicrous. Insp. Kelly Carroll of SFPD asked me why Qvale would have become Zodiac. Since I had no answer, SFPD didn't take me seriously despite any evidence I may have had.

I had no idea at the time; I just had evidence as early as April 2000 that pointed to the possibility that he was. In 1969, the profiling technique of crime scene assessment didn't exist. This absence led to the erroneous profile of a "loser" at the time, which has persisted to this day. But had crime scene assessment existed when Zodiac was active and the killer was immediately described as a wealthy and powerful man who killed for even more power and control, people would have been much quicker to accept Qvale as a legitimate suspect. He would have come to the attention of the authorities long before 1999, since the search for Zodiac may have eventually centered in places like Presidio Heights, and people like Qvale may have been subject to greater scrutiny years before I came along.

I am just a researcher, and as such, as I told Mr. Qvale in 2006, I am a slave to my facts. And those facts show that Qvale, for all the good

208 Bill James and Rachel McCarthy James, *The Man from the Train*, (New York: Scribner, 2018), pp. 346–48.

he did in other aspects of his life, was harboring a shocking, almost unimaginable secret. As stated earlier, his unusual attention-seeking behavior from 1947 is a Rosetta stone that translates events of his early life into the basic behavioral language of the Zodiac and allows us to imagine how the Qvale of that era could easily have evolved into the Zodiac of 1969.

Using the methodology of creating a profile of a killer and then finding the person who fits that profile doesn't require DNA, fingerprints, or, most of all, handwriting. In my opinion, Qvale fits Richard Walter's power-assertive behavioral profile of the Zodiac. And when you add to the profile the killer's obsession with cars, it places immediate and tremendous distance between Qvale and virtually any other suspect who has ever been named since 1969 on the ladder of probability that he was the Zodiac.

A behavioral profile can generally only take us so far, in that it only identifies the *type* of individual we are looking for as a suspect. However, Mr. Walter's profile of the Zodiac, due to its specificity, brings us very close to identifying Kjell Qvale alone as the person responsible for the Zodiac crimes. The truth is, even if he didn't leave his physical fingerprints behind at any of the crime scenes, *Mr. Qvale certainly left his "behavioral fingerprints" all over the Zodiac case.* And when we combine that profile with the circumstantial evidence that I have developed since 1999, they undeniably link Qvale to the innermost workings of the Zodiac case.

Now we turn to the role of the defense attorneys. They must account for the same circumstantial evidence the prosecution weaves into a story to convict a defendant and then retell that story in such a manner as to *exonerate* their client. The many circumstances I have developed about Qvale since 1999, especially since they do collectively tell the story of the Zodiac, could not be overcome by the defense in court. They would not be able to formulate an innocent alternative explanation of the facts used by prosecutors to demonstrate that Qvale *was* the Zodiac.

In other words, I believe the reader will now agree with me and with Mr. Walter, as he stated in *The Murder Room*, that Kjell Qvale was the Zodiac. There is no version of the collective weight of the behavioral and circumstantial evidence presented in this book that would place him in a light that would tend to exonerate him.

...

So where did Zodiac get his name? The possibilities are seemingly as endless as there are investigators looking into the case. I already spoke about Dr. Zodiac in *Charlie Chan at Treasure Island* as one possibility due to the presence of Dr. Z on opening night of Holly's Comedy Club. However, now that we understand the killer's obsession with cars, here is one possibility that is particularly relevant to Qvale: By the late 1960s, Qvale already had an over-twenty-year association with England. At the time that Zodiac named himself, there was a popular British television show called *ZCars*. This was a police show that featured two Ford automobiles that began with the letter Z—the Zephyr and the Zodiac. Qvale may well have seen this popular show on British television when he was in the country on his countless business trips there.

The Ford Zodiac Mark IV was a high-performance car that had a more powerful engine than the Zephyr, making it more in line with the concept of a "sports car." It was used by police to chase suspects who had taken to the highways to make their escape. The Ford Zodiac also had a hood ornament that evoked Zodiac's own crossed-circle symbol.

Was this car the inspiration for Zodiac's name? In this context, the name Zodiac is clearly associated with *cars*, which we know were near and dear to the killer. Aside from being akin to a sports car, the name Zodiac is also linked with a symbol reminiscent of Zodiac's infamous signature. The TV show *ZCars* may well have drawn the killer's attention due to the prominent role of cars in the show as well as the fact that the title itself serves to wed the letter Z with the concept of cars. While no proof can be offered that the Ford Zodiac was the inspiration of the killer's name, it's certainly true that a Zodiac-brand wristwatch isn't the *only* place where the name Zodiac and a symbol reminiscent of the killer's crossed-circle signature can be found together (Exhibit 44).[209]

...

I believe that, given who we now know he was, the only way in which the Zodiac would have ever been identified was through a "back door" idea like the one I had in 1999. I find it hard to believe that anyone at *any* time would have otherwise named Mr. Qvale as a serious suspect, due to his public persona and stellar reputation as an entrepreneur. I don't know how or why the simple idea to look through the letters to the editor occurred to me—or more precisely why it had never occurred to anyone else before. But if I had not, I am resigned to the fact that the identity of the Zodiac would likely have forever remained out of our grasp.

There is one last issue I wish to touch on briefly. While it makes the most sense to imagine that Zodiac's victims were chosen completely at random based on where they were at a given time, there is one other intriguing possibility: it's possible that these weren't *completely* random victims, but that *he was drawn to them based on what they were driving*. Given Zodiac's clear obsession with cars, this is a theory that deserves closer examination.

At Lake Herman, Zodiac may have intended to kill at 11:17 PM. However, in order to scout the area, he likely got to Gate #10 early and drove past the turnout at 9:30 PM. When he did, a different opportunity presented itself. He spotted the British sports car parked in the exact spot he had planned the attack. This is the car that Zodiac either chased or followed to the east end of Lake Herman Road. Given that Qvale

209 While Zodiac's symbol is not an exact replica of the Ford Zodiac hood ornament, it is worth noting that the hood ornament is so distinctive that, had Zodiac used it, he may have feared that it would eventually be traced back to the car—and to his British automotive roots.

was a British sports car dealer, killing people in a new British sports car, like the Triumph or MG, while also planting a cryptic clue to the killer's identity, would have represented tremendous irony. And we know that, like Mr. Qvale (and his rescheduling of our 2006 meeting to September 27), Zodiac loved irony. But when that opportunity failed to come to fruition, he may have gone back to his original plans at 11:17 PM, resulting in the deaths of Faraday and Jensen.

At Blue Rock Springs, according to police reports from that time, Mike Mageau stated that the killer pulled up to them in what was possibly a brown Corvair similar or even *identical to* the one Darlene was driving that night.[210] Was Zodiac also driving a Corvair that evening? We can't rule that out. If he was being truthful in his taunting phone call to the police, he was at the very least driving a brown car that night. Again, given his love of irony, what better thing to do in that case than to attack a couple sitting in *the same make, model, and color of car you were driving?*

At Lake Berryessa, we know that Bryan Hartnell was driving a Volkswagen Karmann-Ghia. Qvale, as Zodiac, immediately recognized it as one he had imported through Riviera Motors and made the couple his victims and then autographed the car.

Finally, Paul Stine was killed in a taxi. But what is the connection between Qvale and taxi drivers?

In a passage early in Qvale's 2005 autobiography,[211] he states that when he was a youth in Norway, a local taxi driver had taught him to drive a car. Qvale specifically stated that the cabbie would allow him to *sit in his lap* and take the wheel while the cabbie worked the pedals. Ironically, at the Stine murder scene, it is pretty much universally accepted that Zodiac laid taxi driver Paul Stine across *his own lap* in order to get the tail of his shirt to send with his subsequent letters.[212]

---

210 Det. Sgt. Ed Rust, Vallejo Police Department Report on Blue Rock Sprints Attack, undated and page not numbered.

211 Qvale, p. 9.

212 I noticed that in the early scene at the mansion of Robert Vaughn's char-

The circle, started in Norway in the 1920s, had closed decades later in Presidio Heights.

Finally, because I know there will be an onslaught of detractors who will accuse me of gratuitously trying to besmirch Mr. Qvale's good name, let me provide a partial list of the people who have read over and been impressed with and/or supported my research since 1999:

- Richard Walter of the Vidocq Society

- The late Solano County Superior Court judge Eric Uldall, who called Qvale "the only true prime suspect ever developed in the history of the case" in 2001

- Detective Patrick Grate (Ret.) of the Solano County SO

- Tim Armistead, formerly of the San Francisco City Attorney's Office

- Detective Jim Dean (Ret.) of the Vallejo Police Department, who worked on the Zodiac investigation in the 1970s and has supported my efforts since 2001

- The late SFPD homicide inspector Gus Coreris, who worked with the Stine eyewitnesses

- Pete Noyes, retired news producer at CBS and Fox for forty years, who in 2005 called my research the "biggest" investigative

---

acter in the 1968 movie *Bullitt*, which was shot in San Francisco, there was a Bentley along with some Jaguars. There are many VWs in the movie parked on the streets, and in the famous chase scene a green VW Beetle shows up repeatedly in various scenes due to apparent editing mistakes. Jacqueline Bisset's character drives a VW Karmann-Ghia. All of these cars may well have been supplied by Kjell Qvale's dealership, since he imported Bentleys and Jaguars and was the exclusive importer of VWs in Northern California. I noticed that in another early scene, a man hails a yellow-colored cab #6912. Zodiac, who had a virtual sea of cabs with all manner of different numbers on them from which to choose on the night of the Stine murder, chose Yellow Cab #912. It's possible that Zodiac chose the cab with the number *closest to the number of the cab in the movie*. Stine's cab lacked only the first digit of cab #6912. The credits in the movie aren't detailed enough to show who supplied vehicles to the production.

story he had seen in his lengthy career

- Insp. Vincent Repetto (Ret.) of the SFPD, who brought my report to the attention of the chief in 2012 and later called my research "interesting . . . compelling" at a gathering of Zodiac researchers in Presidio Heights in 2014

I wish to emphasize that after all of my years of research, I have no reason to believe, nor have I ever unearthed any evidence whatsoever to indicate, that any of Mr. Qvale's immediate relatives knew anything about his double life as the Zodiac. Like Zodiac, Qvale was a very aloof person. And aloof people are very good at keeping secrets. Even from their own families.

In May 2020, I did correspond with a relative of Qvale's on social media. This person clearly did not view me as being out of line in any way for looking at Kjell as the Zodiac. They were, in short, open to the possibility that Qvale could have been the killer. They said that Qvale displayed certain personality traits that, in their mind, resonated with the personality of the Zodiac. In addition, because of property he owned overseas, they told me to look at him as possibly being yet another well-known serial killer who has yet to be identified. I was gratified that this member of the family seems to have an open mind about my research and that they didn't simply dismiss my claims out of hand. This was something I had hoped to hear for many years.

EPILOGUE

ON NOVEMBER 4, 2013, I received an email from a fellow Zodiac researcher telling me that Kjell Qvale had died the previous day. Frankly, I was stunned. For even though he was ninety-four years old, I had never considered the prospect of him dying before my research had reached a final resolution. I always knew, however, that, barring a miracle, I wouldn't be able to tell my story while Kjell was still alive.

As I looked back that day on the years I'd spent trying to prove that Qvale was the Zodiac, I had many regrets. The biggest was that the Zodiac, through no fault of my own, was a very wealthy and powerful man. This made me walk a narrow tightrope between getting my story out to the public and not incurring a huge defamation lawsuit. I can't think of any other researcher in the case who had to do the balancing act I was forced to engage in every day. Qvale's wealth not only intimidated the police, as noted in chapter 19, but it also made the media cautious to write about my research, even though people like Pete Noyes knew this was a huge story.

420 · MIKE RODELLI

The most discouraging thing I have heard is that Zodiac researchers who put in twenty years trying to prove their case are "obsessed" with
the case. This is used to subtly discredit someone like me. With all the
obstacles a person who has a suspect in the case faces along the way—
overly skeptical detectives, like Insp. Kelly Carroll (Ret.) of SFPD, who
knew key Zodiac eyewitness Lindsey Robbins personally but wouldn't
show Lindsey a photo of Qvale from the 1960s prior to Jim and me
doing so in 2003; police departments that are more interested in politics
than justice; other amateur researchers, who elevate their own suspects
by putting both your suspect *and* you down; and last but not least, the
outrageous DNA sample from the front of a stamp, one that the letter
writer probably never even licked, from SFPD/ABC that seemed to end
my quest in 2002—the truth is that it's impossible to solve a case like
this unless you have a huge helping of perseverance and old-fashioned
stick-to-it-iveness, which others then use to denigrate you by putting
their nose in the air and calling you "obsessive." Conversely, a police
detective with similar traits is admiringly called a "pit bull" who "never
gives up," et cetera.

On the DVD that accompanied *Zodiac: The Director's Cut*, in the
discussion of the film, screenwriter James Vanderbilt comments that
obsessive types are "the ones who keep us safe." We're the ones who
notice that a gate looks slightly ajar or that something else looks strange
or out of place and go to investigate. So I wear any obsessive part of my
nature not as a stigma but as a badge of honor.

Had the police taken me more seriously and been less fearful of
Qvale and his political and financial power in 1999 and 2000, maybe
the case would have been solved when I first came along. And by 2006,
I had even set a baseline for police interviewers by meeting with Qvale
and having him give me untrue answers to my simple questions. SFPD
certainly was aware of my conversation with Qvale and could easily
have gone out and asked him the same questions I had to see if his story
changed. And if it did and he placed himself out walking on the streets
of Presidio Heights immediately after the Stine murder, despite telling

me he "should have been in England," might that not have piqued their curiosity to dig some more? I truly don't know.

All I do know is that the totality of my research, along with Richard Walter's profile of the killer, has provided a left-brained and defensible solution to the case of the Zodiac Killer. Might evidence come along one day that proves me wrong? Of course that is always a possibility. However, to date such evidence does not exist, and I believe that since nearly every aspect of Mr. Qvale's life story also tells the story of the Zodiac saga, this is the best solution to the case proposed thus far.

Acknowledgments

WHEN YOU SPEND TWENTY YEARS OF YOUR LIFE putting together a story, there are necessarily many people to thank. I hope to include everyone, but I fear that I will forget some. Just know that if you assisted me in any way along my journey, I am grateful for that assistance.

First I must thank my family for their support, encouragement, and, most of all, patience. In my early research in the summer of 1999, I'm sure they got tired of hearing me go on day after day about my latest findings on either the case or my suspect. Those were incredibly exciting times for me, but, in retrospect, maybe not so much for non–Zodiac researchers like them. I can also recall in August 1999 running my interpretation of Zodiac's first bus bomb by my then twelve-year-old niece and nephew, figuring that if they could understand the way I was presenting my theory, I was presenting my theory clear enough for all. My brother, John Rodelli, a retired New York Police Department lieutenant who was a first responder at the World Trade Center attack on September 11, 2001, and who is currently a federal police officer, noticed in 2005 that Zodiac had described the sounds of the police search in his letters. I thank him for that important observation.

Next I need to thank my friend, confidant, and collaborator retired Vallejo Police Department detective Jim Dean and his wife, Chris, and their family. What hasn't Jim done for me? He has opened doors, gotten me access to otherwise inaccessible eyewitnesses with his badge, acted as my "second" at the 2006 face-to-face meeting with Qvale, and tirelessly championed my conclusions about the identity of the Zodiac since 2001. In 2002 he, along with my European friends, kept me on my task after the 2002 ABC News show seemed to have ruled Qvale out against DNA. Dutch Zodiac researcher Eduard Versluijs, who had previously worked in a DNA lab, pointed out the errors in lab technique he spotted on the 2002 ABC show. Had all of them not urged me to keep going despite that setback, I would have walked away from the case at that time.

I want to thank Richard Walter, world-renowned expert on criminal profiling and crime scene assessment, for accepting me into his circle of acquaintances in 2004, which I know is extremely rarefied air for a rank amateur investigator like me. Mr. Walter's profile input gave context to my circumstantial evidence, and he has lent a willing and patient ear to my many and sometimes irritating questions about crime scene assessment and to my profiling ideas with respect to various other cases since we met. His acknowledgement of my research in *The Murder Room* in 2010 gave me tremendous confidence that I was on the right track.

Speaking of Eduard Versluijs, he has been a reliable friend, confidant, and colleague since I first came along in 1998. He had already formed an opinion that Zodiac was at least Scandinavian, if not Norwegian, so when I named Qvale he felt that I was someone who had come up with a viable suspect. He then used his ingenuity, outside-the-box thinking, and tremendous research skills to help me assemble my case. Among other things, Eduard was the first to recognize the Avery return address as being comprised of Norse runes. He also discovered Qvale's Modena building with the crossed circle on the facade, as well as many other contributions as footnoted in this book.

Next in line is Tim Armistead, a private investigator and former member of the San Francisco City Attorney's Office, for his friendship, his helpful insights, his thoughtful analysis of my research, his advice, and for other things he did for me behind the scenes, such as getting me the first color photograph I had ever seen of Qvale, in 2004.

I also want to think Joey Franks for her support and guidance behind the scenes as an advisor, sounding board, and confidant. Thanks also to Tom Zoellner, formerly of the *San Francisco Chronicle* and now a published author, who now teaches at Chapman University in California. Tom was courageous enough to write the first article about my research in 2001, and when I later approached him for advice on getting published, he introduced me to Margot Atwell of Kickstarter, who ultimately introduced me to my literary agent. He then wrote the May 2018 article "The Serial Killer as Marketing Genius" for the *Los Angeles Review of Books*.

Next I want to thank Tracy Ertl of Titletown Publishing, who was the first person in the publishing world to express an interest in representing me when I was referred to her by Margot Atwell in 2015. I appreciate her unwavering and total belief and faith in my research and conclusions and for introducing me to my literary agent and publisher, Francesca Minerva of Changing Lives Press. I am thankful to Francesca and Changing Lives Press for all the hard work on this project, including publishing my research in e-book format in 2017, so that I could add my research to the public discussion of the identity of the Zodiac.

Mike Capuzzo believed in my research enough to include a reference to me, as well as Mr. Walter's acknowledgement, in his 2010 bestselling book, *The Murder Room*, where others may have backed away from writing about such a controversial suspect. Caitlin Rother reviewed a very early draft of one of my chapters and provided me with needed guidance on how to approach the writing of my book.

Thanks to Pat Grate, formerly of the Solano County Sheriff's Office for not only supporting my research in 2001 when I first approached him but for providing me with the SO's Lake Herman Road files in 2001 and for his continued support in phone calls and emails as recently as 2019, Kevin Fagan of the *San Francisco Chronicle*, and Charlie Goodyear, also formerly of the *Chronicle*. Gracious thanks to the late captain Ken Narlow of the Napa County Sheriff's Office for his friendship and guidance until his death in 2010, Marie Narlow for her support, and Roger and Joanie Wilson for their friendship and hospitality. Thanks to the late judge Rick Uldall for his guiding hand and for being such a great raconteur of stories about the early days of law enforcement in Solano County before his untimely death in 2006. Only the good die young, as they say, and never was that truer. Thanks to retired SFPD inspector Vince Repetto for his friendship and for defending my work to the amateur researchers gathered at Washington and Cherry Streets on the forty-fifth anniversary of the Stine murder, October 11, 2014. Thanks also go to the late SFPD homicide inspector Gus Coreris for all his assistance early in my research. The man who is considered the dean of San Francisco private investigators, the late David Fechheimer, assisted me gratis several times at the behest of Margo St. James. It was he who put me in touch with Don Fouke in 2004. I want to thank Sgt. Fouke (Ret.) for speaking to me several times beginning in 2004 and giving me his version of the events of October 11, 1969. It was David who made me aware of the legal wranglings in the San Francisco court system with regard to Qvale's $100 million estate after he died. Ed Neil was instrumental in assisting me in the early research on Qvale from 1999 to 2000. Mike Butterfield set up my 2006 interview with Qvale, which led to important information relating to Qvale's guilt coming into my hands when Qvale was untruthful with me in response to many of my questions. He was of tremendous assistance in moving my case forward. Tom Voigt's (zodiackiller.com) and Mike Morford's (zodiackillersite.com) websites serve as clearinghouses for new information and lively discussion about the case, so thanks to both of them. A shout-out to my old friend Jake Wark, whose Zodiac website in the late 1990s was one of the first ones I encountered. Thanks to Dr. Mike Kelleher for his insights and his early support of my research.

Dr. Cyril Wecht, the world-renowned former medical examiner of Allegheny County, Pennsylvania, took time to review some of my early evidence in 2000 and offered encouraging comments on my findings.

Denis Pettee (aka Jonathan Zychowski Jr.) has been my friend, confidant, cheerleader, and webmaster for many years. I owe him a huge debt of gratitude. He flattered me by supporting my work even though he had named his own suspect in the Zodiac mystery, which he ultimately abandoned in favor of the case I had amassed against my own suspect. Denis has been a cryptographer, a commercial airline pilot, an inventor, and a computer genius at various times in his life—a true Renaissance man.

Dr. David Van Nuys has been a friend and an advisor behind the scenes for many years and wrote a positive review of my e-book on Amazon. Dr. Mike Kelleher kindly gave me his ear in the very early days of my research, in 1998, and also encouraged me to keep digging on Qvale and learn as much about him before I ever tried to confront him about the case. I did just that leading up to my 2006 face-to-face encounter with Qvale. In 1999 Mike reviewed my solution to Zodiac's first bus-bomb diagram and, to his surprise, could find no fault with my explanation. He then challenged me to come up with an equally satisfying solution to the second diagram, which took me another five years. I hope my solution to the second bus-bomb diagram also meets with his approval.

Karoline Kjesrud of the University of Oslo introduced me to *bumerker* in 2014, which made sense of the batwing symbol on the Avery Halloween card and demonstrated once again that Zodiac was heavily steeped in Norse culture.

I want to thank Debbie McKillop, the manager of the Contra Costa Sheriff's Office Crime Lab for her insights into DNA science.

Thanks to Mehul Patel, who encouraged me as early as 2011 to write a book on my research, and to John Di Giorgio, who read my original manuscript and suggested many improvements to my story. Thanks also to Rich Bodisco, who offered me much encouragement and tons of support after he read my e-book.

This book would not be possible if not for my team at Indigo River Publishing. My thanks for all the hard work put into restructuring and editing my book. River Chau graciously took the time to advise me behind the scenes and encouraged me to sign on with Indigo River. Special thanks to acquisitions editor Georgette Green, who introduced me to Indigo River and shepherded my book through the acceptance process. Jackson Haynes, the former executive editor, encouraged me to restructure the contents of my book to make it friendlier to the reader. Operations manager Bobby Dunaway quarterbacked my editing and layout teams. Tim Neller, my lead editor, left my writing and presentation much better and more polished than it was when he found it. Regina Cornell, my detail editor (aptly named), taught me that I need to get much better acquainted with *The Chicago Manual of Style*. If I considered myself a "writer-researcher" before these talented people edited my book, I definitely consider myself only a "researcher" with a lot to learn about the art and process of writing now! However, I came to realize that the amount of care they demonstrated and the scrupulous editing my team did on my behalf shows that Indigo River truly cares about making my book a success and wants it to be presented to the public in the best way possible. For that I am indebted to them!

Finally, this book is the product of years of library research. I want to extend my thanks to the 2000–2001 staff of the microfilm reading room of the New York City Public Library on Fifth Avenue and Forty-Second Street. I have many fond memories of time I spent there waiting about fifteen minutes for my number to come up on the old board saying my material was ready. It was in that room that I made many crucial discoveries within the microfilmed pages of the *San Francisco Chronicle*. I also want to think the Interlibrary Loan staff at the Morris County,

New Jersey, library for their assistance in obtaining microfilm resources from California newspapers and other places. Also, many thanks to the staff of the Denville, New Jersey, public library, especially Jen.

And if after all that I forgot anyone, I sincerely apologize!

EXHIBITS

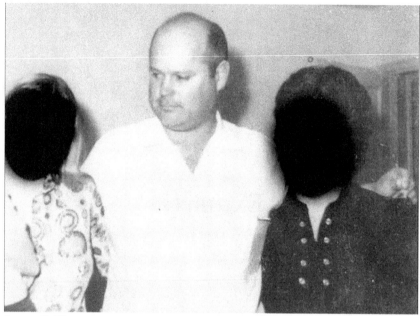

Source: zodiackiller.com

Exhibit 1

ODIN'S CROSS

Exibit 2

Hartnell and Shepard on picnic blanket here.

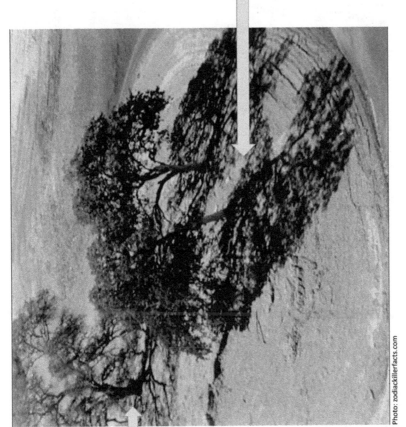

Photo: zodiackillerfacts.com

Zodiac donned hood behind this tree.

Exhibit 3

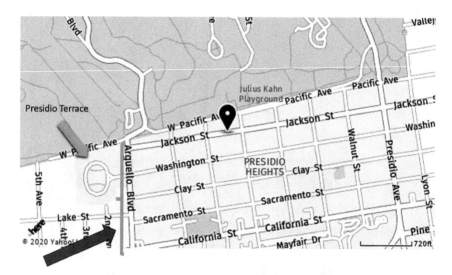

Exhibit 4

Five east–west-running streets

Source: http://www.2040-parts.com

Exhibit 5

Ford Galaxie door handle. To open door, one would wrap their (left) hand around the handle and push button with thumb. To leave distal fingertip prints on the handle, Zodiac would have had to wrap his hand around it in such a way as to dig the very tips of his fingers into the side of the handle facing the door. This is an awkward and painful way to open the door. (Note: This is a driver's-side door handle. Since the passenger's-side door handle is a mirror image of this handle, one would use their right hand and thumb to open it.)

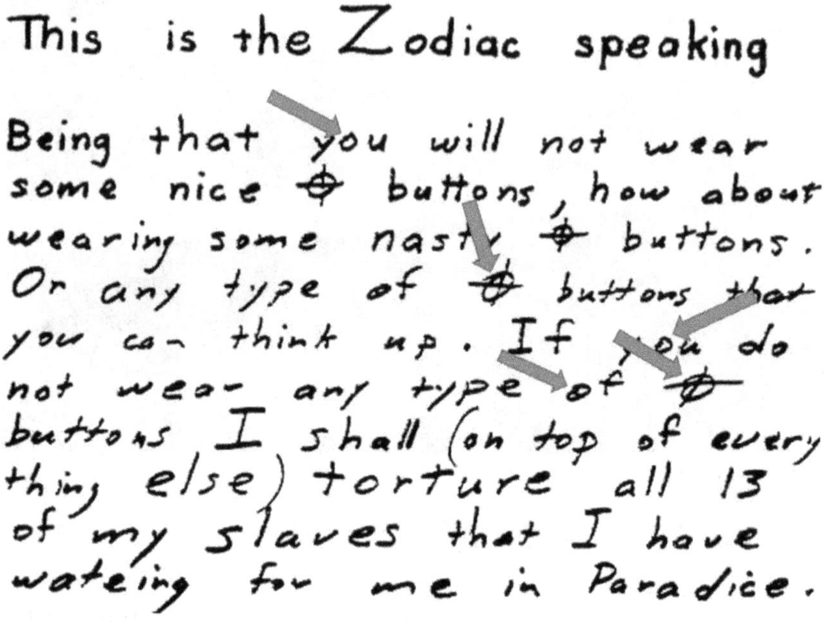

This is the Zodiac speaking

Being that you will not wear some nice ⊕ buttons, how about wearing some nasty ⊕ buttons. Or any type of ⊕ buttons that you can think up. If you do not wear any type of ⊕ buttons I shall (on top of every thing else) torture all 13 of my slaves that I have wateing for me in Paradice.

Exhibit 6a

Arrows point to "eleven o'clock" circles within text of letter. Even the embedded crossed circles are of this variety.

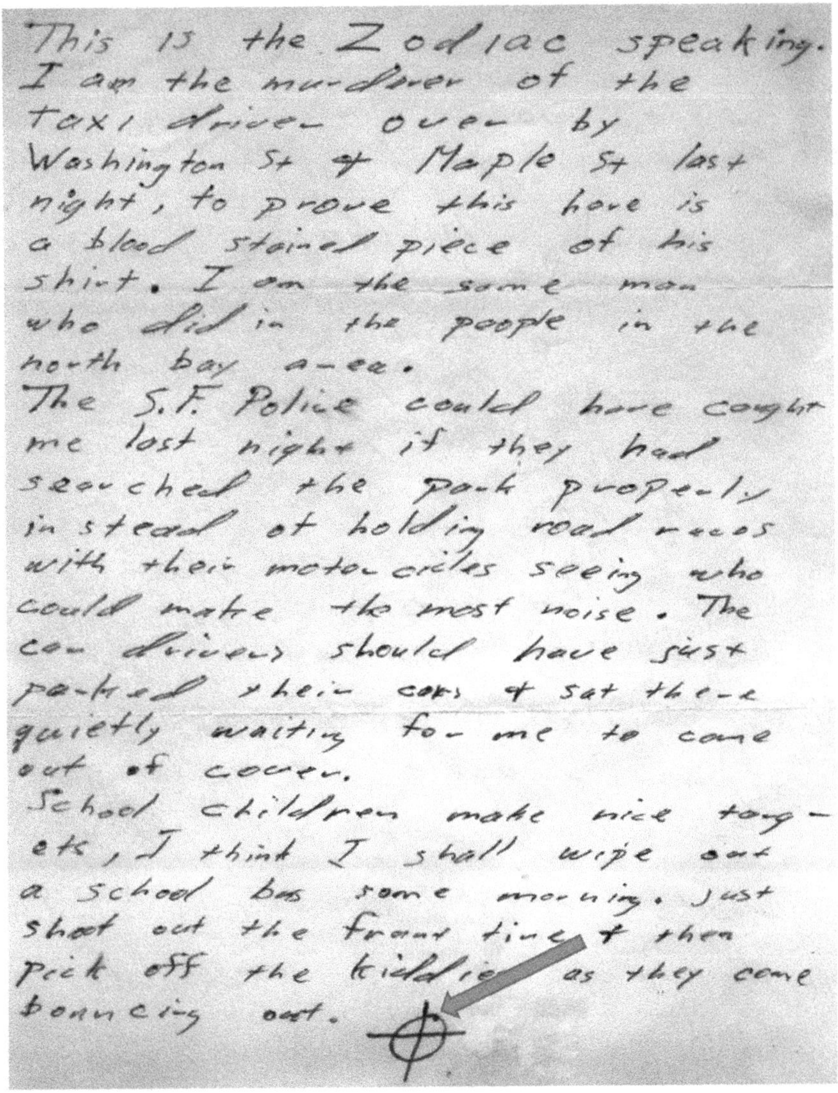
This is the Zodiac speaking.
I am the murderer of the
taxi driver over by
Washington St & Maple St last
night, to prove this here is
a blood stained piece of his
shirt. I am the same man
who did in the people in the
north bay area.
The S.F. Police could have caught
me last night if they had
searched the park properly
instead of holding road races
with their motorcicles seeing who
could make the most noise. The
car drivers should have just
parked their cars & sat there
quietly waiting for me to come
out of cover.
School children make nice targets, I think I shall wipe out
a school bus some morning. Just
shoot out the front tire & then
pick off the kiddies as they come
bouncing out.

Source: zodiackiller.com

Exhibit 6b

One example of a Zodiac-signature crossed circle beginning and ending at 1 o'clock.

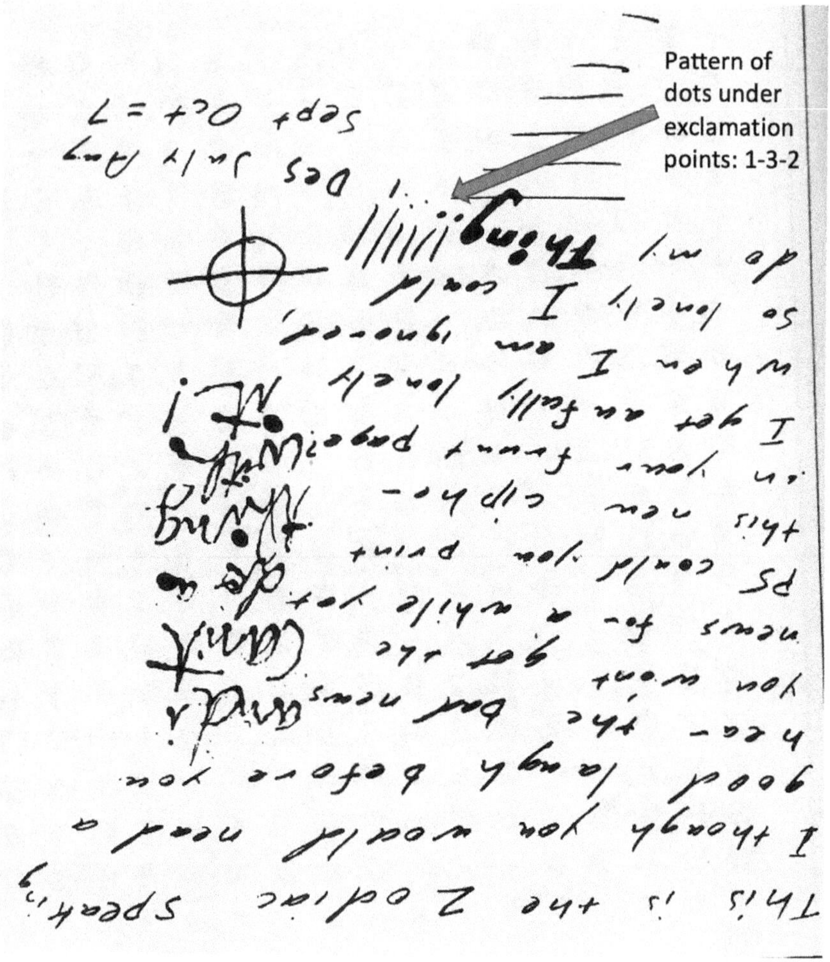

Exhibit 7

This is the Zodiac speaking,
I though you would need a
good laugh before you.
hea- the bad news.and i
you wont got the Cant
news for a while yet do a
PS could you print thing.
this new ciphe- with
.n your frount page? it!
I get aufully lonely
when I am ignored,
So lonely I could
do my **Thing!!!!!!**

Des July Aug
Sept Oct = 7

Pattern of
dots under
exclamation
points: 1-3-2

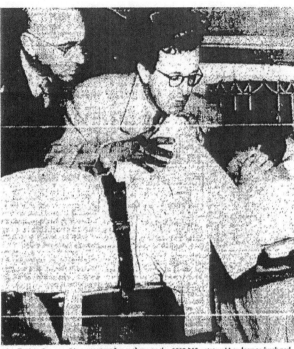

12/1/45
Oakland Tribune

William
Peek-A-Boo
Pennington

standing next to
Melvin Belli

Mrs. Evelyn Bowers, 36, contestant for a share in the $500,000 estate of her former husband, Oscar Bowers, tavern operator, is seen in an ambulance being transferred to Berkeley Hospital after her collapse at the Martinez trial. She is being comforted by her attorney (center).

Exhibit 8

REVERSE
LAGUZ

ANSUZ

Exhibit 9

Exibit 10a

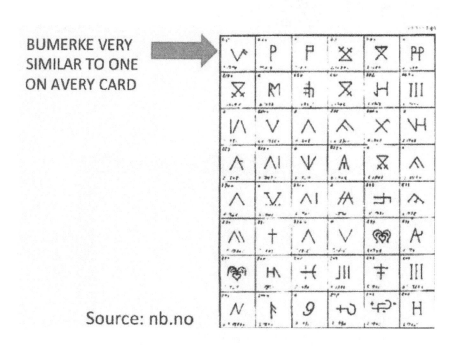

Exhibit 10b

Exhibit 10c

BUMERKE USING BOTH
DOTS AND LINES

Exhibit 10d

Source: Oakland, CA Yellow Pages 1946

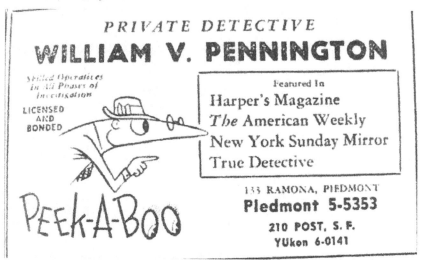

Exhibit 11

LETTERS TO THE EDITOR

Taxpayers' Property

Editor — I must be very simple-minded, but what is the difference between the young people in Berkeley who want to take some land (which belongs to the taxpayer) and build a park serving people, and the old people in Sacramento who want to take 565 million (which belongs to the taxpayer) and build a 24-story twin tower which would give the legislators private privvies, private quarters and lush accommodations?

ROSE M LUCEY

Oakland

Who's to Blame

Editor -- As most citizens of today, I am extremely concerned about the direction our society is heading. It should be obvious to anyone now that a bloody confrontation is a probability in the near future.

The Chronicle's biased covering of the news, and the support of militants and lawbreakers, in my opinion has been, an important factor in the present developing trend. When these young people lie dead or wounded in the street you, your publisher, and some of your columnists must take a large share of the blame.

It has been the opinion of most people that the policy of The Chronicle for years has been to write anything that sells: newspapers, and I am afraid that, in the long run, this will turn out to be rather expensive for all the people of northern California.

On May 28 your editorial featured a statement made by Adolph Hitler. It is obvious that both the ex-Highway Patrol sergeant and the editor missed the entire point of that statement. The only thing missing from our situation is Hitler. The rest of the description seems to fit perfectly. It should be very plain to anyone then that these situations create a Hitler — it did then, so it obviously could again. If it does, you and people like you will be mainly responsible.

As the editor of northern California's largest newspaper, you wield more opinion-making power than any other single individual. This is a tremendous public trust. It is a power that must be wielded with excruciating care and a careful analysis of the potential consequences.

Is this what you are doing? I doubt it

KJELL H QVALE

San Francisco

Who Will Scream?

Editor — Senator William Proxmire is doing a yeoman's job in wringing testimony out of reluctant witnesses to point up the appalling waste and graft in our defense program. He is to be both applauded and supported by every one concerned. The incredible testimony before his Joint Economic sub-committee ... is enough to make any rational citizen scream for reforms and an end to such corruption.

But will he? Only 60 per cent of those eligible voted in the last election. Groaning under the burden of the highest taxes in history, the only other groaning most Americans do is in their living rooms to family and friends. This counts for nothing. But the weight of public opinion does and it does not have to be in the form of a literary masterpiece. Get a stack of postcards and let your congressmen know that if they do not get behind Senator Proxmire in his up-hill battle to trim the fat from this inexcusable defense program you have no desire to return them to the Congress.

FREDERICA DREYFUSS

Los Altos.

A Tearjerker

Editor — It must give you great pleasure to malign the drug industry I refer to the column June 21 by Milton Moskowitz titled "Drug Prices Aren't for the Old Folks," a real tearjerker.

Did it ever occur to your Mr. Moskowitz that the drug compa-

nies he went to great l... condemn are responsible research and development that have helped these "... to stay alive and in relative comfort until they have attained age he speaks of? Is Mr. ... is aware that according to Bureau of Labor Statistics ... ing the time that the cost ... index has risen 14 per c... prescription price index ... risen 9 per cent? Is Mr. ... is aware of the numbers ... who have spent a couple of drugs, while gainfully employed treat an illness that formerly have hospitalized them for weeks?

GORDON D OL...

Turlock

Paths in the Park

Editor — Last Sunday ... and I availed ourselves of ... bicycle path in Golden G... At the same time my daughter friend went horseback ... in the park. At the conclusion of our outings, we compared notes. We all realized that present bicycle path is to ... extent no more than a portion of what had previously been the horse-riding path, that no additional paths have been made available for the new use of horses in the park.

I wonder now that the paths have been paved ... make room for the bicycle, the automobile paths be used to make room for the horses, would be a great step toward returning the park to the people.

VICTOR HO...

San Francisco

Fuzzy Wuzzy

Editor — Fuzzy wuzzy a bear, Fuzzy wuzzy had no hair. Then Fuzzy wuzzn't wuzzy. Wuz he?

BARBARA WITT

Berkeley

Exhibit 12

Exhibit 13

WANTED

SAN FRANCISCO POLICE DEPARTMENT

NO. 90-69   WANTED FOR MURDER   OCTOBER 18, 1969

ORIGINAL DRAWING   AMENDED DRAWING

Supplementing our Bulletin 87-69 of October 13, 1969. Additional information has
developed the above amended drawing of murder suspect known as "ZODIAC".

WMA, 35-45 Years, approximately 5'8", Heavy Build, Short Brown Hair, possibly with
Red Tint, Wears Glasses. Armed with 9 mm Automatic.

Available for comparison: Slugs, Casings, Latents, Handwriting.

ANY INFORMATION:
Inspectors Armstrong & Toschi
Homicide Detail
CASE NO. 696314

THOMAS J. CAHILL
CHIEF OF POLICE

Exhibit 13

Exhibit 14

Qvale's 1969 home at 3636 Jackson Street (see marker) gave him a commanding view of both the Presidio and the Julius Kahn Playground, where the police search for Zodiac centered.

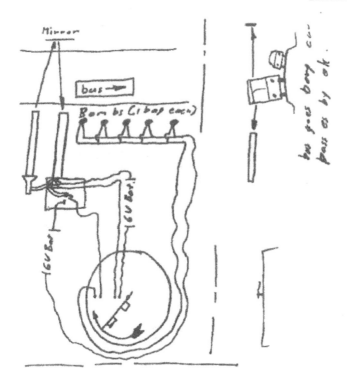

Exhibit 15a

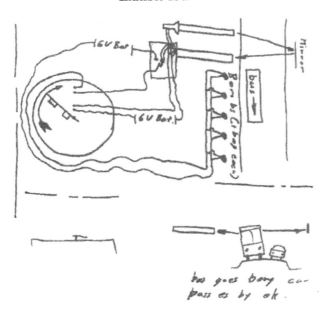

Exhibit 15b

JACKSON STREET (STREET WITH "BUS")

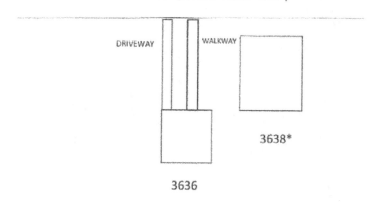

*Note that front of 3636 Jackson is even with rear of 3638 Jackson.

3636 Jackson Street Separated From Street by Parallel Walkway and Driveway

Exhibit 16

Exhibit 17

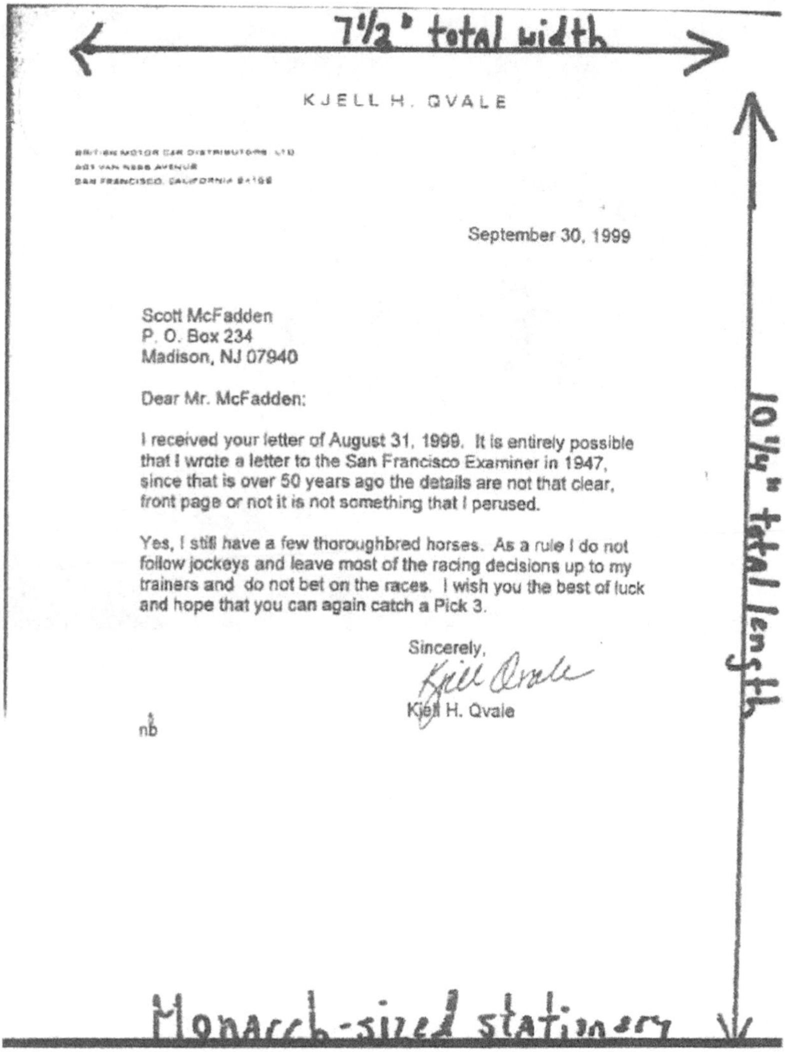

7½" total width

KJELL H. QVALE

BRITISH MOTOR CAR DISTRIBUTORS LTD
901 VAN NESS AVENUE
SAN FRANCISCO, CALIFORNIA 94109

September 30, 1999

Scott McFadden
P. O. Box 234
Madison, NJ 07940

Dear Mr. McFadden:

I received your letter of August 31, 1999. It is entirely possible
that I wrote a letter to the San Francisco Examiner in 1947,
since that is over 50 years ago the details are not that clear,
front page or not it is not something that I perused.

Yes, I still have a few thoroughbred horses. As a rule I do not
follow jockeys and leave most of the racing decisions up to my
trainers and do not bet on the races. I wish you the best of luck
and hope that you can again catch a Pick 3.

Sincerely,

Kjell H. Qvale

nb

10½" total length

Monarch-sized stationery

Exhibit 18

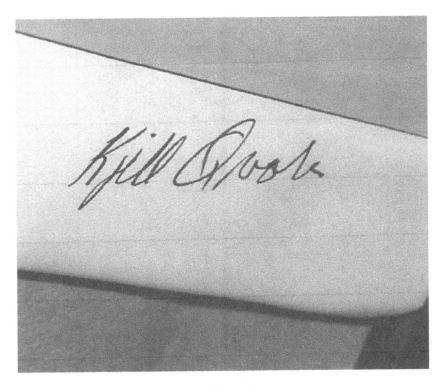

Exhibit 19

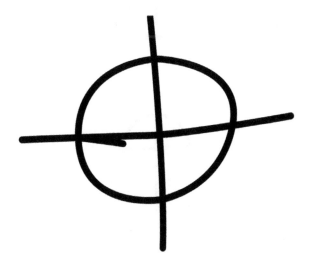

Exhibit 20a

Q

V

A

L

E

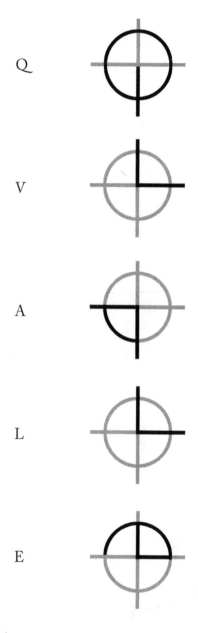

Exhibit 20b

Source: qvalemotors.com

Exhibit 21

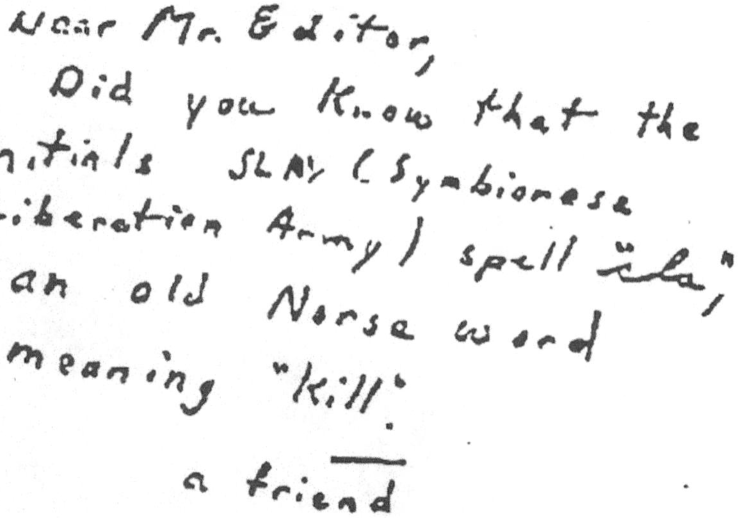

Dear Mr. Editor,
Did you Know that the initials SLAY (Symbionese Liberation Army) spell "sla," an old Norse word meaning "kill".

a friend

Exhibit 22

Source: zodiackiller.com

Paul Averly
S.F. Chronicle
5th - Mission
S.F.

Source: zodiackiller.com

Exhibit 23

PEBBLE BEACH
Nov. 5th, 1950
*
Four Races
THRILLING EUROPEAN STYLE
ROAD RACE FEATURING
THE WORLDS FASTEST
SPORTS CARS
FIRST RACE 12:00 NOON
SPONSORED BY SPORTS CAR CLUB OF AMERICA
Tickets $1.00   Free Parking

Exhibit 24

Original Destination of Cab, Washington Street and Maple Street

Site of Stine Murder, opposite 3899 Washington Street

Fouke Spots Man Walking East, 3712 Jackson Street

Pelissetti Encounters Man Walking Dog, Jackson Street and Maple Street

Home of Kjell Qvale, 3636 Jackson Street

Exhibit 25

Photo by Author

Gate in wall of home just east of 3636 Jackson Street (1999)

Exhibit 26

The new bomb is set up like this

Sun light in early morning

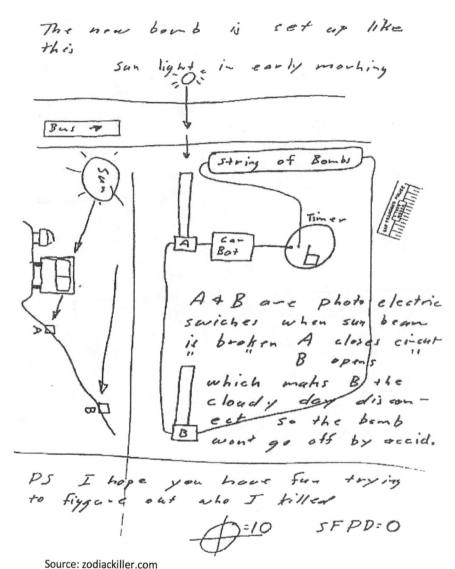

Bus →

String of Bombs

Sun

Timer

A

Car Bot

A & B are photo electric swiches when sun beam is broken A closes circut B opens which maks B + the cloudy day disconect so the bomb wont go off by accid.

B

PS I hope you have fun trying to figgur out who I killed

⊕ = 10   SFPD : 0

Exhibit 27

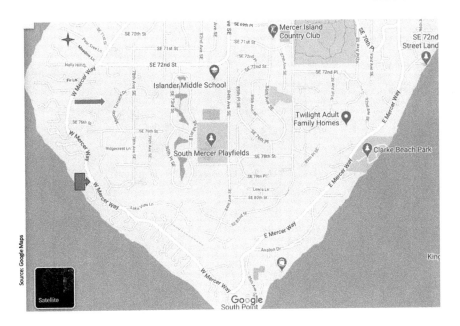

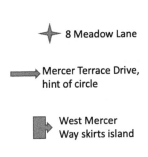

✦ **8 Meadow Lane**

➔ **Mercer Terrace Drive, hint of circle**

West Mercer Way skirts island

Exhibit 28

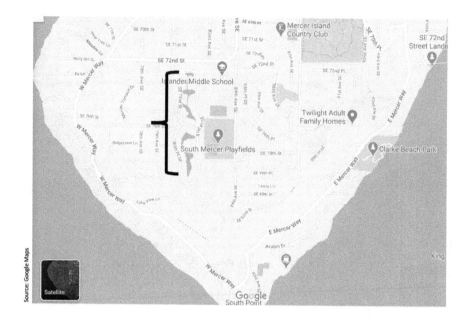

Exhibit 29

Area known as "The Lakes" today. Analogous to "String of Bombs" on second bus-bomb diagram, but in 1970 this was just a wooded area.

WOODED AREA FROM
WHICH "THE LAKES"
WOULD BE FORMED.

RUNNING TRACK

Source: King County, WA Assessor's Office

Exhibit 30

1963 aerial photo of Southern Mercer Island

Smaller insert diagram inverted so "Sun" is shining down and
diagram can be read without turning page 180 degrees. Both
"Suns" shine from same direction.

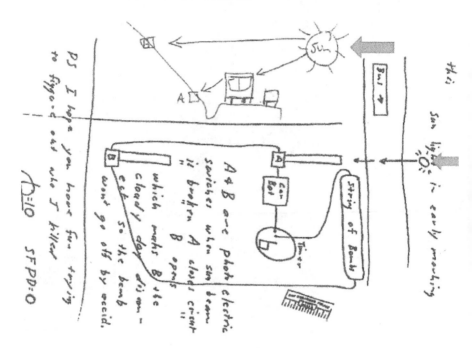

Exhibit 31

Exhibit 32

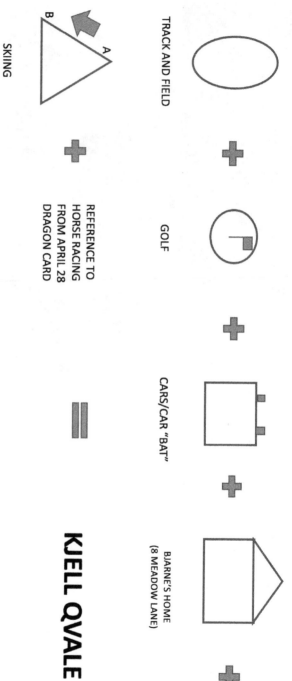

TRACK AND FIELD

GOLF

CARS/CAR "BAT"

BIARNE'S HOME
(8 MEADOW LANE)

SKIING

REFERENCE TO
HORSE RACING
FROM APRIL 28
DRAGON CARD

KJELL QVALE

A
B

Exhibit 33

8 Meadow Lane, "B" for Bjarne Qvale

Mercer Terrace Drive. Hint of circle like "Timer"

Running track analogous to "String of Bombs"

West Mercer Way encircles island analogous to "wire" from "B" to "String of Bombs"

Source: Matthew Parsons Univ. of Washington Libraries

Exhibit 34

Source: San Francisco Examiner, November 20, 1955

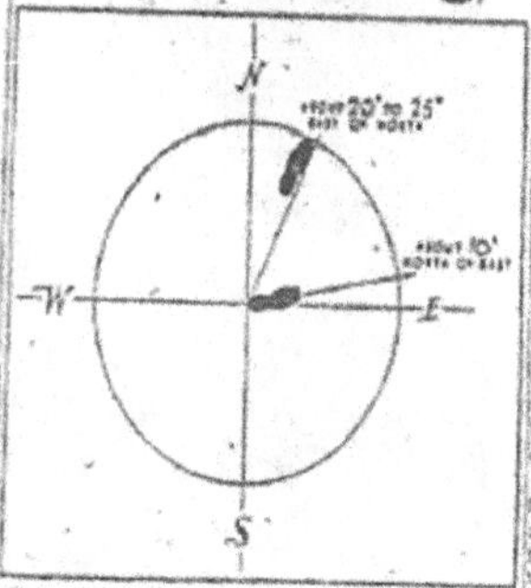

Exhibit 35

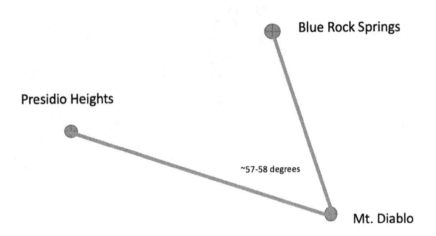

Exhibit 36

Exhibit 37

Exhibit 38

Source: *I Never Look Back*

Exhibit 39

(Above) Cadets take pride in a good target score. Wishing to make each shot count these cadets take their stance and "draw a bead" on the bullseye.

Source: *Mark II of the Slipstream*

Exhibit 40

#2004-45

UNITED STATES OF AMERICA
DEPARTMENT OF THE TREASURY
OFFICE OF THE COMPTROLLER OF THE CURRENCY

In the Matter of:	)	
First National Bank of Marin	)	AA-EC-2004-61
Las Vegas, Nevada	)	
	)	

STIPULATION AND CONSENT TO THE ISSUANCE OF A CONSENT ORDER

WHEREAS, the Comptroller of the Currency of the United States of America

("Comptroller" or "OCC"), through his National Bank Examiners, has examined First National

Bank of Marin, Las Vegas, Nevada ("Bank"), and his findings have been communicated to the

Bank; and

WHEREAS, the Bank, by and through its duly elected and acting Board of Directors

("Board"), desiring to cooperate with the OCC, has executed this Stipulation and Consent to the

Issuance of a Consent Order ("Stipulation and Consent"), dated May 21, 2004, which is accepted

by the Comptroller. By this Stipulation and Consent, the Bank has consented to the issuance of a

Consent Order ("Order") by the Comptroller dated May 21, 2004, and incorporated herein by

this reference as though fully set forth.

In consideration of the above premises, the Comptroller, through his authorized

representative, and the Bank, by and through its Board, hereby stipulate and agree to the

following:

Exhibit 41a

IN TESTIMONY WHEREOF, the undersigned, authorized by the Comptroller, has

hereunto set his hand on behalf of the Comptroller

/s/ Jennifer C. Kelly   3.24.04
Jennifer C. Kelly   Date
Deputy Comptroller
For Mid-Size and Credit Card Bank Supervision

IN TESTIMONY WHEREOF, the undersigned, as the duly elected Board of

Directors of the Bank, have hereunto set their hands on behalf of the Bank.

Signed   3-21-04
Kjell Qvale, Director   Date

Signed   6-21-04
       Date

Signed   5-21-04
       Date

Signed   5-21-04
       Date

Signed   5-21-04
       Date

Signed   5-21-04
       Date

Exhibit 41b

Exhibit 42

Source: *I Never Look Back*

VEHICLE REPORT

| VEHICLE REPORT | ☒ IMPOUNDED | ☐ RECOVERED | ☐ STORED | ☐ RELEASED | Use Reverse Side for Stolen or Embezzled Vehicles. |

DESCRIPTION OF VEHICLE

REPORTING DEPT. NAPA SHERIFF DEPT.   AREA/LOCATION LAKE BERRYESSA   DATE 9-27-69   FILE NO. 105907

| BLK | MAKE KARMANN GHIA | BODY TYPE 2 DR | LICENSE NO. (S) 1 MU 2040 2 4U 2040 | YEAR 1970 | STATE OREGON | COLOR (COMBINATION) BLK |
| WHT | Volks Wagon | COUPE | | | | OREGON |

VEHICLE IDENTIFICATION NO. (TYPE) 86412213   SPEEDOMETER READING 6216

REGISTERED OWNER BRUCE L. CHRISTIE   ADDRESS 3339 NE BROADWAY PORTLAND OREGON   PHONE

LEGAL OWNER   ADDRESS   PHONE

DRIVER OR LAST PERSON IN POSSESSION BRYAN HARTNELL   ADDRESS RT 2, BOX 252 TRCUTDALE, ORE BLUE LAKE   PHONE

CIRCUMSTANCES

NAME OF GARAGE BIAVA MOTORS   ADDRESS 466 SOSCOL, NAPA   PHONE 224-3191

TOWED   HELD AS EVIDENCE ☐ YES ☒ NO   TIME AND DATE TOWED 9-27-69

TOWED FROM (LOC.) BERRYESSA 4 DOORS   TIME AND DATE REPORTED 9-27-69

FIRM REMOVING OCCURRENCE MR. RON FONG   ADDRESS SAN FRANCISCO   PHONE

CONDITION OF VEHICLE FAIR   IMPOUNDABLE ☒ YES ☐ NO   WRECKED ☐ YES ☒ NO   STRIPPED ☐ YES ☒ NO

VEHICLE INVENTORY

	YES	NO		YES	NO	CONDITION	LIST PROPERTY FOUND, OTHER ITEMS
CUSHION (FRONT)	X		SPOTLIGHTS		X	POOR	GIRLS RED COAT
CUSHION (REAR)	X		FLOOR MATS		X	POOR	" SHOES
REAR VIEW MIRROR	X		BUMPER (FRONT)	X		POOR	1 TOOL BOX
ONE SIDE MIRROR		X	BUMPER (REAR)	X		POOR	KNIFE
CHOKE CONTROL		X	MOTOR	X		POOR	1 PR. MENS
RADIO	X		BATTERY	X		FAIR	SHORTS
CLOCK		X	AIR CONDITIONER		X	FAIR	L HARTNELL
HEATER		X	HUB CAPS	X		FAIR	BANK BOOK
KEYS	X		FINISH WHITE		X	FAIR	
SPEEDOMETER	X		TRANSMISSION	X		FAIR	
WINDSHIELD WIPER	X		TIRES	X		FAIR	

OFFICER IMPOUNDING VEH. STORED (SIGNATURE) X R.M. Lonkey   25.68 X   GARAGE RECEIVED OR SIGNED (SIGNING VEH. AND DELIVERY)   TIME AND DATE

IMPOUNDING OFFICER'S BADGE NO. (OFFICER NO.)   TIME AND DATE X   APPRAISED VALUE   TIME AND DATE OF APPRAISAL

IMPOUND RELEASE NOTIFICATION

TO   ADDRESS   DATE

RELEASE VEHICLE TO   ADDRESS

SIGNATURE OF CLERK OR OFFICER RELEASING   CERTIFICATION: I, the undersigned, do hereby certify that I am legal authorized and entitled to take possession of above described vehicle.

Exhibit 43

Source: zodiackillersite.com

Exhibit 44

CPSIA information can be obtained
at www.ICGtesting.com
Printed in the USA
LVHW081145020921
696776LV00011B/271

9 781950 906871